Alexander Pope, Joseph Warton

Works

With notes and illus. by Joseph Warton, and others. Vol. 3

Alexander Pope, Joseph Warton

Works
With notes and illus. by Joseph Warton, and others. Vol. 3

ISBN/EAN: 9783337426057

Printed in Europe, USA, Canada, Australia, Japan

Cover: Foto ©Lupo / pixelio.de

More available books at **www.hansebooks.com**

THE

WORKS

OF

Alexander Pope, Efq.

IN NINE VOLUMES, COMPLETE.

WITH

NOTES AND ILLUSTRATIONS
By JOSEPH WARTON, D.D.
AND OTHERS.

VOLUME THE THIRD.

LONDON:

Printed for B. Law, J. Johnson, C. Dilly, G. G. and J. Robinson,
J. Nichols, R. Baldwin, H. L. Gardner, F. and C. Rivington,
J. Sewell, T. Payne, J. Walker, R. Faulder, J. Scatcherd,
B. and J. White, Ogilvy and Son, T. N. Longman,
Cadell jun. and Davies, and E. Potz.

1797.

CONTENTS

OF THE

THIRD VOLUME.

ESSAY ON MAN, in Four Epistles.   Page
EPISTLE   I. Of the Nature and State of Man with
     refpect to the Univerfe   -   1
EPISTLE   II. Of the Nature and State of Man with
     refpect to Himfelf, as an Individual   53
EPISTLE   III. Of the Nature and State of Man with
     refpect to Society   -   85
EPISTLE   IV. Of the Nature and State of Man with
     refpect to Happinefs   -   123
The Univerfal Prayer   -   -   165

MORAL ESSAYS.
EPISTLE   I. Of the Knowledge and Characters of
     MEN   -   -   175
EPISTLE   II. Of the Characters of WOMEN   209
EPISTLE   III. Of the Ufe of RICHES   -   233
EPISTLE   IV. Of the Ufe of RICHES   -   271
EPISTLE   V. To Mr. Addifon, occafioned by his
     Dialogues on MEDALS   -   301

APPEN-

CONTENTS.

APPENDIX.

	Page
An ESSAY on SATIRE	313
Part I.	317
Part II.	324
Part III.	331
A Letter to a Noble Lord, on occasion of some Libels written and propagated at Court, in the Year 1732-3	339

ERRATA in VOL. III.

Page 24. notes, line 15, *for* even *read* ever
    49. notes, —— 33, *for* may *read* might
    50. notes, —— 7, *for* Meli *read* Mali
    63. notes, —— 20, *for* Burtamaqui *read* Burlamaqui
    84. notes, —— 11, *for* sous mille *read* fourmille
    91. notes, —— 7, *for* Maiscaux *read* De Maiseaux
   203. notes, —— 14, *dele* son's
   212. notes, —— 15, *for* Eubultus *read* Eubulus
   350. notes, —— ult. *for* for *read* Mr.

AN

ESSAY ON MAN,

IN FOUR EPISTLES.

TO

H. ST. JOHN, LORD BOLINGBROKE.

THE DESIGN.

HAVING propofed to write fome pieces on Human Life and Manners, fuch as (to ufe my Lord Bacon's expreffion) *come home to Men's Bufinefs and Bofoms*, I thought it more fatisfactory to begin with confidering *Man* in the abftract, his *Nature* and his *State*; fince, to prove any moral duty, to enforce any moral precept, or to examine the perfection or imperfection of any creature whatfoever, it is neceffary firft to know what *condition* and *relation* it is placed in, and what is the proper *end* and *purpofe* of its *being*.

The fcience of Human Nature is, like all other fciences, reduced to a *few clear points*: There are not *many certain truths* in this world. It is therefore in the Anatomy of the Mind as in that of the Body; more good will accrue to mankind by attending to the large, open, and perceptible parts, than by ftudying too much fuch finer nerves and veffels, the conformations and ufes of which will for ever efcape our obfervation. The *difputes* are all upon thefe laft, and, I will venture to fay, they have lefs fharpened the *wits* than the *hearts* of men againft each other, and have diminifhed the practice, more than advanced the theory, of Morality. If I could flatter myfelf that this Effay has any merit, it is in fteering betwixt the extremes of doctrines feemingly oppofite, in paffing over terms utterly unintelligible, and in forming a *temperate*, yet not *inconfiftent*, and a *fhort*, yet not *imperfect*, fyftem of Ethics.

This I might have done in profe; but I chofe verfe, and even rhyme, for two reafons. The one will appear obvious; that principles, maxims, or precepts fo written, both ftrike the reader more ftrongly at firft, and are more eafily retained by him afterwards: The other may feem odd, but is true. I found I could exprefs them more *fhortly* this way than in profe itfelf; and nothing is more certain, than that much of the *force* as well as *grace* of arguments or inftruction depends on their *concifenefs*. I was unable to treat this part of my fubject more in *detail*, without becoming dry and tedious; or more *poetically*, without facrificing perfpicuity to ornament, without wandering from the precifion, or breaking the chain of reafoning: If any man can unite all thefe without diminution of any of them, I freely confefs he will compafs a thing above my capacity.

What is now publifhed, is only to be confidered as a *general Map* of MAN, marking out no more than the *greater parts*, their *extent*, their *limits*, and their *connection*, but leaving the particular to be more fully delineated in the charts which are now to follow. Confequently thefe Epiftles in their progrefs (if I have health and leifure to make any progrefs) will be lefs dry, and more fufceptible of poetical ornament. I am here only opening the *fountains*, and clearing the paffage. To deduce the *rivers*, to follow them in their courfe, and to obferve their effects, may be a tafk more agreeable.   P.

ARGUMENT OF EPISTLE I.

Of the Nature and State of Man, with respect to the UNIVERSE.

OF Man *in the abstract.*—I. *That we can judge only with regard to our* own *system, being ignorant of the* relations *of systems and things,* Ver. 17, &c. II. *That Man is not to be deemed* imperfect, *but a Being suited to his* place *and* rank *in the creation, agreeable to the* general Order *of things, and conformable to* Ends and Relations *to him unknown,* Ver. 35, &c. III. *That it is partly upon his* ignorance *of* future *events, and partly upon the* hope *of a* future *state, that all his happiness in the present depends,* Ver. 77, &c. IV. *The* pride *of aiming at more knowledge, and pretending to more perfection, the cause of Man's error and misery. The* impiety *of putting himself in the place of* God, *and judging of the fitness or unfitness, perfection or imperfection, justice or injustice, of his dispensations,* Ver. 109, &c. V. *The* absurdity *of conceiting himself the* final cause *of the creation, or expecting that perfection in the* moral world, *which is not in the* natural, Ver. 131, &c. VI. *The* unreasonableness *of his complaints against* Providence, *while on the one hand he demands the Perfections of the Angels, and on the other the bodily qualifications of the Brutes ; though, to possess any of the* sensitive *faculties in a higher degree, would render him miserable,* Ver. 173, &c. VII. *That throughout the whole sensible world, an universal* order *and* gradation *in the sensual and mental faculties is observed, which causes a* subordination *of creature to creature, and of all creatures to Man. The gradations of* sense, instinct, thought, reflection,

flection, reason: *that Reason alone countervails all the other faculties,* Ver. 207. VIII. *How much further this order and subordination of living creatures may extend, above and below us; were any part of which broken, not that part only, but the whole connected* creation *must be destroyed,* Ver. 233. IX. *The* extravagance, madness, *and pride of such a desire,* Ver. 250. X. *The consequence of all, the* absolute submission *due to Providence, both as to our* present *and* future state, Ver. 281, &c. *to the end.*

IF it be a true obfervation, that for a poet to write happily and well, he muſt have feen and felt what he defcribes, and muſt draw from living models alone; and if modern times, from their luxury and refinement, afford not manners that will bear to be defcribed; it will then follow, that thofe fpecies of poetry bid faireſt to fucceed at prefent, which deliver doctrines, not difplay events. Of this fort is didactic and defcriptive poetry. Accordingly the moderns have produced many excellent pieces of this kind. We may mention the Syphilis of Fracaſtorius, the Silkworms and Chefs of Vida, the Ambra of Politian, the Agriculture of Alamanni, the Art of Poetry of Boileau, the Gardens of Rapin, the Cyder of Phillips, the Chafe of Somerville, the Pleafures of Imagination, the Art of preferving Health, the Fleece, the Religion of Racine the younger, the elegant Latin poem of Brown on the Immortality of the Soul, the Latin poems of Stay and Bofcovick, and the philofophical poem before us; to which, if we may judge from fome beautiful fragments, we might have added Gray's didactic poem on Education and Government, had he lived to finiſh it: And the Engliſh Garden of Mr. Mafon muſt not be omitted.

Pope informs us, in his firſt preface to this Effay, " that he chofe this epiſtolary way of writing, notwithſtanding his fubject was high, and of dignity, becaufe of its being mixed with argument which of its nature approacheth to profe." He has not wandered into any ufelefs digreffions; has employed no fictions, no tale or ſtory, and has relied chiefly on the poetry of his ſtyle for the purpofe of intereſting his readers. His ſtyle is concife and figurative, forcible and elegant. He has many metaphors and images, artfully interfperfed in the drieſt paffages, which ſtood moſt in need of fuch ornaments. Neverthelefs there are too many lines, in this performance, plain and profaic. The meaner the fubject is of a preceptive poem, the more ſtriking appears the art of the poet: It is even of ufe, perhaps, to choofe a low fubject. In this refpect Virgil has the advantage over Lucretius; the latter, with all his vigour and fublimity of genius, could hardly fatisfy and come up to the grandeur of his theme. Pope labours under the fame difficulty. If any beauty in this Effay be uncommonly tranfcendent

cendent and peculiar, it is brevity of diction; which, in a few inſtances, and thoſe perhaps pardonable, has occaſioned obſcurity. It is hardly to be imagined how much ſenſe, how much thinking, how much obſervation on human life, is condenſed together in a ſmall compaſs. He was ſo accuſtomed to confine his thoughts in rhyme, that he tells us he could expreſs them more ſhortly this way than in proſe itſelf. On its firſt publication Pope did not own it, and it was given by the public to Lord Paget, Dr. Young, Dr. Deſaguliers, and others. Even Swift ſeems to have been deceived. There is a remarkable paſſage in one of his letters: " I confeſs I did never imagine you were ſo deep in morals, or that ſo many and excellent rules could be produced ſo advantageouſly and agreeably in that ſcience, from any one head. I confeſs in ſome places I was forced to read twice. I believe I told you before what the Duke of D———— ſaid to me on that occaſion; how a judge here, who knows you, told him, that, on the firſt reading thoſe Eſſays, he was much pleaſed, but found ſome lines a little dark: On the ſecond, moſt of them cleared up, and his pleaſure increaſed: On the third, he had no doubt remaining, and then he admired the whole."

The ſubject of this Eſſay is a vindication of Providence; in which the poet propoſes to prove, That, of all poſſible ſyſtems, Infinite Wiſdom has formed the beſt: That in ſuch a ſyſtem, coherence, union, ſubordination, are neceſſary; and if ſo, that appearances of evil, both moral and natural, are alſo neceſſary and unavoidable; That the ſeeming defects and blemiſhes in the univerſe conſpire to its general beauty: That as all parts in an animal are not eyes; and as in a city, comedy, or picture, all ranks, characters, and colours are not equal or alike; even ſo exceſſes and contrary qualities contribute to the proportion and harmony of the univerſal ſyſtem: That it is not ſtrange that we ſhould not be able to diſcover perfection and order in every inſtance; becauſe, in an infinity of things mutually relative, a mind which ſees not infinitely, can ſee nothing fully. This doctrine was inculcated by Plato and the Stoics, but more amply and particularly by the later Platoniſts, and by Antoninus and Simplicius.

In illuſtrating his ſubject, Pope has been much more deeply indebted to the Theodicée of Leibnitz, to Archbiſhop King's Origin of Evil, and to the Moraliſts of Lord Shafteſbury, (particularly to the laſt,) than to the philoſophers above mentioned. The late Lord Bathurſt repeatedly aſſured me, that he had read the whole ſcheme of the Eſſay on Man, in the hand-writing of Bolingbroke,

lingbroke, and drawn up in a series of propositions, which Pope was to amplify, verfify, and illuftrate. In doing which, our poet, it muft be confeffed, left feveral paffages fo expreffed, as to be favourable to fatalifm and neceffity, notwithftanding all the pains that can be taken, and the artful turns that can be given to thofe paffages, to place them on the fide of religion, and make them coincide with the fundamental doctrines of revelation. How could Pope, in the letter which he wrote to Racine, the fon, 1742, venture to fay, that his opinions were exactly conformable to thofe of Pafcal, who, throughout all his Thoughts, is inceffantly inculcating the abfolute neceffity of believing that man is in a fallen and degraded ftate; an opinion which is ftrongly denied in every line of the Effay on Man? And which opinion of Pope, Racine has juftly ftated in the following lines; *La Religion*, Chant. 2.

 Quelque abftrait Raifonneur, qui ne fe plaint de rien,
 Dans fon flegme Anglican, repondra, 'Tout eft bien.
 " Le grand Ordannateur dont le deffein fi fage,
 " De tant d'etres divers ne forme qu'un ouvrage;
 " Nous place à notre rang pour orner fon tableau!"

Pope has indeed inadvertently borrowed fome paffages from Pafcal, but they have only ferved to make this fyftem more inconfiftent. For how can man be a " chaos of thought and paffion all confus'd, and yet be as perfect a being as he ought to be?" The doctrine obviously intended to be inculcated in this Effay is, " That the difpenfations of Providence in the diftribution of good and evil, in this life, ftand in no need of any hypothefis to juftify them; all is adjufted in the moft perfect order; whatever is, is right; and we have no occafion to call in the notion of a future life to vindicate the ways of God to man, becaufe they are fully and fufficiently benevolent and juft in the prefent." If we cannot fubfcribe, on one hand, to Dr. Warburton's opinion, " that thefe epiftles have a precifion, force, and clofenefs of connection rarely to be met with, even in the moft formal treatifes of philofophy;" yet neither can we affent to the fevere fentence that Dr. Johnfon has paffed on the other hand; namely, " that penury of knowledge, and vulgarity of fentiment, were never fo happily difguifed as in this Effay; the reader feels his mind full, though he learns nothing; and, when he meets it in his new array, no longer knows the talk of his mother and his nurfe."

 It has been alleged that Pope did not fully comprehend the drift of the fyftem communicated to him by Bolingbroke; but the following remarkable words of his intimate friend, Mr. Jonathan Richardson, a man of known integrity and honour, clearly evince that he did: " As for this Essay on Man, as I was witness to the whole conduct of it in writing, and actually have his original manuscripts for it, from the first scratches of the four books, to the several finished copies (of his own neat and elegant writing these last); all which, with the manuscript of his Essay on Criticism, and several of his other works, he gave me himself, for the pains I took in collating the whole with the printed editions, at his request, on my having proposed to him the making an edition of his works in the manner of Boileau's. As to this noblest of his works, I know that he never dreamed of the scheme he afterwards adopted; perhaps for good reasons; for he had taken terror about the clergy, and Warburton himself, at the general alarm of its fatalism and deistical tendency; of which, however, we talked with him (my father and I) frequently at Twickenham, without his appearing to understand it otherwise, or even thinking to alter those passages, which he suggested as what might seem the most exceptionable."

To this testimony of Richardson, which is decisive, I will now add, that Lord Lyttelton, with his usual frankness and ingenuity, assured me, that he had frequently talked with Pope on the subject, whose opinions were at that time conformable to his own; before he had written his Observations on the Conversion of St. Paul, when he and his friends (not excepting Mr. Gilbert West) were, as he most candidly confessed, too much inclined to deism, but had fortunately become a most serious and earnest believer of Christianity. Is it not more probable and reasonable to suppose, that Pope might also change his opinion, though, at the time of writing the Essay on Man, he was tinctured with principles of another kind? and that he was equally in earnest when he was a disciple of Bolingbroke, as he afterwards was when he became a disciple of Warburton? It is incredible that he should not be acquainted with the objections that Bolingbroke held against revealed religion; which objections are perpetually repeated, and pervade all his works. But Pope might not indeed know the real opinions of his guide concerning a particular important topic—the moral attributes of the Deity. These two cases are widely different; and there lies a vast space betwixt these two species of infidelity. A man may be unhappily and unjustly prejudiced against the Christian religion, and yet be fully and firmly persuaded of the belief of a God, and his moral attributes. Mr. Harte

more

more than once affured me, that he had feen the preffing letter Dr. Young wrote to Pope, urging him to write fomething on the fide of revelation; to which he alluded in the firft Night-thought:

"O had he prefs'd his theme, purfu'd the track
Which opens out of darknefs into day!
O had he mounted on his wing of fire,
Soar'd when I fink, and fung immortal man!"

And when Harte frequently made the fame requeft, he ufed to anfwer, "No, no! you have already done it;" alluding to Harte's Effay on Reafon, which Harte thought a lame apology, and hardly ferious. With refpect to what has juft been mentioned, that Pope was not acquainted with the opinions of his philofophic guide, on the fubject of the moral attributes of the Deity, it feems rather ftrange and incredible that he fhould not underftand the following, among many other paffages, to this purpofe:

"Clarke, after repeating over and over all the moral attributes, that they are the fame in God as they are in our ideas, and that he who denies them to be fo, may as well deny the divine phyfical attributes, infifts only on two of the former, on thofe of juftice and goodnefs. He was much in the right to contract the generality of his affertion. The abfurdity of afcribing temperance, for inftance, or fortitude, to God, would have been too grofs and too rifible, even to eyes that prejudice had blinded the moft. But that of afcribing juftice and goodnefs to him, according to our notions of them, might be better covered, and was enough for his purpofe, though not lefs really abfurd." Vol. iv. p. 298. It is fomewhat remarkable, that this very opinion, that we have no clear and adequate ideas of God's moral attributes, is ftrongly maintained by that excellent man and writer, Archbifhop King, in his fermon on Divine Predeftination, 1709, which was anfwered by Anthony Collins, author of the Effay on Free-thinking. The perfon who wrote the fpirited and elegant anonymous letter to Dr. Warburton on the fuppofed feverity with which he was thought to have treated Lord Bolingbroke in the View of his Philofophy, was the late Lord Manslield; and this letter was anfwered by Dr. Warburton, with much force and apparent mortification, in the Apology prefixed to the laft edition of this View.

EPISTLE I.

AWAKE, my St. John! leave all meaner things
To low ambition, and the pride of Kings.
Let us (since Life can little more supply
Than just to look about us and to die)
Expatiate free o'er all this scene of Man;   5
A mighty maze! but not without a plan;
A wild, where weeds and flow'rs promiscuous shoot,
Or Garden, tempting with forbidden fruit.
Together let us beat this ample field,
Try what the open, what the covert yield;   10
The latent tracts, the giddy heights, explore
Of all who blindly creep, or sightless soar;
Eye Nature's walks, shoot Folly as it flies,
And catch the manners living as they rise;
                                              Laugh

NOTES.

Ver. 12. *Of all who blindly creep, &c.*] *i. e.* Those who only follow the blind guidance of their passions; or those who leave behind them common sense and sober reason, in their high flights through the regions of Metaphysics. Both which follies are exposed in the fourth epistle, where the popular and philosophical errors concerning Happiness are detected. The figure is taken from *animal* life.   W.

Ver. 13. *Eye Nature's walks,*] These metaphors, drawn from the field sports of setting and shooting, seem much below the dignity of the subject, and an unnatural mixture of the ludicrous and serious.

Laugh where we muſt, be candid where we can; 15
But vindicate the ways of God to Man.
  I. Say firſt, of God above, or Man below,
What can we reaſon, but from what we know?
Of Man, what ſee we but his ſtation here,
From which to reaſon, or to which refer?   20
Thro' worlds unnumber'd tho' the God be known,
'Tis ours to trace him only in our own.
He, who through vaſt immenſity can pierce,
See worlds on worlds compoſe one univerſe,
Obſerve how ſyſtem into ſyſtem runs,   25
What other planets circle other ſuns,
What vary'd Being peoples ev'ry ſtar,
May tell why Heav'n has made us as we are.
                              But

NOTES.

  VER. 15. *Laugh where we muſt,*] " La ſottiſe (ſays old Montaigne) eſt une mauvaiſe qualité; mais ne la pouvoir ſupporter, & s'en dépiter & rouger, comme il m'advient, c'eſt une autre ſorte de maladie, qui ne doit gueres à la ſottiſe en importunité."

  VER. 16. *But vindicate the ways*] Hinting, by this alluſion to the well-known line of Milton,

      " And juſtify the ways of God to man;"

that he intended his poem for a defence of Providence as well as Milton, but he took a very different method in purſuing that end. It cannot be doubted that Warburton ſeriouſly intended to do ſervice to religion, by endeavouring to place this poem on the ſide of Revelation, and to take Pope out of the hands of the infidels. But he laboured in vain, and with an ill-grounded zeal; as would evidently appear if we were to undertake the unpleaſing taſk of collecting all the paſſages which he has tortured and turned into meanings never dreamt of, or deſigned by the poet.

  VER. 19, 20. *Of Man, what ſee we but his ſtation here,*
          From which to reaſon, or to which refer?
The ſenſe is, " we ſee nothing of Man but as he ſtands at preſent in his ſtation here: From which ſtation, all our reaſonings on his

nature

But of this frame, the bearings and the ties,
The strong connections, nice dependencies, 30
Gradations juſt, has thy pervading foul
Look'd through? or can a part contain the whole?
Is the great chain, that draws all to agree,
And drawn ſupports, upheld by God, or thee?

II. Pre-

NOTES.

nature and *end* muſt be drawn; and to this ſtation they muſt all be referred." The conſequence is that our reaſonings on his *nature* and *end* muſt needs be very imperfect. W.

VER. 29. *But of this frame, the bearings*] " Imagine only ſome perſon entirely a ſtranger to navigation, and ignorant of the nature of the ſea or waters, how great his aſtoniſhment would be, when finding himſelf on board ſome veſſel anchoring at ſea, remote from all land-proſpect; whilſt it was yet a calm, he viewed the ponderous machine firm and motionleſs in the midſt of the ſmooth ocean, and conſidered its foundations beneath, together with its cordage, maſts, and ſails above. How eaſily would he ſee the whole one regular ſtructure, all things depending on one another; the uſes of the rooms below, the lodgments, and the conveniencies of men and ſtores? But being ignorant of the intent, or of all above, would he pronounce the maſts and cordage to be uſeleſs and cumberſome, and for this reaſon condemn the frame and deſpiſe the architect? O my friend! let us not thus betray our ignorance; but conſider where we are, and in what univerſe. Think of the many parts of the vaſt machine, in which we have ſo little inſight, and of which it is impoſſible we ſhould know the ends and uſes: when, inſtead of ſeeing to the higheſt pendants, we ſee only ſome lower deck, and are in this dark caſe of fleſh, confined even to the hold and meaneſt ſtation of the veſſel." I have inſerted this paſſage at length, becauſe it is a noble and poetical illuſtration of the foregoing lines, as well as of many other paſſages in this Eſſay. Characteriſtics, vol. ii. p. 188.

The whole doctrine of Plato is contained in this one ſhort ſentence: Μέρος μὲν ἕνεκα ὅλε, καὶ ὐχ᾽ ὅλον ἕνεκα μέρες; ἀπιργάζεται. See a very fine paſſage in A. Gellius, lib. 6. cap. 1. containing the opinion of Chryſippus on the origin of evil.

VER. 32. *Can a part contain the whole?*] " HOBBES (ſays Dr. Campbell) acknowledged God the author of all things, but thought, or at leaſt pretended he thought, too reverently of him

to

II. Presumptuous Man! the reason would'st thou
find, 35
Why form'd so weak, so little, and so blind?
First, if thou can'st, the harder reason guess,
Why form'd no weaker, blinder, and no less?
Ask of thy mother Earth, why oaks are made
Taller or stronger than the weeds they shade? 40
Or ask of yonder argent fields above,
Why Jove's Satellites are less than Jove?

Of

NOTES.

to believe his nature could be comprehended by human understanding. But what gave a handle to some to treat him as an atheist, was, the contempt he expressed for many of those scholastic terms, invented by assuming men, who would impose their own crude notions of the Divine Being, on their fellow-creatures, as so many articles of faith." One of the most false and pernicious tenets of Hobbes was the debasing and disparaging human nature, and saying, that man was to man a wolf; and attempting, as Cudworth expresses it, to " villanize mankind."

VER. 35. *Presumptuous Man!*] Voltaire, tom. iv. p. 227. has the following remarkable words: I own it flatters me to see that Pope has fallen upon the very same sentiment which I had entertained many years ago: Vous vous étonnez que Dieu ait fait l'homme si borné, si ignorant, si peu heureux. Que ne vous etonnez-vous, qu'il ne l'ait pas plus borné, plus ignorant, et plus malheureux? Quand un Français et un Anglais pensent de meme, il fait bien qu'ils ayent raison.

VER. 41. *Or ask of yonder, &c.*] On these lines M. Voltaire thus descants: " Pope dit que l'homme ne peut savoir pourquoi les Lunes de Jupiter sont moins grandes que Jupiter? Il se trompe en cela, c'est une erreur pardonable. Il n'y a point de Mathematicien qui n'ent fait voir," &c. [Vol. ii. p. 384. Ed. Gen.] And so goes on to shew, like a great mathematician as he is, that it would be very inconvenient for the Page to be as big as his Lord and Master. It is pity all this fine reasoning should proceed on a ridiculous blunder. The poet thus reproves the impious complainer of the order of Providence: " You are dissatisfied with the weakness of your condition; But, in your situation, the nature

ESSAY ON MAN.

Of Syſtems poſſible, if 'tis confeſt
That Wiſdom infinite muſt form the beſt,
Where all muſt full or not coherent be,   45
And all that riſes, riſe in due degree;
Then, in the ſcale of reaſ'ning life, 'tis plain,
There muſt be, ſomewhere, ſuch a rank as Man:
And all the queſtion (wrangle e'er ſo long)
Is only this, if God has plac'd him wrong?   50
Reſpecting Man, whatever wrong we call,
May, muſt be right, as relative to all.
In human works, tho' labour'd on with pain,
A thouſand movements ſcarce one purpoſe gain;

In

NOTES.

ture of things requires juſt ſuch a creature as you are; in a different ſituation, it might have required that you ſhould be ſtill weaker. And though you ſee not the reaſon of this in your own caſe; yet, that reaſons there are, you may ſee in the caſe of other of God's creatures.

" Aſk of thy mother Earth, why oaks are made
Taller or ſtronger than the weeds they ſhade?
Or aſk of yonder argent fields above,
Why Jove's Satellites are leſs than Jove?"

Here (ſays the Poet) the ridicule of the *weeds*' and the *Satellites*' complaint, had they the faculties of ſpeech and reaſoning, would be obvious to all; becauſe their very ſituation and office might have convinced them of their folly. Your folly, ſays the Poet to his complainers, is as great, though not ſo evident, becauſe the reaſon is more out of ſight; but that a reaſon there is, may be demonſtrated from the attributes of the Deity. This is the Poet's clear and ſtrong reaſoning; from whence, we ſee, he was ſo far from ſaying, that Man could not know the cauſe *why Jove's Satellites were leſs than Jove*, that all the force of his reaſoning turns upon this, that Man did ſee and know it, and ſhould from thence conclude, that there was a cauſe of this inferiority as well in the *rational*, as in the *material* Creation.   W.

VER. 53. *In human works,*] Verbatim from Bolingbroke. Fragments 43 and 63.

In God's, one single can its end produce; 55
Yet serves to second too some other use.
So Man, who here seems principal alone,
Perhaps acts second to some sphere unknown,
Touches some wheel, or verges to some goal;
'Tis but a part we see, and not a whole. 60
When

NOTES.

VER. 60. *'Tis but a part*] A new method of accounting for the origin of evil has been advanced by Hume in his Dialogues, p. 196. " I scruple not to allow," said Cleanthes, " that I have been apt to suspect the frequent repetition of the word infinite, which we meet with in all theological writers, to favour more of panegyric than of philosophy; and that any purposes of reasoning, and even of religion, would be better served, were we to rest content with more accurate and more moderate expressions. The terms, admirable, excellent, superlatively great, wise, and holy, these sufficiently fill the imaginations of men; and any thing beyond, besides that it leads into absurdities, has no influence on the affections or sentiments. Thus, in the present subject, if we abandon all human analogy, as it seems your intention, Demea, I am afraid we abandon all religion, and retain no conception of the great object of our adoration. If we preserve human analogy, we must for ever find it impossible to reconcile any mixture of evil in the universe with infinite attributes; much less can we ever prove the latter from the former. But supposing the Author of Nature to be finitely perfect, though far exceeding mankind, a satisfactory account may then be given of natural and moral evil, and every untoward phenomenon be explained and adjusted. A less evil may then be chosen, in order to avoid a greater: inconveniencies be submitted to, in order to reach a desirable end: and, in a word, benevolence, regulated by wisdom and limited by necessity, may produce just such a world as the present." This seems to have been borrowed from Voltaire. Questions sur l'Encyclopedie, 9 Partie, p. 348. I have heard Dr. Adam Smith say, that these Dialogues concerning Natural Religion were the most laboured of all Hume's works. They were the occasion of Dr. Balguy's publishing that capital treatise, intitled, *Divine Benevolence*: which benevolence he undertakes to vindicate like this Essay on Man, but with greater consistency and closeness of reasoning, without having recourse to a future existence. Wollaston,

in

When the proud steed shall know why Man restrains
His fiery course, or drives him o'er the plains;
When the dull Ox, why now he breaks the clod,
Is now a victim, and now Egypt's God:
Then shall Man's pride and dulness comprehend   65
His actions', passion's, being's, use and end;
Why doing, suff'ring, check'd, impell'd; and why
This hour a slave, the next a deity.
Then say not Man's imperfect, Heaven's in fault;
Say rather, Man's as perfect as he ought: 70
His knowledge measur'd to his state and place;
His time a moment, and a point his space.

If

VARIATIONS.

VER. 64. In the former Editions,
  Now wears a garland an Egyptian God:
altered as above for the reason given in the note.

NOTES.

in a celebrated passage, has given a striking and pathetic picture of the evils and miseries of this present life, in order to shew (as many divines do in their discourses) the absolute necessity of another, for the defence of the dispensations of Providence. Dr. Balguy, from p. 110 to p. 127, has minutely, and step by step, confuted every part of this statement of the evils and miseries of life; and ends by saying, " that Wollaston has only attended to one side of the question. He has dwelt largely on the melancholy parts of human life; but in great measure overlooked its enjoyments. A pen like his could, with equal ease and success, have painted the happiness of our present state, and given it the appearance of a paradise." This is the passage of Wollaston, which Bolingbroke has so much ridiculed. Works, vol. ii. p. 110.

VER. 64.—*Egypt's God:*] Called so, because the God *Apis* was worshipped universally over the whole land of Egypt.   W.

VER. 70. *As he ought :*] Consequently man is not in a lapsed or degenerate state. He is as perfect a being as ever his Creator intended him to be; nor, consequently, did he stand in need of

If to be perfect in a certain sphere,
What matter, soon or late, or here or there?
The blest to day is as completely so, 75
As who began a thousand years ago.
 III. Heav'n from all creatures hides the book of Fate,
All but the page prescrib'd, their present state:
From brutes what men, from men what spirits know:
Or who could suffer Being here below? 80
The lamb thy riot dooms to bleed to day,
Had he thy Reason, would he skip and play?
Pleas'd to the last, he crops the flow'ry food,
And licks the hand just rais'd to shed his blood.
Oh blindness to the future! kindly giv'n, 85
That each may fill the circle mark'd by Heav'n:
           Who

NOTES.

any redemption or atonement. The expression, as *he ought*, is imperfect; for, ought *to be*.

 VER. 74. *What matter, soon*] But surely, the sooner and the later, with respect to communicating happiness to any being, is, and must be, a circumstance of great consequence.

 VER. 77. *The book of Fate,*] It would obviate the heavy difficulties in which we are involved, when we argue on the Divine Prescience, and consequent Predestination, if we were to adopt Archbishop King's opinion, and say, " that the knowledge of God is very different from the knowledge of Man, which implies succession, and seeing objects one after another; but the existence and the attributes of the Deity can have no relation to time; for that all things, past, present, and to come, are all at once present to the Divine Mind."

 VER. 81. *The lamb thy riot dooms*] The tenderness of this striking image, and particularly the circumstance in the last line, has an artful effect in alleviating the dryness of the argumentative parts of the Essay, and interesting the reader. No happier passage can be found in our author's works, though Johnson thought otherwise.

Who sees with equal eye, as God of all,
A hero perish, or a sparrow fall,
Atoms or systems into ruin hurl'd,
And now a bubble burst, and now a world. 90
Hope humbly then; with trembling pinions soar;
Wait the great teacher Death; and God adore.
What future bliss, he gives not thee to know,
But gives that Hope to be thy blessing now.
Hope springs eternal in the human breast: 95
Man never Is, but always To be blest.
The soul (uneasy, and confin'd) from home,
Rests and expatiates in a life to come.

Lo,

VARIATIONS.

After Ver. 88, in the MS.
   No great, no little; 'tis as much decreed
   That Virgil's Gnat should die as Cæfar bleed.
Ver. 93, 94. In the first Fol. and Quarto,
   What bliss *above* he gives not thee to know,
   But gives that Hope to be thy bliss *below*.

NOTES.

VER. 87. *Who sees with equal eye, &c.*] Matth. x. 29.
VER. 97. *The soul (uneasy, and confin'd)*] " In the old editions,
it was, confin'd *at home*, which was altered at the perfuasion of the
divine, against the sense of the poet. The point to be illustrated
is, that hope is implanted in man, to enable him to bear all the
evils of life, though it is merely visionary, and has no foundation :
   " What future bliss he gives not thee to know,
      But gives that hope to be thy blessing now."
Thus man, confined on his own earth, dreams of imaginary mansions in another world. Hope supplies the reality of them. He hopes, upon the same ground as the Indian does, for a heaven, where his dog shall accompany him. Sorry am I to give this view of the author's creed; but it is too true a reprefentation of it. He makes no difference between the certainty of the

> Lo, the poor Indian! whose untutor'd mind
> Sees God in clouds, or hears him in the wind; 100
> His

NOTES.

Christian's heaven and the Indian's. It will be presumption in me to go further; and yet I cannot help observing, that, allow Mr. Pope this doctrine, and he will go near to overthrow the whole argument of the divine legation of Moses. God has implanted in mankind a religious fear, and a foreboding of a future state. The divine says, he had this from revelation: the deist, that it supplies the want of one; that it has kept the world in awe from the beginning of the creation, seconded with an opinion of Providence prevailing even in this world." From MS. notes of our learned printer Mr. Bowyer.

VER. 99. *Lo, the poor Indian! &c.*] The Poet having bid Man comfort himself with expectation of future happiness; having shewn him that this HOPE is an earnest of it; and put in one very necessary caution,

"Hope *humbly* then, with *trembling* pinions soar;"

provoked at those miscreants whom he afterwards (Ep. iii. Ver. 263.) describes as building *Hell on spite, and Heaven on pride*, he upbraids them (from Ver. 98 to 113.) with the example of the poor Indian, to whom also Nature hath given this *common* HOPE of *Mankind:* But though his untutor'd mind had betrayed him into many childish fancies concerning the nature of that future state. yet he is so far from excluding any part of his own species (a vice which could proceed only from the *pride* of false Science) that he humanely, though simply, admits even his *faithful dog to bear him company.* W.

Pope has indulged himself in but few digressions in this piece; this is one of the most poetical. Representations of undisguised nature and artless innocence always amuse and delight. The simple notions which uncivilized nations entertain of a future state are many of them beautifully romantic, and some of the best subjects for poetry. It has been questioned, whether the circumstance of the dog, although striking at the first view, is introduced with propriety, as it is known that this animal is not a native of America. The notion of seeing God in clouds, and hearing him in the wind, cannot be enough applauded. Buffon says, the Americans had no domestic animals about them when that continent was discovered.

His foul, proud Science never taught to ſtray
Far as the ſolar walk, or milky way;
Yet ſimple Nature to his hope has giv'n,
Behind the cloud-topt hill, an humbler heav'n;
Some ſafer world in depth of woods embrac'd,　105
Some happier iſland in the wat'ry waſte,
Where ſlaves once more their native land behold,
No fiends torment, no Chriſtians thirſt for gold.
To Be, contents his natural deſire,
He aſks no Angel's wing, no Seraph's fire;　110
But thinks, admitted to that equal ſky,
His faithful dog ſhall bear him company.

IV. Go, wiſer thou! and, in thy ſcale of ſenſe,
Weigh thy Opinion againſt Providence;
Call imperfection what thou fancy'ſt ſuch,　115
Say, Here he gives too little, there too much:
Deſtroy all creatures for thy ſport or guſt,
Yet cry, If Man's unhappy, God's unjuſt;
If Man alone ingroſs not Heav'n's high care,
Alone made perfect here, immortal there:　120

Snatch

VARIATIONS.

After Ver. 108. in the firſt Ed.
But does he ſay the Maker is not good,
Till he's exalted to what ſtate he wou'd:
Himſelf alone high Heav'n's peculiar care,
Alone made happy when he will, and where?

NOTES.

VER. 120. *Alone made perfect here,*] The obvious meaning is,
" Be content with the preſent life; it is your pride only that
makes you think yourſelf ill-treated, and induces you to look for
another and more perfect ſtate."

Bolingbroke

Snatch from his hand the balance and the rod,
Rejudge his juſtice, be the GOD of GOD.
In Pride, in reas'ning Pride, our error lies;
All quit their ſphere, and ruſh into the ſkies.
Pride ſtill is aiming at the bleſt abodes, 125
Men would be Angels, Angels would be Gods.

Aſpiring

NOTES.

Bolingbroke is for ever repeating the ſame note, and ſaying, " It is profane even to inſinuate, and much more to affirm peremptorily, that the proceedings of God towards man, in the preſent life, are unjuſt; and, if that could be admitted, it would be abſurd to admit that this may be ſet right; which means, if the words have any meaning, that this injuſtice muſt ceaſe to be injuſtice, on the received hypotheſis of his proceedings towards man in another life. One is profane, notwithſtanding all the queſtions they beg to ſupport the charge: the other is abſurd, on the very principles on which they argue, and according to our cleareſt and moſt diſtinct ideas or notions of human juſtice."

It is a ſingular fact, and not ſufficiently attended to, that neither the ancient philoſophers nor poets, though they abound in complaints of the unequal diſtribution of good and evil at preſent, yet do not even infer or draw any arguments, from this ſuppoſed inequality, for the neceſſity of a future life, where ſuch inequality will be rectified, and Providence vindicated.

VER. 126. *Men would be Angels*,] Verbatim from Bolingbroke, vol. v. p. 465.; as are many other paſſages. How are we to interpret the aſſertion, that Pope did not really underſtand the principles of Bolingbroke, when the latter ſays to him, " Theſe ſubjects have been ſo often treated of between you and me, that I ſhall ſay nothing of them here." The following paſſage, relating to the caution and timidity of Pope, may give us a key to his conduct, vol. iv. p. 190. " Read," ſays Bolingbroke to him, " the entire paſſage; conſult your memory; look round you, and then you ſhall tell me what you think of Clarke's argument. You ſhall tell it in my ear: I expect no more; for I know how deſirous you are to keep fair with orders, whatever liberties you take with particular men."

Ep. I.   ESSAY ON MAN.   25
Afpiring to be Gods, if Angels fell,
Afpiring to be Angels, Men rebel:
And who but wifhes to invert the laws
Of ORDER, fins againſt th' Eternal Caufe.   130
                                                V. Alk

NOTES.

VER. 127. *If Angels fell,*] It may mortify our pride to confider how little we know of the Fall of Angels; on which event depends the Fall of Man, effected by the agency of the chief of thefe
Fallen Angels. Revelation is not exprefs on this important fubject. All is imperfect conjecture. We have only a few hints on
the fubject: Such as that in Ifaiah, c. xiv. v. 12.; and in Eze-
kiel, c. xxviii. v. 14.; and in the Apocalypfe, concerning the
feven-headed dragon. " I had rather know the hiſtory of Lucifer," fays Burnet, in his Theory, " than of all the Babylonian
and Perfian kings; nay, than of all the kings of the earth: what
the birthright was of that mighty prince; what his dominions;
where his imperial court and refidence; how he was depofed; for
what crime, and by what power; how he ſtill wages war againſt
heaven in his exile; what confederates he hath; what is his power
over mankind, and how limited."

Milton, in book v. copies from the Rabbinical writers, from
the fathers, and fome of the fchoolmen, the caufes of the rebellion
of Satan and his affociates; but feems more particularly to have
in view an obfcure Latin poem written by Odoricus Valmarana,
and printed at Vienna in 1627, intitled, " Dæmonomachiæ, five
de Bello Intelligentiarum fuper Divini Verbi Incarnatione;" in
which the revolt of Satan, or Lucifer, is exprefsly afcribed to his
envy at the exaltation of the Son of God. See Newton's Milton,
vol. i. p. 407. But the commentators on Milton have not obferved that there is ſtill another poem which he feems to have copied, " L'Angeleida di Erafmo di Valvafone," printed at Venice,
in quarto, in 1590, defcribing the battle of the Angels againſt
Lucifer, and which Gordon de Porcel, in his Library of Ro-
mances, tom. ii. p. 190. thought related to Angelica, the heroine
of Boiardo and Arioſto. I beg leave to add, that Milton feems
alfo to have attended to a poem of Taffo, not much noticed, on
the Creation, " Le Sette Giornate del Mondo Creato," in 1607.

V. Aſk for what end the heav'nly bodies ſhine,
Earth for whoſe uſe ? Pride anſwers, " 'Tis for mine :
" For me kind Nature wakes her genial pow'r,
" Suckles each herb, and ſpreads out ev'ry flow'r ;
" Annual for me, the grape, the roſe renew,   135
" The juice nectareous, and the balmy dew ;
" For me, the mine a thouſand treaſures brings ;
" For me, health guſhes from a thouſand ſprings ;
" Seas roll to waft me, ſuns to light me riſe ;
" My foot-ſtool earth, my canopy the ſkies."   140
But errs not Nature from this gracious end,
From burning ſuns when livid deaths deſcend,

When

NOTES.

VER. 131. *Aſk for what end, &c.*] If there be any fault in theſe lines, it is not in the general ſentiment, but in the ill choice of inſtances made uſe of in illuſtrating it. It is the higheſt abſurdity to think that *Earth is* man's *foot-ſtool,* his *canopy the Skies,* and the *heavenly bodies* lighted up principally for his uſe ; yet, ſurely, it is very excuſable to ſuppoſe fruits and minerals given for this end.   W.

There is moſt aſſuredly a fault.

VER. 141. *But errs not Nature*] The whole of this doctrine is thus clearly ſtated in ſome valuable manuſcripts of the late James Harris, Eſq.

" Whence evil in the univerſe, and why ? Some things, perhaps, which thou thinkeſt ſuch, are not evil, but in appearance. Where the whole is vaſtly great, the connections will be innumerable. When, therefore, a part only is ſeen, many of theſe connections will be inexplicable. Being inexplicable, they will often exhibit appearances of evil, where yet in fact is no evil, but only good, not underſtood.

" Again, throughout the whole there is more good than evil : For in the ſyſtem of the heavens we know of no evil at all. The

ſame

When earthquakes fwallow, or when tempefts fweep
Towns to one grave, whole nations to the deep?

"No

NOTES.

fame perhaps is true in many other parts of the whole. And with
refpect even to men, 'tis their intereft to be good, if it be true
that by Nature they are rational and focial. So that if, by vice
of any kind, they chance to introduce evil, 'tis by deviating from
Nature, and thwarting her original purpofe. Indeed, all evil in
general appears to be of the cafual kind; not fomething intended
by the Maker of the world, (for all his preparations plainly tend
towards good,) but fomething which follows, without being intended, and that perhaps necefarily, from the nature and effence
of things. Indeed, the nature and effence of every being is immutable; and, while it exifts itfelf, all its attributes will exift
likewife. To fay, therefore, a thing fhould be, without its infe-
parable and conftitutive attributes, is the fame as to fay, it fhould
be, and not be. A miller works in his mill, and becomes white:
a collier works in his mine, and becomes black: yet were neither
of thefe incidents intended by either; but, other and better ends
being purpofed to be anfwered, they were necefarily attended by
thefe collateral incidents. So it is in the univerfe. The good
leads, the evil follows: the good is always defigned, the evil only
admitted: the good has exiftence, by being the final caufe of all
things; the evil has exiftence, becaufe it cannot be avoided: the
good appears to be fomething in character and form, which all
beings fome way or other are framed to enjoy: the evil, on the
contrary, appears to be fomething which all beings fome way or
other are framed to avoid; fome by talons, others by teeth; fome
by wings, others by fins; and, laftly, man, by genius ripened
into arts, which alone is fuperior to the fum of all other preparations.

" Again, fome evil, though evil, is yet productive of good,
and therefore had better be, than not be, elfe there had not been
the good. For example, human nature is infirm; expofed to
many and daily hardfhips; to pinching colds and fcorching heats;
to famines, droughts, difeafes, wounds. Call this all of it evil,
if you pleafe. Yet what a variety of arts arife from this evil, and
which, if this evil had not urged, had never exifted? Where had
been agriculture, architecture, medicine, weaving, with a thou-

fand

" No ('tis reply'd) the first Almighty Cause   145
" Acts not by partial, but by gen'ral laws;
" Th'

NOTES.

sand other arts too many to enumerate, had man been born a self-sufficient animal, superior to the sensations of want or evil? Where had been that noble activity, that never-ceasing energy of all his various powers, had not the poignancy of evil awakened them from the very birth, and dispelled all symptoms of lethargy and drowsiness? Nay more; courage, magnanimity, prudence, and wise indifference; patience, long-suffering, and acquiescence in our lot; a calm and manly resignation to the will of God, whatever he dispenses, whether good or bad; these heroic virtues could never have had existence, had not those things called evils first established them into habit, and afterwards given occasion for them to energize, and become conspicuous. But the most important circumstance of all is, that the very being and essence of society itself is derived from the wants and infirmities of human nature. 'Tis these various infirmities, so much more numerous and lasting in man than in other animals, which make human societies so eminently necessary; which extend them so far beyond all other animal associations, and knit them together with such indissoluble bands. Let each individual be supposed self-sufficient, and society at once is dissolved and annihilated. For why associate without a cause? And what need of society, if each can support himself? But mark the consequence; if society be lost, with it we lose the energy of every social affection; a loss, in which every man loses something, but in which a good man loses his principal and almost his only happiness: For what then becomes of friendship, benevolence, love of country, hospitality, generosity, forgiveness, with all the charities

Of father, son, and brother?

A man detached from human connections and relations (if such a monster may indeed be supposed) is no better than an ignorant inhuman savage; a mere Cyclops, devoid of all that is amiable and good."

In another part of the same manuscripts he adds, " But a few days ago, and 'twas a lovely world. All was florid, cheerful, and gay. Yesterday my friend's house was burnt. To-day arrived

"Th' exceptions few; fome change fince all began:
"And what created perfect?—Why then Man?
If

NOTES.

rived the news of the death of an old fervant, who was diligent, careful, and of long-approved fidelity. Now 'tis all difaftrous, black, and difmal. Wretched man! Wretched univerfe! how miferable a manfion, and how helplefs its inhabitants! Happy exiftence may indeed well be defired; but what value in exiftence only pregnant with anxiety? Wifely murmured! cries the leading principle, the god-like particle of reafon and common fenfe. The events which thou lamenteft are ftrange and unheard of. Thou never kneweft before that thy fpecies was mortal, or that fire could do any thing but prepare thee thy food. Murmur on, and grieve thee with a laudable obftinacy. 'Twill infallibly cancel what is gone and over; render paft, not paft; and done, not done: For what fo eafy, fo practicable, and obvious? Befides thou, for thy part, haft no defire to acquire thofe virtues which none can learn, but who have been partakers of the pains, the croffes, and calamities, and difafters of human life. Man-like conftancy, brave fteady endurance, a cheerful acquiefcence in the univerfal difpenfation, are to thee but trifles of mean importance. They are only of ufe in a buftling world, when the winds rage, the ftorms defcend, thunders roll,

"With terror thro' the dark aerial hall."

Thou haft never dreamt of a world like this: thou haft never framed thyfelf but for a fine Elyfian one, where fpring perpetual fmiles with verdant flowers; where funfhine and zephyrs are happily blended; juft exactly fuch a fpot as thou haft ever found old England, where never was a froft, never a fog, never a day but was delicious and ferene. But hold, Reafon! we have never found old England that paradife which thou defcribeft.—Fools then, and idiots! why act you as though you had? Why are your tempers and manners adapted to one kind of world, while your real fituation is found to be in another?—Would you travel to Greenland in your fhirt, and not be cold?—to Guinea in your cloak, and not be warm? Muft things fubmit to you, or you to things? Or is it not as abfurd to fuppofe that the world fhould be new-modelled, that it might correfpond to the weaknefs and caprices of mankind, as that the foot fhould be fitted to the fhoe,

and,

If the great end be human Happiness,
Then Nature deviates; and can Man do less?   150
As much that end a constant course requires
Of show'rs and sun-shine, as of Man's desires;
As much eternal springs and cloudless skies,
As Men for ever temp'rate, calm, and wise.
If plagues or earthquakes break not Heaven's design,   155
Why then a Borgia, or a Catiline?
                                                  Who

NOTES.

and not the shoe to the foot; the horse to the saddle, and not the saddle to the horse?—Be thankful rather to that Divine Providence, who hath given thee powers to make even this life a happy one; who hath wisely contrived, that, where proper care is had, from the greatest of calamities may be learnt, if thou wilt endeavour, the noblest of all virtues."

VER. 148. *And what created perfect?*] No position can be more true and solid; for perfect happiness is as incommunicable as omnipotence. But the objector will not be equally satisfied by being told, that there can be any exceptions or any change under the guidance of a gracious and powerful Creator. Bayle is for ever repeating, in answer to his antagonists, " I only maintain, that the objections concerning the origin of evil cannot be solved by the mere strength of reason; and I always believed that this was saying no more than what all our divines confess concerning the incomprehensibility of predestination."

VER. 150. *Then Nature deviates, &c.*] " While comets move in very eccentric orbs, in all manner of positions, blind Fate could never make all the planets move one and the same way in orbs concentric; some inconsiderable irregularities excepted, which may have risen from the mutual actions of comets and planets upon one another, and which will be apt to increase, till this system wants a reformation." *Sir Isaac Newton's Optics, Quæst. ult.*

VER. 155. *If plagues, &c.*] What hath misled Mr. De Croufaz in his censure of this passage, is his supposing the comparison to be between the effects of *two things in this sublunary world;* when not only the elegancy, but the justness of it, consists in its being between

Ep. I. ESSAY ON MAN. 31

Who knows but He, whofe hand the light'ning forms,
Who heaves old Ocean, and who wings the ftorms;
Pours

NOTES.

tween the effects of a thing in the *univerfe at large*, and the familiar known effects of one *in this fublunary world*. For the pofition inforced in thefe lines is this, *that partial evil tends to the good of the whole:*

" Refpecting Man, whatever wrong we call,
" May, muft be right, as relative to all." Ver. 51.

How does the Poet inforce it? If you will believe this Critic, in illuftrating the effects of partial moral evil in a particular fyftem, by that of partial natural evil in the *fame* fyftem, and fo he leaves his *pofition* in the lurch. But the Poet reafons at another rate: The way to prove his point, he knew, was to illuftrate the effect of partial moral evil in the *univerfe*, by partial natural evil in a *particular fyftem*. Whether partial moral evil tend to the good of the Univerfe, being a queftion which, by reafon of our ignorance of *many* parts of that Univerfe, we cannot decide but from known effects; the rules of good reafoning require that it be proved by analogy, *i. e.* fetting it by, and comparing it with, a thing *clear and certain;* and it is a thing *clear and certain*, that partial natural evil tends to the good of our *particular fyftem*. W.

" All ills arife from the order of the univerfe, which is abfolutely perfect. Would you wifh to difturb fo divine an order for the fake of your own particular intereft? What if the ills I fuffer arife from malice or oppreffion? But the vices and imperfections of men are alfo comprehended in the order of the univerfe.

" If plagues," &c.

Let this be allowed, and my own vices will be alfo a part of the fame order."

Such is the commentary of the academift on thefe famous lines.

Voltaire, having written his poem on the dreadful earthquake at Lifbon, in direct oppofition to the maxim of " Whatever is, is right," fpeaks of it thus in a letter to his friend, M. de Cideville, 1756: " Comme je ne fuis pas en tout de l'avis de Pope, malgré l'amitié que j'ai eue pour fa perfonne, et l'eftime fincere que je conferverai toute ma vie pour fes ouvrages, j'ai cru devoir lui rendre juftice dans ma preface, auffi-bien qu'à notre illuftre ami M.

l'Abbé

Pours fierce Ambition in a Cæsar's mind,
Or turns young Ammon loose to scourge man-
    kind? 160
From pride, from pride, our very reas'ning springs;
Account for moral, as for nat'ral things:
Why charge we Heav'n in those, in these acquit?
In both, to reason right is to submit.

    Better for Us, perhaps, it might appear, 165
Were there all harmony, all virtue here;
That never air or ocean felt the wind;
That never passion discompos'd the mind.
                                     But

NOTES.

l'Abbé du Resnel, qui lui a fait l'honneur de le traduire, et souvent lui a rendu le service d'adoucir les duretés des ses sentimens."

Ver. 157. *Who knows but He, &c.*] The sublimity with which the great Author of Nature is here characterised, is but the second beauty of this fine passage. The greatest is the making the very dispensation objected to, the periphrasis of his title. W.

Ver. 162. *Account for moral,*] Their natures are so very dissimilar, that they cannot, and ought not, to be accounted for by the same arguments. Men suffer and feel; elements, and unconscious inanimate beings, cannot. Evil must be felt before it is evil. Such different objects require different treatment. " If Nature," says the commentator, " or the inanimate system on which God hath imposed his laws, which it obeys, as a machine obeys the hand of the workman, may, in course of time, deviate from its first direction, as the best philosophy shews it may, where is the wonder that man, who was created a free agent, and hath it in his power every moment to transgress the eternal rule of right, should sometimes go out of order?" Are free agents, and beings accountable, because they are free, to be put on the same footing as the inanimate system? The infidel is for ever asking, Why was man endowed with a faculty so dangerous, and so easily abused?

Ver. 167. *That never air or ocean*] An acute critic asks if it should not be—That never earth or ocean?—not air.

But ALL subsists by elemental strife;
And passions are the elements of Life. 170
The gen'ral ORDER, since the whole began,
Is kept in Nature, and is kept in Man.
VI. What would this Man? Now upward will he
soar,
And little less than Angels, would be more;
Now looking downwards, just as griev'd appears 175
To want the strength of bulls, the fur of bears.
Made

NOTES.

VER. 169. *But All subsists, &c.*] See this subject extended in Epistle ii. from Ver. 90 to 112, 155, &c.

VER. 171. *The general Order,*] It seems utterly impossible to explain these two remarkable lines in a way at all reconcileable to the doctrine of a lapsed condition of man, which opinion is the chief foundation of the Christian revelation, and the capital argument for the necessity of redemption.

"That system of philosophy," says an able writer, "which professes to justify the ways of God to man, without having recourse to the doctrine of a future state, must ever be considered as in the highest degree inimical to religion, whose very nature and essence it is to direct our views beyond the narrow limits of the present state of existence." See Essays Philosophical, Historical, and Literary, p. 399. for some very acute observations on the Essay on Man.

Pope in these lines uses almost the very words of Bolingbroke: "To think worthily of God, we must think that the natural order of things has always been the same; and that a being of infinite wisdom and knowledge, to whom the past and the future are like the present, and who wants no experience to inform him, can have no reason to alter what infinite wisdom and knowledge have once done." Section 58. Essays to Pope.

VER. 174. *And little less than Angels, &c.*] *Thou hast made him a little lower than the Angels, and hast crowned him with glory and honour.* Psalm viii. 9.

Made for his ufe all creatures if he call,
Say, what their ufe, had he the pow'rs of all;
Nature to thefe, without profufion, kind,
The proper organs, proper pow'rs affign'd; 180
Each feeming want compenfated of courfe,
Here with degrees of fwiftnefs, there of force;
All in exact proportion to the ftate;
Nothing to add, and nothing to abate,
Each beaft, each infect, happy in its own: 185
Is Heav'n unkind to Man, and Man alone?
Shall he alone, whom rational we call,
Be pleas'd with nothing, if not blefs'd with all?

   The blifs of Man (could Pride that bleffing find)
Is not to act or think beyond mankind; 190
No pow'rs of body or of foul to fhare,
But what his nature and his ftate can bear.
Why has not Man a microfcopic eye?
For this plain reafon, Man is not a Fly.

Say

NOTES.

VER. 182. *Here with degrees of fwiftnefs, &c.*] It is a certain axiom in the anatomy of creatures, that in proportion as they are formed for ftrength, their fwiftnefs is leffened; or as they are formed for fwiftnefs, their ftrength is abated. P.

VER. 183. *All in exact proportion*] I cannot forbear thinking, that a little French treatife on Providence, publifhed at Paris, 1728, formed on the principles of Leibnitz, fomewhat moderated, had fallen into the hands both of Bolingbroke and Pope, from the great fimilarity of the reafoning there employed.

VER. 186. *Is Heav'n unkind to Man,*] Cudworth, Leibnitz, King, Shaftefbury, Hutchefon, Balguy, have all ftrenuoufly argued for the prepollency of good to evil in our prefent fyftem; but none more forcibly than Balguy from p. 103 to p. 125 of his Divine Benevolence.

Say what the ufe, were finer optics giv'n, 195
T' infpect a mite, not comprehend the heav'n?
Or touch, if tremblingly alive all o'er,
To fmart and agonize at ev'ry pore?
Or quick effluvia darting through the brain,
Die of a rofe in aromatic pain? 200
If Nature thunder'd in his op'ning ears,
And ftunn'd him with the mufic of the fpheres,
How would he wifh that Heav'n had left him ftill
The whifp'ring Zephyr, and the purling rill?
Who finds not Providence all good and wife, 205
Alike in what it gives, and what denies?
   VII. Far as Creation's ample range extends,
The fcale of fenfual, mental pow'rs afcends:
                                        Mark

NOTES.

VER. 202. *And ftunn'd him*] The argument certainly required an inftance drawn from real found, and not from the imaginary mufic of the fpheres. Locke's illuftration of this doctrine is not only proper but poetical: "If our fenfe of hearing were but one thoufand times quicker than it is, how would a perpetual noife diftract us; and we fhould, in the quieteft retirement, be lefs able to fleep or meditate, than in the middle of a fea-fight." In line before 193, the expreffion of microfcopic eye is from Locke.

VER. 207. *Far as Creation's ample range extends,*] He tells us (from Ver. 206 to 233.) that the complying with fuch extravagant defires would not only be ufelefs and pernicious to Man, but would be breaking into the order, and deforming the beauty of God's Creation, in which *this* animal is fubject to *that*, and every one to Man; who by his Reafon enjoys the fum of all their powers. W.

In the prefent improved ftate of Reafon, poets of philofophy will be preferred to poets of fancy. It may be doubted whether our author has excelled Dryden in the art of reafoning in rhyme,
whofe

Mark how it mounts, to Man's imperial race,
From the green myriads in the peopled grafs: 210
                                                What

NOTES.

whofe Religio Laici, and Hind and Panther, are in this refpect admirable; though the fable of the latter abounds in abfurdities and inconfiftencies.

VER. 209. *Mark how it mounts,*] When it is faid that Pope was guilty of fome contradictions and fome inconfiftencies in his reafonings on the *beft*, let us alfo remember that fo alfo was his guide and philofophical friend, who, it is to be wifhed, had always expreffed himfelf as in the following terms, p. 121. v. 5.

" Methinks I hear a fincere and devout theift, in the midft of fuch meditations as thefe, cry out, " No; the world was not made for man, nor man only to be happy. The objections urged by atheifts and divines againft the wifdom and goodnefs of the Supreme Being, on thefe arbitrary fuppofitions, deftroy their own foundations. Mankind is expofed, as well as other animals, to many inconveniencies and to various evils, by the conftitution of the world. The world was not, therefore, made for him, nor he to be happy. But he enjoys numberlefs benefits, by the fitnefs of his nature to this conftitution, unafked, unmerited, freely beftowed. He returns, like other animals, to the duft; yet neither he nor they are willing to leave the ftate wherein they are placed here. The wifdom and the goodnefs of God are therefore manifeft. I thank thee, O my Creator! that I am placed in a rank, low in the whole order of being, but the firft in that animal fyftem to which I belong: a rank wherein I am made capable of knowing thee, and of difcovering thy will, the perfection of my own nature, and the means of my own happinefs. Far be it from me to repine at my prefent ftate, like thofe who deny thee; or like thofe who own thee, only to cenfure thy works and the difpenfations of thy providence. May I enjoy thankfully the benefits beftowed on me by thy divine liberality! May I fuffer the evils, to which I ftand expofed, patiently, nay willingly! None of thy creatures are made to be perfectly happy like thyfelf; nor did thy goodnefs require that they fhould be fo. Such of them as are more worthy objects of it than thy human creatures, fuperior natures that inhabit other worlds, may be affected in fome degree or other by phyfical evils, fince thefe are effects of the general laws of

ESSAY ON MAN.

What modes of fight betwixt each wide extreme,
The mole's dim curtain, and the lynx's beam :
Of fmell, the headlong lionefs between,
And hound fagacious to the tainted green :

Of

NOTES.

matter and motion. They muft be affected too, in fome degree or other, by moral evil, fince moral evil is the confequence of error, as well as of diforderly appetites and paffions, and fince error is the confequence of imperfect underftanding. Lefs of this evil may prevail among them. But all that is finite, the moft exalted intelligences, muft be liable to fome errors. Thou, O God! that Being who is liable to none, and to whom infallibility and impeccability belong,

" Duc me, parens celfique dominator poli,
" Quocumque placuit. Nulla parendi mora eft,
" Affum impiger *."

VER. 210. *From the green myriads*] Thefe lines are admirable patterns of forcible diction. The peculiar and difcriminating expreffivenefs of the epithets ought to be particularly regarded. Perhaps we have no image in the language more lively than that of the laft verfe : " To live along the line," is equally bold and beautiful. In this part of the epiftle the poet feems to have remarkably laboured his ftyle, which abounds in various figures, and is much elevated. Pope has practifed the great fecret of Virgil's art, which was to difcover the very fingle epithet that precifely fuited each occafion. If Pope muft yield to other poets in point of fertility of fancy, or harmony of numbers, yet in point of propriety, clofenefs, and elegance of diction, he can yield to none. Very inferior is the tranflation of Abbé du Refnel, of all this fine paffage, to the original, though it is evident he took pains about it. See his four lines on the fpider :

Contemplez l'araignée en fon réduit obfcur ;
Que fon toucher eft vif, qu'il eft prompt, qu'il eft fur ;
Sur ces pieges, tendus fans ceffe vigilante,
Dans chacun de fes fils elle paroit vivante.

VER. 213. *The headlong lionefs*] The manner of the lions hunting their prey in the defarts of Africa is this : At their firft going

---

* Sen. Ep. 107.

Of hearing, from the life that fills the flood, 215
To that which warbles through the vernal wood?
The spider's touch, how exquisitely fine!
Feels at each thread, and lives along the line:
In the nice bee, what sense so subtly true
From pois'nous herbs extracts the healing dew? 220
How Instinct varies in the grov'ling swine,
Compar'd, half-reas'ning elephant, with thine!
'Twixt that, and Reason, what a nice barrier?
For ever sep'rate, yet for ever near!
Remembrance and Reflection, how ally'd; 225
What thin partitions Sense from Thought divide?
And

NOTES.

out in the night-time they set up a loud roar, and then listen to the noise made by the beasts in their flight, pursuing them by the ear, and not by the nostril. It is probable the story of the jackall's hunting for the lion, was occasioned by the observation of this defect of scent in that terrible animal. P.

VER. 224. *For ever sep'rate, &c.*] *Near*, by the similitude of the operations; *separate* by the immense difference in the nature of the powers. W.

VER. 226. *What thin partitions, &c.*] So *thin*, that the Atheistic Philosophers, as Protagoras, held that THOUGHT *was only* SENSE; and from thence concluded, that *every imagination or opinion of every man was true:* Πᾶσα Φαντασία ἐςὶν ἀληθής. But the Poet determines more philosophically; that they are really and essentially different, how *thin* soever the partition be by which they are *divided*. Thus, (to illustrate the truth of this observation,) when a geometer considers a triangle, in order to demonstrate the equality of its three angles to two right ones, he has the picture or image of some sensible triangle in his mind, which is *sense*; yet notwithstanding, he must needs have the motion or idea of an intellectual triangle likewise, which is *thought*; for this plain reason, because every image or picture of a triangle must needs be obtusangular, or rectangular, or acutangular; but that which, in his mind, is the subject of his proposition is the ratio of a triangle,

undetermined

And Middle natures, how they long to join,
Yet never pafs th' infuperable line!
Without this juft gradation, could they be
Subjected, thefe to thofe, or all to thee?   230
The pow'rs of all fubdu'd by thee alone,
Is not thy Reafon all thefe pow'rs in one?
 VIII. See, through this air, this ocean, and this earth,
All matter quick, and burfting into birth.
Above, how high, progreffive life may go!   235
Around, how wide, how deep extend below!
Vaft chain of Being! which from God began,
Natures ethereal, human, angel, man,
                                                        Beaft,

VARIATIONS.

VER. 238. Ed. 1ft.
   Ethereal effence, fpirit, fubftance, man.

NOTES.

undetermined to any of thefe fpecies. On this account it was that Ariftotle faid, Νοηματα τιπ διοισει, τῳ μη Φαηλασματα ειναι, η δε ταυτα Φαηλασματα, αλλ' εκ ανευ Φαηλασματων. *The conceptions of the mind differ fomewhat from fenfible images; they are not fenfible images, and yet not quite free or difengaged from fenfible images.*

VER. 232. *Is not thy Reafon*] "Such then is the admirable diftribution of nature, her adapting and adjufting not only the ftuff or matter to the fhape itfelf and form, to the circumftance, place, element, or region; but alfo the affections, appetites, fenfations, mutually to each other, as well as the matter, form, action, and all befides; all managed for the beft, with perfect frugality and juft referve: profufe to none, but bountiful to all: never employing in one thing more than enough; but with exact œconomy retrenching the fuperfluous, and adding force to what is principal in every thing: And is not thought and reafon principal in man? would we have no referve for thefe; no faving for this part of his engine?" Shaftfbury, in the Moralift, vol. ii. p. 99.

VER. 235. *Above, how high,*] This is a magnificent paffage. Thomfon had before faid, in Summer, v. 333.

Beaſt, bird, fiſh, inſect, what no eye can ſee,
No glaſs can reach; from infinite to thee,   240
From thee to Nothing.—On ſuperior pow'rs
Were we to preſs, inferior might on ours:
Or in the full creation leave a void,
Where, one ſtep broken, the great ſcale's deſtroy'd:
From Nature's chain whatever link you ſtrike,   245
Tenth, or ten thouſandth, breaks the chain alike.
  And, if each ſyſtem in gradation roll
Alike eſſential to th' amazing Whole,
The leaſt confuſion but in one, not all
That ſyſtem only, but the Whole muſt fall.   250
                                                Let

NOTES.

————Has any ſeen
The mighty chain of beings, leſſening down
From infinite Perfection, to the brink
Of dreary Nothing, deſolate abyſs!
From which aſtoniſh'd thought recoiling turns?
See alſo Locke, vol. ii. p. 49.

VER. 240. *No glaſs can reach;*] "There are," ſays Hooke the naturaliſt, " 8,280,000 *animalcula* in one drop of water." " Nature, in many inſtances," ſays Themiſtius, " appears to make her tranſitions ſo imperceptibly, and by little and little, that in ſome beings it may be doubted whether they are animal or vegetable.

VER. 244. *The great ſcale's deſtroy'd:*] All that can be ſaid of the ſuppoſition of a ſcale of beings gradually deſcending from perfection to non-entity, and complete in every rank and degree, is to be found in the third chapter of King's Origin of Evil, and in a note of the Archbiſhop, marked G, p. 137. of Law's tranſlation, ending with theſe emphatical words: " Whatever ſyſtem God had choſen, all creatures in it could not have been equally perfect; and there could have been but a certain determinate multitude of the moſt perfect; and, when that was completed, there would have been a ſtation for creatures leſs perfect, and it would ſtill have been an inſtance of goodneſs to give them a being as well as others."

VER. 245. *From Nature's chain*] Almoſt the words of Marcus Antoninus, l. v. c. 8.; as alſo v. 265. from the ſame.

ESSAY ON MAN.

Let Earth unbalanc'd from her orbit fly,
Planets and ſtars run lawleſs through the ſky;
Let ruling Angels from their ſpheres be hurl'd,
Being on Being wreck'd, and world on world;
Heav'n's whole foundations to their centre nod, 255
And Nature trembles to the throne of God.

All

NOTES.

VER. 251. *Let Earth unbalanc'd*] *i. e.* Being no longer kept within its orbit by the different directions of its progreſſive and attractive motions; which, like equal weights in a balance, keep it in an equilibre. W.

It is obſervable, that theſe noble lines were added after the firſt folio edition. It is a pleaſing and uſeful amuſement to trace out the alterations that a great and correct writer gradually makes in his works. At firſt it ran,

How inſtinct varies! What a hog may want
Compar'd with thine, half-reaſoning Elephant.

And again;

What the advantage if his finer eyes
Study a mite, not comprehend the ſkies.

Which lines at preſent ſtand thus:

How inſtinct varies in the growling ſwine,
Compar'd, half-reas'ning Elephant, with thine:
Say what the uſe were finer optics given,
T" inſpect a mite, not comprehend the Heav'n.

Formerly it ſtood thus:

No ſelf-confounding faculties to ſhare,
No ſenſes ſtronger than his brain can bear.

At preſent;

No pow'rs of body or of ſoul to ſhare,
But what his nature and his ſtate can bear.

It appeared at firſt very exceptionably;

Expatiate far o'er all this ſcene of Man,
A mighty maze! of walks without a plan.

Which contradicted his whole ſyſtem, and it was altered to,

A mighty maze! but not without a plan!

All this dread ORDER break—for whom? for thee?
Vile worm!—oh Madnefs! Pride! Impiety!

IX. What if the foot, ordain'd the duft to tread,
Or hand, to toil, afpir'd to be the head?   260
What if the head, the eye, or ear repin'd
To ferve mere engines to the ruling mind?
Juft as abfurd for any part to claim
To be another, in this gen'ral frame :
Juft as abfurd, to mourn the tafks or pains,   265
The great directing MIND OF ALL ordains.
All are but parts of one ftupendous whole,
Whofe body Nature is, and God the foul;

That,

NOTES.

VER. 265. *Juft as abfurd, &c.*] See the profecution and application of this in Ep. iv.   P.

VER. 266. *The great directing Mind, &c.*] "Veneramur autem et colimus ob dominium. Deus enim fine dominio, providentia, et caufis finalibus, nihil aliud eft quam FATUM et NATURA." *Newtoni Princip. Schol. gener. fub finem.*

VER. 267. *All are but parts*] Thefe are lines of a marvellous energy and clofenefs of expreffion. They are exactly like the old Orphic verfes quoted in Ariftotle, De Mundo. Edit. Lugd. folio, 1590, p. 378.; and line 289 as minutely refembles the doctrine of the fublime hymn of Cleanthes the Stoic; not that I imagine Pope or Bolingbroke ever read that hymn, efpecially the latter, who was ignorant of Greek.

VER. 268. *Whofe body Nature is, &c.*] Mr. de Croufaz remarks, on this line, that "A Spinozift would exprefs himfelf in this manner." I believe he would; for fo the infamous Toland has done, in his Atheift's Liturgy, called PANTHEISTICON: But fo would St. Paul likewife, who, writing on this fubject, the omniprefence of God in his Providence, and in his Subftance, fays, in the words of a pantheiftical Greek Poet, *In him we live, and move, and have our being; i. e.* we are parts of him, *his offspring:*

And

That, chang'd through all, and yet in all the fame;
Great in the earth, as in th' ethereal frame;   270
Warms

NOTES.

And the reafon is, becaufe a religious theift and an impious pantheift both profefs to believe the omniprefence of God. But would Spinoza, as Mr. Pope does, call God *the great directing Mind of all*, who hath intentionally created a perfect Univerfe? Or would a Spinozift have told us,

" The workman from the work diftinct was known?"
a line that overturns all Spinozifm from its very foundations.

But this fublime defcription of the Godhead contains not only the *divinity* of St. Paul; but, if that will not fatisfy the men he writes againft, the *philofophy* likewife of Sir Ifaac Newton.

The Poet fays,
" All are but parts of one ftupendous whole,
Whofe body Nature is, and God the foul;" &c.

The Philofopher:—" In ipfo continentur et moventur univerfa, fed abfque mutua paffione. Deus nihil patitur ex corporum motibus; illa nullam fentiunt refiftentiam ex omnipræfentia Dei.—Corpore omni et figura corporea deftituitur.—Omnia regit et omnia cognofcit—Cum unaquæque Spatii particula fit femper, et unumquodque Durationis indivifibile momentum, ubique certe rerum omnium Fabricator ac Dominus non erit nunquam, nufquam."

Mr. Pope;
" Breathes in our foul, informs our mortal part,
" As full, as perfect, in a hair as heart;
" As full, as perfect, in vile Man that mourns,
" As the rapt Seraph that adores and burns:
" To him, no high, no low, no great, no fmall;
" He fills, he bounds, connects, and equals all."

Sir Ifaac Newton:—" Annon ex phænomenis conftat effe entem incorporeum, viventem, intelligentem, omnipræfentem, qui in fpatio infinito, tanquam fenforio fuo, res ipfas intime cernat, penitufque perfpiciat, totafque intra fe præfens præfentes complectatur."

But now admitting there were an ambiguity in thefe expreffions, fo great that a Spinozift might employ them to exprefs his own

particular

Warms in the sun, refreshes in the breeze,
Glows in the stars, and blossoms in the trees,
                                            Lives

NOTES.

particular principles; and such a thing might well be, because the Spinozists, in order to hide the impiety of their principle, are wont to express the Omnipresence of God in terms that any religious Theist might employ; in this case, I say, how are we to judge of the Poet's meaning? Surely by the whole tenor of his argument. Now take the words in the sense of the Spinozists, and he is made, in the conclusion of his epistle, to overthrow all he had been advancing throughout the body of it: For Spinozism is the destruction of an Universe, where every thing tends, by a foreseen contrivance in all its parts, to the perfection of the Whole. But allow him to employ the passage in the sense of St. Paul, *That we and all creatures live, and move, and have our being in God;* and then it will be seen to be the most logical support of all that had preceded. For the Poet having, as we say, laboured through his Epistle to prove, that every thing in the Universe tends, by a foreseen contrivance, and a present direction of all its parts, to the perfection of the Whole; it might be objected, that such a disposition of things implying in God a painful, operose, and inconceivable extent of Providence, it could not be supposed that such care extended to *all*, but was confined to the more noble parts of the creation. This gross conception of the First Cause the Poet exposes, by shewing that God is equally and intimately present to every particle of Matter, to every sort of Substance, and in every instant of Being.   W.

Ver. 269. *That, chang'd thro' all*] "Every ear," says a critic of the truest taste, "must feel the ill effect of the monotony in these lines. The cause of it is obvious. This verse consists of ten syllables, or five feet. When the pause falls on the fourth syllable, we shall find that we pronounce the six last in the same time that we do the four first; so that the couplet is not only divided into two equal lines, but each line, with respect to time, is divided into two equal parts." Webb's Remarks on the Beauties of Poetry.

Ver. 270. *Great in the earth,*] It is remarkable that perhaps the most solid refutation of Spinoza is in the 5th volume of Bayle's Dictionary, p. 199.

Lives through all Life, extends through all extent,
Spreads undivided, operates unspent;
Breathes in our soul, informs our mortal part, 275
As full, as perfect, in a hair as heart;
As full, as perfect, in vile Man that mourns,
As the rapt Seraph, that adores and burns:
                                                    To

NOTES.

VER. 274. *Operates unspent;*] To Lucretius, who, in these very bold and magnificent lines, has asked,

"Quis? regere immensi summam; quis habere profundi
Indu manu validas potis est moderanter habenas?
Quis pariter coelos omneis convertere? et omneis
Ignibus aetheriis terras suffire feraceis?
Omnibus inque locis esse omni tempore praesto?

To this question, I say, we may answer, "That Great Being who is so powerfully described by Pope in this passage."

See on this subject the fine and convincing Discourse of Socrates with Aristodemus, in the first book of Xenophon's Memorabilia.

VER. 276. *In a hair as heart;*] How much superior to a conceit of Cowley, addressed to J. Evelyne, Esq.

"If we could open and intend our eye,
We all, like Moses, should espy,
E'en in a Bush, the radiant Deity!"

Very sublime is the idea of the Great First Cause in a fragment of Empedocles:

———Φρην ιερη, και αθεσφατος επλετο μονον,
Φροντισι κοσμον απαντα καταισσουσα θοησι.

                                                    Ammonius, p. 199.

M. du Resnel has translated all this passage of Pope unfairly and absurdly.

Our author strove hard to excel four fine lines of his master Dryden, and has succeeded in the attempt; they are in a speech of Raphael in the "State of Innocence," amidst much trash:

"Where'er thou art, he is; th' eternal Mind
Acts thro' all places; is to none confin'd:
Fills ocean, earth, and air, and all above,
And thro' the universal mass does move."

To him no high, no low, no great, no small;
He fills, he bounds, connects, and equals all.   280

X. Ceafe

NOTES.

VER. 280. *He fills, he bounds,*] This is a noble paffage. Akenfide entered the lifts on this fubject with our author. It will be pleafant to compare two fuch writers:

   ——" Thee, O Father, this extent
Of matter; Thee, the fluggifh earth and tract
Of feas, the heavens and heavenly fplendors feel
Pervading, quickening, moving. From the depth
Of thy great effence, forth did'ft thou conduct
Eternal Form; and there, where Chaos reign'd,
Gav'ft her dominion to erect her feat,
And fanctify the manfion. All her works
Well-pleas'd thou did'ft behold. The gloomy fires
Of ftorm or earthquake, and the pureft light
Of Summer; foft Campania's new-born rofe;
And the flow weed, which pines on Ruffian hills,
Comely alike to thy full vifion, ftand:
To thy furrounding vifion, which unites
All effences and powers of the great world
In one fole order; fair alike they ftand,
As features well confenting, and alike
Requir'd by Nature ere fhe could attain
Her juft refemblance to the perfect fhape
Of univerfal beauty, which with Thee
Dwelt from the firft."——

   Book i. 569. The Pleafures of Imagination.

I will here add, as the beft commentary on the prevailing doctrines of this firft Epiftle, a very exalted paffage from Plotinus, in which he has introduced a fublime profopopœia of Nature, or the Univerfe, fpeaking of the defign of Creation; and I will give it in the forcible and energetic tranflation of Cudworth, book i. p. 881. without apology for any antiquated expreffions that this truly great divine and philofopher has made ufe of:

" That which God made was the Whole, as One thing; which he that attends to may hear it fpeaking to him after this manner:
" God Almighty hath made Me, and from thence came I perfect and complete, and ftanding in need of nothing, becaufe in Me are contained

X. Ceafe then, nor ORDER Imperfection name:
Our proper blifs depends on what we blame.
                                                Know

VARIATIONS.
After Verfe 282. in the MS.
Reafon, to think of God when fhe pretends,
Begins a Cenfor, an Adorer ends.

NOTES.
contained all things; plants and animals, and good fouls, and men happy with virtue; and innumerable demons, and many gods. Nor is the earth alone in me adorned with all manner of plants and variety of animals; or does the power of foul extend at moft no further than to the feas, as if the whole air, and æther, and heaven, in the mean time, were quite devoid of foul, and altogether unadorned with living inhabitants. Moreover, all things in me defire good, and every thing reaches to it, according to its power and nature. For the whole world depends upon that firft and higheft good, the gods themfelves who reign in my feveral parts, and all animals and plants, and whatfoever feems to be inanimate in me. For fome things in me partake only of being, fome of life alfo, fome of fenfe, fome of reafon, and fome of intellect above reafon. But no man ought to require equal things from unequal; nor that the finger fhould fee, but the eye; it being enough for the finger to be a finger, and to perform its own office. As an artificer would not make all things in an animal to be eyes; fo neither has the Divine λογος, or Spermatic Reafon of the World, made all things gods; but fome gods, and fome demons, and fome men, and fome lower animals: not out of envy, but to difplay its own variety and fecundity: but we are like unfkilful fpectators of a picture, who condemn the limner, becaufe he hath not put bright colours every where: whereas he had fuited his colours to every part refpectively, giving to each fuch as belonged to it. Or elfe are we like thofe who would blame a comedy or tragedy, becaufe they were not all kings or heroes that acted in it, but fome fervants and ruftic clowns introduced alfo, talking after their rude fafhion. Whereas the dramatic poem would neither be complete, nor elegant and delightful, were all thofe worfer parts taken out of it."

The learned reader will be highly gratified by turning to a fine paffage on this fubject in Plutarch, De Animi Tranquillitate,
                                                                                                            vol.

48   ESSAY ON MAN.   Ep. I.

Know thy own point : This kind, this due degree
Of blindnefs, weaknefs, Heav'n beftows on thee.
Submit.—In this, or any other fphere,   285
Secure to be as bleft as thou canft bear :
Safe in the hand of one difpofing Pow'r,
Or in the natal, or the mortal hour.
All Nature is but Art, unknown to thee;
All Chance, Direction, which thou canft not fee; 290
All Difcord, Harmony not underftood ;
All partial Evil, univerfal Good :

And,

NOTES.

vol. ii. p. 473. folio, 1620, and to the noble lines of Euripides there quoted : and would be gratified ftill more by attentively perufing the fhort treatife of Ariftotle, Περὶ Κοσμε̃, concerning the beauty and concord of the Univerfe arifing from Contrarieties ; which treatife, notwithftanding the different form of its compofition, ought to be afcribed to this philofopher, for the reafons affigned by Petit in his Obfervations, b. ii. ; and by a differtation of Daniel Heinfius, as well as the opinion of our truly learned Bifhop Berkeley.

VER. 287. *Safe in the hand*] " Be there two worlds, or be there twenty, the fame God is the God of all; and wherever we are, we are equally in his power. Far from fearing my Creator, that all-perfect Being whom I adore, I fhould fear to be no longer his creature." Bolingbroke.

Si fic omnia dixiffet !

VER. 289. *All Nature is but Art,*] Cudworth obferves, upon Lucretius's having faid,

" Ufque adeo res humanas vis abdita quædam
Obterit,"——

that here he reeled and ftaggered in his atheifm ; or was indeed a Theift, and knew it not.

" Nature is the art whereby God governs the world," fays Hobbes.

VER. 291. *All Difcord, Harmony*] The words of Plato, in the Thæot. are, καὶ τὸ μέγιστη; τέχνης ἀγαθὸ ποιεῖ τὰ κακὰ. This
muft

ESSAY ON MAN.

And, fpite of Pride, in erring Reafon's fpite,
One truth is clear, WHATEVER IS, IS RIGHT.

NOTES.

muft be acknowledged to be the greateft of all arts, to be able to bonific evils, or tincture them with good."
                            Cudworth, p. 221. Intellectual Syftem.

I was furprifed to fee this philofophical doctrine amply illuftrated in one of our quaint old writers, Feltham, in his Refolves, p. 130. 1633.

" The whole world is kept in order by Difcord; and every part of it is but a more particular compofed jarre. Not a man, not a beaft, not a creature, but have fomething to ballaft their lightneffe. One fcale is not alwaies in depreffion, nor the other lifted ever high, but the alternate wave of the beame keepes it ever in the play of motion. From the pifmire on the tufted hill, to the monarch in the raifed throne, nothing but hath fomewhat to awe it. Wee are all here like birds that boyes let flye in ftrings: when we mount too high, wee have that which puls us downe againe. What man is it which lives fo happily, which feares not fomething that would fadden his foule if it fell? Nor is there any whom calamity doth fo much triftitiate, as that hee never fees the flafhes of fome warming joy. Beafts with beafts are terrified and delighted. Man with man is awed and defended. States with ftates are bounded and upholded. And, in all thefe, it makes greatly for the Maker's glory that fuch an admirable harmony fhould bee produced out of fuch an infinite difcord. The world is both a perpetuall warre, and a wedding. Heraclitus call'd a Difcord and Concord the univerfall Parents. And to raile on Difcord," faies the Father of the Poets, " is to fpeake ill of Nature. As in muficke fometimes one ftring is lowder, fometimes another; yet never one long, nor never all at once. So fometimes one ftate gets a monarchy, fometimes another: fometimes one element is violent, now another: yet never was the whole world under one long; nor were all the elements raging together. Every ftring has his ufe, and his tune, and his turne."

Feltham, we may imagine, did not know that this was a doctrine fo old as Heraclitus, who fpeaks of Παλίντροπος ἁρμονίη κόσμου, a verfatile harmony of the world, whereby things reciprocate backwards and forwards, &c.; quoted by Cudworth, chap. iv. b. i. from Plutarch, De Iſide & Ofiride, of two principles, a good God and an evil Dæmon; the Manichean doctrine.

* * * *

BAYLE was the person who, by stating the difficulties concerning the Origin of Evil, in his Dictionary, 1695, with much acuteness and ability, revived the Manichean controversy that had been long dormant. He was soon answered by Le Clerc in his Parrhasiana, and by many articles in his Bibliotheques. But by no writer was Bayle so powerfully attacked, as by the excellent Archbishop King, in his Treatise de Origine Mcli, 1702. About 1705, Lord Shaftesbury frequently visited Bayle at Rotterdam, whose wit and learning he admired, and made him a present of an elegant watch by a delicate stratagem; and offered him a fine collection of books, which that philosopher declined to accept. He had many conversations and disputes with Bayle on the Manichæan controversy; and in 1709 wrote the famous Dialogue intitled, The Moralists, as a direct confutation of the opinions of Bayle; though he had before touched on this subject, 1699, when the first edition of the Enquiry concerning Virtue and Merit was published: as did his disciple Hutcheson, 1725. In 1710, Leibnitz wrote his famous Theodicée; without entering into the metaphysical refinements of that piece, it may be more amusing to our reader just to mention the agreeable fiction with which he ends his philosophical disquisition. He feigns, (in continuance of a Dialogue of Laurentius Valla,) that Sextus the son of Tarquin goes to Dodona to complain to Jupiter of the crime which he was destined to commit, the rape of Lucretia. Jupiter answers him, that he had nothing to do but to abstain from going to Rome: but Sextus declares positively, that he could not renounce the hope of being a king, and accordingly to Rome he goes. After his departure, the high priest, Theodorus, asks Jupiter, why he did not give another will to Sextus? Jupiter sends Theodorus to Athens to consult Minerva; she shews to Theodorus the great palace of the Destinies, in which were placed all the pictures and representations of all possible worlds, from the worst model to the best. Theodorus beholds, in the latter, the crime which Sextus was doomed to commit; from which crime arose the liberty of Rome, and a mighty empire; an event so interesting to a great part of the human race. Theodorus was silenced.

In 1720 Dr. John Clarke published his Enquiry into the Cause and Origin of Evil, a work full of sound reasoning; but almost every argument on this most difficult of all subjects had been urged many years before any of the above-mentioned treatises appeared,

peared, namely, 1678, by that truly great scholar and divine Cudworth, in that inestimable treasury of learning and philosophy his Intellectual System, to which so many authors have been indebted, without owning their obligations.

I thought this little account of the writers who had preceded Pope, on the subject of this Essay, not improper to be subjoined in this place.

Voltaire wrote his Candide with the professed design of ridiculing the fundamental doctrine of this Essay; and in his Philosophical Dictionary; in his poem on the Destruction of Lisbon; in his Additions to the Encyclopedie; and in many parts of his Works and Letters; he seized every opportunity of combating and exposing the opinion of Optimism. And he joined with Hume in saying, " That the only solid method of accounting for the Origin of Evil, consistently with the other attributes of God, is not to allow that his power is infinite." " Sa puissance est très grande; mais qui nous a dit qu'elle est infinie, quand ses ouvrages nous montrent le contraire ? Certes, j'aime mieux l'adorer borné que mechant. Il ne reste que d'avouer que Dieu ayant agi pour le mieux, n'a pu agir mieux. Cette necessité tranche toutes les difficultés & finit toutes les disputes. Nous n'avons pas le front de dire, Tout est bien ; nous disons tout est le moins mal qu'il se pouvait." " We ought," says Hume, " to allow that the Creator of the universe possesses that precise degree of power, intelligence, and benevolence which actually appears in his workmanship ; nothing farther can ever be justly proved ; and the supposition of farther attributes is mere hypothesis." Thus endeavouring to deprive us of our most comfortable hopes, and most salutary expectations. But he should remember, that, if this be all that reason and philosophy can be able to prove, life and immortality are brought to light by the gospel. Notwithstanding these loose principles of Voltaire, yet one is glad to find, from the same hand, a full confutation of the impious tenets advanced in the Systeme de la Nature. Tom. iv. of Questions sur l'Encyclopedie, page 285. And in the beginning of this article, in the same volume, he has confuted Spinoza, and pointed out his many contradictions, sophisms, and obscurities; proving clearly that he did not understand his own opinions. In vol. vii. of the same work, page 283. he has demolished the artful arguments of Bayle, who endeavoured to prove that atheism was a tenet less mischievous to the happiness of man than idolatry.

ARGUMENT OF EPISTLE II.

Of the Nature and State of Man with respect to Himself, as an Individual.

I. *THE business of Man not to pry into* God, *but to study himself. His* Middle Nature; *his Powers and Frailties,* Ver. 1 to 19. *The Limits of his* Capacity, Ver. 19. &c. II. *The two Principles of Man,* Self-love *and* Reason, *both necessary,* Ver. 53, &c. Self-love *the stronger, and why,* Ver. 67, &c. *Their end the same,* Ver. 81, &c. III. *The* PASSIONS, *and their use,* Ver. 93 to 130. *The* Predominant Passion, *and its force,* Ver. 132 to 160. *Its Necessity, in directing Men to different purposes,* Ver. 165, &c. *Its providential Use, in fixing our* Principle, *and ascertaining our* Virtue, Ver. 177. IV. Virtue *and* Vice *joined in our* mixed Nature; *the limits near, yet the things* separate *and* evident: *What is the Office of* Reason, Ver. 202 to 216. V. *How odious* Vice *in itself, and how we deceive ourselves in it,* Ver. 217. VI. *That, however, the* Ends *of* Providence *and* general Good *are answered in our* Passions *and* Imperfections, Ver. 238, &c. *How usefully these are distributed to all* Orders of Men, Ver. 241. *How useful they are to* Society, Ver. 251. *And to* Individuals, Ver. 263. *In every* state, *and every* age *of life,* Ver. 273, &c.

EPISTLE II.

I. KNOW then thyſelf, preſume not God to ſcan,
   The proper ſtudy of Mankind is Man.
   Plac'd

VARIATIONS.

VER. 2. Ed. 1ſt.
The only ſcience of Mankind is Man.

NOTES.

VER. 1. *Know then thyſelf,*] Not content with the fame acquired by writing thoſe fine tragedies, Zaire, Alzire, Merope, and Mahomet, Voltaire muſt needs deſcend to didactic poetry; for a deſcent it is; out of an ambition to be an univerſal genius; and produced, in emulation of Pope, five Diſcourſes on Man: the firſt is, on the Equality of Happineſs in the different Conditions of Man; the ſecond, on the Freedom of Man; the third, on the Miſchiefs of Envy, and that it is the chief Obſtacle to our Happineſs; the fourth, to ſhew that, to be Happy, we muſt be moderate in all Things; the fifth, that Pleaſure muſt proceed from God; the ſixth, that Perfect Happineſs cannot be attained in this Life, and that Men ought not to complain; the ſeventh and laſt is, to ſhew that Virtue chiefly conſiſts in Acts of Beneficence to our Fellow-creatures. A cloſe reſemblance is viſible in the following lines of the ſixth diſcourſe to the Eſſay on Man. Ep. i. v. 173.

" Un vieux Lettre Chinois, qui toujours ſur les bancs
Combattit la raiſon par de beaux argumens,
Plein de Confucius, et ſa Logique en tête,
Diſtinguant, concluant, préſenta ſa requête.
Pourquoi ſuis-je en un point reſſerré par le tems?
Mes jours devraient aller par-delà vingt mille ans;
Ma taille pour le moins dût avoir cent condées,
D'où vient que je ne puis, plus promt que mes idées,
Voyager dans la Lune, et reformer ſon cours?
Pourquoi faut-il dormir un grand tiers de mes jours;
Pourquoi ne puis-je, au gré de ma pudique flâme;
Faire au moins en trois mois cent enfans à ma femme;

Pourquoi

Plac'd on this ifthmus of a middle ftate,
A Being darkly wife, and rudely great:
With too much knowledge for the Sceptic fide,   5
With too much weaknefs for the Stoic's pride,
He hangs between; in doubt to act, or reft;
In doubt to deem himfelf a God, or Beaft;

In

NOTES.

Pourquoi pis-je en un jour fi las de fes attraits?
T'es pourquoi, dit le Dieu, ne finiraient jamais
Bientot tes queftions vont etre decidées:
Vas chercher ta réponfe au pays des idées;
Pars!"——

Though there are many fenfible and fprightly paffages in thefe difcourfes, yet their inferiority to Pope is indifputable. As much as we may lament and reprobate the loofe and libertine principles wantonly fcattered up and down in the writings of Voltaire, yet is it impoffible not to admire the fertility of his genius, the brilliancy of his wit, and the variety of his talents? It is vain to think it poffible to deftroy and depreciate the man who, with fuch an unparalleled verfatility of mind, could produce, not only the tragedies juft mentioned, and fome parts of the Henriade, but Comic Tales, a certain Mock Heroic Poem, and Familiar Epiftles in verfe, equal to the facility and naiveté of La Fontaine; as well as fuch hiftories as that of Charles XII. Louis XIV. and the Effay on General Hiftory; which laft work has had the great merit of giving a new turn to hiftorical compofitions, and carrying them from accounts of battles, and fieges, and negotiations alone, to inveftigations of the progrefs of manners, laws, and arts; and this in a ftyle of marvellous perfpicuity and precifion; fo that his profe is quite equal to his verfe, perhaps fuperior. They who are fond of attributing the diforders and enormities in France to the influence of Voltaire's writings, ought in common juftice to be reminded, that even in one of his moft exceptionable works, the Dictionaire Philofophique, are various paffages, ftrongly pointed, againft Atheifm, Equality, and Democracy, and the very impious tenets of the Syfteme de la Nature.

VER. 3. *On this ifthmus*] From Cowley, in the Ode on Life and Fame. As alfo line 205. in the 4th Epiftle,

To Kings, or to the Favorites of Kings.

Ep. II.   ESSAY ON MAN.   57

In doubt his Mind or Body to prefer;
Born but to die, and reas'ning but to err;   10
Alike in ignorance, his reafon fuch,
Whether he thinks too little, or too much:
Chaos of Thought and Paffion, all confus'd;
Still by himfelf abus'd, or difabus'd;
Created half to rife, and half to fall;   15
Great Lord of all things, yet a prey to all;
Sole judge of truth, in endlefs error hurl'd:
The glory, jeft, and riddle of the world!
                                                  Go,

VARIATIONS.

After Ver. 18. in the MS.
   For more perfect'on than this ftate can bear
   In vain we figh, Heav'n made us as we are.
   As wifely fure a modeft Ape might aim
   To be like Man, whofe faculties and frame
                                                  He

NOTES.

VER. 11. *Alike in ignorance, &c.*] *i. e.* The proper fphere of his reafon is fo narrow, and the exercife of it fo nice, that the too immoderate ufe of it is attended with the fame ignorance that proceeds from the not ufing it at all. Yet though, in both thefe cafes, he is *abufed by himfelf*, he has it ftill in his own power to *difabufe himfelf*, in making his paffions fubfervient to the *means*, and regulating his Reafon by the *end* of life.   W.

VER. 12. *Whether he thinks too little,*] It was obferved by Bayle, above an hundred years ago, " that philofophy might be compared to certain powders, fo very corrofive, that, having confumed the proud and fpongy flefh of a wound, they would corrode even the quick and found flefh, rot the bones, and penetrate to the very marrow. Philofophy is proper at firft to confute errors, but if fhe be not ftopped there, fhe attacks truth itfelf; and, when fhe has her full fcope, fhe generally goes fo far that fhe lofes herfelf, and knows not where to ftop." What would Bayle have faid if he had feen the ufes to which philofophy has been applied in the prefent times?

Go, wond'rous creature! mount where Science guides,
Go, measure earth, weigh air, and state the tides; 20
Instruct the planets in what orbs to run,
Correct old Time, and regulate the Sun;
Go, soar with Plato, to th' empyreal sphere,
To the first good, first perfect, and first fair;
                                                                Or

VARIATIONS.

He sees, he feels, as you or I to be
An Angel thing we neither know nor see.
Observe how near he edges on our race;
What human tricks! how risible of face!
It must be so—why else have I the sense
Of more than monkey charms and excellence?
Why else to walk on two so oft essay'd?
And why this ardent longing for a Maid?
So Pug might plead, and call his Gods unkind,
Till set on end and married to his mind.
Go, reas'ning thing! assume the Doctor's chair,
As Plato deep, as Seneca severe:
Fix moral fitness, and to God give rule,
Then drop into thyself, &c.——

VER. 21. Ed. 4th and 5th.
Show by what rules the wand'ring planets stray,
Correct old Time, and teach the Sun his way.

NOTES.

VER. 20. *Go, measure earth, &c.*] Alluding to the noble and useful labours of the modern Mathematicians, in measuring a degree at the equator and the polar circle, in order to determine the true figure of the earth; of great importance to astronomy and navigation; and which proved of equal honour to the wonderful sagacity of Newton.   W.

VER. 22. *Correct old Time, &c.*] This alludes to Newton's Grecian Chronology, which he reformed on those two sublime conceptions, the difference between the reigns of kings, and the generations of men; and the position of the colours of the equinoxes and solstices at the time of the Argonautic expedition.   W.

Or tread the mazy round his follow'rs trod, 25
And quitting fenfe call imitating God ;
As eaftern priefts in giddy circles run,
And turn their heads to imitate the Sun.
Go, teach Eternal Wifdom how to rule—
Then drop into thyfelf, and be a fool. 30
Superior Beings, when of late they faw
A mortal Man unfold all Nature's law,
          Admir'd

NOTES.

VER. 29, 30. *Go, teach Eternal Wifdom, &c.*] Thefe two lines are a conclufion from all that had been faid from Ver. 18. to this effect: Go now, vain Man, elated with thy acquirements in *real* fcience, and *imaginary* intimacy with God ; go, and run into all the extravagancies I have exploded in the firft epiftle, where thou pretendeft to teach Providence how to govern ; then drop into the obfcurities of thy own nature, and thereby manifeft thy ignorance and folly.   W.

VER. 31. *Superior beings, &c.*] In thefe lines the Poet fpeaks to this effect : " But to make you fully fenfible of the difficulty of this ftudy, I fhall inftance in the great Newton himfelf ; whom, when fuperior beings, not long fince, faw capable of unfolding the whole law of Nature, they were in doubt whether the owner of fuch prodigious fagacity fhould not be reckoned of their order ; juft as men, when they fee the furprifing marks of Reafon in an Ape, are almoft tempted to rank him with their own kind." And yet this wondrous Man could go no further in the knowledge of himfelf than the generality of his fpecies. M. Du Refnel, who underftood nothing of all this, tranflates thefe four celebrated lines thus,

 " Des celeftes Efprits la vive intelligence
 Regarde *avec pitie notre foible Science ;*
 Newton, le grand Newton, que nos admirons tous
 Eft peut être pour eux, *ce qu'un Singe eft pour nous.*"

But it is not the *pity*, but the *admiration* of thofe celeftial Spirits which is here fpoken of. And it was for no flight caufe they admired ; it was *to fee a mortal man unfold the whole law of Nature.* By which we fee it was not Mr. Pope's intention to bring any of the Ape's *qualities*, but its *fagacity*, into the comparifon. W.

Admir'd such wisdom in an earthly shape,
And shew'd a NEWTON as we shew an Ape.

Could he, whose rules the rapid Comet bind, 35
Describe or fix one movement of his Mind?
Who saw its fires here rise, and there descend,
Explain his own beginning, or his end?
Alas, what wonder! Man's superior part
Uncheck'd may rise, and climb from art to art; 40
But when his own great work is but begun,
What Reason weaves, by Passion is undone.

Trace

VARIATIONS.

VER. 35. Ed. 1st.
Could he, who taught each Planet where to roll,
Describe or fix one movement of the Soul?
Who mark'd their points to rise, or to descend,
Explain his own beginning, or his end?

NOTES.

VER. 34. *As we shew an Ape.*] Evidently borrowed from the following passage in the Zodiac of Palingenius, and not, as hath been suggested by Dr. Hurd, from Plato. Pope was a reader and publisher of the modern Poets of Italy who wrote in Latin. The words are,

" Simia Cœliolûm risusq; jocusq; Deorum est
 Tunc Homo, cum temerè ingenio confidit, et audet
 Abdita Naturæ scrutari, arcanaq; Divum."

VER. 37. *Who saw its fires here rise, &c.*] Sir Isaac Newton, in calculating the velocity of a Comet's motion, and the course it describes, when it becomes visible in its descent to, and ascent from, the Sun, conjectured, with the highest appearance of truth, that Comets revolve perpetually round the Sun, in ellipses vastly eccentrical, and very nearly approaching to parabolas. In which he was greatly confirmed, in observing between two Comets a coincidence in their perihelions, and a perfect agreement in their velocities. W.

Trace Science then, with Modefty thy guide:
Firſt ſtrip off all her equipage of Pride;
Deduct what is but Vanity, or Dreſs, 45
Or Learning's Luxury, or Idleneſs;
Or tricks to ſhew the ſtretch of human brain,
Mere curious pleaſure, or ingenious pain;
Expunge

NOTES.

VER. 44. *Firſt ſtrip off*] The abuſes of learning are enumerated with brevity and elegance in theſe few lines. It was a favourite ſubject with our author; and it is ſaid he intended to have written four epiſtles on it, wherein he would have treated of the extent and limits of human reaſon; of arts and ſciences uſeful and attainable; of the different capacities of different men; of the knowledge of the world; and of wit. Such cenſures, even of the moſt unimportant parts of literature, ſhould not, however, be carried too far; and a ſenſible writer obſerves, that there is not indeed any part of knowledge which can be called entirely uſeleſs. "The moſt abſtracted parts of mathematics, and the knowledge of mythological hiſtory, or ancient allegories, have their own pleaſures, not inferior to the more gay entertainments of painting, muſic, or architecture; and it is for the advantage of mankind that ſome are found who have a taſte for theſe ſtudies. The only fault lies in letting any of thoſe inferior taſtes engroſs the whole man to the excluſion of the nobler purſuits of virtue and humanity *."
We may here apply an elegant obſervation of Tully, who ſays, in his Brutus, " Credo, ſed Athenienſium quoque plus interfuit firma tecta in domiciliis habere, quam Minervæ ſignum ex ebore pulcherrimum : tamen ego me Phidiam eſſe mallem quam vel optimum fabrum lignarium ; quare non quantum quiſque profit, ſed quanti quiſque ſit, ponderandum eſt : præſertim cum pauci pingere egregiè poſſint aut fingere, operarii autem aut bajuli deeſſe non poſſint."

VER. 47. *Or tricks to ſhew the ſtretch of human brain,*] 'Such as the mathematical demonſtrations concerning the *ſmall quantity of matter;* the *endleſs diviſibility* of it, &c. W.

VER. 48. *Mere curious pleaſure, or ingenious pain;*] *i. e.* when *Admiration* has ſet the mind on the rack. W.

* Hutcheſon's Nature and Conduct of the Paſſions, p. 179.

Expunge the whole, or lop th' excrescent parts
Of all our Vices have created Arts;   50
Then see how little the remaining sum,
Which serv'd the past, and must the times to come!

II. Two Principles in human nature reign;
Self-love, to urge, and Reason, to restrain;

Nor

NOTES.

VER. 49. *Expunge the whole, or lop th' excrescent parts Of all our Vices have created Arts;*] i. e. Those parts of natural Philosophy, Logic, Rhetoric, Poetry, &c. which administer to luxury, deceit, ambition, effeminacy, &c.

VER. 53. *Two Principles, &c.*] The Poet having shewn the difficulty which attends the study of Man, proceeds to remove it, by laying before us the elements or true principles of this science, in an account of the *Origin*, *Use*, and *End* of the PASSIONS; which, in my opinion, contains the truest, clearest, shortest, and consequently the best system of Ethics that is any where to be met with. He begins (from Ver. 52 to 59.) with pointing out the two grand Principles in human nature, SELF-LOVE and REASON. Describes their general nature: The first sets Man upon acting, the other regulates his action. However, these principles are *natural*, not *moral*; and therefore, in themselves, neither good nor evil, but so only as they are directed. This observation is made with great judgment, in opposition to the desperate folly of those Fanatics, who, as the Ascetic, vainly pretend to eradicate Self-love; or, as the Mystic, are more successful in stifling Reason; and both, on the absurd fancy of their being *moral*, not *natural*, principles.   W.

VER. 54. *Self-love, to urge,*] Such popular writers as Pascal, Nicole, and Rochefoucault, having given a wrong and improper definition of Self-love, and mistaken the origin of it for its end, have argued unfairly and inconclusively on the subject, and represented this first spring of all human actions, as base, mean, and disgraceful. Our Author, more wise and temperate, has endeavoured to reconcile Self-love with social, and private good with universal happiness. He had the hint from Shaftesbury: " If

there

Nor this a good, nor that a bad we call, 55
Each works its end, to move or govern all :
And to their proper operation ſtill,
Aſcribe all Good ; to their improper Ill.
Self-love, the ſpring of motion, acts the ſoul ;
Reaſon's comparing balance rules the whole. 60
Man, but for that, no action could attend,
And, but for this, were active to no end :
Fix'd

NOTES.

there can poſſibly be ſuppoſed in a creature ſuch an affection towards ſelf-good, as is actually, in its natural degree, conducing to his private intereſt, and at the ſame time inconſiſtent with the public good ; this may indeed be called ſtill a vitious affection. And on this ſuppoſition a creature cannot really be good and natural in reſpect of his ſociety or public, without being ill and unnatural towards himſelf. But if the affection be then only injurious to ſociety when it is immoderate, and not ſo when it is moderate, duly tempered, and allay'd, then is the immoderate degree of the affection truly vicious, but not the moderate. Characteriſtics, vol. ii. p. 22. He had ſaid before, vol. i. p. 120. ſpeaking of thoſe who had written on Self-love, " If theſe gentlemen who delight ſo much in the play of words, but are cautious how they grapple cloſely with definitions, would tell us only what Self-intereſt was, and would determine Happineſs and Good, there would be an end of this enigmatical wit." See alſo pages 78, 79, 80, 87, 139, 140, of volume the ſecond. Pope does not appear to have read, though publiſhed before this Eſſay, Hutcheſon's admirable Illluſtrations and Defence of the Moral Senſe, and his fine Treatiſe on the Paſſions. Burtamaqui's work, Principes du Droit Natural, was not yet publiſhed, by which our Author might have profited much.

VER. 59. *Self-love, the ſpring of motion, acts the ſoul ;*] The Poet proceeds (from Ver. 58 to 67.) more minutely to mark out the diſtinct offices of theſe two Principles, which offices he had before aſſigned only in general ; and here he ſhews their neceſſity ; for without Self-love, as the *ſpring*, Man would be unactive : and without Reaſon, as the *balance*, active to no purpoſe. W.

Fix'd like a plant on his peculiar spot,
To draw nutrition, propagate, and rot;
Or, meteor-like, flame lawless through the void, 65
Destroying others, by himself destroy'd.

Most strength the moving principle requires:
Active its task, it prompts, impels, inspires.
Sedate and quiet, the comparing lies,
Form'd but to check, delib'rate, and advise. 70
Self-love still stronger, as its objects nigh;
Reason's at distance, and in prospect lie:
That sees immediate good by present sense;
Reason, the future and the consequence.
Thicker than arguments, temptations throng, 75
At best more watchful this, but that more strong.
The action of the stronger to suspend
Reason still use, to Reason still attend.
Attention, habit and experience gains;
Each strengthens Reason, and Self-love restrains. 80

Let subtle schoolmen teach these friends to fight,
More studious to divide than to unite;

And

NOTES.

VER. 81. *Let subtle schoolmen, &c.*] From this description of Self-love and Reason it follows, as the Poet observes (from Ver. 80 to 93.) that both conspire to one end, namely, human happiness, though they be not equally expert in the choice of the means; the difference being this, that the first hastily seizes every thing which hath the appearance of good; the other weighs and examines whether it be indeed what it appears.

This shews, as he next observes, the folly of the schoolmen, who consider them as two opposite principles, the one good and the other evil. The observation is seasonable and judicious; for this dangerous school-opinion gives great support to the Manichean

ESSAY ON MAN.

And Grace and Virtue, Senſe and Reaſon ſplit,
With all the raſh dexterity of wit.
Wits, juſt like Fools, at war about a name, 85
Have full as oft no meaning, or the ſame.
Self-love and Reaſon to one end aſpire,
Pain their averſion, Pleaſure their deſire;
But greedy That, its object would devour,
This taſte the honey, and not wound the flow'r: 90
Pleaſure, or wrong or rightly underſtood,
Our greateſt evil, or our greateſt good.
  III. Modes of Self-love the Paſſions we may call:
'Tis real good, or ſeeming, moves them all:
But ſince not ev'ry good we can divide, 95
And Reaſon bids us for our own provide;
Paſſions, though ſelfiſh, if their means be fair,
Liſt under Reaſon, and deſerve her care;
Thoſe, that imparted, court a nobler aim,
Exalt their kind, and take ſome Virtue's name. 100
  In

VARIATIONS.

After Ver. 86. in the MS.
  Of good and evil Gods what frighted Fools,
  Of good and evil Reaſon puzzled ſchools,
  Deceiv'd, deceiving, taught——

NOTES.

chean or Zoroaſtrian error, the confutation of which was one of the Author's chief ends in writing. For if there be *two principles* in Man, a *good* and *evil*, it is natural to think him the joint product of the two Manichean Deities (the firſt of which contributed to this *Reaſon*, the other to his *Paſſions*) rather than the creature of one Individual Cauſe. This was Plutarch's opinion, and, as we may ſee in him, of ſome of the more ancient theiſtical Philoſophers. It was of importance, therefore, to reprobate and ſubvert a notion that ſerved to the ſupport of ſo dangerous an error: And this the Poet hath done with much force and clearneſs. W.

In lazy Apathy let Stoics boast
Their Virtue fix'd; 'tis fix'd as in a frost;
Contracted all, retiring to the breast;
But strength of mind is Exercise, not Rest:
The rising tempest puts in act the soul,   105
Parts it may ravage, but preserves the whole.

On

NOTES.

VER. 101. *In lazy Apathy*] Swift observes, that "the Stoical scheme of supplying our wants by lopping off our passions, is like cutting off our legs for want of shoes." How easy is it to expose assertions which were never asserted; to refute tenets which were never held; to become St. George when we make our own dragons? What says old Epictetus, who knew Stoicism better than these men? ὐ γαρ δεῖ με ἔιναι ΑΠΑΘΗ ὡς Ανδριάντα, &c. "I am not to be Apathetic, or void of passions, like a statue. I am to discharge all the relations of a social and friendly life, the parent, the husband, the brother, the magistrate." These words are copied from a valuable manuscript of my late excellent friend James Harris, Esq. author of Hermes, and other admirable treatises. Perhaps a stronger example cannot be found, of taking notions upon trust without any examination, than the universal censure that has been passed upon the Stoics, as if they constantly and strenuously inculcated a total insensibility with respect to passion, to which these lines of Pope allude; when it is certain the Stoics meant only, a freedom from strong perturbation, from irrational and excessive agitations of the soul; and no more.

VER. 105. *The rising tempest puts in act the soul,*] As it was from observation of the evils occasioned by the passions, that the Stoics thus extravagantly projected their extirpation, the Poet recurs (from Ver. 104 to 111.) to his grand principle so often before, and to so good purpose, insisted on, that *partial Ill is universal Good;* and shews, that though the tempest of the passions, like that of the air, may tear and ravage some few parts of nature in its passage, yet the salutary agitation produced by it preserves the Whole, in life and vigour. This is his *first* argument against the Stoics, which he illustrates by a very beautiful similitude, on a hint taken from Scripture:

" Nor God alone in the still calm we find,
He mounts the storm, and walks upon the wind."   W.

From

On life's vast ocean diverfely we fail,
Reafon the card, but paffion is the gale;
Nor God alone in the ftill calm we find,
He mounts the ftorm, and walks upon the wind. 110
Paffions,

VARIATIONS.

After Ver. 108. in the MS.
A tedious Voyage! where how ufelefs lies
The compafs, if no pow'rful gufts arife?

NOTES.

From factions, and ferments, and political agitations, and commotions, and wars, arife the moft ftriking and vigorous exertions of the human mind. Witnefs what happened in Greece, and Rome, and modern Italy; in France after the league; and in England after, and in, our civil war. Great occafions call forth great and latent abilities; and every man becomes capable of every exertion. A Socrates and a Sophocles were found, alone, in the time of Themiftocles and Thrafybulus. The dead calm of defpotifm, in fuch a government as China, for inftance, crufhes and overwhelms all effort and all emulation.

VER. 108. *Reafon the card,*] This paffage is exactly copied from Fontenelle, tom. i. p. 109.

" Ce font les paffions qui font et qui defont tout. Si la raifon dominoit fur la terre, il ne s'y pafferoit rien. On dit que les pilotes craignent au dernier point ces mers pacifiques, ou l'ont ne peut naviger, et qu'ils veulent du vent, au hazard d'avoir des tempêtes. Les paffions font chez des hommes des vents qui font neceffaires, pour mettre tout en mouvement, quoiqu'ils caufent fouvent les orages." He had alfo copied Fontenelle before, in Epiftle i. v. 290.

All chance direction which thou canft not fee,

" Tout eft hazard dans le monde, pourvû que l'on donne ce nom à un ordre que l'on ne connoit point." Tom. i. p. 81.

VER. 109. *Nor God alone* in the ftill calm *we find,*
He mounts the ftorm, *and walks upon the wind.*]

The tranflator turns it thus,
" Dieu lui-même, Dieu fort de *fon profond repos.*"
And fo, makes an *Epicurean* God, of the Governor of the Univerfe. M. De Croufaz does not fpare this expreffion of *God's*

coming

Passions, like elements, tho' born to fight,
Yet, mix'd and soften'd, in his work unite:
These, 'tis enough to temper and employ;
But what composes Man, can Man destroy?
Suffice that Reason keep to Nature's road, 115
Subject, compound them, follow her and God.
Love, Hope, and Joy, fair Pleasure's smiling train,
Hate, Fear, and Grief, the family of Pain,
These

VARIATIONS.

After Ver. 112. in the MS.
The soft reward the virtuous, or invite ;
The fierce, the vicious punish or affright.

NOTES.

coming out of his profound repose. " It is," says he, " excessively poetical, and presents us with ideas which we ought not to dwell upon," &c. and then, as usual, blames the Author for the blunder of his Translator. *Comm. p.* 158. W.

VER. 109. *Nor God alone, &c.*] These words are only a simple affirmation in the poetic dress of a similitude, to this purpose: Good is not only produced by the subdual of the Passions, but by the turbulent exercise of them. A truth conveyed under the most sublime imagery that poetry could conceive or paint. For the author is here only shewing the providential issue of the Passions; and how, by God's gracious disposition, they are turned away from their natural destructive bias, to promote the Happiness of Mankind. As to the method in which they are to be treated by Man, in whom they are found, all that he contends for, in favour of them, is only this, that they should not be quite rooted up and destroyed, as the Stoics, and their followers, in all Religions, foolishly attempted. For the rest, he constantly repeats this advice,

" The action of the stronger to suspend,
Reason still use, to Reason still attend." W.

VER. 110. *Walks upon the wind.*] In Dryden's Ceyex and Alcione is,

" And now sublime she rides upon the wind."

VER. 117. *Love, Hope, and Joy,*] This beautiful group of allegorical personages, so strongly contrasted, how does it act?
The

These mix'd with art, and to due bounds confin'd,
Make and maintain the balance of the mind : 120
The lights and shades, whose well-accorded strife
Gives all the strength and colour of our life.
Pleasures are ever in our hands or eyes;
And when, in act, they cease, in prospect, rise :
Present to grasp, and future still to find, 125
The whole employ of body and of mind.
All spread their charms, but charm not all alike;
On diff'rent senses diff'rent objects strike;
Hence diff'rent Passions more or less inflame,
As strong or weak, the organs of the frame; 130
And

NOTES.

The prosopopœia is unfortunately dropped, and the metaphor changed immediately in the succeeding lines, viz.

" These mix'd with art," &c.

VER. 128. *On diff'rent senses*] A didactic poet, who has happily indulged himself in bolder flights of enthusiasm, supported by a more figurative style than our Author used, has thus nobly illustrated this very doctrine :

    ———" Diff'rent minds
Incline to diff'rent objects: one pursues
The vast alone, the wonderful, the wild;
Another sighs for harmony, and grace,
And gentlest beauty. Hence, when lightning fires
The arch of heaven, and thunders rock the ground;
When furious whirlwinds rend the howling air,
And Ocean, groaning from the lowest bed,
Heaves his tempestuous billows to the sky;
Amid the mighty uproar, while below
The nations tremble, Shakespeare looks abroad
From some high cliff, superior, and enjoys
The elemental war. But Waller longs
All on the margin of some flow'ry stream,
To spread his careless limbs, amid the cool
Of plantane shades."———

And hence one MASTER PASSION in the breast,
Like Aaron's serpent, swallows up the rest.
As Man, perhaps, the moment of his breath,
Receives the lurking principle of death;
The young disease, that must subdue at length, 135
Grows with his growth, and strengthens with his
  strength:
So, cast and mingl'd with his very frame,
The Mind's disease, its RULING PASSION came;
Each vital humour which should feed the whole,
Soon flows to this, in body and in soul: 140
Whatever warms the heart, or fills the head,
As the mind opens, and its functions spread,
Imagination plies her dang'rous art,
And pours it all upon the peccant part.
  Nature its mother, Habit is its nurse; 145
Wit, Spirit, Faculties, but make it worse;
Reason itself but gives it edge and pow'r;
As Heav'n's blest beam turns vinegar more sow'r.

We,

NOTES.

VER. 133. *As Man, perhaps, &c.*] "Antipater Sidonius Poeta omnibus annis uno die natali tantum corripiebatur febre, et eo consumptus est satis longa senecta." *Plin.* l. vii. *N. H.* This *Antipater* was in the times of Crassus; and is celebrated for the quickness of his parts by Cicero. W.

VER. 147. *Reason itself, &c.*] The Poet, in some other of his epistles, gives examples of the doctrines and precepts here delivered. Thus, in that *Of the Use of Riches*, he has illustrated this truth in the character of Cotta. W.

VER. 148. *Turns vinegar*] Taken from Bacon, De Calore; and the preceding verse, and comparison, 132.

" Like Aaron's serpent,"————
is from Bacon likewise.

We, wretched fubjects, tho' to lawful fway,
In this weak queen, fome fav'rite ftill obey: 150
Ah! if fhe lend not arms, as well as rules,
What can fhe more than tell us we are fools?
Teach us to mourn our Nature, not to mend,
A fharp accufer, but a helplefs friend!
Or from a judge turn pleader, to perfuade 155
The choice we make, or juftify it made;
Proud of an eafy conqueft all along,
She but removes weak Paffions for the ftrong:
So, when fmall humours gather to a gout,
The doctor fancies he has driv'n them out. 160
    Yes, Nature's road muft ever be preferr'd;
Reafon is here no guide, but ftill a guard:
'Tis her's to rectify, not overthrow,
And treat this paffion more as friend than foe:
A mightier Pow'r the ftrong direction fends, 165
And fev'ral Men impels to fev'ral ends:
Like varying winds, by other paffions toft,
This drives them conftant to a certain coaft.
                                          Let

NOTES.

VER. 149. *We, wretched fubjects,*] The weaknefs and infufficiency of Human Reafon is here painted in the ftrongeft colours: from whence the neceffity and the utility of Revelation may be juftly inferred.

VER. 157. *Proud of an eafy*] From the Duc de la Rochefoucault, Maxim. 10.; as is alfo Verfe 170. from Maxim. 266.; and alfo Verfe 272. from the fame author, Maxim. 36.

The late excellent Duke de la Rochefoucault, in a letter to Dr. Adam Smith, dated Paris, 3 Mars. 1778, fpeaks thus of the Maxims of his ingenious grandfather, as too fevere on Human Nature: " Perhaps it may be urged to excufe him, that he had feen and known men chiefly in a court, or in the time of a civil war; deux theatres fur lefquels ils font certainement plus mauvais qu'ailleurs."

Let pow'r or knowledge, gold or glory, pleafe,
Or (oft more ftrong than all) the love of eafe; 170
Through life 'tis follow'd, even at life's expence;
The merchant's toil, the fage's indolence,
The monk's humility, the hero's pride,
All, all alike, find reafon on their fide.

Th' Eternal Art educing good from ill, 175
Grafts on this Paffion our beft principle:
'Tis thus the Mercury of Man is fix'd,
Strong grows the Virtue with his nature mix'd;
The drofs cements what elfe were too refin'd,
And in one int'reft body acts with mind. 180

As fruits, ungrateful to the planter's care,
On favage ftocks inferted, learn to bear;
The fureft Virtues thus from Paffions fhoot,
Wild Nature's vigour working at the root.
What crops of wit and honefty appear 185
From fpleen, from obftinacy, hate, or fear!
See anger, zeal, and fortitude fupply;
Ev'n avarice, prudence; floth, philofophy;
Luft, through fome certain ftrainers well refin'd,
Is gentle love, and charms all womankind; 190
Envy, to which th' ignoble mind's a flave,
Is emulation in the learn'd or brave;
Nor Virtue, male or female, can we name,
But what will grow on pride, or grow on fhame.

Thus

VARIATIONS.

After Ver. 194. in the MS.

How oft with Paffion, Virtue points her charms!
Then fhines the Hero, then the Patriot warms.

Peleus'

Thus Nature gives us (let it check our pride) 195
The virtue neareſt to our vice ally'd :
Reaſon the bias turns from good to ill,
And Nero reigns a Titus, if he will.

The

VARIATIONS.

Peleus' great Son, or Brutus, who had known,
Had Lucrece been a Whore, or Helen none!
But Virtues oppoſite to make agree,
That, Reaſon! is thy taſk; and worthy Thee.
Hard taſk, cries Bibulus, and Reaſon weak.
—Make it a point, dear Marqueſs! or a pique.
Once, for a whim, perſuade yourſelf to pay
A debt to Reaſon, like a debt at play.
For right or wrong have mortals ſuffer'd more
B— for his prince, or * * for his Whore?
Whoſe ſelf-denials Nature muſt controul?
His, who would ſave a Sixpence, or his Soul?
Web for his health, a Chartreux for his Sin,
Contend they not which ſooneſt ſhall grow thin?
What we reſolve, we can : but here's the fault,
We ne'er reſolve to do the thing we ought.

NOTES.

VER. 197. *Reaſon the bias, &c.*] But leſt it ſhould be objected that this account favours the doctrine of Neceſſity, and would inſinuate that men are only acted upon, in the production of good out of evil ; the Poet teacheth (from Ver. 196 to 203.) that Man is a free agent, and hath it in his power to turn the natural paſſions into virtues or into vices, properly ſo called :

" Reaſon the bias turns to good from ill,
 And Nero reigns a Titus, if he will."

Secondly, If it ſhould be objected, that though he doth, indeed, tell us ſome actions are beneficial and ſome hurtful, yet he could not call thoſe *virtuous*, nor theſe *vicious*, becauſe, as he hath deſcribed things, the motive appears to be only the gratification of ſome paſſion ; give me leave to anſwer for him, that this would be miſtaking the argument, which (to Ver. 249. of this epiſtle) conſiders the paſſions only with regard to *Society*, that is, with regard to their *effects* rather than their *motives :* That, however, it is his deſign to teach that actions are *properly virtuous and vicious* ; and

though

The fiery foul abhorr'd in Catiline,
In Decius charms, in Curtius is divine: 200
The same ambition can destroy or save,
And makes a patriot as it makes a knave.

This light and darkness in our chaos join'd,
What shall divide? The God within the mind.

Extremes in Nature equal ends produce,   205
In Man they join to some mysterious use;
Tho' each by turns the other's bound invade,
As, in some well-wrought picture, light and shade,
And

NOTES.

though it be difficult to distinguish genuine virtue from spurious, they having both the same appearance, and both the same public effects, yet that they may be disentangled. If it be asked, by what means? He replies (from Ver. 202 to 205.) by conscience;—*the God within the mind;*—and this is to the purpose; for it is a Man's own concern, and no one's else, to know whether his virtue be pure and solid; for what is it to others, whether this virtue (while, as to them, the effect of it is the same) be real or imaginary?   W.

VER. 205. *Extremes in Nature equal ends produce, &c.*] But still it will be said, Why all this difficulty to distinguish true virtue from false? The Poet shews why, (from Ver. 204 to 211.) That though indeed vice and virtue so invade each other's bounds, that sometimes we can scarce tell where one ends and the other begins, yet great purposes are served thereby, no less than the perfecting the constitution of the Whole, as lights and shades, which run into one another insensibly in a well-wrought picture, make the harmony and spirit of the composition. But on this account to say there is neither vice nor virtue, the Poet shews (from Ver. 210 to 217.) would be just as wise as to say, there is neither black nor white; because the shade of that, and the light of this, often run into one another, and are mutually lost:

> " Ask your own heart, and nothing is so plain;
> "'Tis to mistake them, costs the time and pain."

This is an error of *speculation*, which leads men so foolishly to conclude, that there is neither vice nor virtue.   W.

And oft so mix, the diff'rence is too nice
Where ends the Virtue, or begins the Vice.   210
Fools! who from hence into the notion fall,
That Vice or Virtue there is none at all.
If white and black blend, soften, and unite
A thousand ways, is there no black or white?
Ask your own heart, and nothing is so plain;   215
'Tis to mistake them, costs the time and pain.
Vice is a monster of so frightful mien,
As, to be hated, needs but to be seen;
Yet seen too oft, familiar with her face,
We first endure, then pity, then embrace.   220
But where th' Extreme of Vice, was ne'er agreed:
Ask where's the North? at York, 'tis on the Tweed;
In Scotland, at the Orcades; and there,
At Greenland, Zembla, or the Lord knows where.

No

VARIATIONS.

After Ver. 220. in the 1st Edition, followed these,
A Cheat! a Whore! who starts not at the name,
In all the Inns of Court or Drury-lane?

NOTES.

VER. 217. *Vice is a monster, &c.*] There is another Error, an error of *practice*, which hath more general and hurtful effects; and is next considered (from Ver. 216 to 221.) It is this, that though, at the first aspect, Vice be so horrible as to fright the beholder, yet, when by habit we are once grown familiar with her, we first suffer, and in time begin to lose the memory of her nature; which necessarily implies an equal ignorance in the nature of virtue. Hence men conclude, that there is neither one nor the other. W.

" Hence we find," says that amiable moralist Hutcheson, " that the basest actions are drest in some tolerable mask:" " What others call avarice, appears to the agent a prudent care of a family or friends; fraud, artful conduct; malice and revenge, a just sense of honour; fire, and sword, and desolation among enemies, a just thorough

No creature owns it in the firſt degree, 225
But thinks his neighbour farther gone than he;
Ev'n thoſe who dwell beneath its very zone,
Or never feel the rage, or never own;
What happier natures ſhrink at with affright,
The hard inhabitant contends is right. 230
Virtuous and vicious ev'ry Man muſt be,
Few in th' extreme, but all in the degree;
The rogue and fool by fits is fair and wiſe;
And ev'n the beſt, by fits, what they deſpiſe.

'Tis

VARIATIONS.

After Ver. 226. in the MS.
  The Col'nel ſwears the Agent is a dog,
  The Scriv'ner vows th' Attorney is a rogue.
  Againſt the Thief, th' Attorney loud inveighs,
  For whoſe ten pound the County twenty pays.
  The Thief damns Judges, and the Knaves of State;
  And dying, mourns ſmall Villains hang'd by great.

NOTES.

thorough defence of our country; perſecution, a zeal for truth, and for the eternal happineſs of men, which heretics oppoſe."

VER. 231. *Virtuous and vicious*] A fine and juſt reflection, and well calculated to ſubdue and extinguiſh that petulant contempt and unmerited averſion which men too generally entertain of each other, and which gradually diminiſh and deſtroy the ſocial and kind affections. " Our emulation," ſays the amiable and ſagacious Hutcheſon, " our jealouſy or envy, ſhould be reſtrained in a great meaſure by a conſtant reſolution of bearing always in our minds the lovely ſide of every character." And Plato obſerves, in the Phædon, that there is ſomething amiable in almoſt every man living. This charitable doctrine of putting candid conſtructions on actions that appear blameable, nay, deteſtable and deformed, is illuſtrated and enforced, with great ſtrength of argument and of benevolence, by King, in the 5th ch. of the Origin of Evil, when he endeavours to evince the prevalence of moral good in the world.

VER. 234. *By fits, what they deſpiſe.*] Χαλεπὸν ἐσθλὸν ἔμμεναι, was a ſaying of Pittacus, quoted and commented upon by Plato, in the Protagoras.

'Tis but by parts we follow good or ill ; 235
For, Vice or Virtue, Self directs it still ;
Each individual seeks a sev'ral goal ;
But HEAV'N's great view is One, and that the Whole.
That counter-works each folly and caprice ;
That disappoints th' effect of ev'ry vice ; 240
That, happy frailties to all ranks apply'd ;
Shame to the virgin, to the matron pride,
Fear to the statesman, rashness to the chief,
To kings presumption, and to crowds belief :
That, Virtue's ends from Vanity can raise, 245
Which seeks no int'rest, no reward but praise ;
And build on wants, and on defects of mind,
The joy, the peace, the glory of Mankind.
    Heav'n forming each on other to depend,
A master, or a servant, or a friend, 250
                                            Bids

NOTES.

VER. 239. *That counter-works each folly and caprice ;*] The mention of this principle, that *Self* directs vice and virtue, and its consequence, which is, that
    " Each individual seeks a sev'ral goal,"
leads the Author to observe,
    " That HEAV'N's great View is One, and that the Whole."
And this brings him naturally round again to his main subject, namely, *God's producing good out of ill*, which he prosecutes from Ver. 238 to 249.   W.

VER. 249. *Heav'n forming each on other to depend,*] I. Hitherto the Poet hath been employed in discoursing of the use of the Passions, with regard to Society at large ; and in freeing his doctrine from objections : This is the *first* general division of the subject of this epistle.

II. He comes now to shew (from Ver. 248 to 261.) the use of these Passions, with regard to the more confined circle of our
                                                                    friends,

Bids each on other for affiftance call,
Till one Man's weaknefs grows the ftrength of all.
Wants

NOTES.

friends, relations, and acquaintance: and this is the *fecond* general divifion.

III. The Poet having thus fhewn the ufe of the Paffions in *Society*, and in *Domeftic* life, comes, in the laft place, (from Ver. 260 to the end) to fhew their ufe to the *Individual*, even in their illufions; the imaginary happinefs they prefent, helping to make the real miferies of life lefs infupportable: And this is his *third* general divifion:

———" OPINION gilds with varying rays
Thofe painted clouds that beautify our days;
One profpect loft, another ftill we gain;
And not a VANITY is giv'n in vain."

Which muft needs vaftly raife our idea of God's goodnefs; who hath not only provided more than a counterbalance of *real happinefs* to human miferies, but hath even, in his infinite compaffion, beftowed on thofe who were fo foolifh as not to have made this provifion, an *imaginary happinefs;* that they may not be quite overborne with the load of human miferies. This is the Poet's great and noble thought; as ftrong and folid as it is new and ingenious: It teaches, that thefe illufions are the faults and follies of Men, which they wilfully fall into; and thereby deprive themfelves of much happinefs, and expofe themfelves to equal mifery: but that ftill, God (according to his univerfal way of working) gracioufly turns thefe faults and follies fo far to the advantage of his miferable creatures, as to become, for a time, the folace and fupport of their diftreffes:

———" Tho' Man's a fool, yet God is wife."   W.

It was an objection conftantly urged by the ancient Epicureans, that Man could not be the creature of a benevolent Being, as he was formed in a ftate fo helplefs and infirm: Montague took it, and urged it alfo. They never confidered or perceived that this very infirmity and helpleffnefs were the caufe and cement of fociety; that if men had been perfect and felf-fufficient, and had ftood in no need of each other's affiftance, there would have been no occafion for the invention of the arts, and no opportunity for the exertion of the affections. The lines, therefore, in which Lucretius

Wants, frailties, paffions, clofer ftill ally
The common int'reft, or endear the tie.

To

NOTES.

cretius propofes this objection, are as unphilofophical and inconclufive, as they are highly pathetic and poetical.

" Tum porrò puer, ut fævis projectus ab undis
Navita, nudus humi jacet, infans, indigus omni
Vitali auxilio, cùm primùm in luminis oras
Nixibus ex alvo matris natura profudit ;
Vagitúque locum lugubri complet, ut æquum eft,
Cui tantum in vitâ reftet tranfire malorum *."

There is a paffage in the Moralifts which I cannot forbear thinking Pope had in his eye, and which I muft not therefore omit, as it ferves to illuftrate and confirm fo many parts of the Effay on Man ; I fhall therefore give it at length, without apology :

" The young of moft other kinds are inftantly helpful to themfelves, fenfible, vigorous, know how to fhun danger, and feek their good : a human infant is of all the moft weak, helplefs, infirm. And wherefore fhould it not have been fo ordered ? Where is the lofs in fuch a fpecies ? Or what is Man the worfe for that defect, amidft fuch large fupplies ? Does not this defect engage him the more ftrongly to fociety, and force him to own that he is purpofely, and not by accident, made rational and fociable ; and can no otherwife increafe or fubfift than in that focial intercourfe and community which is his natural ftate ? Is not both conjugal affection, and natural affection to parents, duty to magiftrates, love of a common city, community, or country, with the other duties and focial parts of life, deduced from hence, and founded in thefe very wants ? What can be happier than fuch a deficiency, as it is the occafion of fo much good ? What better, than a want fo abundantly made up, and anfwered by fo many enjoyments ? Now, if there are ftill to be found among mankind, fuch as even, in the midft of thefe wants, feem not afhamed to affect a right of independency, and deny themfelves to be by nature fociable ; where would their fhame have been had nature otherwife fupplied their wants ? What duty or obligation had been ever thought of ? What refpect or reverence of parents, magiftrates, their country, or their kind ? Would not their full and felf-fufficient ftate more

---

* Lib. v. ver. 223.

To these we owe true friendship, love sincere, 255
Each home-felt joy that life inherits here;
Yet from the same we learn, in its decline,
Those joys, those loves, those int'rests to resign;
Taught half by Reason, half by mere decay,
To welcome death, and calmly pass away. 260

Whate'er the Passion, knowledge, fame, or pelf,
Not one will change his neighbour with himself.
The learn'd is happy nature to explore,
The fool is happy that he knows no more;
The rich is happy in the plenty giv'n, 265
The poor contents him with the care of Heav'n.
See the blind beggar dance, the cripple sing,
The sot a hero, lunatic a king;

The

NOTES.

strongly have determined them to throw off nature, and deny the ends and author of their creation?"

VER. 253. *Wants, frailties, passions, closer still ally*
The common int'rest, &c.]

As these lines have been misunderstood, I shall give the reader their plain and obvious meaning. To these frailties (says he) we owe all the endearments of private life; yet, when we come to that age, which generally disposes men to think more seriously of the true value of things, and consequently of their provision for a future state, the consideration, that the grounds of those joys, loves, and friendships, are wants, frailties, and passions, proves the best expedient to wean us from the world; a disengagement so friendly to that provision we are now making for another state. The observation is new, and would in any place be extremely beautiful, but has here an infinite grace and propriety, as it so well confirms, by an instance of great moment, the general thesis, *That God makes Ill, at every step, productive of Good.* W.

VER. 266. *With the care of Heav'n.*] It is, alas! with difficulty we can persuade the Poor that they are as much the favourites of Heaven as the Rich.

The ſtarving chemiſt in his golden views
Supremely bleſt, the poet in his Muſe. 270
See ſome ſtrange comfort ev'ry ſtate attend,
And pride beſtow'd on all, a common friend:
See ſome fit paſſion ev'ry age ſupply,
Hope travels through, nor quits us when we die.
                                                Behold

NOTES.

VER. 270. *The poet in his Muſe.*] The Author having ſaid, that no one could change his own profeſſion or views for thoſe of another, intended to carry his obſervation ſtill further, and ſhew that men were unwilling to exchange their own acquirements even for thoſe of the ſame kind, confeſſedly larger, and infinitely more eminent, in another.

To this end he wrote,
  " What partly pleaſes, totally will ſhock:
   I queſtion much, if *Toland* would be *Locke*."
But wanting another proper inſtance of this truth, he referred the lines above for ſome following edition of this Eſſay; which he did not live to give.   W.

VER. 271. *See ſome ſtrange comfort*] How exquiſite is this ſtanza of an unfiniſhed Ode of Gray?
  " Still where roſy Pleaſure leads
    See a kindred Grief purſue;
    Behind the ſteps that Miſery treads,
    Approaching Comfort view:
    The hues of Bliſs more brightly glow,
    Cheriſh'd by ſabler tints of Woe;
    And blended form, with artful ſtrife,
    The ſtrength and harmony of life."

VER. 272. *And pride*] From La Rochefoucault, whoſe words are: " Nature, who ſo wiſely has fitted the organs of our body to make us happy, ſeems likewiſe to have beſtowed pride on us, on purpoſe, as it were, to ſave us the pain of knowing our own imperfections." Maxim 36.

VER. 274. *Hope travels through,*] Is this Hope then no more than one of thoſe ſtrange comforts, thoſe deluſive pleaſures, thoſe ſorts of groundleſs happineſs, that conſtitute the chief enjoyment of the ſot, the chemiſt, the poet, and the lunatic?

Behold the child, by nature's kindly law, 275
Pleas'd with a rattle, tickled with a straw:
Some livelier play-thing gives his youth delight,
A little louder, but as empty quite:
Scarfs, garters, gold, amuse his riper stage,
And beads and pray'r-books are the toys of age: 280
Pleas'd with this bauble still, as that before,
Till tir'd he sleeps, and Life's poor play is o'er.
  Mean-while opinion gilds with varying rays
Those painted clouds that beautify our days;
Each want of happiness by Hope supply'd, 285
And each vacuity of sense by Pride:

These

NOTES.

VER. 280. *And beads and pray'r-books are the toys of age:*] A Satire on what is called, in Popery, the *Opus operatum.* As this is a description of the circle of human life returning into itself by a second child-hood, the Poet has with great elegance concluded his description with the same image with which he set out—*And life's poor play is o'er.* W.

VER. 280. *The toys of age:*] Exactly what Fontenelle says,
  "Il est des hochets pour tout age."
And Prior,
  " Give us play-things for old age."
Yet it is certain that Fontenelle could not have taken this verse from Prior, for he did not understand English, though Prior wrote it more than twenty years before Fontenelle.

  De Lisle, whose translation of Virgil's Georgics is so frequently and so unjustly praised by Voltaire, has also translated, but not published, the Essay on Man. Millot has given another, published 1762.

VER. 286. *And each vacuity of sense by Pride:*] An eminent Casuist, *Father Francis Garasse,* in his *Somme Theologique,* has drawn a very charitable conclusion from this principle; which he hath well illustrated: " Selon la Justice" (says this equitable Divine) " tout travail honnête doit être recompensé de loüange

ou

Thefe build as faft as knowledge can deftroy;
In folly's cup ftill laughs the bubble, joy;
One profpect loft, another ftill we gain;
And not a vanity is giv'n in vain; 290
Ev'n mean Self-love becomes, by force divine,
The fcale to meafure others wants by thine.
                                                See!

NOTES.

ou de fatisfaction. Quand les bons efprits font un ouvrage excellent, ils font juftement recompenfez par les fuffrages du Public. Quand un pauvre efprit travaille beaucoup, pour fair un mauvais ouvrage, il n'eft pas jufte ni raifonable, qu'il attende des loüanges publiques; car elles ne lui font pas dues. Mais afin que fes travaux ne demeurent pas fans recompenfe, Dieu lui donne une fatisfaction perfonnelle, que perfonne ne lui peut envier fans une injuftice plus que barbare; tout ainfi que Dieu, qui eft jufte, donne de la fatisfaction aux Grenoüilles de leur chant. Autrement la blâme public, joint' à leur mécontentement, feroit fuffifant pour les réduire au defefpoir."   W.

VER. 290. *And not a vanity*] Dr. Balguy has given us fome bold and original thoughts on this fubject:

" In fingle perfons, it muft be owned, the balance of the paffions is very frequently deftroyed; feldom indeed preferved with exactnefs and truth. But then the defects to be found in one man are fupplied by the exceffes in another. So that, if you confider the *whole* fpecies, you will neither find too much, nor too little, of any one principle in the human mind. Indolence and ambition, avarice and fenfuality, refentment and compaffion, if not in the fame perfons, yet in different perfons, counteract and balance each other. Nor is there a fingle fentiment implanted in our nature which can either be increafed, or leffened, in the *whole* race of mankind, without lofs or harm to the human fpecies; unlefs, indeed, you affume a liberty of altering *many* things at a time; of forming a new and fantaftic fyftem, perhaps made up of inconfiftent parts, and beyond the bounds of poffibility itfelf. So true is that celebrated paffage of Cicero, de Nat. Deorum, lib. ii. c. 34; " Si quis corrigere aliquid volet, aut deterius faciet, aut id, quod fieri non potuit, defiderabit." Divine Benevolence, p. 100.

See! and confess, one comfort still must rise;
'Tis this, Tho' Man's a fool, yet GOD IS WISE.

NOTES.

VER. 294. *'Tis this, Tho' Man's a fool,*] A little time after the second edition of this Epistle was published, Voltaire writes thus, July 24, 1733, to Monf. Thiriot, his friend, in London:

" A propos d'epitre, dites à M. Pope, que je l'ai très-bien reconnu, in his Essay on Man (which Pope had not owned at that time); 'tis certainly his style; now and then there is some obscurity: but the whole is charming." Lettres de M. Voltaire, tome i. p. 165. And, speaking of it again, p. 291. he says, " C'est un ouvrage qui donne quelquefois de la peine aux lecteurs Anglois." And in a long letter to La Marquise du Deffant, in the year 1736, p. 337. he tells her, " Tout l'ouvrage de Pope, sous mille de pareille obscurités. Il y a cent eclairs admirables qui percent à tous momens cette nuit, et votre imagination brillante doit les aimer." I am informed by Lord Orford, an intimate friend of this accomplished lady, that she communicated a great number of Voltaire's letters to the publishers of his Works, which they returned, and would not insert, because they bore very hard on many of the philosophers of Paris, and particularly on Helvetius.

ARGUMENT OF EPISTLE III.

Of the Nature and State of Man with respect to Society.

I. THE *whole Universe one system of Society*, Ver. 7, &c. *Nothing made wholly for* itself, *nor yet wholly for* another, Ver. 27. *The happiness of* Animals *mutual*, Ver. 49. II. Reason *or* Instinct *operate alike to the good of each Individual*, Ver. 79. Reason *or* Instinct *operate also to Society, in all animals*, Ver. 109. III. *How far* Society *carried by* Instinct, Ver. 115. *How much farther by Reason*, Ver. 128. IV. *Of that which is called the* State *of* Nature, Ver. 144. *Reason instructed by Instinct in the Invention of* Arts, Ver. 166; *and in the Forms of* Society, Ver. 176. V. *Origin of Political Societies*, Ver. 196. *Origin of Monarchy*, Ver. 207. *Patriarchal Government*, Ver. 212. VI. *Origin of true Religion and Government, from the same principle, of Love*, Ver. 231, &c. *Origin of Superstition and Tyranny, from the same principle, of Fear*, Ver. 237, &c. *The Influence of Self-love operating to the* social *and* public *Good*, Ver. 266. *Restoration of true Religion and Government on their first principle*, Ver. 285. *Mixt Government*, Ver. 288. *Various Forms of each, and the true end of all*, Ver. 300, &c.

EPISTLE III.

H<small>ERE</small> then we reſt: " The Univerſal Cauſe
" Acts to one end, but acts by various laws."
In all the madneſs of ſuperfluous health,
The trim of pride, the impudence of wealth,

Let

V A R I A T I O N S.

V<small>ER</small>. 1. In ſeveral Edit. in 4to.
Learn, Dulneſs, learn! " The Univerſal Cauſe," &c.

N O T E S.

V<small>ER</small>. 1. *The Univerſal Cauſe*] Voltaire concludes his objections to Optimiſm with the following words: " Ce ſyſtême, du tout eſt bien, ne repreſente l'auteur de toute la nature que comme un roi puiſſant et mal-faiſant, qui ne s'embarraſſe pas qu'il en coute la vie à quatre ou cinq cent mille hommes, et que les autres trainent leurs jours dans la diſette et dans les larmes, pourvû qu'il vienne à tout de ſes deſſeins. Loins donc que l'opinion du meilleur des mondes poſſible conſole, elle eſt déſeſpérante pour les philoſophes qui l'embraſſent. La queſtion du bien et du mal demeure un cahos indebrouillable pour ceux qui cherchent de bonne foi; c'eſt un jeu d'eſprit pour ceux qui diſputent; ils ſont des forçats qui jouent avec leurs chaînes. Pour le peuple non penſant, il reſ-ſemble aſſez à des poiſſons qu'on a tranſporter d'une rivière dans un reſervoir; ils ne ſe doutent pas qu'ils ſont là pour être man-gés le carême; auſſi ne ſçavons-nous rien du tout par nous-mêmes des cauſes de notre deſtinée. Mettons à la fin de preſque tous les chapitres de Metaphyſique les deux lettres des juges Romains quand ils n'entendant pas une cauſe. N. L. non liquet, cela n'eſt pas clair."

V<small>ER</small>. 3. *Superfluous health,*] Immoderate labour and immode-rate ſtudy are equally the impairers of health: They, whoſe ſta-

tion

Let this great truth be prefent night and day; 5
But moſt be prefent, if we preach or pray.
Look round our World; behold the chain of Love
Combining all below and all above.

See

NOTES.

tion fets them above both, muſt needs have an abundance of it, which not being employed in the common ſervice, but waſted in Luxury and Folly, the Poet properly calls a *fuperfluity*. W.

VER. 4. *Impudence of wealth*,] Becauſe *wealth* pretends to be wifdom, wit, learning, honeſty, and, in ſhort, all the virtues in their turns. W.

VER. 3, 4, 5, 6. M. Du Refnel, not feeing into the admirable purpofe of the caution contained in thefe four lines, hath quite dropped the moſt material circumſtances contained in the laſt of them; and, what is worfe, for the fake of a foolifh antitheſis, hath deſtroyed the whole propriety of the thought in the two firſt: and fo, between both, hath left his Author neither fenfe nor fyſtem.

" Dans le fein du bonheur, *ou de l'adverſité.*"
Now of all men, thofe in adverfity have leaſt need of this caution, as being leaſt apt to forget, *That God confults the good of the whole, and provides for it by procuring mutual happineſs by means of mutual wants;* it being feen that fuch who yet retain the fmart of any freſh calamity, are moſt compaſſionate to others labouring under diſtreſſes, and moſt prompt and ready to relieve them. W.

VER. 7. *Look round our World, &c.*] He introduceth the fyſtem of human Sociability (Ver. 7, 8.) by fhewing it to be the dictate of the Creator; and that Man, in this, did but follow the example of general Nature, which is united in one clofe fyſtem of benevolence. W.

" The bufh protects that acorn which becomes an oak. The grafs maintains the nobleſt animals. Thus does the vegetable nature both help itfelf and help the animal. Again, blights and blaſts deſtroy the tender plant, and breed contagions and peſts among animals. Thus does the vegetable, or at leaſt inanimate nature, both hurt itfelf and hurt the animal. By the induſtry of man and the dung of animals, the vegetable nature is fertilized and cultivated. The parent animal nouriſhes its young, and defends

ESSAY ON MAN.

See plaſtic Nature working to this end,
The ſingle atoms each to other tend, 10
Attract, attracted to, the next in place
Form'd and impell'd its neighbour to embrace.
See Matter next, with various life endu'd,
Preſs to one centre ſtill, the gen'ral Good.
See dying vegetables life ſuſtain, 15
See life diſſolving vegetate again :
All

NOTES.

fends them at a feaſon when of themſelves defencelefs. Thus does the animal nature both keep itſelf and help the vegetable. Again, by man and beaſt are vegetables deſtroyed; and by man and beaſt are man and beaſt deſtroyed. Thus does the animal nature both hurt itſelf and hurt the vegetable. Friendſhip and ſtrife are concurrent principles. By friendſhip are prevented chaos and confuſion; by ſtrife are prevented ſloth and lethargy. By ſtrife all powers are rouſed to action; and by friendſhip they are tempered into harmony and concord." MSS. of Harris.—And again;

" Hence we perceive the meaning of what Heraclitus ſays in Plutarch, when he calls War the father, and king, and lord of all things; and aſſerts that, when Homer prayed

" That ſtrife be baniſh'd both from God and men,"

he was not aware that he was curſing the generation of all things, as, in fact, they deduce their riſe out of conteſt and antipathy."

VER. 12. *Form'd and impell'd, &c.*] To make Matter ſo cohere as to fit it for the uſes intended by its Creator, a proper *configuration* of its infenſible parts is as neceſſary as that quality ſo equally and univerſally conferred upon it, called *Attraction*. To expreſs the firſt part of this thought, our Author ſays *form'd;* and to expreſs the latter, *impell'd.* W.

VER. 15. *See dying vegetables*] Pope has again copied Shafteſbury ſo cloſely in this paſſage, as to uſe almoſt his very words:
" Thus, in the feveral terreſtrial forms, a reſignation is required; a ſacrifice, and mutual yielding of nature, one to another. The vegetables, by their death, ſuſtain the animals; and the animal bodies diſſolved enrich the earth, and raiſe again the vegetable world. The numerous inſects are reduced by the ſuperior kinds of birds or beaſts: and theſe again are checked by man, who, in his turn,

ſubmits

All forms that perish other forms supply,
(By turns we catch the vital breath, and die,)
                                                        Like

NOTES.

submits to other natures, and resigns his form a sacrifice in common to the rest of things. And if in natures, so little exalted or pre-eminent above each other, the sacrifice of interest can appear so just; how much more reasonably may all inferior natures be subjected to the superior nature of the world!" The Moralist, p. 130.

    Whatever censures Shaftesbury has incurred for his many indecent and groundless objections against the Christian religion, yet we ought candidly to confess, that two of his treatises, the Enquiry concerning Virtue, and the Moralists, deserve attention and applause. The former is written with great perspicuity of method and closeness of argument, and with a purity and simplicity of style very different from the over-ornamented, tumid style of many of his other works. The latter is perhaps the finest imitation of the manner of Plato, as Lord Monboddo has shewn at large, in our language. In both are advanced the most cogent arguments for an Intelligent First Cause, and the benevolence, wisdom, and goodness of a superintending Providence. Our Author has therefore been guilty of manifest injustice in insinuating, in the last book of the Dunciad, ver. 418. that the very Theocles, from whom he has copied so much, and so many of whose sentiments and arguments he has adopted, is a preacher of Fate and Naturalism. And, what is still more inexcusable, the words of Theocles are imperfectly quoted in the note of this passage of the Dunciad, in order to give a colour to the insinuation; for, after the words "impowered Creatress," the two following ones—"or Thou," are unfairly omitted. See Characteristics, vol. ii. p. 345. The first book of the Enquiry ends with a sentence far remote from irreligion and epicurism: "Hence we may determine justly the relation which virtue has to piety; the first being not complete without the latter; since, where the latter is wanting, there can be neither the same benignity, firmness, nor constancy; the same good composure of the affections, nor uniformity of mind. And thus the perfection and height of virtue must be owing to the belief of a God!" Vol. ii. p. 76.

    In a letter of Dr. Warburton, transcribed from the manuscripts of Dr. Birch, in the British Museum, by the late Mr. Maty, are
                                                                          these

Like bubbles on the fea of Matter born,
They rife, they break, and to that fea return. 20
Nothing is foreign; Parts relate to whole;
One all-extending, all-preferving Soul
                                             Connects

NOTES.

thefe remarkable words: " As to the paffages of Mr. Pope that correfpond with Leibnitz, you know he took them from Shaftefbury; and that Shaftefbury and Leibnitz had one common original, Plato, whofe fyftem of the beft, when pufhed as far as Leibnitz has carried it, muft end in Fate." A ftrange opinion once prevailed, that Leibnitz was not ferious in his Theodicée. Le Clerc and De Maifeaux were of this opinion. But Mr. Jourdan, in his entertaining Voyage Literaire, p. 150. has produced a letter of the celebrated and learned Mr. Le Croze, that effectually deftroys this abfurd fuppofition.

I fhall add to this long note, that it feems to be an infufferable inftance of affectation in Bolingbroke, never once to have mentioned Shaftefbury, who was much his fuperior in learning and philofophy, and from whom he has borrowed fo many fentiments and opinions. See alfo Letters of Shaftefbury to a Young Clergyman.

VER. 19, 20. *Like bubbles, &c.*] M. Du Refnel tranflates thefe two lines thus:

" *Sort du neant y rentre*, et reparoit au jour."

He is here, indeed, confiftently wrong: for having (as we faid) miftaken the Poet's account of the *prefervation* of *Matter* for the *creation* of it, he commits the very fame miftake with regard to the *vegetable* and *animal* fyftems; and fo talks now, though with the lateft, of the *production of things out of nothing*. Indeed, by his fpeaking of their *returning into nothing*, he has fubjected his Author to M. Du Croufaz's cenfure. " Mr. Pope defcends to the moft vulgar prejudices, when he tells us that *each being returns to nothing:* the Vulgar think that what difappears is annihilated," &c. *Comm. p.* 221.   W.

VER. 22. *One all-extending, all-preferving Soul*] Which, in the language of Sir Ifaac Newton, is, " Deus omnipræfens eft, non per virtutem folam, fed etiam per fubftantiam: nam virtus fine fubftantia fubfiftere non poteft." *Newt. Princ. Schol. gen. fub fin.*   W.

Connects each being, greatest with the least;
Made Beast in aid of Man, and Man of Beast;
All serv'd, all serving: nothing stands alone; 25
The chain holds on, and where it ends, unknown.

 Has God, thou fool! work'd solely for thy good,
Thy joy, thy pastime, thy attire, thy food?
Who for thy table feeds the wanton fawn,
For him as kindly spread the flow'ry lawn: 30
Is it for thee the lark ascends and sings?
Joy tunes his voice, joy elevates his wings.
Is it for thee the linnet pours his throat?
Loves of his own and raptures swell the note.
The bounding steed you pompously bestride, 35
Shares with his lord the pleasure and the pride.
Is thine alone the seed that strews the plain?
The birds of Heav'n shall vindicate their grain.
Thine the full harvest of the golden year?
Part pays, and justly, the deserving steer: 40
The hog, that ploughs not, nor obeys thy call,
Lives on the labours of this Lord of all.

 Know, Nature's children all divide her care;
The fur that warms a monarch, warm'd a bear.

While

NOTES.

VER. 23. *Greatest with the least;*] As acting more strongly and immediately in beasts, whose instinct is plainly an external reason; which made an old school-man say, with great elegance, " Deus est anima brutorum:"

" In this 'tis God directs"— W.

VER. 43. *Know, Nature's children all*] The poetry of these lines is as beautiful as the philosophy is solid. " They who imagine that all things in this world were made for the immediate use of Man alone, run themselves into inextricable difficulties. Man, indeed,

While Man exclaims, " See all things for my ufe!"
" See man for mine!" replies a pamper'd goofe : 46
And juft as fhort of reafon he muft fall,
Who thinks all made for one, not one for all.
Grant that the pow'rful ftill the weak controul ;
Be Man the Wit and Tyrant of the whole :   50
                                                      Nature

VARIATIONS.
After Ver. 46. in the former Editions,
   What care to tend, to lodge, to cram, to treat him!
   All this he knew ; but not that 'twas to eat him.
   As far as Goofe could judge, he reafon'd right ;
   But as to Man, miftook the matter quite.

NOTES.
deed, is the head of this lower part of the creation ; and perhaps it was defigned to be abfolutely under his command. But that all things here tend directly to his own ufe, is, I think, neither eafy nor neceffary to be proved. Some manifeftly ferve for the food and fupport of others, whofe fouls may be neceffary to prepare and preferve their bodies for that purpofe, and may at the fame time be happy in a confcioufnefs of their own exiftence. It is probable they are intended to promote each other's good reciprocally : Nay, Man himfelf contributes to the happinefs, and betters the condition of the brutes in feveral refpects, by cultivating and improving the ground ; by watching the feafons ; by protecting and providing for them, when they are unable to protect and provide for themfelves." Thefe are the words of Dr. Law, in his learned Commentary on King's Origin of Evil, firft publifhed in Latin, 1701, a work of penetration and clofe reafoning ; which, it is remarkable, Bayle had never read, but only fome extracts from it, when he firft wrote his famous article of the Paulicians, in his Dictionary.

   VER. 45. *See all things for my ufe!*] On the contrary, the wife man hath faid, *The Lord hath made all things for himfelf.* Prov. xvi. 4.   W.

   VER. 46. *Replies a pamper'd goofe :*] Taken from Peter Charron ; but fuch a familiar and burlefque image is improperly introduced among fuch folid and ferious reflections.

   VER. 50. *Be Man the Wit and Tyrant of the whole :*] Alluding to the *witty* fyftem of that Philofopher, which made Animals
                                                                                                                                 mere

Nature that Tyrant checks; He only knows,
And helps, another creature's wants and woes.
Say, will the falcon, ftooping from above,
Smit with her varying plumage, fpare the dove?
Admires the jay the infect's gilded wings?   55
Or hears the hawk when Philomela fings?
Man cares for all: to birds he gives his woods,
To beafts his paftures, and to fifh his floods;
For fome his int'reft prompts him to provide,
For more his Pleafure, yet for more his Pride: 60
All feed on one vain patron, and enjoy
Th' extenfive bleffing of his luxury.
That very life his learned hunger craves,
He faves from famine, from the favage faves;
Nay, feafts the animal he dooms his feaft,   65
And, till he ends the being, makes it bleft;
Which fees no more the ftroke, or feels the pain,
Than favour'd Man by touch ethereal flain.
The creature had his feaft of life before;
Thou too muft perifh, when thy feaft is o'er!   70

To

NOTES.

mere Machines, infenfible of pain or pleafure; and fo encouraged Men in the exercife of that *Tyranny* over their fellow-creatures, confequent on fuch a principle.   W.

VER. 51. *Nature that Tyrant checks;*] What an exquifite affemblage is here (down to Ver. 70.) of deep reflection, humane fentiments, and poetic imagery! It is finely obferved, that compaffion is exclufively the property of Man alone.

VER. 68. *Than favour'd Man, &c.*] Several of the ancients, and many of the Orientals fince, efteemed thofe who were ftruck by lightning as facred perfons, and the particular favourites of Heaven.   P.

VER. 68. *By touch ethereal flain.*] The expreffion is from Milton's Comus.

To each unthinking being, Heav'n a friend,
Gives not the uſeleſs knowledge of its end:
To Man imparts it, but with ſuch a view
As, while he dreads it, makes him hope it too:
The hour conceal'd, and ſo remote the fear,   75
Death ſtill draws nearer, never ſeeming near.
Great ſtanding miracle! that Heav'n aſſign'd
Its only thinking thing this turn of mind.

II. Whether with Reaſon or with Inſtinct bleſt,
Know, all enjoy that pow'r which ſuits them beſt;   80
To bliſs alike by that direction tend,
And find the means proportion'd to their end.
Say, where full Inſtinct is th' unerring guide,
What Pope or Council can they need beſide?
Reaſon, however able, cool at beſt,   85
Cares not for ſervice, or but ſerves when preſt,
Stays till we call, and then not often near;
But honeſt Inſtinct comes a volunteer,
Sure never to o'erſhoot, but juſt to hit;
While ſtill too wide or ſhort is human Wit;   90
Sure by quick Nature happineſs to gain,
Which heavier Reaſon labours at in vain.
This too ſerves always, Reaſon never long;
One muſt go right, the other may go wrong.
See then the acting and comparing pow'rs   95
One in their nature, which are two in ours;

And

VARIATIONS.

After Ver. 84. in the MS.
  While Man, with op'ning views of various ways
  Confounded, by the aid of knowledge ſtrays.
  Too weak to chuſe, yet chuſing ſtill in haſte,
  One moment gives the pleaſure and diſtaſte.

And Reason raise o'er Instinct as you can,
In this 'tis God directs, in that 'tis Man.

Who

NOTES.

VER. 97. *And Reason raise o'er Instinct*] Charron, of whom Pope and Bolingbroke were so fond, has treated this subject with so much freedom of thought, and endeavoured to raise Instinct so much above Reason, that Stanhope, his translator, deemed it necessary to obviate the tendency of his tenets, by a long Appendix to the 34th chapter of the first book. It appears a little strange, that so orthodox a divine as Stanhope should translate two books that are supposed to favour libertinism and scepticism—the Wisdom of Charron and the Maxims of Rochefoucault. Bayle has stated the difficulties, that arise in accounting to the actions of brutes, with his usual acuteness and force of argument.

Hume has gone farther than any other writer on the subject: " Though animals," he says, " learn many parts of their knowledge from observation and experience, there are also many parts of it which they derive from the original hand of Nature, which much exceed the share of capacity they possess on ordinary occasions, and in which they improve little or nothing by the longest practice and experience. These we denominate Instincts, and are so apt to admire as something very extraordinary and inexplicable by all the disquisitions of human understanding. But our wonder will perhaps cease or diminish, when we consider that the experimental reasoning itself, which we possess in common with beasts, and on which the whole conduct of life depends, is nothing but a species of Instinct, or mechanical power, that acts in us unknown to ourselves ; and, in its chief operations, is not directed by any such relations or comparisons of ideas as are the proper objects of our intellectual faculties. Though the Instinct be different, yet still it is an Instinct which teaches a man to avoid the fire ; as much as that which teaches a bird with such exactness the art of incubation, and the whole economy and order of its nursery." Of the Reason of Animals, Essay, p. 432.

Father Bougeant's little treatise on the Language of Beasts is an amusing work ; in which he has placed the notion of Des Cartes, that they are mere machines, in a strong light, as well as the difficulties that arise from the opinion of their having immortal souls. Bougeant was severely censured by his brother jesuits for this little work. He had better have kept to politics. He wrote the History

Who taught the nations of the field and wood
To fhun their poifon, and to chufe their food? 100
Prefcient, the tides or tempefts to withftand,
Build on the wave, or arch beneath the fand?
Who made the fpider parallels defign,
Sure as De-moivre, without rule or line?
Who bid the ftork, Columbus-like, explore 105
Heav'ns not his own, and worlds unknown before?
Who calls the council, ftates the certain day,
Who forms the phalanx, and who points the way?
  III. God, in the nature of each being, founds
Its proper blifs, and fets its proper bounds: 110
                                                But

NOTES.

tory of the Treaty of Weftphalia. Pofterity will look on this as a curious work: the ftate of Europe being now fo totally changed, this hiftory will read like a romance.

  VER. 99. *Who taught*] This paffage is highly finifhed: fuch objects are more fuited to the nature of poetry than abftract ideas. Every verb and epithet has here a defcriptive force. We find more imagery from thefe lines to the end of the epiftle, than in any other parts of this Effay. The origin of the connections in focial life, the account of the ftate of nature, the rife and effects of fuperftition and tyranny, and the reftoration of true religion and juft government; all thefe ought to be mentioned as paffages that deferve high applaufe, nay, as fome of the moft exalted pieces of Englifh poetry.

  VER. 109. *God, in the nature of each being, &c.*] The Author now cometh to the main fubject of his epiftle, the proof of Man's SOCIABILITY, from the two general focieties compofed by him; the *natural*, fubject to *paternal* authority; and the *civil*, fubject to that of a *magiftrate*. This he hath the addrefs to introduce, from what had preceded, in fo eafy and natural a manner, as fheweth him to have the art of giving all the grace to the drynefs and feverity of Method, as well as wit to the ftrength and depth of
                                                  Reafon.

But as he fram'd the Whole, the Whole to blefs,
On mutual Wants built mutual Happinefs:
So from the firft, eternal ORDER ran,
And creature link'd to creature, man to man.
Whate'er of life all quick'ning ether keeps, 115
Or breathes thro' air, or fhoots beneath the deeps,
Or pours profufe on earth, one nature feeds
The vital flame, and fwells the genial feeds.
Not man alone, but all that roam the wood,
Or wing the fky, or roll along the flood, 120
Each loves itfelf, but not itfelf alone,
Each fex defires alike, till two are one.
Nor ends the pleafure with the fierce embrace!
They love themfelves, a third time, in their race.

Thus

NOTES.

Reafon. The philofophic nature of his work requiring he fhould fhew by what means thofe Societies were introduced, this affords him an opportunity of fliding gracefully and eafily from the preliminaries into the main fubject; and fo of giving his work that perfection of method, which we find only in the compofitions of great writers. For having juft before, though to a different purpofe, defcribed the power of beftial Inftinct to attain the happinefs of the *Individual*, he goeth on, in fpeaking of Inftinct as it is ferviceable both to that, and to the *Kind* (from Ver. 108 to 147.), to illuftrate the original of *Society*. He fheweth, that though, as he had before obferved, God had founded the proper blifs of each creature in the nature of its own exiftence; yet thefe not being independent individuals, but parts of a Whole, God, to blefs that Whole, built mutual happinefs on mutual wants: Now, for the fupply of mutual wants, creatures muft neceffarily come together: which is the firft ground of Society amongft Men. He then proceeds to that called *natural*, fubject to *paternal* authority, and arifing from the union of the two fexes; defcribes the imperfect image of it in brutes; then explains it at large in all its caufes and

effects.

Thus beaſt and bird their common charge attend, 125
The mothers nurſe it, and the ſires defend;
The young diſmiſs'd to wander earth or air,
There ſtops the Inſtinct, and there ends the care;
The link diſſolves, each ſeeks a freſh embrace,
Another love ſucceeds, another race. 130
A longer care Man's helpleſs kind demands;
That longer care contracts more laſting bands:
Reflection, Reaſon, ſtill the ties improve,
At once extend the int'reſt, and the love;
With choice we fix, with ſympathy we burn; 135
Each Virtue in each Paſſion takes its turn;
And ſtill new needs, new helps, new habits riſe,
That graft benevolence on charities.
Still as one brood, and as another roſe,
Theſe nat'ral love maintain'd, habitual thoſe: 140
The laſt, ſcarce ripen'd into perfect Man,
Saw helpleſs him from whom their life began:
Mem'ry and forecaſt juſt returns engage,
That pointed back to youth, this on to age;
While pleaſure, gratitude, and hope, combin'd, 145
Still ſpread the int'reſt, and preſerv'd the kind.
 IV. Nor think, in NATURE's STATE they blindly
  trod;
The State of Nature was the reign of God:
            Self-

NOTES.

effects. And laſtly ſhews, that, as in *fact*, like mere animal Society, it is founded and preſerved by mutual wants, the ſupplial of which cauſeth mutual happineſs; ſo is it likewiſe in *right*, as a rational Society, by equity, gratitude, and the obſervance of the relation of things in general. W.

Self-love and Social at her birth began,
Union the bond of all things, and of Man.   150
Pride then was not; nor Arts, that Pride to aid;
Man walk'd with beast, joint-tenant of the shade;
The same his table, and the same his bed;
No murder cloath'd him, and no murder fed.
In the same temple, the resounding wood,   155
All vocal beings hymn'd their equal God:
The

NOTES.

Ver. 152. *Man walk'd with beast,*] Lucretius, agreeably to his more uncomfortable system, has presented us with a different and more horrid picture of this state of Nature. The calamitous condition of Man is exhibited by images of much energy and wildness of fancy; see ver. 980. book v.; and particularly when he represents, at ver. 991. some of these wretched mortals mangled by the wild beasts, into whose caverns they had retreated for shelter in tempestuous seasons, and running distracted with pain through the woods, with their wounds undressed and putrifying:

—tremulas super ulcera tetra tenentes
Palmas, horriferis accibant vocibus Orcum.

Pain is most forcibly expressed by the action here described, and by the epithet " tremulas."

The continuance and universality of the savage state of Man, in the earliest ages of the world, has been the favourite opinion of many late philosophical writers, particularly of Lord Kaims, in his Sketches, which has been answered with much learning and acuteness by Dr. Doig, 1792.

Ver. 156. *All vocal beings, &c.*] This may be well explained by a sublime passage of the Psalmist, who, calling to mind the age of Innocence, and full of the great ideas of those

" Chains of Love
Combining all below and all above,
Which to one point, and to one centre bring,
Beast, Man, or Angel, Servant, Lord, or King;"

breaks out into this rapturous and divine apostrophe, to call back the devious Creation to its pristine rectitude; that very state our author describes above: " Praise the Lord, all angels; praise him all ye hosts. Praise ye him, sun and moon; praise him, all ye stars of light," &c.   W.

Ep. III.   ESSAY ON MAN.   101

The fhrine with gore unftain'd, with gold undreft,
Unbrib'd, unbloody, ftood the blamelefs prieft :
Heav'n's attribute was Univerfal Care,
And Man's prerogative to rule, but fpare.   160
Ah ! how unlike the Man of times to come!
Of half that live the butcher and the tomb ;
Who, foe to Nature, hears the gen'ral groan,
Murders their fpecies, and betrays his own.
But juft difeafe to luxury fucceeds,   165
And ev'ry death its own avenger breeds ;
The Fury-paffions from that blood began,
And turn'd on Man a fiercer favage, Man.
See him from Nature rifing flow to Art !
To copy Inftinct then was Reafon's part ;   170
Thus then to Man the voice of Nature fpake—
" Go, from the Creatures thy inftructions take :
                                        " Learn

NOTES.

VER. 157. *Undreft, unbrib'd, unbloody,*] Alliteration is here ufed with effect. But is the affertion confiftent with the ufual interpretation of the Scripture account of the origin of facrifice ?

VER. 158. *Unbrib'd, unbloody, &c.*] *i. e.* the ftate defcribed from Ver. 262 to 269, was not yet arrived. For then, when Superftition was become fo extreme as to bribe the Gods with *human facrifices ;* Tyranny became neceffitated to woo the prieft for a favourable anfwer.   W.

VER. 162. *The butcher and the tomb ;*] Plutarch has written a treatife againft animal food ; tom. ii. 995. Thomfon, with his ufual tendernefs, has done the fame ; Spring, v. 330.

VER. 171. *Thus then to Man the voice of Nature fpake*——
      " *Go, &c.*]
M. Du Refnel has tranflated the lines thus,
   " La Nature *indigné* alors fe fit entendre ;
   " Va, *malheureux* mortel, va, lui dit elle, apprendre."
One would wonder what fhould make the Tranflator reprefent
                                                    Nature

"Learn from the birds what food the thickets yield;
"Learn from the beasts the physic of the field;
                                        " Thy

NOTES.

Nature in such a passion with Man, and calling him names, at a time when Mr. Pope supposed her in her best good-humour. W.

VER. 171. *The voice of Nature*] The prosopopœia is magnificent, and the occasion important, no less than the origin of the arts of life. Nature is personified by Lucretius, and introduced speaking with suitable majesty and elevation: She is chiding her foolish and ungrateful children for their vain and impious discontent:

" Quid tibi tantopere est, mortalis, quod nimis ægris
   Luctibus indulges? quid mortem congemis, ac fles?—
   Aufer abhinc lacrymas, barathro et compesce querelas."

There is an authoritative air in the brevity of this sentence, as also in the concluding line of her speech; and particularly in the very last words:

" Æquo animoque, agedum, jam aliis concede:—necesse est."

This fine prosopopœia in our Author is not, as Dr. Warburton asserted, the most sublime that ever entered into the human imagination, for we see Lucretius used it before.

The Romans have left us scarcely any piece of poetry so striking and original as the beginning and progress of arts, at the end of the fifth book of Lucretius; who perhaps, of all the Roman poets, had the strongest imagination. The Persians distinguish the different degrees of Fancy in different poets, by calling them painters or sculptors. Lucretius, from the force of his images, should be ranked among the latter. He is in truth a Sculptor Poet. His images have a bold relief. Of this noble prosopopœia, in Lucretius, Addison seems to have thought, in a well-known passage of Cato:

——" All Nature cries aloud
     Thro' all her Works."——

VER. 173. *Learn from the birds, &c.*] It is a caution commonly practised amongst Navigators, when thrown upon a desert coast, and in want of refreshments, to observe what fruits have been touched by the Birds: and to venture on these without further hesitation.   P.

VER. 173. *Learn from the birds*] Taken, but finely improved, from Bacon's Advancement of Learning, p. 48. " They who
                                                        discourse

" Thy arts of building from the bee receive ; 175
" Learn of the mole to plough, the worm to weave ;
" Learn of the little Nautilus to fail,
" Spread the thin oar, and catch the driving gale.
" Here too all forms óf focial union find,
" And hence let Reafon, late, inftruct Mankind :
" Here fubterranean works and cities fee ; 181
" There towns aerial on the waving tree.
" Learn

NOTES.

difcourfe of the inventions and originals of things, refer them rather to Beafts, Birds, and Fifhes, and Serpents, than to Men. So that it was no marvaile (the manner of antiquity being to confecrate Inventors) that the Ægyptians had fo few human idols in their temples, but almoft all brute. Who taught the raven in a drowth to throw pebbles into a hollow tree when fhe fpied water, that the water might rife fo as fhe might come to it ? Who taught the bee to fayle thro' fuch a vaft fea of air, and to find the way from a field in flower a great way off to her hive ? Who taught the ant to bite every graine of corne fhe burieth in her hill, leaft it fhould take roote and grow ?" See, in the Philofophical Tranfactions, the marvellous account of the white ants in Africa, and their buildings and arts.

It is fomewhat remarkable, that Solomon, in the Proverbs, when he fpeaks of the wonderful inftincts of certain animals, does not mention the bee.

VER. 174. *Learn from the beafts, &c.*] See Pliny's *Nat. Hift.* l. viii. c. 27. where feveral inftances are given of Animals difcovering the medical efficacy of herbs, by their own ufe of them; and pointing out to fome operations in the art of healing, by their own practice. W.

VER. 177. *Learn of the little Nautilus, &c.*] Oppian Halieur, lib. ii. defcribes this fifh in the following manner : " They fwim on the furface of the fea, on the back of their fhells, which exactly refemble the hulk of a fhip ; they raife two feet like mafts, and extend a membrane between, which ferves as a fail ; the other two feet they employ as oars at the fide. They are ufually feen in the Mediterranean." P.

"Learn each small People's genius, policies,
"The Ants' republic, and the realm of Bees;
"How those in common all their wealth bestow, 185
"And Anarchy without confusion know;
"And these for ever, tho' a Monarch reign,
"Their sep'rate cells and properties maintain.
"Mark what unvary'd laws preserve each state,
"Laws wise as Nature, and as fix'd as Fate. 190
"In vain thy Reason finer webs shall draw,
"Entangle Justice in her net of Law,
"And right, too rigid, harden into wrong,
"Still for the strong too weak, the weak too strong.
"Yet go! and thus o'er all the creatures sway, 195
"Thus let the wiser make the rest obey;
"And for those Arts mere Instinct could afford,
"Be crown'd as Monarchs, or as Gods ador'd."

V. Great Nature spoke; observant Men obey'd;
Cities were built, Societies were made: 200
Here rose one little state; another near
Grew by like means, and join'd, thro' love or fear.

Did

VARIATIONS.

VER. 197. In the first Editions,
Who for those Arts they learn'd of BRUTES before,
As Kings shall crown them, or as Gods adore.

" Les Sauvages racontent que ce fut *Michabou* [le DIEU des Eaux] qui apprit à leurs Ancêtres à pêcher, qu'il inventa les Rêts, et que ce fut la toile d'ARAIGNE'E qui lui en donne l'idée."
——*Journal d'un Voyage dans l'Amerique Sept. par Charlevoix.* Vol. v. p. 417. *Par.* 1744. 8vo.   W.

VER. 201. *Here rose one little state, &c.*] In the MS. thus,
The neighbours leagu'd to guard their common spot;
And Love was Nature's dictate, Murder, not.

For

Did here the trees with ruddier burthens bend,
And there the ſtreams in purer rills deſcend?
What War could raviſh, Commerce could beſtow,
And he return'd a friend, who came a foe.   206
Converſe and Love mankind may ſtrongly draw,
When Love was Liberty, and Nature Law.
Thus States were form'd; the name of King unknown,
Till common int'reſt plac'd the ſway in one.   210

'Twas

VARIATIONS.

For want alone each animal contends;
Tigers with Tigers, that remov'd, are friends.
Plain Nature's wants the common mother crown'd,
She pour'd her acorns, herbs, and ſtreams around.
No Treaſure then for rapine to invade;
What need to fight for ſun-ſhine, or for ſhade?
And half the cauſe of conteſt was remov'd,
When beauty could be kind to all who lov'd.

NOTES.

VER. 208. *When Love was Liberty,*] *i. e.* When men had no need to guard their native liberty from their governors by civil paƈtions; the love which each maſter of a family had for thoſe under his care being their beſt ſecurity.   W.

VER. 209. *Thus States were form'd;*] Having thus explained the original of Civil Society, he ſhews us next (from Ver. 208 to 215.) that to this Society a *civil magiſtrate*, properly ſo called, did belong: And this in confutation of that idle hypotheſis, which pretends that God conferred the regal title on *the Fathers* of families; from whence men, when they had inſtituted Society, were to fetch their Governors. On the contrary, our Author ſhews, that a King was unknown, till common intereſt, which led men to inſtitute civil government, led them at the ſame time to inſtitute a Governor. However, that it is true that the ſame wiſdom or valour, which gained regal obedience from ſons to the ſire, procured kings a paternal authority, and made them conſidered as fathers of their people. Which probably was the original (and,

while

'Twas Virtue only (or in arts or arms,
Diffusing blessings, or averting harms)
The same which in a Sire the Sons obey'd,
A Prince the Father of a People made.
VI. Till then, by Nature crown'd, each Patriarch
 sate,   215
King, priest, and parent of his growing state;
                                                  On

NOTES.

while mistaken, continues to be the chief support) of that slavish error: Antiquity representing its earliest monarchs under the idea of a common father, πατὴρ ἀνδρῶν. Afterwards, indeed, they became a kind of foster-fathers, ποιμένα λαῶν, as Homer calls one of them: Till at length they began to devour that flock they had been so long accustomed to shear; and, as Plutarch says of Cecrops, ἐκ χρηστοῦ βασιλέως ἄγριον καὶ ὀρκοιτόδη γενόμενον ΤΥΡΑΝΝΟΝ. W.

From the manuscripts of James Harris, Esq. "The highest order of men are wise and honest legislators: next to them come wise and honest magistrates: next to these, military commanders, whether naval or terrestrial: next to these, the tribe of artists, as well the elegant as the necessary: next to these, farmers, hinds, and labourers: then come idle men of great family, patent-gatherers, knights, and baronets, mumpers, fortune-tellers, gypsies, gentlemen without possessions; all who injure society either by fraud or rapine, or at least by ingratitude, in partaking of its benefits, without regarding the great duty of contributing their own endeavours."

Ver. 211. *'Twas Virtue only, &c.*] Our Author hath good authority for this account of the origin of kingship. Aristotle assures us, that it was Virtue only, or in arts or arms: Καθίσταται Βασιλεὺς ἐκ τῶν ἐπιεικῶν καθ' ὑπεροχὴν ἀρετῆς, ἢ πρᾶξιν τῶν ἀπὸ τῆς ἀρετῆς, ἢ καθ' ὑπεροχὴν τοιούτου γένους.   W.

Ver. 214. *A Prince the Father*] Joinville relates, that he had frequently seen St. Louis, after having heard mass in the summer, seat himself at the foot of an old oak in the forest of Vincennes, where any one of his subjects might approach him, and lay his business or complaint before this good king. Our Author would have much improved all that he says of Government, if he had lived to have read one of the best, perhaps, of all treatises on politics, that of the President Montesquieu.

Ep. III.   ESSAY ON MAN.   107

On him, their fecond Providence, they hung,
Their law his eye, their oracle his tongue.
He from the wond'ring furrow call'd the food,
Taught to command the fire, controul the flood,   220
Draw forth the monfters of th' abyfs profound,
Or fetch the aerial eagle to the ground.
Till drooping, fick'ning, dying, they began
Whom they rever'd as God to mourn as Man:
Then, looking up from fire to fire, explor'd   225
One great firft father, and that firft ador'd.

Or

NOTES.

VER. 219. *He from the wond'ring*] A finer example can perhaps fcarce be given of a compact and comprehenfive ftyle. The manner in which the four elements were fubdued is comprifed in thefe four lines alone. Pope is here, as Quintilian fays of another, " denfus et brevis, et inftans fibi." There is not an ufelefs word in this paffage; there are but three epithets, wondering, profound, aerial; and they are placed precifely with the very fubftantive that is of moft confequence: if there had been epithets joined with the other fubftantives, it would have weakened the nervoufnefs of the fentence. This was a fecret of verfification Pope well underftood, and hath often practifed with peculiar fuccefs.

VER. 225. *Then, looking up, &c.*] The Poet here maketh their more ferious attention to Religion to have arifen, not from their gratitude amidft abundance, but from their inability in diftrefs; by fhewing, that, in profperity, they refted in *fecond caufes*, the immediate authors of their bleffings, *whom they revered as God;* but that, in adverfity, they reafoned up to the *Firft:*

" Then, looking up from fire to fire," &c.

This, I am afraid, is but too true a reprefentation of humanity. W.

VER. 225 to Ver. 240.] M. Du Refnel, not apprehending that the Poet was here returned to finifh his defcription of the State of Nature, has fallen into one of the groffeft errors that ever was committed. He has miftaken this account of *true Religion* for an account of the *origin of Idolatry;* and thus he fatally embellifhes his own blunder:

" Jaloux

Or plain tradition that this All begun,
Convey'd unbroken faith from fire to fon;
                                                    The

NOTES.

" Jaloux d'en conferver les traits et la figure,
Leur zèle induftrieux inventa la peinture.
Leurs neveux, attentifs à ces hommes fameux,
Qui par le droit du fang avoient régné fur eux,
Trouvent-ils dans leur fuite *un grand, un premier pere,*
Leur aveugle refpect l'adore et le révere."
Here you have one of the finest pieces of reafoning turned at once into a heap of nonfenfe. The unlucky term of *Great firft Father,* was miftaken by our Tranflator to fignify a *Great Grand Father.* But he fhould have confidered, that Mr. Pope always reprefents God under the idea of a FATHER: He fhould have obferved that the Poet is here defcribing thofe men who

" To *Virtue,* in the paths of pleafure trod,
And own'd a *Father,* where they own'd a *God.*"   W.

VER. 226. *That firft ador'd.*] In Hume's celebrated difcourfe on the Natural Hiftory of Religion, he endeavours to prove, that, " confidering the improvement of human fociety, from rude beginnings to a ftate of greater perfection, Polytheifm or Idolatry was, and neceffarily muft have been, the firft religion of mankind: And that the firft ideas of religion arofe not from a contemplation of the works of Nature, but from a concern with regard to the events of life, and from the inceffant hopes and fears which actuate the human mind." This was anfwered by Bifhops Warburton and Hurd.

VER. 227. *That this All begun,*]
" Some few, whofe lamp fhone brighter, have been led
From caufe to caufe, to Nature's fecret head;
And found that one firft Principle muft be:
But what, or who, that Univerfal He;
Whether fome foul incompaffing this ball
Unmade, unmov'd; yet making, moving All;
Or various atoms interfering dance,
Leapt into form (the noble work of Chance);
Or this great All was from eternity;
Not e'en the Stagirite himfelf could fee;
And Epicurus guefs'd as well as he:
                                                    }
                                                    As

The worker from the work diſtinct was known,
And ſimple Reaſon never ſought but one : 230
Ere Wit oblique had broke that ſteddy light,
Man, like his Maker, ſaw that all was right;
To Virtue, in the paths of pleaſure trod,
And own'd a Father when he own'd a God.
Love all the faith, and all th' allegiance then; 235
For Nature knew no right divine in Men,
No ill could fear in God; and underſtood
A ſov'reign being but a ſov'reign good.
True faith, true policy, united ran,
That was but love of God, and this of Man. 240
    Who firſt taught ſouls enſlav'd, and realms undone,
Th' enormous faith of many made for one;

That

NOTES.

As blindly grop'd they for a future ſtate ;
As raſhly judg'd of Providence and Fate.
Thus anxious thoughts in endleſs circles roll
Without a centre where to fix the ſoul :
In this wild maze their vain endeavours end ;
How can the leſs the greater comprehend ?
Or finite Reaſon reach infinity ?
For what cou'd fathom God were more than he."

This paſſage is from the Religio Laici of Dryden. It is a pleaſing and uſeful amuſement, to compare the didactic ſtyle of Pope with that of his maſter, and ſee which of them has the art of reaſoning beſt in verſe.

VER. 231. *Ere Wit oblique, &c.*] A beautiful alluſion to the effects of the priſmatic glaſs on the rays of light. W.

VER. 232. *Man, like his Maker,*] It was before the Fall of Man, as the ſacred hiſtorian tells us, that God pronounced—That all was good. But we muſt bear in mind that our Author never adverts to, or argues from, or ſuppoſes, any lapſed condition of Man.

VER. 241. *Who firſt taught*] " What flatterers of princes often tell us, that monarchy was the earlieſt form, is rather diſhonour-
able

That proud exception to all Nature's laws,
T' invert the world, and counter-work its Cause?
Force first made Conquest, and that conquest, law;
Till Superstition taught the Tyrant awe,   246
                                                Then

NOTES.

able to it; importing, indeed, that it at first pleased a rude and unexperienced populace, but could not continue to please upon experience and the increase of wisdom. And indeed in nothing could one less expect that the first essays could be perfect, than in a constitution of civil policy; a work requiring the greatest knowledge and prudence, to be acquired only by much thought and experience of human life. The several great inconveniencies attending each of the simple forms, shew the necessity of having recourse to the mixt and complex; and the several great advantages peculiar to each of the simple, shew that those mixed forms are best where all the three kinds are artfully compounded: and this was the opinion of the wisest men of antiquity—Plato, Aristotle, Zeno, Cicero."

These are the words of that most amiable and candid philosopher, Hutcheson.

VER. 242. *Th' enormous faith, &c.*] In this Aristotle placeth the difference between a King and a Tyrant, that the first supposeth himself made for the People: the other, that the People are made for him: Βυλεται δ' ὁ ΒΑΣΙΛΕΥΣ εἶναι φύλαξ, ὅπως οἱ μὲν κεκλημένοι τὰς ἡσίας μηθὲν ἄδικον πάσχωσιν, ὁ δὲ δῆμος μὴ ὑβρίζηται μηθὲν ἡ δὲ ΤΥΡΑΝΝΙΣ πρὸς; οὐδὲν ἀποβλέπει κοινὸν, εἰ μὴ τῆς ἰδίας ὠφελείας χάριν. Pol. lib. v. cap. 10.   W.

VER. 245. *Force first made Conquest, &c.*] All this is agreeable to fact, and shews our Author's knowledge of human nature. For that *Impotency* of mind, (as the Latin writers call it,) which gives birth to the enormous crimes necessary to support a Tyranny, naturally subjects its owner to all the vain, as well as real, terrors of Conscience: Hence the whole machinery of SUPERSTITION.

It is true, the Poet observes, that afterwards, when the Tyrant's fright was over, he had cunning enough, from the experience of the effect of Superstition upon himself, to turn it, by the assistance of the Priest (who for his reward went shares with him in the Tyranny) against the justly dreaded resentment of his subjects. For a Tyrant naturally and reasonably supposeth all his Slaves to be his Enemies.

                                                Having

Then shar'd the Tyranny, then lent it aid,
And Gods of Conqu'rors, Slaves of subjects made:
She 'midst the light'ning's blaze, and thunder's sound,
When rock'd the mountains, and when groan'd the
    ground,   250
She taught the weak to bend, the proud to pray,
To Pow'r unseen, and mightier far than they:
She, from the rending earth and bursting skies,
Saw Gods descend, and fiends infernal rise:
Here fix'd the dreadful, there the blest abodes;   255
Fear made her Devils, and weak Hope her Gods;
Gods partial, changeful, passionate, unjust,
Whose attributes were Rage, Revenge, or Lust;
                                                      Such

NOTES.

Having given the Causes of Superstition, he next describeth its objects:

" Gods partial, changeful, passionate, unjust," &c.
The ancient Pagan Gods are here very exactly described. This fact evinces the truth of that original, which the Poet gives to Superstition; for if these phantasms were first raised in the imagination of Tyrants, they must needs have the qualities here assigned to them. For Force being the Tyrant's Virtue, and Luxury his Happiness, the attributes of his God would of course be *Revenge* and *Lust*; in a word, the antitype of himself. But there was another, and more substantial cause, of the Resemblance between a Tyrant and a Pagan God; and that was the making *Gods of Conquerors*, as the Poet says; and so canonizing a tyrant's vices with his person.   W.

VER. 246. *Till Superstition taught*] Notwithstanding these Verses are so spirited and splendid, yet how much are they excelled by the sublime and terrific figure painted by Lucretius with such force and energy, that Michael Angelo might have worked from the sketch of the gigantic Demon of Superstition putting out his head from the heavens, and looking down with an horrible aspect on the miserable and trembling sons of men!

" Quæ caput à cœli regionibus ostendebat,
    Horribili super aspectû mortalibus instans!"

Such as the souls of cowards might conceive,
And, form'd like tyrants, tyrants would believe. 260
Zeal then, not charity, became the guide;
And hell was built on spite, and heav'n on pride.
Then sacred seem'd th' ethereal vault no more;
Altars grew marble then, and reek'd with gore:
Then first the Flamen tasted living food; 265
Next his grim idol smear'd with human blood;
With heav'n's own thunders shook the world below,
And play'd the God an engine on his foe.
 So drives Self-love, through just and through unjust,
To one Man's pow'r, ambition, lucre, lust: 270

NOTES.

VER. 257. *Gods partial, changeful,*] "It were better," says Bacon, in his 17th Essay, "to have no opinion of God at all, than such an opinion as is unworthy of Him; for the one is unbelief, the other is contumely: and certainly superstition is the reproach of the Deity. And as the contumely is greater towards God, so the danger is greater towards men. Atheism leaves a man to sense, to philosophy, to natural piety, to laws, to reputation; all which may be guides to an outward moral virtue, though religion were not; but superstition dismounts all these, and erecteth an absolute monarchy in the minds of men. Therefore Atheism did never perturbe states; for it makes men wary of themselves, as looking no farther."

It is extremely remarkable, that this last paragraph comprehends all that Bayle has said of the effects of Atheism in his celebrated Thoughts on Comets. And yet Bacon has never been censured for it, nor numbered among Infidels.

VER. 262. *And hell was built on spite,*] How mortifying is it to consider, says one, that Locke, Newton, and Clarke would have been persecuted in France, imprisoned at Rome, and burnt at Lisbon?

VER. 269. *So drives Self-love, &c.*] The inference our Author draws from all this (from Ver. 268 to 283.) is, that SELF-LOVE driveth through right and wrong; it causeth the Tyrant to violate

Ep. III.   ESSAY ON MAN.

The fame Self-love, in all, becomes the caufe
Of what reftrains him, Government and Laws.
For, what one likes if others like as well,
What ferves one will, when many wills rebel?
How fhall we keep, what, fleeping or awake,   275
A weaker may furprize, a ftronger take?

His

NOTES.

late the rights of mankind; and it caufeth the People to vindicate that violation. For Self-love being common to the whole fpecies, and fetting each individual in purfuit of the fame objects, it became neceffary for each, if he would fecure his own, to provide for the fafety of another's. And thus Equity and Benevolence arofe from that fame Self-love which had given birth to Avarice and Injuftice:

" His Safety muft his Liberty reftrain ;
All join to guard what each defires to gain."

The Poet hath not any where fhewn greater addrefs, in the difpofition of this work, than with regard to the inference before us; which not only giveth a proper and timely fupport to what had been advanced in the fecond epiftle concerning the nature and effects of Self-love, but is a neceffary introduction to what follows, concerning the Reformation of Religion and Society: as we fhall fee prefently.   W.

VER. 272. *Government and Laws.*] " However men might fubmit voluntarily, in the fimplicity of early ages, or be fubjected by conqueft, to a government without a conftitution; yet they were never long in difcovering," in the words of Hooker, " that to live by one man's will, became the caufe of all men's mifery ; and therefore they foon rejected the yoke, or made it fit eafy on their necks."

VER. 273. *For, what one likes*] Thefe two lines exprefs with brevity and clearnefs the following fentiments of Hooker : " The like natural inducement hath brought men to know that it is no lefs their duty to love others than themfelves; for feeing thofe things which are equal muft needs all have one meafure; if I cannot but wifh to receive good, even as much at every man's hands as any man can wifh unto his own foul, how fhould I look to have any part of my defire herein fatisfied, unlefs my felf be careful to fatisfy the like defire which is undoubtedly in other men ?"

His safety must his liberty restrain:
All join to guard what each desires to gain.
Forc'd into virtue thus by Self-defence,
Ev'n Kings learn'd justice and benevolence: 280
Self-love forsook the path it first pursu'd,
And found the private in the publick good.
  'Twas then, the studious head, or gen'rous mind,
Follow'r of God, or friend of human-kind,

POET

NOTES.

Ver. 283. *'Twas then, the studious head, &c.*] The Poet hath now described the rise, perfection, and decay of civil Policy and Religion in the more early times. But the design had been imperfect, had he dropt his discourse here: There was, in after ages, a recovery of these from their several corruptions. Accordingly, he hath chosen that happy æra for the conclusion of his Song. But as good and ill Governments and Religions succeed one another without ceasing, he now leaveth facts, and turneth his discourse (from Ver. 282 to 295.) to speak of a more lasting reform of mankind, in the Invention of those philosophic Principles, by whose observance, a Policy and a Religion may be for ever kept from sinking into Tyranny and Superstition:

  " 'Twas then, the studious head, or gen'rous mind,
  Follow'r of God, or friend of human-kind,
  Poet or Patriot, rose but to restore
  The Faith and Moral, Nature gave before;" &c.

The easy and just transition into this subject from the foregoing is admirable. In the foregoing he had described the effects of Self-love; and now, with great art, and high probability, he maketh Men's *observations* on these effects the occasion of those discoveries which they have made of the true principles of Policy and Religion, described in the present paragraph; and this he evidently hinteth at in that fine transition,

  " 'Twas THEN, the studious head," &c.

The Poet seemeth here to mean the polite and flourishing age of Greece; and those benefactors to Mankind, which he had principally in view, were SOCRATES and ARISTOTLE; who, of all the pagan world, spoke best of God, and wrote best of Government. W.

Poet or Patriot, rofe but to reftore 285
The Faith and Moral, Nature gave before;
Re-lum'd her ancient light, not kindled new;
If not God's image, yet his fhadow drew:
Taught Pow'r's due ufe to People and to Kings,
Taught nor to flack, nor ftrain its tender ftrings,
The lefs, or greater, fet fo juftly true, 291
That touching one muft ftrike the other too;
Till jarring int'refts, of themfelves create
Th' according mufic of a well-mix'd State.
Such

NOTES.

Ver. 285. *Poet or Patriot, rofe*] " No conftitution is formed by concert; no government is copied from a plan. The members of a fmall ftate contend for equality; the members of a greater find themfelves claffed in a certain manner that lays a foundation for monarchy. They proceed from one form of government to another; by eafy tranfitions, and frequently under old names, adopt a new conftitution. The feeds of every form are lodged in human nature; they fpring up and ripen with the feafon. The prevalence of a particular fpecies is often derived from an imperceptible ingredient mingled in the foil. We are therefore to receive, with caution, the traditionary hiftories of ancient legiflators and founders of ftates. Their names have long been celebrated; their fuppofed plans have been admired; and what were probably the confequences of an early fituation, is, in every inftance, confidered as an effect of defign. An author and a work, like caufe and effect, are perpetually coupled together. This is the fimpleft form under which we can confider the eftablifhment of nations: and we afcribe to a previous defign what came to be known only by experience, what no human wifdom could forefee, and what, without the concurring humour and difpofition of his age, no authority could enable an individual to execute." Fergufon, in his Hiftory of Civil Society; a work highly commended by the late Lord Mansfield.

Ver. 294. *Th' according mufic*] This is the very fame illuftration that Tully ufes in that beautiful fragment, De Republicâ:
" Ut

Such is the World's great Harmony, that springs
From Order, Union, full Consent of things :   296
Where

NOTES.

" Ut in fidibus, ac tibiis, atque cantu ipso, ac vocibus, concentus est quidam tenendus ex distinctis tonis, quem immutatum, ac discrepantem aures eruditæ ferre non possunt, isque concentus ex dissimillarum vocum moderatione concors tamen efficitur et congruens; sic, ex summis et infimis, et mediis interjectis ordinibus, ut tonis, moderata ratione civitas consensu dissimili morum concinit, et quæ harmonia a musicis dicitur in cantu, ea est in civitate concordia, arctissimum atque optimum omni in Republicâ vinculum incolumitatis ; quæ sine justitiâ, nullo pacto esse potest."

Such is the happy and inestimable constitution of Great Britain! Let those, who talk and think of absolute equality, remember the words of one whom they must allow was a lover of freedom :

———" And if not equal all, yet free,
Equally free; for orders and degrees
Jar not with liberty, but well consist."
            Par. Lost. Book V. v. 791.

Thucydides, in three words, describes a just and well-poised government, which ought to be, αὐτόνομοι, αὐτοδίκοι, αὐτοτελῆ.

VER. 295. *Such is the World's great Harmony, &c.*] This doctrine was taken up by Leibnitz ; but it was to ingraft upon it a most pernicious fatalism. Plato said, God *chose* the best : Leibnitz said, he *could not but* choose the best, as he could not act without, what this philosopher called, a *sufficient reason*. Plato supposed freedom in God to choose one of two things equally good : Leibnitz held the supposition to be absurd : however, admitting the case, he still held that God could *not* choose one of two things equally good. Thus it appears, the first went on the system of Freedom ; and that the latter, notwithstanding the most artful disguises of his principles, in his *Theodicée*, was a thorough Fatalist : for we cannot well suppose he would give that freedom to Man which he had taken away from God. The truth of the matter seems to be this : he saw, on the one hand, the monstrous absurdity of supposing, with Spinoza, that blind Fate was the author of a coherent Universe ; but yet, on the other, he could not conceive with Plato, how God could foresee and conduct, according to an archetypal idea, a World, of all possible Worlds the
                                                                          best,

Where small and great, where weak and mighty made
To serve, not suffer, strengthen, not invade;
More pow'rful each as needful to the rest,
And, in proportion as it blesses, blest;   300
Draw to one point, and to one centre bring
Beast, Man, or Angel, Servant, Lord, or King.
For Forms of Government let fools contest;
Whate'er is best administer'd is best:

For

NOTES.

best, inhabited by *free Agents*. This difficulty therefore, which made the Socinians take Prescience from God, disposed Leibnitz to take Free-will from Man: And thus he fashioned his fantastical hypothesis; he supposed that when God made the body, he impressed on his new-created Machine a certain series or suite of *motions*; and that when he made the fellow soul, he impressed a correspondent series of *ideas*; whose operations, throughout the whole duration of the union, were so exactly timed, that whenever an *idea* was excited, a correspondent *motion* was ever ready to satisfy the volition. Thus, for instance, when the mind had the *will* to raise the arm to the head, the body was so pre-contrived, as to raise, at that very moment, the part required. This he called the PRE-ESTABLISHED HARMONY; and with this he promised to do wonders.   W.

VER. 297. *Where small and great,*] Swift's opinion about property is remarkable, in his Various Thoughts, p. 394. " In all well-instituted commonwealths, care has been taken to limit men's possessions; which is done for many reasons, and, among the rest, for one, which is perhaps not often considered; that when bounds are set to men's desires, after they have acquired as much as the laws will permit them, their private interest is at an end, and they have nothing to do but to take care of the public."

VER. 303. *For Forms of Government*] But surely some Forms of Government are better calculated to produce and continue a good administration than others, or alter and reform bad administrations. " It is a great question with several, Whether there be any essential difference," says Hume, " betwixt one form of Government and

For Modes of Faith let gracelefs zealots fight ;   305
His can't be wrong whofe life is in the right :
                                                In

NOTES.

and another? and, Whether every form may not become good or bad, according as it is well adminiftered? Were it once admitted, that all Governments are alike, and that the only difference confifts in the character and conduct of the governors, moft political difputes would be at an end, and all zeal for one conftitution above another, muft be efteemed mere bigotry and folly. But, though a friend to moderation, I cannot forbear condemning this fentiment, and fhould be very forry to think that human affairs admit of no greater ftability than what they receive from the cafual humours and characters of particular men.

" 'Tis true, thofe who maintain that the goodnefs of all Government confifts in the goodnefs of the adminiftration, may cite many particular inftances in hiftory, where the very fame Government, in different hands, has varied fuddenly into the oppofite extremes of good and bad. Compare the French Government under Henry III. and under Henry IV. Oppreffion, levity, artifice, on the part of the rulers : faction, fedition, treachery, rebellion, difloyalty, on the part of the fubjects : thefe compofe the character of the former miferable æra. But when the patriot and heroic prince, who fucceeded, was once firmly feated on the throne, the government, the people, every thing feemed to be totally changed, and all from the difference of the temper and fentiments of thefe two fovereigns. An equal difference of a contrary kind may be found on comparing the reigns of Elizabeth and James, at leaft with regard to foreign affairs : and inftances of this kind may be multiplied, almoft without number, from ancient as well as modern hiftory.

" But here I would beg leave to make a diftinction. All abfolute Governments (and fuch that of England was, in great meafure, till the middle of the laft century, notwithftanding the numerous panegyrics on ancient Englifh liberty) muft very much depend on the adminiftration : and this is one of the great inconveniencies of that form of Government. But a republican and free Government would be a moft obvious abfurdity, if the particular checks and controuls, provided by the conftitution, had really no influence, and made it not the intereft, even of bad men, to ope-
                                                rate

In Faith and Hope the world will difagree,
But all Mankind's concern is Charity:

All

NOTES.

rate for the public good. Such is the intention of thefe forms of Government, and fuch is their real effect where they are wifely conftituted: As, on the other hand, they are the fources of all diforders, and of the blackeft crimes, where either fkill or honefty has been wanting in their original frame and inftitution.

" So great is the force of laws, and of particular forms of Government, and fo little dependance have they on the humours and temper of men, that confequences almoft as general and certain may be deduced from them, on moft occafions, as any which the mathematical fciences afford us."

Hear alfo the opinion of the Cambridge Profeffor, Dr. Rutherforth, on this fubject, which is an important one: " Politicians are very well employed in comparing and balancing the advantages and inconveniencies of each form of Government with one another. For though the refult of their inquiries will never determine what form it is which any particular nation has agreed to eftablifh, yet it may ferve to fhew every nation what is the moft defireable form, and may lead them, as they have opportunity, to make fuch alterations in their own as will bring them nearer to that point, if they cannot quite reach it. Certainly our Englifh Poet has but little reafon on his fide, when he reprefents fuch an inquiry as the bufinefs of fools; and maintains, that the only difference between civil conftitutions of Government confifts in the better or worfe adminiftration of them: for that conftitution is, in his judgment, to be called the beft, let it be what it will, which is beft adminiftered. Whatever public benefit depends upon the character of the perfons in power, it is derived from their wifdom and goodnefs, and not from the nature of the form of government. So that to call that form the beft, which is beft adminiftered, feems to be fpeaking improperly. Or if we will call it the beft, we muft in the mean time allow, that it is the beft by accident only, and not in its own nature. In the common courfe of human affairs it is almoft impoffible to prevent the civil power from coming into the hands of weak and bad men, whatever the conftitution is. That form of Government, therefore, is beft in itfelf, which guards moft effectually againft this evil; or if this evil ever does

happen,

All muſt be falſe that thwart this One great End;
And all of God, that bleſs Mankind or mend.   310
                                            Man,

NOTES.

happen, which lays the perſons in power under ſuch checks and reſtraints as are moſt likely to prevent them from abuſing their truſt; or, laſtly, if this truſt is abuſed, which has provided the readieſt means for correcting the abuſes. An abſolute monarchy is a conſtitution which has ſo little title to theſe characters, that it can have no pretenſion to be thought the only natural, and much leſs the only poſſible, form of Government, upon account of its being the beſt form." In that elegant and valuable publication, intitled Athenian Letters, written by ſome of the moſt reſpectable perſons of the preſent age, and in which ſubjects of literature, philoſophy, and politics are treated with uncommon candour and penetration, is an excellent diſcourſe on Forms of Government, by the honourable Charles Yorke, p. 216. London. 4to. 1781.

A penetrating writer has well obſerved, " that all Forms of Government, in fact, mutually approach each other, or recede, by many, and often inſenſible gradations?" Ariſtotle is of opinion, in the ſeventh chapter of the ſeventh book of his Politics, that there are ſome nations who cannot live under a free Government.

VER. 305. *For Modes of Faith let gracelefs zealots fight;*] Theſe latter ages have ſeen ſo many ſcandalous contentions for *modes of faith*, to the violation of Chriſtian Charity, and diſhonour of ſacred Scripture, that it is not at all ſtrange they ſhould become the object of ſo benevolent and wiſe an Author's reſentment.   W.

He borrowed this from Cowley; who, extolling the piety of his friend Craſhaw, the Poet, who went over to the Romiſh Church, and died a Canon of Loretto, ſays,

" Pardon, my Mother Church, if I conſent
That Angels led him, when from thee he went;
For e'en in error ſure no danger is,
When join'd to ſo much piety as his:—
His Faith, perhaps, in ſome nice tenets might
Be wrong; his life, I'm ſure, was in the right."

Cowley alſo, poſſibly, might take the hint from Lord Herbert of Cherbury; who hath this diſtich in his works:

                                          " Digladient

Man, like the gen'rous vine, fupported lives;
The ftrength he gains is from th' embrace he gives.
On their own Axis as the Planets run,
Yet make at once their circle round the Sun;
So two confiftent motions act the Soul; 315
And one regards Itfelf, and one the Whole.
Thus God and Nature link'd the gen'ral frame,
And bade Self-love and Social be the fame.

NOTES.

" Digladient alii circa res religionis:
Quod credas nihil eft, fit modo vita proba."
But " digladient is a barbarifm; he fhould have faid, digladien-
tur, or contendant," fays Dr. Jortin.

VER. 313. *On their own Axis*] This illuftration is plainly taken
from the Spectator, No. 588, faid to be written by Mr. Grove:
" Is therefore Benevolence inconfiftent with Self-love? Are their
motions contrary? No more than the diurnal rotation of the earth
is oppofed to its annual; or its motion round its own centre;
which might be improved as an illuftration of Self-love; that
whirls it about the common centre of the world, anfwering to
univerfal benevolence. Is the force of Self-love abated, or its intereft prejudiced by benevolence? So far from it, that benevolence, though a diftinct principle, is extremely ferviceable to Self-
love, and then doth moft fervice when it is leaft defigned."

VER. 315. *Act the Soul;*] It fhould certainly be actuate, or act
upon. He has ufed this expreffion again, Iliad xv. v. 487.
" —— This acted by a God."
Such inaccuracies are not worth remarking, but in writers fo correct and eminent as our author, leaft they fhould give a fanction
to errors. Dr. Lowth in his Grammar has pointed out feveral in
our Author's Works.

VER. 318. *And bade Self-love*] The Remarks of Warburton on
the Effay on Man, on the Moral Epiftles, and the Alliance betwixt
Church and State, were tranflated into French by M. De Silhouette; for which tranflation, fuppofing it contained opinions
unfavourable to the defpotic government of France, he was much
cenfured,

NOTES.

censured, and had nearly been prosecuted, when he became Controller General of the Finances; and he immediately bought up and destroyed all the copies of this work that could be found.

Voltaire, writing to M. De Cideville, in June 1759, says of M. De Silhouette, " Le genie de M. De Silhouette est Anglais, calculateur, et courageux; mais si on nous prend des Guadeloupe, si ces mandits Anglois ont plus de vaisseaux que nous, et meilleurs, si les frais de la visite qu'on veut leur rendre sont perdus, si les depenses immenses d'une guerre juste, mais ruineuse, absorbent les revenus de l'état, ni M. De Silhouette, ni Pope, n'y pourront suffire."

In this passage, (Ver. 318.) Pope uses the very words of Bolingbroke: " Thus it happens that Self-love and Social are divided, and set in opposition to one another in the conduct of particular men, whilst in the making laws, and the regulation of government, they continue the same." Minutes of Essays, section 51. addressed to Pope.

EPISTLE IV.

OUR Poet having, in the three former Epistles, treated of Man in all the three respects in which he can be considered; namely, first, Of his Nature and State with respect to the Universe; secondly, With respect to Himself; thirdly, With respect to Society: seems to have finished his subject in the three foregoing Epistles. This fourth Epistle, therefore, on Happiness, may be thought to be adscititious, and out of its proper place, and ought to have made part of the second Epistle, where Man is considered with respect to Himself. I formerly mentioned this to Dr. Akenside and Mr. Harris, who were of my opinion.

ARGUMENT OF EPISTLE IV.

Of the Nature and State of MAN, *with respect to* Happiness.

I. FALSE *Notions of Happiness, Philosophical and Popular, answered from* Ver. 19 to 27. II. *It is the End of all Men, and attainable by all,* Ver. 30. *God intends Happiness to be equal; and to be so it must be* social, *since all particular Happiness depends on general, and since he governs by* general, *not* particular Laws, Ver. 37. *As it is necessary for* Order, *and the peace and welfare of* Society, *that* external goods *should be* unequal, *Happiness is not made to consist in these,* Ver. 51. *But, notwithstanding that inequality, the* balance *of Happiness among Mankind is kept even by Providence, by the two Passions of* Hope *and* Fear, Ver. 70. III. *What the Happiness of* Individuals *is, as far as is consistent with the constitution of this world; and that the* good Man *has here the advantage,* Ver. 77. *The error of imputing to* Virtue *what are only the calamities of* Nature, *or of* Fortune, Ver. 94. IV. *The folly of expecting that God should alter his general Laws in favour of particulars,* Ver. 121. V. *That we are not judges who are good; but that whoever they are, they must be happiest,* Ver. 133, &c. VI. *That* external goods *are not the proper rewards, but often inconsistent with, or destructive of,* Virtue, Ver. 165. *That even these can make no Man happy without Virtue: Instanced in* Riches, Ver. 183. Honours, Ver. 191. Nobility, Ver. 203. Greatness, Ver. 215. Fame, Ver. 235. Superior Talents, Ver. 257, &c. *With pictures of human Infelicity in Men possessed of them all,* Ver. 267, &c. VII. *That* Virtue *only constitutes a Happiness, whose object is* universal, *and whose prospect* eternal, Ver. 307, &c. *That the* perfection *of* Virtue *and* Happiness *consists in a* conformity *to the* ORDER *of* PROVIDENCE *here, and a* Resignation *to it here and hereafter,* Ver. 326, &c.

EPISTLE IV.

OH HAPPINESS! our being's end and aim!
Good, Pleasure, Ease, Content! whate'er thy
    name:
That something still which prompts th' eternal sigh,
For which we bear to live, or dare to die,
Which still so near us, yet beyond us lies, 5
O'erlook'd, seen double, by the fool, and wise.
                                            Plant

VARIATIONS.

VER. 1. *Oh Happiness! &c.*] In the MS. thus:
Oh Happiness! to which we all aspire,
Wing'd with strong hope, and borne by full desire:
That ease, for which in want, in wealth we sigh;
That ease, for which we labour and we die.

NOTES.

VER. 1. *Oh Happiness!*] He begins his address to Happiness after the manner of the ancient hymns, by enumerating the titles and various places of abode of this goddess. He has undoubtedly personified her at the beginning, but he seems to have dropped that idea in the seventh line, where the deity is suddenly transformed into a plant; from thence this metaphor of a vegetable is carried on distinctly through the eleven succeeding lines, till he suddenly returns to consider Happiness again as a person, in the eighteeenth line,

" And fled from Monarchs, ST. JOHN! dwells with thee."
For to fly and to dwell, cannot justly be predicated of the same subject, that immediately before was described as twining with laurels, and being reaped in harvests.

                                            Of

Plant of celeſtial ſeed! if dropt below,
Say, in what mortal ſoil thou deign'ſt to grow?
Fair op'ning to ſome Court's propitious ſhine,
Or deep with di'monds in the flaming mine?   10
Twin'd with the wreaths Parnaſſian laurels yield,
Or reap'd in iron harveſts of the field?
Where grows?—where grows it not? If vain our toil,
We ought to blame the culture, not the ſoil:
Fix'd to no ſpot is happineſs ſincere,   15
'Tis no where to be found, or every where:

'Tis

NOTES.

Of the numberleſs treatiſes that have been written on Happineſs, one of the moſt ſenſible is that of Fontenelle, in the third volume of his works. Our Author's leading principle is, that Happineſs is attainable by all men;

" For mourn our various portions as we pleaſe,
    Equal is Common Senſe, and Common Eaſe."
So Horace alſo in Epiſt. xviii. b. 1.

" Æquam mi animum ipſe parabo."

" But Horace," ſays a penetrating obſerver on human life, " was groſsly miſtaken: the thing for which he thought he ſtood in no need of Jupiter's aſſiſtance, was what he could leaſt expect from his own ability. It is much more eaſy to get even riches and honours by one's induſtry, than a quiet and contented mind. If it be ſaid, that riches and honours depend on a thouſand things which we cannot diſpoſe of at pleaſure, and that therefore it is neceſſary to pray to God that he would turn them to our advantage; I anſwer, that the ſilence of the paſſions, and the tranquillity and eaſe of the mind, depend on a thouſand things that are not under our juriſdiction. The ſtomach, the ſpleen, the lymphatic veſſels, the fibres of the brain, and a hundred other organs, whoſe ſeat and figure are yet unknown to the anatomiſts, produce in us many uneaſineſſes, jealouſies, and vexations. Can we alter theſe organs? Are they in our own power?"

Seneca, by writing De Beatâ Vitâ, made neither his readers nor himſelf happy.

'Tis never to be bought, but always free,
And fled from Monarchs, ST. JOHN! dwells with
thee.
Afk of the Learn'd the way? The Learn'd are
blind;
This bids to ferve, and that to fhun mankind; 20
Some place the blifs in action, fome in eafe,
Thofe call it Pleafure, and Contentment thefe;
Some funk to Beafts, find pleafure end in pain;
Some fwell'd to Gods, confefs ev'n Virtue vain!
                                                Or

NOTES.

VER. 18. ST. JOHN! *dwells with thee.*] Among the many paffages in Bolingbroke's Pofthumous Works that bear a clofe refemblance to the tenets of this Effay, are the following: Vol. iv. octavo edition, pp. 223. 324. 388. 389. alfo pp. 49. 316. 328. 336, 337. 339. And in Vol. v. pp. 5, 6. 17. 92. 51. 113. 310.

VER. 21, 23. *Some place the blifs in action,——
Some funk to Beafts, &c.*]
1. Thofe who place Happinefs, or the *fummum bonum*, in Pleafure, Ἡδονή; fuch as the Cyreniac fect, called, on that account, the Hedonic. 2. Thofe who place it in a certain tranquillity or calmnefs of Mind, which they call Εὐθυμία; fuch as the Democritic fect. 3. The Epicurean. 4. The Stoic. 5. The Protagorean, which held that Man was πάντων χρημάτων μέτρον, *the meafure of all things;* for that all things which *appear* to him, *are*, and thofe things which *appear not* to any Man, *are not;* fo that every imagination or opinion of every Man was true. 6. The Sceptic: Whofe abfolute doubt is, with great judgment, faid to be the effect of Indolence, as well as the abfolute truft of the Protagorean: For the fame dread of labour attending the fearch of truth, which makes the Protagorean prefume it is always at hand, makes the Sceptic conclude it is never to be found. The only difference is, that the lazinefs of the one is defponding, and the lazinefs of the other fanguine; yet both can give it a good name, and call it HAPPINESS.   W.

VER. 23. *Some funk to Beafts, &c.*] Thefe four lines added in
                                                                the

Or indolent, to each extreme they fall, 25
To truſt in ev'ry thing, or doubt of all.
  Who thus define it, ſay they more or leſs
Than this, that Happineſs is Happineſs?
  Take Nature's path, and mad Opinion's leave;
All ſtates can reach it, and all heads conceive; 30
Obvious her goods, in no extreme they dwell;
There needs but thinking right, and meaning well;
And mourn our various portions as we pleaſe,
Equal is Common Senſe, and Common Eaſe.
  Remember, Man, " the Univerſal Cauſe 35
" Acts not by partial, but by gen'ral laws:"
And makes what Happineſs we juſtly call
Subſiſt not in the good of one, but all.
There's not a bleſſing Individuals find,
But ſome way leans and hearkens to the kind; 40
No Bandit fierce, no Tyrant mad with pride,
No cavern'd hermit, reſts ſelf-ſatisfy'd:
Who moſt to ſhun or hate Mankind pretend,
Seek an admirer, or would fix a friend:
Abſtract what others feel, what others think, 45
All pleaſures ſicken, and all glories ſink:
Each has his ſhare; and who would more obtain,
Shall find, the pleaſure pays not half the pain.

ORDER

NOTES.

the laſt Edition, as neceſſary to complete the ſummary of the falſe purſuits after Happineſs among the Greek Philoſophers. W.

  Of which Greek Philoſophers, I imagine, Pope did not think, nor allude to.

  VER. 34. *Equal is Common Senſe,*] The experience of every day and every hour convinces us of the falſehood of this Stoical boaſt.

ORDER is Heav'n's firſt law; and this confeſt,
Some are, and muſt be, greater than the reſt,   50
More rich, more wiſe; but who infers from hence
That ſuch are happier, ſhocks all common ſenſe.
                                                    Heav'n

VARIATIONS.

After Ver. 52. in the MS.
Say not, " Heav'n's here profuſe, there poorly ſaves,
" And for one Monarch makes a thouſand ſlaves."
You'll find, when Cauſes and their Ends are known,
'Twas for the thouſand Heav'n has made that one.

NOTES.

VER. 49. ORDER *is Heav'n's firſt law;*] A writer of uncommon ſagacity and penetration has made the following reflection: " Our notion of order in civil ſociety, is frequently falſe; it is taken from the analogy of ſubjects inanimate and dead; we conſider commotion and action as contrary to its nature; we think it conſiſtent only with obedience, ſecrecy, and the ſilent paſſing of affairs through the hands of a few; the good order of ſtones in a wall, is their being properly fixed in the places for which they were hewn; were they to ſtir, the building muſt fall: but the good order of men in ſociety, is their being placed where they are properly qualified to act. The firſt is a fabric made of dead and inanimate parts; the ſecond is made of living and active members. When we ſeek in ſociety for the order of mere inaction and tranquillity, we forget the nature of our ſubject, and find the order of ſlaves, not of men." Ferguſon.

VER. 50. *Some are, and muſt be,*] So much has of late years been ſaid of the doctrine of Equality, and ſo much has it been perverſely miſinterpreted and miſunderſtood, that it is to be wiſhed, that thoſe who declaim on this ſubject, would only look into the three following faſhionable French authors, who ſurely were ſtaunch lovers of liberty, to ſee the abſurdity of the notion of Equality of Ranks; namely, I. Monteſquieu, in the third Chapter of his eighth Book. II. D'Alembert, in his Comment on this Chapter of Monteſquieu. III. Voltaire, in the Eſſay on the Spirit of Nations, Chapter 67. on Switzerland. " You are not, by this term Equality," ſays the laſt, " to underſtand that abſurd and impoſſible Equality, by which the maſter and the ſervant, the magiſtrate and the artificer, the plaintiff and the judge,

are

Heav'n to Mankind impartial we confefs,
If all are equal in their Happinefs:
But mutual wants this Happinefs increafe;   55
All Nature's diff'rence keeps all Nature's peace.
Condition, circumftance is not the thing;
Blifs is the fame in fubject or in king,
In who obtain defence, or who defend,
In him who is, or him who finds a friend: 60
Heav'n breathes thro' ev'ry member of the whole
One common bleffing, as one common foul.
But Fortune's gifts if each alike poffeft,
And each were equal, muft not all conteft?
If then to all Men Happinefs was meant,   65
God in Externals could not place Content.

 Fortune her gifts may varioufly difpofe,
And thefe be happy call'd, unhappy thofe;
But Heav'n's juft balance equal will appear,
While thofe are plac'd in Hope, and thefe in Fear:
Not prefent good or ill, the joy or curfe,   71
But future views of better, or of worfe.

 Oh fons of earth! attempt ye ftill to rife,
By mountains pil'd on mountains, to the fkies?
Heav'n

VARIATIONS.

After Ver. 66. in the MS.
 'Tis peace of mind alone is at a ftay:
 The reft mad Fortune gives or takes away.
 All other blifs by accident's debar'd;
 But Virtue's, in the inftant, a reward;
 In hardeft trials operates the beft,
 And more is relifh'd as the more diftreft.

NOTES.

are confounded together; but that Equality by which the fubject depends only on the laws."

Heav'n ſtill with laughter the vain toil ſurveys, 75
And buries madmen in the heaps they raiſe.
  Know, all the good that individuals find,
Or God and Nature meant to mere Mankind,
Reaſon's whole pleaſure, all the joys of Senſe,
Lie in three words, Health, Peace, and Competence.
But Health conſiſts with Temperance alone; 81
And Peace, oh Virtue! Peace is all thy own.
The good or bad the gifts of Fortune gain;
But theſe leſs taſte them, as they worſe obtain.
Say, in purſuit of profit or delight, 85
Who riſk the moſt, that take wrong means, or right?
Of Vice or Virtue, whether bleſt or curſt,
Which meets contempt, or which compaſſion firſt?
Count all th' advantage proſp'rous Vice attains,
'Tis but what Virtue flies from and diſdains: 90
And grant the bad what happineſs they wou'd,
One they muſt want, which is, to paſs for good.
                                                  Oh

VARIATIONS.

After Ver. 92. in the MS.
  Let ſober Moraliſts correct their ſpeech,
  No bad man's happy: he is great, or rich.

NOTES.

VER. 84. *But theſe leſs taſte them,*] "A ſelfiſh villain," ſays an acute obſerver, "may poſſeſs a ſpring and alacrity of temper, a certain gaiety of heart, which is indeed a good quality, but which is rewarded much beyond its merit; and when attended with good fortune, will compenſate the uneaſineſs and remorſe ariſing from all the other vices." Hume's Eſſays. The Sceptic.

VER. 88. *Which meets contempt,*] Compaſſion, it will be ſaid, is but a poor compenſation for miſery.

VER. 92. *To paſs for good.*] But are not the one frequently miſtaken for the other? How many profligate hypocrites have paſſed for good?"

K 2

Oh blind to truth, and God's whole scheme below,
Who fancy Bliss to Vice, to Virtue Woe!
Who sees and follows that great scheme the best, 95
Best knows the blessing, and will most be blest.
But fools, the Good alone unhappy call,
For ills or accidents that chance to All.
See FALKLAND dies, the virtuous and the just!
See godlike TURENNE prostrate on the dust! 100
                                                See

NOTES.

VER. 99. *See* FALKLAND] His genius, his learning, his integrity, his patriotism, are eloquently displayed by Cowley, as well as by Clarendon; but Lord Orford thinks the portrait by the latter too flattering and over-charged. If any proofs had been wanting of the violence and haughtiness of archbishop Laud, this virtuous nobleman's opposing him would have been sufficient. He assisted Chillingworth in his great work against Popery; and he wrote some very elegant verses to Sandys, on his Translation of the Psalms. The gallantry of Sir Philip Sidney, mentioned in a succeeding line, (101,) cannot be disputed; but whether the death of this valorous knight was a proper example of suffering virtue to be here introduced, is another question.

VER. 100. *See god-like* TURENNE] This great general was killed July 27, 1675, by a cannon shot, near the village of Saltyback, in going to choose a place whereon to erect a battery. "No one," says Voltaire, "is ignorant of the circumstances of his death; but we cannot here refrain a review of the principal of them, for the same reason that they are still talked of every day. It seems as if one could not too often repeat, that the same bullet which killed him, having shot off the arm of St. Hilaire, lieutenant general of the artillery, his son came and bewailed his misfortune with many tears; but the father, looking towards Turenne, said, 'It is not I, but that great man, who should be lamented.' These words may be compared with the most heroic sayings recorded in all history; and are the best eulogy that can be bestowed upon Turenne. It is uncommon under a despotic government, where people are actuated only by private interests, for those who have served their country to die regretted by the public. Nevertheless, Turenne was lamented both by the soldiers and people; and Louvois was the only one who rejoiced at his death. The honours which the
                                                            king

See SIDNEY bleeds amid the martial ſtrife!
Was this their Virtue, or Contempt of Life?
Say, was it Virtue, more tho' Heav'n ne'er gave,
Lamented DIGBY! ſunk thee to the grave?
Tell me, if Virtue made the Son expire, 105
Why, full of days and honour, lives the Sire?
Why drew Marſeilles' good biſhop purer breath,
When Nature ſicken'd, and each gale was death?
Or

NOTES.

king ordered to be paid to his memory are known to every one; and that he was interred at St. Denis, in the ſame manner as the conſtable du Gueſclin." But how much is the glory of Turenne tarniſhed by his cruel devaſtation of the Palatinate?

VER. 101. *See* SIDNEY *bleeds*] Among the many things related of the life and character of this all-accompliſhed perſon, it does not ſeem to be much known, that he was the intimate friend and patron of the famous atheiſt Giordano Bruno; was in a ſecret club with him and Sir Fulk Greville, held in London in 1587; and that the Spaccio della Beſtia Triumfante was at that time compoſed and printed in London, and dedicated to Sir Philip. See General Dictionary, vol. iii. p. 622.

VER. 107. *Why drew*] M. de Belſance, biſhop of Marſeilles. This illuſtrious prelate was of a noble family in Guienne. In early life he took the vows, and belonged to a convent of Jeſuits. He was made biſhop of Marſeilles in 1709.

In the plague of that city, in the year 1720, he diſtinguiſhed himſelf by his zeal and activity, being the paſtor, the phyſician, and the magiſtrate of his flock, whilſt that horrid calamity prevailed. Louis XV. in 1723, offered him a more conſiderable biſhopric, (to which peculiar feudal honours were annexed,) that of Laon in Picardy. He refuſed, however, to quit that of Marſeilles, giving for a reaſon, that he could not deſert a flock which had been ſo endeared to him by their misfortunes and his own exertions. The king, however, inſiſted upon his accepting of the privilege of appealing, in all his own cauſes, either temporal or ſpiritual, to the Parliament of Paris. The Pope ſent him from Rome an or-

Or why so long (in life if long can be)
Lent Heav'n a parent to the poor and me? 110
What makes all physical or moral ill?
There deviates Nature, and here wanders Will.
God sends not Ill; if rightly understood,
Or partial Ill is universal Good,

Or

NOTES.

nament called Pallium, worn only by archbishops. He died at a very advanced age, in the year 1755, after having founded a college in Marseilles, which bears his name, and after having written the History of the Lives of his Predecessors in that See. When he was grand vicar of Agen, he published the life of a female relation of his, who was eminent for her piety, with this title, "Vie de Susanne Henriette de Foix Candale." Vaniere has finely celebrated him. Lib. iii. of the Prædium Rusticum.

VER. 108. *When Nature sicken'd,*] A verse of marvellous comprehension and expressiveness, adopted from Dryden's Miscellanies, v. 6. The effects of this pestilence are more emphatically set forth in these few words than in forty such Odes as Sprat's on the Plague at Athens. A fine example of what Dion. Halicarnassus calls Πυκνότητος ϗ͗ σεμνότητος.

VER. 110. *Lent Heav'n a parent, &c.*] This last instance of the Poet's illustration of the ways of Providence, the reader sees, has a peculiar elegance; where a tribute of piety to a parent is paid in return of thanks to, and made subservient of his vindication of, the great Giver and Father of all things. The Mother of the Author, a person of great piety and charity, died the year this poem was finished, viz. 1733. W.

VER. 112. *There deviates Nature,*] How can Nature be said to deviate, when we before have been told, that the general "Order has been kept, since the whole began." And as to the wandering of the will, objectors persist in saying, that it is precisely the same thing, whether a God of infinite power and knowledge created beings originally wicked and miserable, or gave them a power to make themselves so; fore-knowing, that they would employ that power to their own destruction.

This is the objection forever repeated by Bayle, and which our limited understandings cannot fully answer,

" But find no end in wand'ring mazes lost."

Ep. IV.   ESSAY ON MAN.

Or Change admits, or Nature lets it fall;   115
Short, and but rare, till Man improv'd it all.
We juft as wifely might of Heav'n complain
That righteous Abel was deftroy'd by Cain,
As that the virtuous fon is ill at eafe
When his lewd father gave the dire difeafe.   120
Think we, like fome weak Prince, th' Eternal Caufe,
Prone for his fav'rites to reverfe his laws?
Shall

VARIATIONS.

After Ver. 116. in the MS.
Of ev'ry evil, fince the world began,
The real fource is not in God, but man.

NOTES.

VER. 115. *Or Change admits,*] How Change can admit, or Nature let fall any evil, however fhort and rare it may be, under the government of an all-wife, powerful, and benevolent Creator, is hardly to be underftood. The reafons affigned for the Origin of Evil, in thefe two lines, are furely not folid and fatisfactory, and the doctrine is expreffed in obfcure and equivocal terms. Thefe fix lines are perhaps the moft exceptionable in the whole Poem, in point both of fentiment and expreffion.

VER. 121. *Think we, like fome weak Prince, &c.*] Agreeable hereunto, Holy Scripture, in its account of things under the common Providence of Heav'n, never reprefents miracles as wrought for the fake of him who is the object of them, but in order to give credit to fome of God's extraordinary difpenfations to Mankind.   W.

Akenfide has thus enlarged on this opinion, book i. p. 120. in a more copious and diffufe ftyle and manner:

—Left blind o'erweening pride
Pollute their offerings: left their felfifh heart
Say to the heavenly ruler, " At our call
Relents thy power: by us thy arm is mov'd!
Fools! who of God as of each other deem:
Who his invariable acts deduce

Shall burning Etna, if a sage requires,
Forget to thunder, and recall her fires?
On air or sea new motions be imprest,   125
Oh blameless Bethel! to relieve thy breast?
When the loose mountain trembles from on high,
Shall gravitation cease, if you go by?
                                                  Or

NOTES.

From sudden counsels transient as their own;
Nor farther of his bounty, than the event
Which haply meets their loud and eager prayer,
Acknowledge; nor, beyond the drop minute,
Which haply they have tasted, heed the source
That flows from all; the fountain of his love;
Which, from the summit where he sits inthron'd,
Pours health and joy, unfailing streams throughout
The spacious region flourishing in view,
The goodly work of his eternal day,
His own fair universe; on which alone
His counsels fix, and whence alone his will
Assumes her strong direction."

VER. 123. *Shall burning Etna, &c.*] Alluding to the fate of those two great Naturalists, Empedocles and Pliny, who both perished by too near an approach to Etna and Vesuvius, while they were exploring the cause of their eruptions.   W.

VER. 125. *On air or sea*] It was observed in the Adventurer, many years before the elegant Letter to Mr. Mason, on the Marks of Imitation, appeared, that this whole passage, and even the expressions, " New motions be imprest," and " Shall gravitation cease," were taken from Wollaston, section v. p. 99.

Wollaston, in this section, endeavours to prove, that, " It is not impossible, that such laws of nature, and such a series of causes and effects may be originally designed; that not only general provisions may be made for the several species of beings, but even particular cases, at least many of them, may also be provided for, without innovations or alterations in the course of nature." From whence he infers the doctrine of a particular Providence, and the reasonableness and efficacy of prayer: a doctrine

for

Or some old temple, nodding to its fall,
For Chartres' head reserve the hanging wall? 130
But still this world (so fitted for the knave)
Contents us not. A better shall we have?
A kingdom of the Just then let it be:
But first consider how those Just agree.
The good must merit God's peculiar care; 135
But who, but God, can tell us who they are?
One thinks on Calvin Heav'n's own spirit fell;
Another deems him instrument of hell;
If Calvin feel Heav'n's blessing, or its rod,
This cries, there is, and that, there is no God. 140
What

NOTES.

for which Bolingbroke, in a variety of passages in his works, is fond of condemning Wollaston, and his Defence of this Duty of Prayer. I have received the most authentic information that Dr. Middleton left behind him, a treatise on this subject; which Mrs. Middleton, by the advice of a judicious friend, was prevailed on not to publish, from the offence it might have given. But it was communicated to Lord Bolingbroke at his earnest request, and returned to Mrs. Middleton after he had kept it a considerable time. After Bolingbroke's death, a copy of it was found in his library.

VER. 130. *The hanging wall?*] Eusebius is weak enough to relate, from the testimonies of Irenæus and Polycarp, that the roof of the building under which Cerinthus the heretic was bathing, providentially fell down and crushed him to death. Lib. 3. cap. 29.

VER. 136. *Tell us who they are?*] This again is exactly copied from Wollaston, section v. p. 110. who quotes Virgil on the occasion,

———Cadit & Ripheus justissimus unus
Qui fuit in Teucris, & servantissimus æqui:
Diis aliter visum.———

VER. 138. *Instrument of hell;*] The hard fate of Servetus will remain for ever as an indelible mark of the violence, cruelty, and intolerance of Calvin.

What shocks one part will edify the rest,
Nor with one system can they all be blest.
The very best will variously incline,
And what rewards your Virtue, punish mine.
WHATEVER IS, IS RIGHT.—This world 'tis true,
Was made for Cæsar—but for Titus too: 146
And which more blest? who chain'd his country? say,
Or he whose Virtue sigh'd to lose a day!
  " But sometimes Virtue starves, while Vice is fed."
What then? Is the reward of Virtue bread?   150
That, Vice may merit, 'tis the price of toil;
The knave deserves it, when he tills the soil,
The knave deserves it when he tempts the main,
Where Folly fights for kings, or dives for gain.
The good man may be weak, be indolent;   155
Nor is his claim to plenty, but content.
But grant him Riches, your demand is o'er?
" No—shall the good want Health, the good want
  " Pow'r?"
Add Health, and Pow'r, and ev'ry earthly thing.
" Why bounded Pow'r? why private? why no
  king?"   160
                              Nay,

VARIATIONS.

After Ver. 142. in some Editions,
  Give each a System, all must be at strife;
  What diff'rent Systems for a Man and Wife?
The joke, though lively, was ill plac'd, and therefore struck out of the text.

NOTES.

VER. 157. *But grant him Riches,*] It does by no means follow, that because he should want riches, wealth, and power, he should want every thing, and never know where to stop.

Nay, why external for internal giv'n?
Why is not Man a God, and Earth a Heav'n?
Who afk and reafon thus, will fcarce conceive
God gives enough, while he has more to give:
Immenfe the pow'r, immenfe were the demand;
Say, at what part of nature will they ftand?   166
What nothing earthly gives, or can deftroy,
The foul's calm fun-fhine, and the heart-felt joy,
                                                Is

NOTES.

VER. 162. *Why is not Man a God,*] The manner in which Ramfay endeavours, but in vain, to explain the doctrine of the Effay, is as follows: " Pope is far from afferting, that the prefent ftate of Man is his primitive ftate, and is conformable to Order: His defign is to fhew, that fince the Fall, all is proportioned with weight, meafure, and harmony, to the condition of a degraded Being, who fuffers, and who deferves to fuffer, and who cannot be reftored but by fufferings; that phyfical evils are defigned to cure moral evil; that the paffions and the crimes of the moft abandoned men are confined, directed, and governed by infinite wifdom, in fuch a manner as to make order emerge out of confufion, light of darknefs, and to call out innumerable advantages from the tranfitory inconveniences of this life; that this fo gracious Providence conducts all things to its own ends, and without either caufing or approving the effects of their deliberate malice; that all is ordained in the phyfical order, as all is free in the moral; that thefe two orders are connected clofely without fatality, and are not fubject to that neceffity which renders us virtuous without merit, and vicious without crime; that we fee at prefent but a fingle wheel of the magnificent machine of the univerfe; but a fmall link of the great chain; and but an infignificant part of that immenfe plan which will one day be unfolded. Then will God juftify all the incomprehenfible proceedings of his wifdom and goodnefs, and will vindicate himfelf, as Milton fpeaks, from the rafh judgment of mortals."

But there are too many paffages in this Effay to fuffer us to admit of the forced interpretation here given by Ramfay.

Is Virtue's prize: A better would you fix?
Then give Humility a coach and fix,   170
Juſtice a Conqu'ror's ſword, or Truth a gown,
Or Public Spirit its great cure, a Crown.
Weak, fooliſh Man! will Heav'n reward us there
With the ſame traſh mad mortals wiſh for here?
The Boy and Man an Individual makes,   175
Yet ſigh'ſt thou now for apples and for cakes?

Go,

VARIATIONS.

After Verſe 172. in the MS.
Say, what rewards this idle world imparts,
Or fit for ſearching heads or honeſt hearts.

NOTES.

VER. 170. *Then give Humility*] In a work of ſo ſerious and ſevere a caſt, in a work of reaſoning, in a work of theology, deſigned to explain the moſt intereſting ſubject that can employ the mind of man, ſurely ſuch ſtrokes of levity, of ſatire, of ridicule, as alſo lines 204. 223. 276. however poignant and witty, are ill placed and diſguſting, are violations of that propriety which Pope in general ſo ſtrictly obſerved. Lucretius preſerves throughout, the dignity he at firſt aſſumed; even his ſarcaſms and irony on the ſuperſtitious, have ſomething auguſt, and a noble haughtineſs in them; as in particular where he aſks, " How it comes to paſs that Jupiter ſometimes ſtrikes his own temples with his thunderbolts; whether he employs himſelf in caſting them in the deſerts for the ſake of exerciſing his arm; and why he hurls them in places where he cannot ſtrike the guilty.

———" Tum fulmina mittat; et ædes
Sæpe ſuas diſturbet; et in deſerta recedens
Sæviat, exercens telum, quod ſæpe nocentes
Præterit, exanimatque indignos, inque merentes."

He has turned the inſult into a magnificent image.

VER. 173. *Weak, fooliſh Man!*] Theſe eight ſucceeding lines were not in former editions; and indeed none of them, eſpecially lines 177 and 179, do any credit to the Author, and rather make us wiſh they had been ſuppreſſed.

Go, like the Indian, in another life
Expect thy dog, thy bottle, and thy wife:
As well as dream fuch trifles are affign'd,
As toys and empires, for a god-like mind.   180
Rewards, that either would to Virtue bring
No joy, or be deftructive of the thing:
How oft by thefe at fixty are undone
The virtues of a faint at twenty-one!
To whom can Riches give Repute, or Truft,   185
Content, or Pleafure, but the Good and Juft?
Judges and Senates have been bought for gold,
Efteem and Love were never to be fold.
Oh fool! to think God hates the worthy mind,
The lover and the love of human-kind,   190
Whofe life is healthful, and whofe confcience clear,
Becaufe he wants a thoufand pounds a year.

Honour and fhame from no Condition rife;
Act well your part, there all the honour lies.

Fortune

NOTES.

VER. 185. *Give Repute, or Truft,*] We fee in the world, alas! too many examples of riches giving repute and truft, content, and pleafure to the worthlefs and profligate.

VER. 189. *God hates the worthy mind,*] The ground of the complaint is, not that the worthy man does not poffefs a large and ample fortue, but becaufe he fometimes wants even neceffaries.

VER. 194. *Act well your part,*] The Antients were very fond of this comparifon of human life with a drama. Epictetus ufes it in a well known paffage, chapter 27. and Arrian alfo recites it: it is repeated twice or thrice in Stobæus; and Antoninus finifhes his meditations with an allufion to it. Ivie has given it from Epictetus in a manner fo truly Horatian, that I cannot forbear repeating it:

" Nos

Fortune in Men has some small diff'rence made, 195
One flaunts in rags, one flutters in brocade;
The

NOTES.

"Nos sumus in scenâ; quin et mandante magistro,
Quisque datas agimus partes; sit longa brevisve
Fabula, nil refert: Tyrio seu dives in ostro
Incedam, pannis seu veler squallidus, imo
Prognatus populo, seu fracto crure humerove
In triviis rogitem æra; placet lex"——

But our Author found the same illustration in his friend's Essay. See Bolingbroke, vol. v. p. 79. "The whole world, nay, the whole universe, is filled with Beings which are all connected in one immense design. The sensitive inhabitants of our globe, like the dramatis personæ, have different characters, and are applied to different purposes of action in every scene. The several parts of the material world, like the machines of a theatre, were contrived not for the actors, but for the action: and the whole order and system of the drama would be disordered and spoiled, if any alteration was made in either. The nature of every creature, his manner of being, is adapted to his state here, to the place he is to inhabit, and, as we may say, to the part he is to act. If man was a creature inferior or superior to what he is, he would be a very preposterous creature in this system. Gulliver's horses made a very absurd figure in the place of men, and men would make one as absurd in the place of horses. I do not think that philosophers have shewn in every instance why every thing is what it is, and as it is, or that nothing could be, in any one case, otherwise than it is, without producing a greater inconveniency to the whole than the particular inconveniency that would be removed. But I am sure this has been proved in so many instances, that it is trifling, as well as profane, to deny it in any. We complain often of our senses, and sometimes of our reasoning faculties: both are defective, weak, fallible: and yet if the former were more extensive, more acute, and more nice, they would not answer the purposes of human life, they would be absolutely inconsistent with them. Just so, if our reasoning faculties were more perfect than they are, the order of intellectual Beings would be broken unnecessarily, and man would be raised above his proper form, without any real advantage to himself, since the reason he has is sufficient for him in the state allotted

ESSAY ON MAN.

The cobler apron'd, and the parſon gown'd,
The frier hooded, and the monarch crown'd.
" What differ more (you cry) than crown and
" cowl?"
I'll tell you, friend! a wiſe man and a fool.   200
You'll find, if once the monarch acts the monk,
Or, cobler-like, the parſon will be drunk,
Worth makes the man, and want of it the fellow;
The reſt is all but leather or prunella.   204
 Stuck o'er with titles, and hung round with ſtrings,
That thou may'ſt be by kings, or whores of kings,
Boaſt the pure blood of an illuſtrious race,
In quiet flow from Lucrece to Lucrece:
But by your fathers' worth if your's you rate,
Count me thoſe only who were good and great. 210
Go!

VARIATIONS.

VER. 207. *Boaſt the pure blood, &c.*] In the MS. thus,
 The richeſt blood, right-honourably old,
 Down from Lucretia to Lucretia roll'd,
 May ſwell thy heart and gallop in thy breaſt,
 Without one daſh of uſher or of prieſt:
 Thy pride as much deſpiſe all other pride
 As Chriſt Church once all colleges beſide.

NOTES.

allotted to him; and ſince higher faculties and greater degrees of knowledge would on one hand increaſe his preſumption, and yet on the other would rather excite than ſate his curioſity, by ſhewing him more clearly the extent of his ignorance."

 VER. 208. *From Lucrece to Lucrece:*] A bad rhyme to the preceding word race. It is taken from Boileau, vol. 85. Satire 5.
 " Et ſi leur ſang tout pur, ainſi que leur nobleſſe,
 Eſt paſſé juſqu'à vous de Lucrece en Lucrece."

 VER. 210. *Count me thoſe*] The following comment is taken from the manuſcripts of James Harris, Eſq.

" If

Go! if your ancient, but ignoble blood
Has crept through scoundrels ever since the flood,
Go! and pretend your family is young;
Nor own, your fathers have been fools so long.
What can ennoble sots, or slaves, or cowards? 215
Alas! not all the blood of all the HOWARDS.
  Look next on Greatness; say where Greatness lies?
" Where, but among the Heroes and the Wise?"
Heroes are much the same, the point's agreed,
From Macedonia's madman to the Swede; 220
                                              The

NOTES.

" If thou art ever touched with the admiration of family, remember that thou too hadst a progenitor in the time of the Holy War, as much as either the Courteneys, the Greys, or the Howards. The difference is no more than that in those wise expeditions thy forefathers were corporals, while theirs were captains: That their forefathers had wealth enough to be benefactors to monkery; while the poverty of thine, if ever they had such intentions, most happily prevented them from making their folly conspicuous."

Pope seems to have been reading Peter Charron's severe Animadversions on Natural and Personal Nobility, in book i. of Wisdom, p. 499.

VER. 220. *From Macedonia's*] He has fallen into the common cant about Alexander the Great. Think of the scene in Darius's tent; of the foundation of the city of Alexandria, and the extent of its commerce; of the many colonies he established; of his refusing to treat the Persians as slaves; of the grief expressed by the Persians at his death; of the encouragement he gave to arts, both useful and elegant; and of his assistance to Aristotle his master, in making experiments and promoting science: The encomiums bestowed on him by two such judges of men as Bacon and Montesquieu, outweigh the censures of Boileau and Pope. Charles XII. deserved not to be joined with him: Charles XII. tore out the leaf in which Boileau had censured Alexander. Robertson, in his Disquisitions on India, has given a fine and comprehensive view of the very grand design which Alexander had formed to annex that extensive and opulent country to his empire. Section 1. Appendix.

Ep. IV. ESSAY ON MAN.

The whole ſtrange purpoſe of their lives to find
Or make, an enemy of all mankind!
Not one looks backward, onward ſtill he goes,
Yet ne'er looks forward further than his noſe.
No leſs alike the Politic and Wiſe;   225
All ſly ſlow things, with circumſpective eyes:
Men in their looſe unguarded hours they take,
Not that themſelves are wiſe, but others weak.
But grant that thoſe can conquer, theſe can cheat;
'Tis phraſe abſurd to call a Villain Great: 230
Who wickedly is wiſe, or madly brave,
Is but the more a fool, the more a knave.
Who noble ends by noble means obtains,
Or failing, ſmiles in exile or in chains,
Like good Aurelius let him reign, or bleed   235
Like Socrates, that Man is great indeed.

What's Fame, a fancied life in other's breath,
A thing beyond us, ev'n before our death.

Juſt

NOTES.

VER. 222. *An enemy of all mankind!*] Had all nations, with regard to their heroes, been of the humour with the Normans, who called Robert II. the greateſt of their Dukes, by the name of ROBERT THE DEVIL, the Races of heroes might have been leſs numerous, or, however, leſs miſchievous.   W.

VER. 235. *Or bleed like Socrates,*] Conſidering the manner in which Socrates was put to death, the word "bleed" ſeems to be improperly uſed. Cudworth has remarked, that it is a common miſtake to aſſert that Socrates was condemned for aſſerting the doctrine of one Supreme Deity; for he alſo acknowledged the exiſtence of inferior created gods; but he was puniſhed for expoſing and ridiculing the common fabulous poetic accounts of theſe inferior and ſubordinate gods, which accounts were held ſacred by the people. It was hence he was accuſed of impiety.

VER. 237. *What's Fame,*] It is the fate of many philoſophical reflections, that, in the ſame proportion with which they diminiſh

Just what you hear, you have, and what's unknown
The same (my Lord) if Tully's, or your own.   240
All that we feel of it begins and ends
In the small circle of our foes or friends;
To all beside as much an empty shade
An Eugene living, as a Cæsar dead:
Alike or when, or where, they shone, or shine, 245
Or on the Rubicon, or on the Rhine.
A Wit's a feather, and a Chief a rod;
An honest Man's the noblest work of God.
Fame but from death a villain's name can save,
As Justice tears his body from the grave;   250
When what t'oblivion better were resign'd,
Is hung on high, to poison half mankind.
All fame is foreign, but of true desert;
Plays round the head, but comes not to the heart:
             One

NOTES.

and destroy vicious passions and pursuits, they also diminish and destroy such as are virtuous and reasonable, and by degrees render the mind callous, indifferent, and inactive: Just as when Fontenelle says, that the true system of astronomy ought to extinguish ambition; "for what a poor thing is the conquest of the whole globe in comparison of the infinite extent of Nature?" Such a reflection would extinguish patriotism as well as ambition. Perhaps our Author, in these fine lines, has carried the matter too far, as Mr. Wollaston has certainly done: "The man is not known ever the more to posterity, because his name is transmitted to them. He doth not live because his name does. Since Pompey is as little known as Cæsar, all that is said of their conquests amounts to this, Somebody conquered somebody." The reader may be highly gratified if he will peruse a very fine speech on this subject, in a poem too much neglected, the Paradise Regained of Milton, book iii. v. 45. Is exposing and depreciating the passion for fame consistent with the doctrine before advanced, that

"Not a vanity is giv'n in vain?"

Ver. 248. *An honest Man's*] Plato says, Πάντων ἐρώτατον ἐστιν ἀνθρωπος· ὁ ἀγαθός.

One self-approving hour whole years outweighs 255
Of stupid starers, and of loud huzzas;
And more true joy Marcellus exil'd feels, ⁓
Than Cæsar with a senate at his heels.
In Parts superior what advantage lies?
Tell (for You can) what is it to be wise? 260
'Tis

NOTES.

VER. 257. *Marcellus exil'd*] "Brutus," said he, "perished untimely, and Cæsar did no more.—'Twas thus, as I remember, not long since, you were expressing yourself: And yet, suppose their fortunes to have been exactly parallel, which would you have preferred? Would you have been Cæsar or Brutus?"

"Brutus," replied I, "beyond all controversy." He asked me, "Why? where was the difference, when their fortunes, as we now supposed them, were considered as the same?"

"There seems," said I, "abstract from their fortunes, something, I know not what, intrinsically preferable in the life and character of Brutus." "If that," said he, "be true, then must we derive it, not from the success of his endeavours, but from their truth and rectitude. He had the comfort to be conscious that his cause was a just one. 'Twas impossible the other should have any such feeling." "I believe," said I, "you have explained it." Harris's Discourse on Happiness, v. 1.

Cicero's fine oration to Cæsar on behalf of Marcellus, is sufficiently known. Middleton has given an elegant account of his enmity to Cæsar, and of his being stabbed by Magius, and his funeral rites at Athens, vol. ii. 286. By Marcellus, Pope was said to mean the Duke of Ormond.

VER. 259. *In Parts superior*] To a person that was praising Dr. Balguy's admirable Discourses on the Vanity and Vexation of our Pursuits after Knowledge, he replied, " I borrowed the whole from ten lines of the Essay on Man, at ver. 259.; and I only enlarged and commented upon what the Poet had expressed with such marvellous concisesness, penetration, and precision." He particularly admired verse 266. " Men value themselves," says Fontenelle, " for having wit, and genius, and talents, more than for the gifts of fortune, riches, and birth, as not depending on hazard.

'Tis but to know how little can be known;
To fee all others faults, and feel our own:
Condemn'd in bufinefs or in arts to drudge,
Without a fecond, or without a judge:
Truths would you teach, or fave a finking land?
All fear, none aid you, and few underftand.   266
Painful pre-eminence! yourfelf to view
Above life's weaknefs, and its comforts too.

 Bring then thefe bleffings to a ftrict account:
Make fair deductions; fee to what they mount; 270
How much of other each is fure to coft;
How each for other oft is wholly loft;
How inconfiftent greater goods with thefe;
How fometimes life is rifqu'd, and always eafe:
Think, and if ftill the things thy envy call,   275
Say, would'ft thou be the Man to whom they fall?
To figh for ribbands if thou art fo filly,
Mark how they grace (Lord Umbra,) or (Sir Billy.)
              Is

NOTES.

But how unjuft and ill-grounded is this? Does not genius confift in a certain conformation of the brain? and is the hazard lefs to be born with a brain fo well difpofed, than to be born the fon of a king? There is therefore no more perfonal merit to be born witty than to be born rich. Let this mortify our pride."

 VER. 266. *All fear, none aid you,*] " A perfecuted man of genius," fays a certain celebrated wit, " is like a flying-fifh; if he rifes above the furface of the water, the birds feize and devour him; if he plunges down, the fifhes eat him."

 VER. 277. *To figh for ribbands*] Why laugh at a modern peer, for his folicitude to obtain two or three yards of ribband, green or blue, more than at an antient champion for his laborious efforts to gain a chaplet of parfley, or crown of oak-leaves?

ESSAY ON MAN.

Is yellow dirt the paffion of thy life?
Look but on Gripus, or on Gripus' wife. — 380
If Parts allure thee, think how Bacon fhin'd,
The wifeft, brighteft, meaneft of mankind:
Or ravifh'd with the whiftling of a Name,
See Cromwell, damn'd to everlafting fame!

If

NOTES.

VER. 279. *Is yellow dirt*] A depreciating idle term, like the concifum argentum in titulos of Juvenal.

VER. 281. *How Bacon*] Can we believe the mortifying account of this great philofopher's vices, given by Sir S. Dewes in Hearne's Richard II.?

VER. 281, 283. *If Parts allure thee,—*
Or ravifh'd with the whiftling of a Name,]
Thefe two inftances are chofen with great judgment. The world, perhaps, doth not afford two fuch other.

BACON difcovered and laid down thofe true principles of fcience, by whofe affiftance Newton was enabled to unfold the whole law of Nature. He was no lefs eminent for the creative power of his imagination, the brightnefs of his conceptions, and the force of his expreffion: Yet being convicted on his own confeffion for bribery and corruption in the adminiftration of juftice, while he prefided in the fupreme Court of Equity, he endeavoured to repair his ruined fortunes by the moft profligate flattery to the Court: Which, indeed, from his very firft entrance into it, he had accuftomed himfelf to practife with a proftitution that difgraceth the very profeffion of letters, or of fcience.

CROMWELL feemeth to be diftinguifhed in the moft eminent manner, with regard to his abilities, from all other great and wicked men, who have overturned the Liberties of their Country. The times in which others have fucceeded in this attempt, were fuch as faw the fpirit of Liberty fuppreffed and ftifled by a general luxury and venality: But Cromwell fubdued his country, when this fpirit was in its height, by a fuccefsful ftruggle againft courtoppreffion; and while it was conducted and fupported by a fet of the greateft Geniufes for Government the world ever faw embarked together in one common caufe. W.

ESSAY ON MAN.   Ep. IV.

If all, united, thy ambition call,   285
From ancient story learn to scorn them all.
There, in the rich, the honour'd, fam'd, and great,
See the false scale of happiness complete!
In hearts of Kings, or arms of Queens who lay,
How happy! those to ruin, these betray.   290
Mark by what wretched steps their glory grows,
From dirt and sea-weed as proud Venice rose;
                                              In

NOTES.

VER. 283. *Or ravish'd with the whistling of a Name,*] And even this fantastic glory sometimes suffers a terrible reverse.—*Sacheverel*, in his *Voyage to Icolumb-kill*, describing the Church there, tells us, that " in one corner is a peculiar inclosure, in which were the monuments of the kings of many different nations, as Scotland, Ireland, Norway, and the *Isle of Man*. THIS (said the person who shewed me the place, pointing to a plain stone) was the monument of the GREAT TEAGUE, king of Ireland. I had never heard of him, and could not but reflect of how little value is *Greatness*, that has barely left a *name* scandalous to a nation, and a grave which the meanest of mankind would never envy."   W,

From Cowley in his imitation of Virgil;
    " Charm'd with the foolish whistlings of a name."
He frequently borrows expressions from Cowley; as did Gray.

VER. 285. *Thy ambition call,*] Candide meets at supper, in an inn at Venice, six dethroned and unfortunate kings. Their number, of late, might be augmented.

VER. 292. *From dirt and sea-weed*] There is something striking in the origin of this extraordinary state :

" No one can reproach the Venetians with having acquired their liberty by revolt," says Voltaire ; " no one could say, I have enfranchised you ; here is the charter of your manumission.

" They did not usurp the territory as the Cæsars usurped the empire ; as so many bishops, to begin with him of Rome, have usurped the regal sceptre. They are lords of Venice, (if one may use such a presumptuous comparison,) as the Supreme Being is Lord of the earth, because they founded it. Attila, who never
                                              took

In each how guilt and greatnefs equal ran,
And all that rais'd the Hero, funk the Man:
Now Europe's laurels on their brows behold, 295
But ftain'd with blood, or ill exchang'd for gold:
Then fee them broke with toils, or funk in eafe,
Or infamous for plunder'd provinces.

Or

NOTES.

took the title of the Scourge of God, carried his ravages over Italy. He had undoubtedly as much right as Charlemagne, Arnold the Baftard, Guy duke of Spoleto, Berenger marquis of Frioul, and the Bifhops who afpired at fovereignty afterwards.

" In thofe days of military and ecclefiaftical depredations, Attila came on like a vulture; and the Venetians, like Halcyons, faved themfelves in the waves. They had no protector but themfelves; they built their nefts in the middle of the waters; they enlarged, they peopled, they defended, they enriched it. I would afk if it be poffible that there fhould be a jufter title to poffeffion?

" I have read Squittinio della Liberta di Venezio, and am highly offended with it.

" What! then, was not Venice originally free, becaufe the foolifh, barbarous, fanatic Emperors of Greece faid, This new city was built on our ancient territory; and becaufe the Germans, having the title of Emperors of the Weft, faid, This, being a weftern city, muft belong to us?

" I here think I fee a poor flying-fifh purfued at the fame time by a falcon above, and a fhark below, and efcaping from both.

" Sannazarius, on comparing Rome to Venice, has very well expreffed himfelf:

' Illam homines dicas, hanc pofuiffe deos.'

" Rome, at the end of five hundred years, loft by Cæfar the liberty fhe had acquired by Brutus. Venice has preferved her's eleven centuries, and I flatter myfelf that fhe will preferve it ftill."

VER. 297. *Or funk in eafe,*] In the MSS. it was thus:

———or funk in years,
Loft in unmeaning, unrepenting tears.

Meaning the great Duke of Marlborough, who funk in the latter

4   part

Oh wealth ill-fated! which no act of fame
E'er taught to shine, or sanctify'd from shame! 300
What greater bliss attends their close of life?
Some greedy minion, or imperious wife,
The trophy'd arches, story'd halls invade,
And haunt their slumbers in the pompous shade.
Alas! not dazzled with their noon-tide ray, 305
Compute the morn and ev'ning to the day?
The whole amount of that enormous fame,
A Tale, that blends their glory with their shame!
  Know then this truth (enough for Man to know)
" Virtue alone is Happiness below." 310
                                                                The

NOTES.

part of his life into a state of perfect childhood and dotage; as did Lord Somers. Our Author always spoke of the Duke with a wonderful degree of acrimony; nay, he once turned into ridicule his sorrow on the death of his only son, the Marquis of Blandford. The Duke having a very effeminate voice, Pope, in some bitter verses which he suppressed, made him lament his loss

  " In accents of a whining ghost!"

  Marlborough among his friends, in some of their familiar letters, used to be called—Silly; as, " Silly says so," &c. This took its rise from an habit he had of crying out, in a shrill and effeminate voice, " Silly, Silly," when he objected to any thing. " Shall the Allies make an attempt upon Lisle?"—" Silly." " Upon Arras then?"—" Silly, Silly." The great Generals, Œtius and Bellisarius, as well as Marlborough and Monk, were governed by their imperious wives. See Ver. 302. The wife of Monk was Anne Clargess, a blacksmith's daughter, who had been Monk's sempstress, when he was a prisoner in the Tower. She was very instrumental in bringing about the Restoration.

  VER. 299. *Oh wealth ill-fated!*] In the journal written to his Stella, Swift speaks in very handsome terms of the Duke of Marlborough, and this too at a time when the Ministry was about to be changed, 1710. And Bolingbroke always mentioned him with respect.

The only point where human blifs ftands ftill,
And taftes the good without the fall to ill;
Where only Merit conftant pay receives,
Is bleft in what it takes, and what it gives;
The joy unequal'd if its end it gain, 315
And if it lofe, attended with no pain:
Without fatiety, though e'er fo blefs'd,
And but more relifh'd as the more diftrefs'd:
The broadeft mirth unfeeling Folly wears,
Lefs pleafing far than Virtue's very tears: 320
Good, from each object, from each place acquir'd,
For ever exercis'd, yet never tir'd;
Never elated, while one man's opprefs'd;
Never dejected, while another's blefs'd;
 And

VARIATIONS.

After Ver. 316. in the MS.
 Ev'n while it feems unequal to difpofe,
 And chequers all the good Man's joys with woes,
 'Tis but to teach him to fupport each ftate,
 With patience this, with moderation that;
 And raife his bafe on that one folid joy,
 Which confcience gives, and nothing can deftroy.
Thefe lines are extremely finifhed. In which there is fuch a foothing fweetnefs in the melancholy harmony of the verfification, as if the Poet was then in that tender office in which he was moft officious, and in which all his foul came out, the condoling with fome good man in affliction. W.

NOTES.

VER. 319. *The broadeft mirth*] It is fingular that this uncommon expreffion, broad mirth, fhould be in Origen. Not that we are to imagine that Pope had read it in this Greek father. There are many fuch coincidences, which muft not be attributed to copying or borrowing. The words in Origen are, γελωΐα πλατυν οφλησομε..

And where no wants, no wishes can remain,   325
Since but to wish more Virtue, is to gain.
  See the sole bliss Heav'n could on all bestow!
Which who but feels can taste, but thinks can know:
Yet poor with fortune, and with learning blind,
The bad must miss; the good, untaught, will find;
Slave to no sect, who takes no private road,   331
But looks through Nature, up to Nature's God;
Pursues that Chain which links th' immense design,
Joins heav'n and earth, and mortal and divine;
Sees, that no Being any bliss can know,   335
But touches some above, and some below;
Learns from this union of the rising Whole,
The first, last purpose of the human soul;
And knows where Faith, Law, Morals, all began,
All end, in LOVE OF GOD, and LOVE OF MAN. 340
  For him alone, Hope leads from goal to goal,
And opens still, and opens on his soul;
                                                    Till

NOTES.

VER. 327. *See the sole bliss Heav'n could on all bestow!*] Having proved that happiness is placed in *Virtue*; he proves next (from Ver. 326 to 329.) that it is *rightly* placed there; for that then, and then only, ALL may partake of it, and ALL be capable of relishing it.   W.

VER. 332. *But looks through Nature,*] Verbatim from Bolingbroke's Letters to Pope.

VER. 341. *For him alone, Hope leads from goal to goal, &c.*] PLATO, in his first book of a Republic, hath a remarkable passage to this purpose: " He whose conscience does not reproach him, has chearful *Hope* for his companion, and the support and comfort of his old age, according to Pindar. For this great Poet, O Socrates, very elegantly says, That he who leads a just and holy life
                                                    has

Till lengthen'd on to FAITH, and unconfin'd,
It pours the blifs that fills up all the mind.
He fees, why Nature plants in Man alone   345
Hope of known blifs, and Faith in blifs unknown:
(Nature, whofe dictates to no other kind
Are giv'n in vain, but what they feek they find;)
Wife is her prefent; fhe connects in this
His greateft Virtue with his greateft Blifs;   250
At once his own bright profpect to be bleft,
And ftrongeft motive to affift the reft.

Self-love

NOTES.

has always amiable *Hope* for his companion, which fills his heart with joy, and is the fupport and comfort of his old age. *Hope*, the moft powerful of the Divinities, in governing the ever-changing and inconftant temper of mortal men." Ἰῳ δε μποιν ιωνιῳ ὁδίκον ξυνιϐοιτι ἡδεια ἐλπις ἁ.ι παρϛι και αγαϐη γηρυϐρτϐου, ως και Πι.δκρος λιγι. Χαριϋως γαρ τοι, ὠ Σωκρατες, τετ' ἐκεινος εἰπ.·, οτι ος ἀν δικαιως και ὁσιως τον βιον διαγαγη γλυκιια οἱ καρδιαν αταλλυσα γηροτρϐος συναορει ἑπ..., ἐ μαλιϛτα ϑναταν ϖλυϛροϐον γνω'ϛαν καϑερα. In the fame manner Euripides fpeaks in his *Hercules furens*,

Οὑτις δ' ἀνηρ αριϛος ὁϛις ελπισιν
Πεποιϐεν αἱει, τι δ' α'τορειν, ἠϐος κακῶ.   Ver. 105.

"He is the good man in whofe *breaft Hope fprings eternally:* But to be *without Hope in the world*, is the portion of the wicked." W.——To this we may add, he hopes, indeed, for another life, but he does not from hence infer the abfolute necef-fity of it, in order to vindicate the juftice and goodnefs of God.

VER. 346. *Faith in blifs unknown:*] Voltaire, having men-tioned the arguments urged by Lucretius againft the Immor-tality of the Soul, adds the following words, which we muft wifh he had never contradicted in any other of his writings: "Mais l'inftinct, la raifon, le befoin d'etre confolé, le bien de la fociété, prevalurent; et les hommes ont toujours eu l'efperance d'une vie à venir: efperance, à la verité fouvent accompagnée de doute. La Revelation detruit le doute, et met la certitude à la place." tom. ii. p. 382.

Self-love thus puſh'd to ſocial, to divine,
Gives thee to make thy neighbour's bleſſing thine.
Is this too little for the boundleſs heart?   355
Extend it, let thy enemies have part:
Graſp the whole worlds of Reaſon, Life, and Senſe,
In one cloſe ſyſtem of Benevolence:
Happier as kinder, in whate'er degree,
And height of Bliſs but height of Charity.   360
 God loves from Whole to Parts: But human ſoul
Muſt riſe from Individual to the Whole.
Self-love

NOTES.

Ver. 360. *But height of Charity.*] " To prove that the diſpenſations of Providence in the preſent ſtate are not unequal, is certainly very deſirable; but there is reaſon to fear, that thoſe who blame divines for admitting an inequality, have not ſucceeded in the attempt. The philoſophers, both antient and modern, who have endeavoured to juſtify the ways of God to Man, by proving that happineſs does not conſiſt in externals, in order to ſhew that his diſpenſations are equal, have yet placed happineſs in virtue chiefly as a principle of active benevolence.
 " Happier as kinder, in each due degree,
  And height of Bliſs but height of Charity."
Now there ſeems to be an inconſiſtency between theſe two principles, of which they are not aware.
 It may reaſonably be aſked, what virtue, as a principle of active benevolence, has to beſtow? Can it beſtow upon others any thing more than externals? If not, it either has not the power of communicating happineſs, or happineſs is to be communicated in externals. If it has not the power of communicating happineſs, it is indeed a mere name; the ſubject receives nothing; the agent gives nothing. The bliſs of charity is founded on a deluſion; on the falſe ſuppoſition of a benefit communicated by externals, which externals cannot communicate. If happineſs can be communicated by externals, and conſequently is dependent upon them, and theſe externals are unequally diſtributed, how is the diſpenſation of Providence with reſpect to happineſs in the preſent ſtate equal?" Hawkſworth on Swift's Works.

ESSAY ON MAN.

Self-love but serves the virtuous mind to wake,
As the small pebble stirs the peaceful lake;
The centre mov'd, a circle straight succeeds, 365
Another still, and still another spreads;
Friend, parent, neighbour, first it will embrace;
His country next; and next all human race;
Wide, and more wide, th' o'erflowings of the mind
Take ev'ry creature in, of ev'ry kind; 370
Earth smiles around, with boundless bounty blest,
And Heav'n beholds its image in his breast.
    Come then, my Friend! my Genius! come along;
Oh master of the poet, and the song!
                                            And

VARIATIONS.

VER. 373. *Come then, my Friend! &c.*] In the MS. thus,
    And now transported o'er so vast a Plain,
    While the wing'd courser flies with all her rein,
    While heav'n-ward now her mounting wing she feels,
    Now scatter'd fools fly trembling from her heels,
    Wilt thou, my ST. JOHN! keep her course in sight,
    Confine her fury, and assist her flight?

NOTES.

VER. 364. *As the small pebble*] It is observable that this similitude, which is to be found in Silius Italicus, l. xiii. v. 24. and also in Du Bartas, and in Shakspeare's Henry VI. and also in Feltham's Resolves, hath been used twice more in the writings of our Poet; in the Temple of Fame, in the four hundred and thirty-sixth line, and in the Dunciad, at the four hundred and fifth. This Essay is not decorated with many comparisons; two, however, ought to be mentioned, on account of their aptness and propriety. The first is, where he compares man to the vine, that gains its strength from the embrace it gives: The second is conceived with peculiar felicity; all Nature does not perhaps afford so fit and close an application. It is observed above, in ver. 313. from whence it is borrowed.

On

And while the Muse now stoops, or now ascends,
To Man's low passions, or their glorious ends, 376
Teach

NOTES.

On their own axis as the planets run,
Yet make at once their circle round the sun:
So two consistent motions act the soul;
And one regards itself, and one the whole.

This simile bears a close resemblance to that in the first act of the tragedy of Cato.

VER. 373. *Come then, my Friend! &c.*] This noble apostrophe, by which the Poet concludes the Essay in an address to his friend, will furnish a critic with examples of every one of those five Species of elocution, from which, as from its sources, Longinus deduceth the Sublime *.

1. The first and chief is *a grandeur and sublimity of conception:*

" Come then, my Friend! my Genius! come along;
Oh Master of the Poet, and the Song!
And while the Muse now stoops, and now ascends,
To Man's low passions, or their glorious ends"——

2. The *second*, that *pathetic enthusiasm*, which, at the same time, melts and inflames:

" Teach me, like thee, in various nature wise,
To fall with dignity, with temper rise;
Form'd by thy converse, happily to steer
From grave to gay, from lively to severe;
Correct with spirit, eloquent with ease,
Intent to reason, or polite to please."

3. *A certain elegant formation and ordonnance of figures:*

" Oh! while along the stream of time thy name
Expanded flies, and gathers all its fame,
Say, shall my little bark attendant sail,
Pursue the triumph, and partake the gale?"

4. *A*

---

*—πέντε πηγαί τινές εἰσιν τ' ὑψηγορίας. 1. Πρῶτον μὲν κỳ κράτιστον τὸ περὶ τὰς νοήσεις ἀδρεπήβολον. 2. Δεύτερον δὲ τὸ σφοδρὸν κỳ ἐνθυσιαστικὸν πάθος. 3. Ποιὰ τῶν σχημάτων πλάσις. 4. Ἡ γενναῖα φράσις. 5. Πέμπτη δὲ μεγέθες αἰτία, κỳ συγκλείουσα τὰ πρὸ ἑαυτῆς ἅπαντα, ἡ ἐν ἀξιώματι κỳ διάρσει σύνθεσις.

Teach me, like thee, in various nature wife,
To fall with dignity, with temper rife;
Form'd by thy converfe, happily to fteer
From grave to gay, from lively to fevere; 380
Correct with fpirit, elegant with eafe,
Intent to reafon, or polite to pleafe.
Oh! while along the ftream of Time thy name
Expanded flies, and gathers all its fame;
Say, fhall my little bark attendant fail, 385
Purfue the triumph, and partake the gale?

When

NOTES.

4. *A fplendid diction:*
" When ftatefmen, heroes, kings, in duft repofe,
Whofe fons fhall blufh their fathers were thy foes,
Shall then this verfe to future age pretend
Thou wert my guide, philofopher, and friend?
That urg'd by thee, I turn'd the tuneful art
From founds to things, from fancy to the heart;
For Wit's falfe mirror held up Nature's light;"

5. And fifthly, which includes in itfelf all the reft, *a weight and dignity in the compofition:*
" Shew'd erring Pride, Whatever is, IS RIGHT;
That REASON, PASSION, anfwer one great AIM;
That true SELF-LOVE and SOCIAL are the fame;
That VIRTUE only makes our BLISS below;
And all our Knowledge is, OURSELVES TO KNOW." W.

I find by a memorandum, written at the time, that it was on the 20th of January 1767, that Lord Bathurft informed me of the fact above mentioned; that he had read the outline of the Effay on Man, the fcheme and tenour of its doctrines, in the hand-writing of Bolingbroke, which fketch he greatly commended.

VER. 383. *Oh! while along*] From the Silvæ of Statius, c. v. v. 120.

———" immenfæ veluti connexa Carinæ
Cymba minor, cum fævit hyems———
———et eodem volvitur Auftro."

ESSAY ON MAN. Ep. IV.

When ſtateſmen, heroes, kings, in duſt repoſe,
Whoſe ſons ſhall bluſh their fathers were thy foes,
Shall then this verſe to future age pretend
Thou wert my guide, philoſopher, and friend? 390
That urg'd by thee, I turn'd the tuneful art
From ſounds to things, from fancy to the heart;
For Wit's falſe mirror held up Nature's light;
Shew'd erring Pride, WHATEVER IS, IS RIGHT;
That REASON, PASSION, anſwer one great aim; 395
That true SELF-LOVE and SOCIAL are the ſame;
That VIRTUE only makes our Bliſs below;
And all our Knowledge is, OURSELVES TO KNOW.

VARIATIONS.

VER. 307. *That Virtue only, &c.*] In the MS. thus,
That juſt to find a God is all we can,
And all the ſtudy of Mankind is Man.

NOTES.

VER. 391. *I turn'd the tuneful art*] Ought the lovers of true genuine poetry to be obliged to his friend, for being inſtrumental in making Pope forſake works of imagination for the didactic! Which of the two ſpecies of compoſition may be the more uſeful and inſtructive, is entirely beſide the queſtion; but, in point of poetic genius, the Rape of the Lock, and The Eloiſa, as far excel the Eſſay on Man, and the Moral Epiſtles, as the Gieruſalemme, ſo unjuſtly depreciated by Boileau, does all his Satires and his Art of Poetry; and as the ſecond and fourth books of Virgil excel the Georgics. To be able to reaſon well in verſe is not the firſt nor the moſt eſſential talent of a poet, great as its merit may be.

VER. 398. OURSELVES TO KNOW.] How unfortunate has our learned commentator been, in all the five examples he has produced, of the five ſpecies of elocution mentioned by Longinus?

In the firſt example there is little grandeur and ſublimity of conception.

In the ſecond, not one ſtroke of the pathetic.

In the third, not that formation and ufe of figures which, in the 16th fection, Longinus infifts upon.

In the fourth example, nothing that can be called τεσπικη κ̣ πεποιημένη λέξις; dictio tropis plena atque facta; i. e. artificio quodam elaborata.

In the fifth and laft, the bare enumeration of the fubjects treated of in thefe four epiftles cannot be juftly given as an example of weight and dignity of compofition, which Longinus calls η ὲν ἀξιώματι κ̣ διάρσει σύνθεσις: magnifica elataque compofitio.

After all, why would the commentator produce thefe five examples of the fources of the fublime, when, in another work, his Doctrine of Grace, he has laboured exceedingly to prove, that there is no fuch thing as fublimity, confidered in itfelf; that fublimity is only the application of fuch images as arbitrary and cafual connexions, rather than their own native grandeur, have dignified and ennobled; thus ftripping, what ages have admired as elegant and great, of its imaginary value, and refolving it into chance, caprice, and fafhion. This paradox, and the Defence of it, have been completely confuted by the learned and ingenious Dr. Leland, in a Differtation on the Principles of Human Eloquence. So truly is Warburton characterized by a nervous writer, who fays, " he had an eager propenfity to ftart afide from the regular and common orbit of opinion, upon every plain, every abftrufe, every trifling, and every important fubject." The fame writer, with a fpirit of impartiality that does him credit, adds, " The Bifhop of Gloucefter, amidft all his fooleries in criticifm, and all his outrages in controverfy, certainly united a moft vigorous and comprehenfive intellect, with an open and a generous heart." I will juft add, that the antiparadifical ftate mentioned by this prelate in the additional book of the Div. Legation, publifhed by the Bifhop of Worcefter, has difpleafed many ferious and able judges.

If, after all, the Divine Legation is a work, as Dr. Hurd affures us it is, " of the moft tranfcendent merit, whether we confider the invention or execution; a work fo embellifhed by a lively fancy, and illuftrated from all quarters by exquifite learning and the moft ingenious difquifition, that, in the whole compafs of modern or ancient theology, there is nothing equal or fimilar to this extraordinary performance;" if, to the authority of Hooker, the acutenefs of Chillingworth, and the perfpicuity of Locke, he added more than all their learning; if thefe rare and admirable qualifications fhone out in him with greater luftre than in any other ornament of our church, Stillingfleet, and Barrow, and Taylor himself not excepted; if, I say, this high encomium of Dr. Hurd, on his all-accomplished friend, be just and well-founded, it surely is of small consequence to an author of such exalted and extraordinary merits to say, that his notes on Shakespeare and Pope are conceited, futile, and frivolous.

In the very last edition of Bishop Law's excellent translation of the Origin of Evil, is the following remarkable passage: " I had now the satisfaction of seeing, that those very principles which had been maintained by Archbishop King, were adopted by Mr. Pope in his Essay on Man: this I used to recollect, and sometimes to relate, with pleasure, conceiving that such an account did no less honour to the poet than to our philosopher; but was soon made to understand, that any thing of that kind was taken highly amiss by one (i. e. Dr. Warburton), who had once held the doctrine of that same Essay to be rank atheism, but afterwards turned a warm advocate for it, and thought proper to deny the account above mentioned, with heavy menaces against those who presumed to insinuate that Pope borrowed any thing from any man whatsoever.

Marmontel, in his Poetique, has given the following judgment on the Essay on Man: " Pope, dans les Epitres qui composent son Essai sur l'Homme, a fait voir combien la poesie pouvoit s'élever sur les ailes de la philosophie. C'est dommage que ce Poete n'ait pas eu autant de methode que de profondeur. Mais il avoit pris un systeme; il failloit le soutenir. Ce systeme lui offroit des difficultés épouvantables; il falloit ou les vaincre, ou les eviter : le dernier parti etoit le plus sur et le plus commode; aussi pour repondre aux plaintes de l'homme sur les malheurs de son etat, lui donne-t-il le plus souvent des images pour des preuves, et des injures pour des raisons."

Still more contemptuous and degrading, than the opinion of this French critic, are the terms in which Dr. Johnson has spoken of this Essay, in which are so many splendid and highly-finished passages. " The subject," he says, " is perhaps not very proper for poetry; and the poet was not sufficiently master of his subject : metaphysical morality was a new study; and he was proud of his acquisitions; and, supposing himself master of great secrets, was in haste to teach what he had not learned. When these wonder-working sounds sink into sense, and the doctrine of the Essay, disrobed of its ornaments, is left to the powers of its naked excellence, what shall we discover? that we are, in comparison with our Creator, very weak and ignorant; that we do not uphold the chain of exiſtence; and that we could not make one another with more ſkill than we are made. We may learn yet more; that the arts of human life were copied from the inſtinctive operations of other animals; that if the world be made for man, it may be ſaid that man was made for geeſe."

This ſort of burleſque abſtract, which may be ſo eaſily but ſo unjuſtly made of any compoſition whatever, is exactly ſimilar to the imperfect and unfair repreſentation which the ſame critic has given of the beautiful imagery in Il Penſeroſo of Milton. Very different was the opinion of the ingenious and acute Dr. Balguy on the Eſſay on Man; who, in various paſſages of his excellent treatiſe, intitled, " Divine Benevolence," has manifeſtly copied many of its doctrines and reaſonings; who has written two ſermons on the vanity of our purſuits after knowledge, which contain, as hath been already obſerved, little more than is comprehended in ten lines of this Eſſay; and who has even done Pope the honour of prefixing to his admirable ſermons, as a motto, the following ſentence from the preface to this Eſſay: " If I could flatter myſelf that theſe Eſſays have any merit, it is in ſteering between the extremes of doctrines ſeemingly oppoſite; in paſſing over terms utterly unintelligible; and in forming a temperate, yet not inconſiſtent ſyſtem."

THE
UNIVERSAL PRAYER.
DEO OPT. MAX.

THE

UNIVERSAL PRAYER.

DEO OPT. MAX.

FATHER of All! in ev'ry Age,
    In ev'ry Clime ador'd,
By Saint, by Savage, and by Sage,
    Jehovah, Jove, or Lord!

Thou

NOTES.

VER. 1. FATHER *of All!*] For clofenefs and comprehenfion of thought, and for brevity and energy of expreffion, few pieces of poetry in our language can be compared with this Prayer. I am furprifed Johnfon fhould not make any mention of it. When it was firft publifhed, many orthodox perfons were, I remember, offended at it, and called it, The Deift's Prayer. It were to be wifhed the Deifts would make ufe of fo good an one.

VER. 4. *Jehovah, Jove, or Lord!*] " It is of very little confequence," fays Seneca, De Beneficiis, " by what name you call the firft Nature, and the divine Reafon, that prefides over the univerfe, and fills all the parts of it. He is ftill the fame God. You may give Him as many names as you pleafe, provided you allow but one Sole Principle every where prefent."

" Notwithftanding all the extravagancies and mifcarriages of the Poets," fays Cudworth, chap. 4. " we fhall now make it plainly appear, that they really afferted, not a multitude of felf-exiftent and independent Deities, but one, only, unmade Deity; and all the other, generated or created gods. This hath been already

UNIVERSAL PRAYER.

Thou Great Firſt Cauſe, leaſt underſtood:
Who all my Senſe confin'd
To know but this, that Thou art Good,
And that myſelf am blind;

Yet gave me, in this dark Eſtate,
To ſee the Good from Ill;
And binding Nature faſt in Fate,
Left free the Human Will.

What

NOTES.

ready proved concerning Orpheus, from ſuch fragments of the Orphic Poems as have been owned and atteſted by Pagan writers." Cudworth proceeds to confirm this opinion by many ſtrong and unconteſted paſſages from Homer, Heſiod, Pindar, Sophocles, and eſpecially Euripides, Book i. chap. iv. ſect. 19.; and Ariſtophanes, in the firſt line of Plutus, diſtinguiſhes betwixt Jupiter and the gods: Ω Ζεῦ κ̀ θεοι.

VER. 6. *My Senſe confin'd*] It ought to be confinedſt, or didſt confine; and afterwards, gaveſt, or didſt give, in the ſecond perſon. See Lowth's Grammar.

VER. 9. *Yet gave me,*] Originally Pope had written another ſtanza, immediately after this;

  Can ſins of moments claim the rod
   Of everlaſting fires?
  And that offend great Nature's God
   Which Nature's ſelf inſpires?

The licentious ſentiment it contains, evidently borrowed from a well-known paſſage of Guarini in the Paſtor Fido, induced him to ſtrike it out. And perhaps alſo the abſurd metaphor of a rod of fires, on examination, diſpleaſed him.

VER. 12. *Left free*] An abſurd and impoſſible exemption, exclaims the Fataliſt; " comparing together the moral and the natural world, every thing is as much the reſult of eſtabliſhed laws in the one as in the other. There is nothing in the whole univerſe

that

What Confcience dictates to be done,
Or warns me not to do,
This, teach me more than Hell to fhun,
That, more than Heav'n purfue.

What Bleffings thy free Bounty gives,
Let me not caft away;
For God is paid when Man receives,
T' enjoy is to obey.

Yet

NOTES.

that can properly be called contingent : nothing loofe or fluctuating in any part of Nature ; but every motion in the natural, and every determination and action in the moral world, are directed by immutable laws ; fo that, whilft thefe laws remain in their force, not the fmalleft link of the univerfal chain of caufes and effects can be broken, nor any one thing be otherwife than it is." All the moft fubtile and refined arguments that can be urged in a difpute on Fate and Free-will, are introduced, in a converfation on this fubject, betwixt the angels Gabriel and Raphael, and Adam, in the fourth act of Dryden's State of Innocence, and ftated with a wonderful precifion and perfpicuity. Reafoning, in verfe, was one of Dryden's moft fingular and predominant excellencies : notwithftanding which, he muft rank as a poet for his Mufic-ode, not for his Religio Laici.

VER. 12. *The Human Will.*] The refult of what Locke advances on this, the moft difficult of all fubjects, is, that we have a power of doing what we will. " Il ferait plaifant," fays a noted wit, " qu'une partie de ce monde fut arrangée, et que l'autre ne le fut point ; qu'une partie de ce qui arrive ne dût pas arriver. Quand on y regarde de pres, on voit que la doctrine contraire à celle du deftin eft abfurde ; mais il y a beaucoup de gens deftinés à raifonner mal, d'autres à ne point raifonner du tout, d'autres à perfecuter ceux qui raifonnent." Let us acquiefce in a better philofophy, which teaches us, " that if Free-will be the origin of evil, it is alfo the origin of good. If it be the occafion of difor-

der,

UNIVERSAL PRAYER.

Yet not to Earth's contracted Span
   Thy Goodnefs let me bound,
Or think Thee Lord alone of Man,
   When thoufand Worlds are round:

Let not this weak, unknowing hand
   Prefume thy bolts to throw,
And deal damnation round the land,
   On each I judge thy Foe.

If

NOTES.

der, it is the caufe of order; of all the moral order that appears in the world. Had Liberty been excluded, Virtue had been excluded with it. And if this had been the cafe, the world could have had no charms, no beauties, fufficient to recommend it to Him who made it. In fhort, all other powers and perfections would have been very defective without this, which is truly the life and fpirit of the whole creation."

VER. 25. *This weak, unknowing hand*] Forbearing one another, and forgiving one another: expreffing neither furprife nor averfion at perfons who hold opinions different from our own, either in religion or politics; knowing that this difference of opinion is as pardonable as it is unavoidable; and convinced that Laud and Milton, Hickes and Burnet, Atterbury and Hoadley, Waterland and Clarke, were all equally fincere in their feveral tenets.

The great Bifhop Butler ufed to fay, that if Lord Shaftefbury had lived to fee the candour, moderation, and gentlenefs of the prefent times in difcuffing religious fubjects, he would have been a good Chriftian.

VER. 27. *Deal damnation*] He cenfures the narrow and illiberal doctrine of popery and bigotry, "the impoffibility of being faved out of the pale of the Church." It is very remarkable, that Mahomet, in the Koran, Surat 2. feverely reprehends the Jews and the Chriftians for condemning each other; and fays, "that, on the day of refurrection, God will judge the merits of their caufe." So that there are Chriftians lefs tolerant than Mahomet.

If I am right, thy grace impart,
　　Still in the right to ſtay;
If I am wrong, oh teach my heart
　　To find that better way.

Save me alike from fooliſh Pride,
　　Or impious Diſcontent,
At aught thy Wiſdom has deny'd,
　　Or aught thy Goodneſs lent.

Teach me to feel another's Woe,
　　To hide the Fault I ſee;
That Mercy I to others ſhow,
　　That Mercy ſhow to me.

Mean though I am, not wholly ſo,
　　Since quicken'd by thy Breath;
Oh lead me whereſoe'er I go,
　　Through this day's Life or Death.

This

NOTES.

VER. 39. *That Mercy*] It has been ſaid that our Poet, in this Prayer, choſe the Lord's Prayer for his model; but there is no reſemblance but in this paſſage, and in the laſt ſtanza but one.

M. Le Franc de Pompignan, a celebrated avocat at Montau-ban, author of Dido a tragedy, was ſeverely cenſured in France for tranſlating this Univerſal Prayer, as a piece of Deiſm; which, having been printed in London, in 4to. by Vaillant, was conveyed to the Chancellor Agueſſau, who immediately ſent a ſtrong repri-mand to M. Le Franc, and he vindicated his orthodoxy in a laboured letter to that learned Chancellor. Voltaire reproached Le Franc with making this tranſlation. His brother, Biſhop of Puy au Velei, has called Locke an atheiſt.

UNIVERSAL PRAYER.

This day, be Bread and Peace my Lot:
　　All elfe beneath the Sun,
Thou know'ſt if beſt beſtow'd or not,
　　And let Thy Will be done.

To thee, whoſe Temple is all Space,
　　Whoſe Altar Earth, Sea, Skies!
One Chorus let all Being raiſe!
　　All Nature's Incenſe riſe!

MORAL ESSAYS,

IN FOUR EPISTLES

TO SEVERAL PERSONS.

Est brevitate opus, ut currat sententia, neu se
Impediat verbis lassis onerantibus aures:
Et sermone opus est modo tristi, sæpe jocoso,
Defendente vicem modo Rhetoris atque Poetæ
Interdum urbani, parcentis viribus, atque
Extenuantis eas consulto.　　　　　　　　Hor.

EPISTLE I.

TO

SIR RICHARD TEMPLE, LORD COBHAM.

ARGUMENT.

Of the Knowledge *and* Characters *of* MEN.

THAT it is not sufficient for this knowledge to consider Man in the Abstract: Books *will not serve the purpose, nor yet our own* Experience *singly,* Ver. 1. *General maxims, unless they be formed upon* both, *will be but notional,* Ver. 10. *Some peculiarity in every man, characteristic to himself, yet varying from himself,* Ver. 15. *Difficulties arising from our own Passions, Fancies, Faculties,* &c. Ver. 31. *The shortness of Life, to observe in, and the uncertainty of the* Principles of Action *in men, to observe by,* Ver. 37, &c. *Our own Principle of action often hid from ourselves,* Ver. 41. *Some few characters plain, but in general confounded, dissembled, or inconsistent,* Ver. 51. *The same man utterly different in different places and seasons,* Ver. 71. *Unimaginable weaknesses in the greatest,* Ver. 77, &c. *Nothing constant and certain but* God *and* Nature, Ver. 95. *No judging of the* Motives *from the actions; the same actions proceeding from contrary* Motives, *and the same Motives influencing contrary actions,* Ver. 100. II. *Yet to form* Characters, *we can only take the* strongest actions *of a man's life, and try to make them* agree: *The utter uncertainty*

tainty of this, from Nature *itself, and from* Policy, Ver. 120. Characters *given according to the* rank *of men of the world,* Ver. 135. *And some reason for it,* Ver. 141. Education *alters the* Nature, *or at least the* Character, *of many,* Ver. 149. Actions, Passions, Opinions, Manners, Humours, *or* Principles, *all subject to change. No judging by* Nature, *from* Ver. 158 *to* 174. III. *It only remains to find (if we can) his* Ruling Passion : *That will certainly influence all the rest, and can reconcile the seeming or real inconsistency of all his actions,* Ver. 175. *Instanced in the extraordinary character of* Clodio, Ver. 179. *A caution against mistaking* second qualities *for* first, *which will destroy all possibility of the knowledge of mankind,* Ver. 210. *Examples of the strength of the* Ruling Passion, *and its continuation to the last breath,* Ver. 222, &c.

EPISTLE I.

Of the Knowledge *and* Characters *of* MEN.

YES, you defpife the man to Books confin'd,
Who from his ftudy rails at human kind;
Tho' what he learns he fpeaks, and may advance
Some gen'ral maxims, or be right by chance.

The

NOTES.

Epiftle I. *Of the Knowledge and Characters of Men.*] Whoever compares this with the former editions of the Epiftle, will obferve, that the order and difpofition of the feveral parts are entirely changed and reverfed; though with hardly the alteration of a fingle word. When the Editor, at the Author's defire, firft examined this epiftle, he was furprifed to find it contain a number of exquifite obfervations, without order, connection, or dependence: but much more fo, when, on an attentive review, he faw, that if the epiftle were put into a different form, on an idea he then conceived, it would have all the clearnefs of method and force of connected reafoning. The Author appeared as much ftruck with the thing as the Editor, and agreed to put the poem into the prefent order; which has given it all the juftnefs of a true compofition. The introduction to the epiftle on Riches was in the fame condition, and underwent the fame reform. W. But this reform is not happily made.

Moral Effays.] The ESSAY ON MAN was intended to be comprifed in four books:

The *Firft* of which, the Author has given us under that title, in four epiftles.

The *Second* was to have confifted of the fame number: 1. Of the extent and limits of human reafon. 2. Of thofe arts and fciences, and the parts of them which are ufeful, and therefore attainable; together with thofe which are unufeful, and therefore unattainable. 3. Of the nature, ends, ufe, and application of the

VOL. III.   N   different

The coxcomb bird, so talkative and grave, 5
That from his cage cries Cuckold, Whore, and
    Knave,
                                              Tho'

NOTES.

different capacities of men. 4. Of the use of learning; of the science of the world; and of wit; concluding with a satire against the misapplication of them; illustrated by pictures, characters, and examples.

The *Third* book regarded civil regimen, or the science of politics; in which the several forms of a Republic were to be examined and explained; together with the several modes of religious worship, so far forth as they affect Society; between which the Author always supposed there was the closest connection and the most interesting relation. So that this part would have treated of Civil and Religious Society in their full extent.

The *Fourth* and last book concerned private ethics, or practical morality; considered in all the circumstances, orders, professions, and stations of human life.

The scheme of all this had been maturely digested, and *communicated* to L. Bolingbroke, Dr. Swift, and one or two more; and was intended for the only work of his riper years; but was, partly through ill health, partly through discouragements from the depravity of the times, and partly on prudential and other considerations, interrupted, postponed, and, lastly, in a manner laid aside.

But as this was the Author's favourite Work, which more exactly reflected the image of his own strong and capacious mind, and as we can have but a very imperfect idea of it from the *disjecta membra Poetæ*, which now remain, it may not be amiss to be a little more particular concerning each of these projected books.

The FIRST, as it treats of man in the abstract, and considers him in general, under every one of his relations, becomes the foundation, and furnishes out the subjects, of the *three* following; so that

The SECOND BOOK was to take up again the *first* and *second* epistles of the first book; and to treat of man in his intellectual capacity at large, as has been explained above. Of this only a small part of the conclusion (which, as we said, was to have contained

Tho' many a paſſenger he rightly call,
You hold him no Philoſopher at all.

And

NOTES.

tained a ſatire againſt the miſapplication of wit and learning) may be found in the *fourth* book of the *Dunciad;* and up and down, occaſionally, in the other *three.*

The THIRD BOOK, in like manner, was to reaſſume the ſubject of the *third* epiſtle of the *firſt,* which treats of Man in his ſocial, political, and religious capacity. But this part the Poet afterwards conceived might be beſt executed in an EPIC POEM, as the Action would make it more animated, and the Fable leſs invidious; in which all the great principles of true and falſe Governments and Religions ſhould be chiefly delivered in feigned examples.

The FOURTH and laſt book was to purſue the ſubject of the *fourth* epiſtle of the *firſt,* and to treat of *Ethics,* or practical morality; and would have conſiſted of many members, of which, the four following epiſtles are detached portions; the *two firſt,* on the *Characters of Men and Women,* being the *introductory* part of this concluding book. W.

VER. 1. *Yes, you deſpiſe*] The patrons and admirers of French literature uſually extol thoſe authors of that nation who have treated of life and manners; and five of them, particularly, are eſteemed to be unrivalled, namely, Montagne, Charron, La Rochefoucault, Boileau, La Bruyere, and Paſcal. Theſe are ſuppoſed to have deeply penetrated into the moſt ſecret receſſes of the human heart, and to have diſcovered the various vices and vanities that lurk in it. I know not why the Engliſh ſhould in this reſpect yield to their polite neighbours more than in any other. Bacon in his Eſſays and Advancement of Learning, Hobbes and Hume in their treatiſes, Prior in his elegant and witty Alma, Richardſon in his Clariſſa, and Fielding in his Tom Jones, (comic writers are not here included,) have ſhewn a profound knowledge of man; and many portraits of Addiſon may be compared with the moſt finiſhed touches of La Bruyere. But the Epiſtles we are now entering upon will place the matter beyond a diſpute; for the French can boaſt of no author who has ſo much exhauſted the ſcience of morals as Pope has in his five Epiſtles. They indeed contain all that is ſolid and valuable in the above-mentioned French

writers,

And yet the fate of all extremes is such,
Men may be read, as well as Books, too much. 10
To obfervations which ourfelves we make,
We grow more partial for th' Obferver's fake;
To written Wifdom, as another's lefs:
Maxims are drawn from Notions, thofe from Guefs.
There's fome Peculiar in each leaf and grain, 15
Some unmark'd fibre, or fome varying vein:
Shall only Man be taken in the grofs?
Grant but as many forts of Mind as Mofs.

That

NOTES.

writers, of whom our Author was remarkably fond. But whatever obfervations he has borrowed from them he has made his own by the dexterity of his application.

VER. 10. *Men may be read,*] " Say what they will of the great Book of the World, we muſt read others to know how to read that." M. De Sevigne to R. Rabutin.

VER. 15. *There's fome Peculiar, &c.*] The Poet enters on the firſt divifion of his fubject, *the difficulties of coming at the Knowledge and true Characters of Men.* The firſt caufe of this difficulty, which he profecutes (from Ver. 14 to 19.) is the great *diverfity of characters;* of which, to abate our wonder, and not difcourage our inquiry, he only defires we would grant him

" —but as many forts of Mind as Mofs."

Hereby artfully infinuating, that if Nature hath varied the moſt worthlefs vegetable into above three hundred fpecies, we need not wonder at a greater diverfity in her higheſt work, the human mind: And if the variety in that vegetable has been thought of importance enough to employ the leifure of a ferious inquirer, much more will the fame circumſtance in this maſter-piece of the fublunary world deferve our ſtudy and attention.

" Shall only Man be taken in the grofs?" W.

VER. 18. *As many forts of Mind*] It is related in Mr. Harris's Manufcripts, that " Newton, hearing Handel play on the harpfichord, could find nothing worthy to remark but the elaſticity of his

That each from other differs, first confefs;
Next, that he varies from himfelf no lefs: 20
Add Nature's, Cuftom's, Reafon's, Paffion's ftrife,
And all Opinion's colours caft on life.
                                                    Our

NOTES.

his fingers. At another time, having afferted that Terence's plays had no plot, and Bentley (in this knowledge his fuperior beyond all controverfy) having copioufly endeavoured to fhew the contrary, he concluded as he began, that Terence's plays had no plot. At another time, being afked his opinion of poetry, he quoted a fentiment of Barrow, that it was ingenious nonfenfe.

" Thus will it neceffarily happen, when men, even the greateft, are (according to the common faying) got out of their element. No genius, perhaps ever exifting, more acute than his in difcovering true from falfe, in the fubjects of colour, quantity, and motion. No one had an abler intellect to difcern what exifted from that which exifted not. But among the number of things exifting, what were fair, beautiful, graceful, elegant, and what the contrary, of this, by thefe ftories, one would imagine he had no conception."

VER. 19. *That each from other differs, &c.*] A fecond caufe of this difficulty (from Ver. 18 to 21.) is *man's inconftancy;* for not only one man differs from another, but the fame man from himfelf.

VER. 20. *Next, that he varies*] A fenfible French writer fays, that the faults and follies of men chiefly arife from this circumftance, qu'ils n'ont pas l'efprit, en equilibre, pour ainfi dire, avec leur charactere : Ciceron, par exemple, etoit un grand efprit et une ame foible ; c'eft pour cela, qu'il fut grand orateur et homme d'etat mediocre.

VER. 21. *Add Nature's, &c.*] A third caufe (from Ver. 20 to 23.) is that *obfcurity* thrown over the characters of men, through the ftrife and conteft between *nature* and *cuftom*, between *reafon* and *appetite*, between *truth* and *opinion*. And as moft men, either through *education*, *temperature*, or *profeffion*, have their characters warp'd by *cuftom*, *appetite*, and *opinion*, the obfcurity arifing from thence is almoft univerfal.   W.

Our depths who fathoms, or our shallows finds,
Quick whirls, and shifting eddies, of our minds?
On human Actions reason tho' you can,   25
It may be Reason, but it is not Man:
His Principle of action once explore,
That instant 'tis his principle no more.
Like following life through creatures you dissect,
You lose it in the moment you detect.   30
   Yet more; the diff'rence is as great between
The optics seeing, as the objects seen.
All Manners take a tincture from our own;
Or come discolour'd through our Passions shown.

Or

NOTES.

VER. 23. *Our depths who fathoms, &c.*] A fourth cause (from Ver. 22 to 25.) is deep *dissimulation*, and restless *caprice;* whereby the shallows of the mind are as difficult to be *found*, as the depths of it are to be *fathomed*.   W.

" A mesure qu'on a plus d'esprit," says the profound Pascal, " on trouve qu'il y a plus d'hommes originaux."

VER. 25. *On human Actions, &c.*] A fifth cause (from Ver. 24 to 31.) is the sudden change of his *principle of action;* either on the point of its being laid open and detected, or when it is reasoned upon, and attempted to be explored.   W.

VER. 31. *Yet more; the diff'rence, &c.*] Hitherto the Poet hath spoken of the causes of difficulty arising from the *obscurity of the object;* he now comes to those which proceed from *defects in the observer*. The first of which, and a sixth cause of difficulty, he shews (from Ver. 30 to 37.) is the perverse *manners, affections,* and *imaginations* of the observer; whereby the characters of others are rarely seen either in their true *light, complexion,* or *proportion*.   W.

VER. 33. *All Manners take*] A deep knowledge of Human Nature is displayed in these four lines. So also in Ver. 42.

Or Fancy's beam enlarges, multiplies, 35
Contracts, inverts, and gives ten thousand dies.
Nor will Life's stream for Observation stay,
It hurries all too fast to mark their way:
In vain sedate reflections we would make,
When half our knowledge we must snatch, not take.
Oft, in the Passions' wide rotation tost, 41
Our spring of action to ourselves is lost:
Tir'd, not determin'd, to the last we yield,
And what comes then is master of the field.

As

NOTES.

VER. 37. *Nor will Life's stream for Observation, &c.*] The seventh cause of difficulty, and the second arising from defects in the Observer, (from Ver. 36 to 41.) is the *shortness of human life*; which will not suffer him to select and weigh out his knowledge, but just to snatch it, as it rolls swiftly by him down the rapid current of Time. W.

VER. 41. *Oft, in the Passions', &c.*] We come now to the eighth and last cause, which very properly concludes the account; as, in a sort, it sums up all the difficulties in one, (from Ver. 40 to 51.) namely, that very often the *man himself is ignorant of his own motive of action;* the cause of which ignorance our Author has admirably explained: When the mind (says he) is now tired out by the long conflict of opposite motives, it withdraws its attention, and suffers the *will* to be seized upon by the first that afterwards obtrudes itself, without taking much notice what that motive is. This is finely illustrated by what he supposes to be the natural cause of dreams; where the fancy, just let loose, possesses itself of the *last image* which it meets with, on the confines between sleep and waking, and on that erects all its ideal scenery; yet this seisure is, with great difficulty, recollected; and never, but when by some accident we happen to have our first slumbers suddenly interrupted. Then (which proves the truth of the hypothesis) we are sometimes able to trace the workings of the Fancy backwards, from idea to idea, in a chain, till we come to that from whence they all arose. W.

As the laſt image of that troubled heap, 45
When Senſe ſubſides, and Fancy ſports in ſleep,
(Tho' paſt the recollection of the thought,)
Becomes the ſtuff of which our dream is wrought:
Something as dim to our internal view,
Is thus, perhaps, the cauſe of moſt we do. 50

True ſome are open, and to all men known;
Others ſo very cloſe they're hid from none;
(So Darkneſs ſtrikes the ſenſe no leſs than Light;)
Thus gracious CHANDOS is belov'd at ſight;
And ev'ry child hates Shylock, tho' his ſoul 55
Still ſits at ſquat, and peeps not from its hole.

At

NOTES.

VER. 48. *Becomes the ſtuff of which our dream is wrought:*] Giraldus Cambrenſis, ſpeaking of a *divine viſion* with which he was favoured, ſeems yet to think that it might be *made out of the ſtuff of his waking thoughts.* His words are theſe: " Cum igitur ſuper univerſis quæ nobis acciderant, mecum non mediocriter anxius extiterim—ſuſpirioſæ mihi multoties cogitationes in animum aſcenderint, noćte quadam in ſomnis EX RELIQUIIS FERTE COGITATIONEM Viſionem vidi," &c. *De rebus a ſe geſtis,* L. II. C. 12. By which we ſee, and it is worth remarking, that to philoſophiſe on our Superſtitions is ſo far from eraſing them, that it engraves them but the more deeply in the mind. The reaſon is plain; it turns the *objection* to them to a *ſolution* in their credit. W.

VER. 56. *Still ſits at ſquat,*] No two characters have been painted with more life and truth, and more circumſtances nicely diſcriminated, than thoſe of the artful Blifield and the open Tom Jones, in Fielding's incomparable Comic Epopée, an original and unrivalled work.

VER. 56. *Peeps not from its hole.*] Which ſhews (ſays Scriblerus, idly) that this grave perſon was content with his preſent ſituation, as finding but ſmall ſatisfaction in what a famous Poet reckons one of the advantages of old age;

" The ſoul's dark cottage, batter'd and decay'd,
Lets in new light through chinks that time has made,"

SCRIBL.

At half mankind when gen'rous Manly raves,
All know 'tis Virtue, for he thinks them knaves:
When univerfal homage Umbra pays,
All fee 'tis Vice, and itch of vulgar praife.   60
When Flatt'ry glares, all hate it in a Queen,
While one there is who charms us with his Spleen.
    But thefe plain characters we rarely find;
Tho' ftrong the bent, yet quick the turns of mind:
Or puzzling Contraries confound the whole;   65
Or Affectations quite reverfe the foul.
The Dull, flat Falfhood ferves for policy;
And in the Cunning, Truth itfelf's a lie:
                                                         Un-

NOTES.

VER. 57. *At half mankind*] The character alluded to is the principal one in the Plain Dealer of Wycherly, a comedy taken from the Mifanthrope of Moliere, but much inferior to the original. Alceftes has not that bitternefs of fpirit, and has much more humanity and honour than Manly. Writers transfufe their own characters into their works: Wycherly was a vain and profligate libertine; Moliere was beloved for his candour, fweetnefs of temper, and integrity. It is remarkable that the French did not relifh this incomparable comedy on the three firft reprefentations. The ftrokes of fatire were too fubtle and delicate to be felt by the generality of the audience, who expected only the grofs diverfion of laughing; fo that, at the fourth time of its being acted, the author was forced to add to it one of his coarfeft farces; but Boileau in the mean time affirmed that it was the capital work of their ftage, and that the people would one time be induced to think fo.

VER. 61. *Hate it in a Queen,*] Meaning Queen Caroline, whom he was fond of cenfuring; as was Bolingbroke. See vol. i. p. 123. of his Works, for a bitter ridicule on her affectation of fcience.

VER. 62. *Who charms us with his Spleen.*] Clofely copied from Boileau;

    " Un efprit né chagrin plait par fon chagrin même."
It is a compliment to Swift.

Unthought-of Frailties cheat us in the Wife;
The Fool lies hid in inconsistencies.   70
                                                        See

NOTES.

VER. 69. *Unthought-of Frailties*] For who could have thought that Xenophon, during his famous retreat, performed many acts of the most vulgar superstition; that Augustus was alarmed and dispirited if he put on a slipper on his right leg which should have been on his left; that Newton once studied astrology; and that Thuanus, Dryden, and the Chancellor Shaftesbury, calculated nativities; that Roger Ascham and Dr. Whitby were devoted lovers of cock-fighting, as was Bayle of mountebanks; that Bishop Hoadley was often rallied by Dr. Clarke for his dread of thunder; that Henry IV. of France was terrified at the jolting of his coach; that Ben Johnson and Addison were hard drinkers, and our Author himself an epicure. The night before the battle of Blenheim, after a council of war had been held in the Duke of Marlborough's tent, at which Prince Louis of Baden and Prince Eugene had assisted, the latter, after the council had broke up, stept back to the tent to communicate something he had forgot to the Duke, whom he found giving orders to his aid-de-camp Colonel Selwyn (who related this fact) at the table, on which there was now only a single taper burning, all the others being extinguished the moment the council was over. "What a man is this," said Prince Eugene, "who at such a time can think of saving the ends of candles." Elizabeth was a coquette, and Bacon received a bribe. Dr. Busby had a violent passion for the stage: it was excited in him by the applauses he received in acting the Royal Slave before the king at Christ-church; and he declared, that, if the rebellion had not broke out, he had certainly engaged himself as an actor. Luther was so immoderately passionate, that he sometimes boxed Melancthon's ears; and Melancthon himself was a believer in judicial astrology, and an interpreter of dreams. Richelieu and Mazarin were so superstitious as to employ and pension Morin, a pretender to astrology, who cast the nativities of those two able politicians. Nor was Tacitus himself, who generally appears superior to superstition, untainted with this folly, as may appear from the twenty-second chapter of the sixth book of his Annals. Men of great genius have been somewhere compared to the pillar of fire that conducted the Israelites, which frequently turned a cloudy side towards the spectator.

Ep. I.   MORAL ESSAYS.   187

See the fame man, in vigour, in the gout;
Alone, in company; in place, or out;
Early at Bus'nefs, and at Hazard late;
Mad at a Fox-chafe, wife at a Debate;
Drunk at a Borough, civil at a ball;   75
Friendly at Hackney, faithlefs at Whitehall.
Catius is ever moral, ever grave,
Thinks who endures a knave, is next a knave,
                                                        Save

NOTES.

VER. 71. *See the fame man, &c.*] Of four *caufes* he here gives EXAMPLES: 1. Of the *vivacity of the imagination* (from Ver. 70 to 77.)—2. Of the *contrariety of Appetites* (from Ver. 76 to 81.)—3. Of *Affectations* (from Ver. 80 to 87.)—and 4. Of the *Inequalities of the human mind* (from Ver. 86 to 95.)   W.

VER. 72. *Alone, in company;*] The unexpected inequalities of our minds and tempers is a fubject that has been exhaufted by Montagne in the 1ft chap. of the 2d book of his Effays, which, it is evident, Pope had been reading. Nothing can be finer than the picture which Tully has given, in his oration for Cælius, of the inconfiftencies and varieties of Catiline's conduct; ending with, " Quis clarioribus viris quodam tempore jucundior? Quis turpioribus conjunctior? Quis civis meliorum partium aliquando? Quis tetrior hoftis huic civitati? Quis in voluptatibus inquinatior? Quis in laboribus patientior? Quis in rapacitate avarior? Quis in largitione effufior?" The learned Markland, in defending Euripides from a well-known objection made to the inconfiftency of the character of Iphigenia, is of opinion, that the Poet's defign, through the whole tragedy, was, in general, to fhew the inequality and inconfiftency of the human character; and gives inftances of this inconfiftency in the behaviour of Agamemnon, Menelaus, Achilles, the Chorus, and all the perfons introduced, except Clytemneftra; intending to difplay humani animi levitatem et inconftantiam in confiliis fuis, et nos omnes æquè effe homines." Eurip. Iphig. Ant. p. 191.

VER. 77. *Ever grave,*] I here add a fenfible reflection of Rochefoucault, that the reader may compare it with one of the great Confucius on the fame fubject: " Gravity," fays the former,

Save juſt at dinner—then prefers, no doubt,
A Rogue with Ven'ſon to a Saint without. 80
Who would not praiſe Patritio's high deſert,
His hand unſtain'd, his uncorrupted heart,
His comprehenſive head! all int'reſts weigh'd,
All Europe ſav'd, yet Britain not betray'd.
He thanks you not, his pride is in Picquette, 85
New-market fame, and judgment at a Bett.
 What made (ſay Montagne, or more ſage Char-
  ron!)
Otho a warrior, Cromwell a buffoon?
          A per-

VARIATIONS.

After Ver. 86. in the former Editions,
 Triumphant leaders, at an army's head,
 Hemm'd round with glories, pilfer cloth or bread;
 As meanly plunder as they bravely fought,
 Now ſave a people, and now ſave a groat.

NOTES.

mer, " is a myſterious carriage of the body to cover the defects of the mind."—" Gravity," ſays the latter, " is indeed only the rind, or bark, of wiſdom; but it preſerves it."

VER. 81. *Patritio's high deſert*,] Meaning Lord Godolphin, of whom, ſays Prior, in an original letter that I have ſeen, " as the wife Earl of Godolphin told me when he turned me out for having ſerved him;—Things change, times change, and men change." Though he was a great gameſter, yet he was an able and honeſt miniſter.

VER. 87. *What made*] One of the reaſons that makes Montagne ſo agreeable a writer is, that he gives ſo ſtrong a picture of the way of life of a country gentleman in the reign of Henry III. The deſcriptions of his caſtle, of his library, of his travels, of his entertainments, of his diet and dreſs, are particularly pleaſing. Malebranche and Paſcal have ſeverely and juſtly cenſured his ſcepticiſm. Peter Charron contracted a very ſtrict friendſhip with
                 him,

A perjur'd Prince, a leaden Saint revere,
A godlefs Regent tremble at a Star ? 90
The

NOTES.

him, infomuch that Montagne permitted him by his will to bear his arms. In his Book of Wifdom, which was publifhed at Bourdeaux in the year 1601, he has inferted a great number of Montagne's fentiments. This treatife has been loudly blamed for its freedom by many writers of France, and particularly Garaffe the Jefuit. Bayle has remarked, in oppofition to thefe cenfurers, that, of a hundred thoufand readers, there are hardly three to be found in any age who are well qualified to judge of a book, wherein the ideas of an exact and metaphyfical reafoning are fet in oppofition to the moft common opinions. Pope has borrowed many fenfible remarks from Charron, of whom Bolingbroke was particularly fond.

Who would imagine, from the boldnefs of Hobbes's fentiments, that he was naturally a great coward.

VER. 89. *A perjur'd Prince,*] Louis XI. of France wore in his hat a leaden image of the Virgin Mary, which, when he fwore by, he feared to break his oath. P.

VER. 90. *A godlefs Regent tremble at a Star ?*] Philip Duke of Orleans, Regent in the minority of Louis XV. fuperftitious in judicial aftrology, though an unbeliever in all religion. P.

The fame has been obferved of many other *politicians.* The Italians, in general, are not more noted for their refined politics, than for their attachment to the dotages of *Aftrology,* under the influence of *Atheifm.* It may be worth while to inquire into the caufe of fo fingular a phenomenon, as it may probably do honour to Religion. Thefe men obferving (and none have equal opportunities of fo doing) how perpetually public events fall out befides their expectation, and contrary to the beft laid fchemes of worldly policy, cannot but confefs that human affairs are ordered by fome power extrinfical. To acknowledge a God and his Providence, would be next to introducing a morality deftructive of that civil fyftem which they think neceffary for the government of the world. They have recourfe therefore to that abfurd fcheme of power which rules by no other law than *Fate* or *Deftiny.* W.

The Duke of Orleans, here pointed at, was an infidel and a libertine, and at the fame time, as well as Bouranvilliers and Cardan, who calculated the nativity of Jefus Chrift, was a bigotted believer

The throne a Bigot keep, a Genius quit,
Faithlefs through Piety, and dup'd through Wit?
Europe a Woman, Child, or Dotard rule,
And juft her wifeft monarch made a fool?
 Know, GOD and NATURE only are the fame: 95
In Man, the judgment fhoots at flying game;
A bird of paffage! gone as foon as found;
Now in the Moon perhaps, now under ground.

II.

In vain the Sage, with retrofpective eye,
Would from th' apparent What conclude the Why,
Infer the Motive from the Deed, and fhew, 101
That what we chanc'd was what we meant to do.
Behold! if Fortune or a Miftrefs frowns,
Some plunge in bus'nefs, others fhave their crowns:
To eafe the Soul of one oppreffive weight, 105
This quits an Empire, that embroils a State:

            The

NOTES.

believer in judicial aftrology; he was faid to be the author, which however has been doubted, of many of thofe flimfy fongs, nugæ canoræ, to which the language and manners of France feem to be peculiarly adapted. He knew mankind. "Quiconque eft fans honneur et fans humeur, eft un courtifan parfaite," was one of his favourite fayings.

 VER. 91. *The throne a Bigot keep, a Genius quit,*] Philip V. of Spain, who, after renouncing the throne for Religion, refumed it to gratify his Queen; and Victor Amadeus II. King of Sardinia, who refigned the Crown, and trying to re-affume it, was imprifoned till his death.   P.

 VER. 93. *Europe a Woman, Child, or Dotard rule,*
   And juft her wifeft monarch made a fool?]
The Czarina, the King of France, the Pope, and the above-mentioned King of Sardinia.   W.

 VER. 95. GOD *and* NATURE] It is not very clear what is precifely meant by Nature in this paffage.

The fame aduſt complexion has impell'd
Charles to the Convent, Philip to the Field.
    Not always Actions ſhew the man : we find
Who does a kindneſs, is not therefore kind ;   110
Perhaps Proſperity becalm'd his breaſt ;
Perhaps the Wind, juſt ſhifted from the eaſt :
Not therefore humble he who ſeeks retreat,
Pride guides his ſteps, and bids him ſhun the Great :
Who combats bravely, is not therefore brave,   115
He dreads a death-bed like the meaneſt ſlave ;
Who reaſons wiſely is not therefore wiſe,
His pride in Reas'ning, not in Acting lies.
    But grant that Actions beſt diſcover man ;
Take the moſt ſtrong, and ſort them as you can.   120
The few that glare each character muſt mark,
You balance not the many in the dark.
What will you do with ſuch as diſagree ?
Supprefs them, or miſcall them Policy ?
Muſt then at once (the character to ſave)   125
The plain rough Hero turn a crafty Knave ?
                                        Alas !

NOTES.

VER. 107. *The ſame aduſt complexion has impell'd
    Charles to the Convent, Philip to the Field.*]
Philip II. was of an atrabilaire complexion. He derived it from his father Charles V. whoſe health, the hiſtorians of his life tell us, was frequently diſordered by bilious fevers. But what was moſt extraordinary, the ſame complexion not only drove them variouſly, but made each act contrary to his character ; Charles, who was an active man when he retired into a Convent ; Philip, who was a man of the cloſet when he gave the battle of St. Quintin.   W.

    All that wants to be known of this Emperor's character may be learned from Robertſon's admirable Hiſtory.

Alas! in truth the man but chang'd his mind,
Perhaps was sick, in love, or had not din'd.
                                                Ask

NOTES.

VER. 127. *Alas! in truth*] "For the destruction of a kingdom," said a man of wit, "nothing more is sometimes requisite than a bad digestion of the prime minister." The Grand Seignior offered to assist Henry IV. against his rebellious subjects, not for any deep political reason, but only because he hated the word League. It is a fault in Davila, as well as Tacitus, never to ascribe great events to whim, caprice, private passions, and petty causes. The Treaty of Utrecht was occasioned, it is said, by a quarrel betwixt the Duchess of Marlborough and Queen Anne about a pair of gloves. The expedition to the island of Ré was undertaken to gratify a foolish and romantic passion of the Duke of Buckingham. The coquetry of the daughter of Count Julien introduced the Saracens into Spain. It is for the honour of many great events, as of many great families, that their origins should be concealed. Bayle, in his Thoughts on the Comet, tome ii. p. 214. has collected a number of entertaining instances to confirm this truth, "that mighty rivers, which desolate or fertilize great tracts of land, issue sometimes from a small and dirty fountain."

Hear the sentiments of one who was well acquainted with life and business. "I have been frequently assured," says Swift, "that politics were nothing but common sense; which, as 'it was the only true thing they spoke, so it was the only thing they could have wished I should not believe. I have been assured, by men long practised in business, that the secrets of a court are much fewer than we generally suppose; and I hold it for the greatest secret of a court that they are so. I could produce innumerable instances, from my own memory and observation, of events imputed to the profound skill and address of the minister, which in reality were either the mere effect of negligence, weakness, humour, passion, or pride; or, at best, but the natural course of things left to themselves." Free Thoughts on the State of Affairs, 1714.

What was the cause of the Reformation in England,
  "When Love could teach a monarch to be wise,
  And Gospel-truth first dawn'd from Bullen's eyes?"

But Burnet gravely labours to prove, that the king had a scruple

Afk why from Britain Cæfar would retreat?
Cæfar himfelf might whifper he was beat. 130
Why

VARIATIONS.

Ver. 129. in the former Editions,
Afk why from Britain Cæfar made retreat?
Cæfar himfelf would tell you he was beat.
The mighty Czar what mov'd to wed a Punk?
The mighty Czar would tell you he was drunk.

Altered as above, becaufe Cæfar wrote his Commentaries of this war, and does *not* tell you he was beat. And as Cæfar afforded an inftance of both cafes, it was thought better to make him the fingle example.

NOTES.

of confcience for having married his brother's widow. It has been faid, that the firft difguft Cæfar gave to the Romans was his not rifing from his feat to receive a deputation from the Senate, which at the moment he could not venture to do, being taken with a dyfentery, and which they interpreted as a mark of haughtinefs, and an air of tyranny, which ultimately occafioned his affaffination.

VER. 129. *Afk why from*] In former Editions, the third and fourth lines were,

The mighty Czar what mov'd to wed a Punk?
The mighty Czar would tell you he was drunk.

But it was altered as above; and altered for the worfe. It is ftrange that Pope, or his learned friends, fhould not have known that drunkennefs was not one of Cæfar's vices. Suetonius fays, " Vini parciffimum ne inimici quidem negaverunt." Verbum M. Catonis eft, " Unum ex omnibus Cæfarem ad evertendam rempublicam fobrium acceffiffe." Vit. D. Julius Cæfar, fection 53. Aaron Hill, in his Letters, faid, he had in his poffeffion fome authentic documents that would redound to the honour of the Czar, for making this match with Catherine, and would place this part of his conduct, which the malice of fome great courts in Europe had taken pains to mifreprefent, in another and very honourable point of view.

VER. 130. *Cæfar himfelf might whifper he was beat.*] Cæfar wrote his *Commentaries*, in imitation of the Greek Generals, for

Why rifk the world's great empire for a Punk?
Cæfar perhaps might anfwer he was drunk.
But, fage hiftorians! 'tis your tafk to prove
One action conduct; one, heroic Love.
'Tis from high Life, high characters are drawn;
A Saint in Crape is twice a Saint in Lawn;   136
A Judge is juft, a Chanc'lor jufter ftill;
A Gownman, learn'd; a Bifhop, what you will;
Wife, if a Minifter; but, if a King,
More wife, more learn'd, more juft, more ev'ry thing.
                                                Court-

NOTES.

the entertainment of the world: But had his friend afked him, in his ear, the reafon of his fudden retreat from Britain, after fo many pretended victories, we have caufe to fufpect, even from his own public relation of that matter, that he would have *whifper'd he was beat*.   W.

VER. 131. *Why rifk the world's great empire for a Punk?*] After the battle of Pharfalia, Cæfar purfued his enemy to Alexandria, where he became infatuated with the charms of Cleopatra, and inftead of pufhing his advantages, and difperfing the relics of the Pharfalian quarrel, brought upon himfelf (after narrowly efcaping the violence of an enraged populace) an unneceffary war, at a time his arms were moft wanted elfewhere.   W.

VER. 133. *But, fage hiftorians!*] " Si on pouvait," fays a fhrewd wit, " confronter Suetone avec les valets de chambre des douze Cefars, penfe-t-on qu'ils feraient toujours d'accord avec lui?—Mallebranche, à cet egard, avait raifon de dire, qu'il ne fefait pas plus de cas de l'Hiftoire, que des nouvelles de fon quartier."

VER. 135. *'Tis from high Life,*] Copied from Boileau, v. 203. Sat. 8.

VER. 137. *A Judge is juft, a Chanc'lor jufter ftill;*
A Gownman, learn'd; a Bifhop, what you will;
Each profeffion is here equally turned into ridicule; but not with equal juftice. The *Lawyer at the Bar* pleads indifferently for right
                                                and

Court-Virtues bear, like Gems, the higheſt rate. 141
Born where Heav'n's influence fcarce can penetrate:
In life's low vale, the foil the Virtues like,
They pleafe as beauties, here as wonders ſtrike.
Tho' the fame fun with all-diffufive rays 145
Bluſh in the Rofe, and in the Di'mond blaze,
We prize the ſtronger effort of his pow'r,
And juſtly fet the Gem above the Flow'r.
'Tis Education forms the common mind,
Juſt as the Twig is bent, the Tree's inclin'd. 150
Boaſtful and rough, your firſt fon is a 'Squire;
The next a Tradeſman, meek, and much a liar;
                                            Tom

NOTES.

and wrong. On the *Bench* he is the moſt zealous Patron and In-
veſtigator of Truth. The *Divine*, on the contrary, while in a
private ſtation, confults only the honour of his Religion; but
when advanced to a public, he is only anxious that *the Miniſtry be
not blamed*. Whence comes this difference? Not from their own
difpofitions, but from that of the times: in which, *Juſtice* is fuppofed to be neceſſary to civil Society; and *Religion*, of no fuch
ufe. Therefore the Lawyer, when advanced into the Magiſtracy,
is invariably attached to the Right; and the Churchman in Authority, muſt give no offence. W.

VER. 141. *Court-Virtues bear, like Gems, &c.*] This whole reflection, and the fimilitude brought to fupport it, have great delicacy of ridicule, together with all the charms of Wit and
Poetry. W.

VER. 151. *Boaſtful and rough,*] How much knowledge of life,
of manners, and characters, is contained in the eleven fucceeding
lines! We are not to afcribe fo much to the powerful influence
of educatian alone, as does Helvetius in his fanciful Treatife de
L'Efprit, who imagines and afferts that all men are born with
equal talents, and that it is education alone that caufes any difference or fuperiority in different men. It is the common mind
that is formed by education; which has not the fame effect on
                                            minds,

Tom ſtruts a Soldier, open, bold, and brave;
Will ſneaks a Scriv'ner, an exceeding knave: 154
Is he a Churchman? then he's fond of pow'r:
A Quaker? ſly: a Preſbyterian? ſour:
A ſmart Free-thinker? all things in an hour.

Aſk men's Opinions: Scoto now ſhall tell
How trade increaſes, and the world goes well;
Strike off his Penſion, by the ſetting ſun,   160
And Britain, if not Europe, is undone.

That gay Free-thinker, a fine talker once,
What turns him now a ſtupid ſilent dunce?
Some God, or Spirit he has lately found;
Or chanc'd to meet a Miniſter that frown'd. 165

Judge

VARIATIONS.

VER. 165. *Or chanc'd to meet Sir Robert when he frown'd.*

NOTES.

minds, on which nature and conſtitution have imprinted deep and ſtrong marks of original genius. It is impoſſible not to lament that Gray did not finiſh the deſign he ſketched out, of an Eſſay on the Alliance of Education and Government, which, from the ſpecimens we find in his life, (page 193.) would doubtleſs have been a maſter-piece of didactic poetry.

VER. 156. *A Preſbyterian? ſour:*] If it be aſked, why *Preſbyterian* Divines, of the puritan ſtamp, took more ſatisfaction, in their ſermons and diſcourſes, to quote the *Old Teſtament* than the *New*; it may be ſaid, that their gloomy *ſour* temper found moſt ſolace in the terrors of the God of Iſrael; and their pride was moſt indulged in having, like the Jews, a God to themſelves. W.———
This is not applicable to the preſent mode of preaching uſed by the diſſenting miniſters.

VER. 164, 165. *Some God, or Spirit he has lately found;*
         Or chanc'd to meet a Miniſter that frown'd.]
Diſaſters the moſt unlooked-for, as they were what the Freethinker's *ſpeculations* and *practice* were principally directed to avoid.
—The

MORAL ESSAYS.

Judge we by Nature? Habit can efface,
Int'reſt o'ercome, or Policy take place:
By Actions? thoſe Uncertainty divides:
By Paſſions? theſe Diſſimulation hides:
Opinions? they ſtill take a wider range: 170
Find, if you can, in what you cannot change.
                                        Manners

NOTES.

—The Poet here alludes to the antient claſſical opinion, that the ſudden viſion of a God was wont to ſtrike the irreverent obſerver ſpeechleſs. He has only a little extended the conceit, and ſuppoſed, that the terrors of a *Court-Deity* might have the like effect on one of theſe devoted worſhippers.   SCRIBL.

VER. 166. *Judge we by Nature?*] We find here, in the compaſs of eight lines, an anatomy of human nature; more ſenſe and obſervation cannot well be compreſſed and concluded in a narrower ſpace. This paſſage might be drawn out into a voluminous commentary, and be worked up into a ſyſtem concerning the knowledge of the world. There ſeems to be an inaccuracy in the uſe of the laſt verb; the natural temperament is by no means ſuddenly changed, or turned, with a change of climate, though undoubtedly the humours are originally formed by it. " Influenced by," would be a more proper expreſſion than " turn with," if the metre would admit it.

I have ſeen a collection of all the paſſages, in Horace and Pope, that relate to men and manners, placed together and compared with each other. The ſuperiority was given to Pope, for a deeper knowledge of human nature than could be found in Horace.

We may juſtly apply to Pope what Cicero ſays ſo finely of Thucydides: " Omnes dicendi artificio, meâ ſententiâ facilè vicit, ut verborum prope numerum, ſententiarum numero conſequatur; ità porro verbis aptus et preſſus, ut neſcias utrum res oratione, an verba ſententiis illuſtrentur."

VER. 171. *In what you cannot change.*] " Combien diverſement jugeons nous de choſes?" ſays honeſt Montaigne. " Combien de fois changeons nous nos fantaſies? Ce que je tien aujourdhuy, ce que je croy, je le tien et le croy, de toute ma creance; mais ne m'eſt-il pas advenu, non une fois mais cent; mais mille et tous les jours, d'avoir

Manners with Fortunes, Humours turn with Climes,
Tenets with Books, and Principles with Times.

III.

Search then the RULING PASSION: There, alone,
The Wild are conſtant, and the Cunning known;
The

NOTES.

d'avoir embraſſé quelque autre choſe?" Montaigne furniſhed many hints for this Epiſtle.

VER. 172. *Manners with Fortunes,*] Are there any two lines in Horace or Boileau ſo replete with ſtrong ſenſe, and ſo condenſed and crowded with matter, as theſe two of our Author? I have often amuſed myſelf by thinking what ſort of magiſtrates Dante and Montaigne made, when the former was mayor of Florence and the latter of Bourdeaux. Did their manners change with their ſtations?

VER. 174. *The* RULING PASSION:] Two eminent writers have attacked our Author's notion of a Ruling Paſſion, Mr. Harris and Dr. Johnſon: The former ſays, " One talks of an univerſal paſſion; as if all paſſions were not univerſal. Another talks of a Ruling Paſſion; and means, without knowing it, certain ruling opinions. Thus, when ſpecious falſehood aſſumes the lyre, we are charmed with the muſic, and worſhip her as truth."

" Of any paſſion," ſays Johnſon, " thus innate and irreſiſtible, the exiſtence may reaſonably be doubted. Human characters are by no means conſtant; men change, by change of place, of fortune, of acquaintance; he who is at one time a lover of pleaſure, is at another a lover of money. Thoſe, indeed, who attain any excellence, commonly ſpend life in one purſuit; for excellence is not often gained upon eaſier terms. But to the particular ſpecies of excellence men are directed, not by an aſcendant planet or predominating humour, but by the firſt book which they read, ſome early converſation which they heard, or ſome accident which excited ardour and emulation.

" It muſt be at leaſt allowed, that this ruling paſſion, antecedent to reaſon and obſervation, muſt have an object independent on human contrivance; for there can be no natural deſire of artificial good. No man, therefore, can be born, in the ſtricteſt acceptation,

MORAL ESSAYS.

The Fool confiftent, and the Falfe fincere; 176
Priefts, Princes, Women, no Diffemblers here.
This clue once found, unravels all the reft,
The profpect clears, and WHARTON ftands confeft.
Wharton, the fcorn and wonder of our days, 180
Whofe Ruling Paffion was the Luft of Praife:

Born

NOTES.

tion, a lover of money; for he may be born where money does not exift: nor can he be born, in a moral fenfe, as a lover of his country; for fociety, politically regulated, is a ftate contradiftinguifhed from a ftate of nature; and any attention to that coalition of interefts which makes the happinefs of a country, is poffible only to thofe whom inquiry and reflection have enabled to comprehend it.

" This doctrine is in itfelf pernicious as well as falfe: its tendency is to produce the belief of a kind of moral predeftination or over-ruling principle which cannot be refifted; he that admits it is prepared to comply with every defire that caprice or opportunity fhall excite, and to flatter himfelf that he fubmits only to the lawful dominion of nature, in obeying the refiftlefs authority of his Ruling Paffion.

" Pope has formed his theory with fo little fkill, that, in the examples by which he illuftrates and confirms it, he has confounded paffions, appetites, and habits."

I fhall add, that the expreffion, Ruling Paffion, was firft ufed by Rofcommon. See how much is attributed to the effects of a Ruling Paffion. Effay on Man, Epiftle ii. v. 132.

VER. 177. *Priefts, Princes, Women, no* DISSEMBLERS *here.*] Infinuating that one common principle, *the purfuit of Power,* gives a conformity of conduct to the moft diftant and different characters. W.

VER. 181. *The Luft of Praife:*] This very well expreffes the *groffnefs* of his appetite for it; where the ftrength of the paffion had deftroyed all the delicacy of the fenfation. W.

Born with whate'er could win it from the Wife,
Women and Fools muſt like him, or he dies;
Tho' wond'ring Senates hung on all he ſpoke,
The Club muſt hail him maſter of the joke.   185
Shall parts ſo various aim at nothing new?
He'll ſhine a Tully and a Wilmot too.
Then turns repentant, and his God adores
With the ſame ſpirit that he drinks and whores;
Enough, if all around him but admire,   190
And now the Punk applaud, and now the Fryer,
Thus with each gift of nature and of art,
And wanting nothing but an honeſt heart;
Grown all to all, from no one Vice exempt;
And moſt contemptible to ſhun contempt;   195
His Paſſion ſtill, to covet gen'ral praiſe,
His Life, to forfeit it a thouſand ways;
A conſtant Bounty which no friend has made;
An angel Tongue, which no man can perſuade!

A Fool,

NOTES.

Ver. 187. John Wilmot, Earl of Rocheſter, famous for his wit and extravagancies in the time of Charles the Second.   W.

Ver. 189. *With the ſame* ſpirit] Spirit for *principle*, not *paſſion*.   W.

Ver. 190. *Enough, if all around him but admire, &c.*] What an able French writer obſerves of *Alcibiades* may be juſtly applied to this nobleman. "Ce n'étoit pas un *ambitieux*, mais un homme *vain*, qui vouloit fair du bruit, et occuper les Atheniens. Il avoit l'*eſprit* d'un grand homme; mais ſon *ame*, dont les reſſorts amollis étoient devenus incapables d'une application conſtante, ne pouvoit s'élever au grand, que par boutade. J'ai bien de la peine à croire, qu'un homme aſſez ſouple, pour être à Sparte auſſi dur et auſſi ſévere, qu'un Spartiate; dans l'Ionie auſſi recherché dans ſes plaiſirs, qu'un Ionien, &c. fût propre à faire un grand homme."   W.

A Fool, with more of Wit than half mankind, 200
Too raſh for Thought, for Action too refin'd:
A Tyrant to the Wife his heart approves;
A Rebel to the very king he loves;
He dies, ſad out-caſt of each church and ſtate,
And, harder ſtill! flagitious, yet not great. 205
Aſk you why Wharton broke thro' ev'ry rule?
'Twas all for fear the Knaves ſhould call him Fool.

Nature

NOTES.

VER. 200. *A Fool, with more of Wit*] *Folly*, joined with much wit, produces that behaviour which we call *abſurdity*; and this abſurdity the Poet has here admirably deſcribed in the words,

" Too raſh for Thought, for Action too refin'd:"

by which we are given to underſtand, that the perſon deſcribed, indulged his fancy when he ſhould have uſed his judgment; and purſued his ſpeculations when he ſhould have truſted to his experience. W.

VER. 205. *And, harder ſtill! flagitious, yet not great.*] To arrive at what the world calls GREATNESS, a wicked man muſt either hide and conceal his vices, or he muſt openly and ſteadily practiſe them in the purſuit and attainment of one important end. This unhappy nobleman did neither. W.

VER. 206. *Aſk you why Wharton*] " This celebrated peer," ſays Lord Orford, " like Buckingham and Rocheſter, comforted all the grave and dull by throwing away the brighteſt profuſion of parts on witty fooleries, debaucheries, and ſcrapes, which may mix graces with a great character, but never can compoſe one. If Julius Cæſar had only rioted with Cataline, he had never been emperor of the world. Indeed the Duke of Wharton was not made for conqueſt; he was not equally formed for a Round-houſe and Pharſalia. In one of his ballads he has bantered his own want of heroiſm; it was in a ſong he made on being ſeized by the guard in St. James's Park, for ſinging the Jacobite air, ' The king ſhall have his own again:'

" The duke he drew out half his ſword,
———The guard drew out the reſt."

Nature well known, no prodigies remain,
Comets are regular, and WHARTON plain.
                                                    Yet,

VARIATIONS.

VER. 208. In the former Editions,
Nature well known, no *Miracles* remain.
Altered as above, for very obvious reasons.

NOTES.

His levities, wit, and want of principles, his eloquence and adventures, are too well known to be recapitulated. With attachment to no party, though with talents to govern any party, this lively man changed the free air of Westminster for the gloom of the Escurial, the prospect of King George's garter for the Pretender's; and, with indifference to all religion, the frolic lord, who had writ the ballad on the Archbishop of Canterbury, died in the habit of a capuchin.

It is difficult to give an account of the works of so mercurial a man, whose library was a tavern, and women of pleasure his muses. A thousand sallies of his imagination may have been lost: he no more wrote for fame than he acted for it. There are two volumes in octavo, called his Life and Writings, but containing of the latter nothing but " seventy four numbers of a periodical paper, called the True Briton," and his celebrated " Speech in the House of Lords on the third reading of the bill to inflict pains and penalties on Francis Lord Bishop of Rochester, May 15, 1723." It is a remarkable anecdote relating to this speech, that his Grace, then in opposition to the Court, went to Chelsea the day before the last debate on that prelate's affair, where acting contrition, he professed being determined to work out his pardon at Court, by speaking against the bishop, in order to which he begged some hints. The minister was deceived, and went through the whole cause with him, pointing out where the strength of the argument lay, and where its weakness. The duke was very thankful, returned to town, passed the night in drinking, and, without going to bed, went to the House of Lords, where he spoke for the bishop, recapitulating, in the most masterly manner, and answering all that had been urged against him. His speech against the Ministry, two years before, on the affair of the South-Sea Company, had a fatal effect, Earl Stanhope answering it with so much warmth that he broke a blood-vessel and died.

Yet, in this search, the wisest may mistake, 210
If second qualities for first they take.
When Catiline by rapine swell'd his store ;
When Cæsar made a noble dame a whore ;
In this the Lust, in that the Avarice
Were means, not ends ; Ambition was the vice. 215
That

NOTES.

VER. 207. *'Twas all for fear, &c.*] To understand this, we must observe, that the *lust of general praise* made the person, whose character is here so admirably drawn, both *extravagant* and *flagitious*; his *madness* was to please the Fools,
" *Women* and *Fools* must like him, or he dies."
And his *crimes*, to avoid the censure of the Knaves,
" 'Twas all for fear the *Knaves* should call him fool."
Prudence and *Honesty* being the two qualities, in which fools and knaves are most interested, and consequently most industrious, to misrepresent. W.

VER. 213. *When Cæsar made*] This was Servilia, the sister of Cato, and the mother of Brutus. " How great," says St. Real, finely, " must have been her affliction at the death of Cæsar her son's lover, massacred by the hand of her own son ! who perhaps hoped to efface this suspicion of his bastardy by this very action ! Historians have neglected to inform us of the fate of this most unhappy mistress and mother. Nothing could have been more interesting than the history of Servilia after this event. Next to Cleopatra, she was the most beloved of all Cæsar's mistresses ; and Suetonius says, Cæsar bought for her a single jewel at the price of 50,000 l.

VER. 214. *In this the Lust,*] The same passion excited Richelieu to throw up the dyke at Rochelle, and to dispute the prize of poetry with Corneille ; whom to traduce was the surest method of gaining the affection of this ambitious minister ; nay, who formed a design to be canonized as a Saint. A perfect contrast to the character of Cardinal Fleury, who shewed that it was possible to govern a great state with moderate abilities and a mild temper. His ministry is impartially represented by Voltaire in the age of Louis XIV.

That very Cæsar born in Scipio's days,
Had aim'd, like him, by Chastity at praise.
Lucullus, when Frugality could charm,
Had roasted turnips in the Sabin farm.
In vain th' observer eyes the builder's toil, 220
But quite mistakes the scaffold for the pile.
  In this one Passion man can strength enjoy,
As Fits give vigour, just when they destroy.
Time, that on all things lays his lenient hand,
Yet tames not this; it sticks to our last sand. 225
Consistent in our follies and our sins,
Here honest Nature ends as she begins.

Old

NOTES.

Ver. 215. *Ambition was the vice.*] *Pride*, *Vanity*, and *Ambition* are such bordering and neighbouring vices, and hold so much in common, that we generally find them going together; and therefore, as generally mistake them for one another. This does not a little contribute to our confounding characters; for they are, in reality, very different and distinct; so much so, that it is remarkable, the three greatest men in Rome, and cotemporaries, possessed each of these passions separately, with very little mixture of the other two: The men I mean were Cæsar, Cato, and Cicero: for Cæsar had *ambition* without either vanity or pride; Cato had *pride* without ambition or vanity; and Cicero had *vanity* without pride or ambition. The aim of these passions too, are very different. Vanity leads men, as it did Cicero, to seek homage from others: Pride, as it did Cato, to seek homage from one's self: And Ambition, as in the case of Cæsar, to dispense with it from all, for the sake of solid interest. W.

Ver. 225. *It sticks to our last sand, &c.*] " M. de Lagny mourut le 12 Avril 1734. Dans les derniers momens, où il ne connoissoit plus aucun de ceux qui etoient autour de son lit, quelqu'un, pour faire une experience philosophique, s'avisa de lui demander quel étoit le quarré de douze: Il repondit dans l'instant, et apparemment sans savoir qu'il repondit, cent quarante quatre." *Fontenelle, Eloge de M. de Lagny.*

Old Politicians chew on wifdom paft,
And totter on in bus'nefs to the laft;
As weak, as earneft; and as gravely out,   230
As fober Lanefb'row dancing in the gout.
                                        Behold

NOTES.

VER. 228. *Old Politicians*] The ftrength and continuance of what our Author calls the Ruling Paffion, concerning which fee ver. 174. and the notes, is ftrongly exemplified in thefe eight characters, namely, the Politician, the Debauchee, the Glutton, the Economift, the Coquet, the Courtier, the Mifer, and the Patriot. Of thefe characters, the moft lively, becaufe the moft dramatic, are the fifth and feventh. There is true humour alfo in the circumftance of the frugal Crone, who blows out one of the confecrated tapers in order to prevent its wafting.—Shall I venture to infert another example or two?—An old ufurer, lying in his laft agonies, was prefented by the prieft with the crucifix. He opened his eyes a moment before he expired, attentively gazed on it, and cried out, " Thefe jewels are counterfeit; I cannot lend more than ten piftoles upon fo wretched a pledge." To reform the language of his country was the ruling paffion of Malherbe. The prieft, who attended him in his laft moments, afked him if he was not affected with the defcription he gave him of the joys of heaven? " By no means," anfwered the incorrigible bard; " I defire to hear no more of them, if you cannot defcribe them in a purer ftyle." Both thefe ftories would have fhone under the hands of Pope.

This doctrine of our Author may be farther illuftrated by the following paffage of Bacon: " It is no lefs worthy to obferve how little alteration, in good fpirits, the approaches of death make, for they appear to be the fame men till the laft inftant. Auguftus Cæfar died in a compliment; Livia, conjugii noftri memor, vive et vale. Tiberius, in diffimulation; as Tacitus faith of him, Jam Tiberium vires et corpus, non diffimulatio deferebant. Vefpafian, in a jeft; Ut puto Deus fio. Galba, with a fentence; Feri, fi ex re fit populi Romani; holding forth his neck. Septimus Severus, in a difpatch; Adefte, fi quid mihi reftat agendum."

This Epiftle concludes with a ftroke of art worthy admiration. The Poet fuddenly ftops the vein of ridicule with which he was flowing, and addreffes his friend in a moft delicate compliment, concealed under the appearance of fatire.

Behold a rev'rend fire, whom want of grace
Has made the father of a namelefs race,
Shov'd from the wall perhaps, or rudely prefs'd
By his own fon, that paffes by unblefs'd: 235
Still to his wench he crawls on knocking knees,
And envies ev'ry fparrow that he fees.

   A falmon's belly, Helluo, was thy fate;
The doctor call'd, declares all help too late:
" Mercy!" cries Helluo, " mercy on my foul! 240
" Is there no hope?——Alas!——then bring the
   " jowl."

   The frugal Crone, whom praying priefts attend,
Still tries to fave the hallow'd taper's end,
                                  Collects

NOTES.

VER. 231. *Lanefb'row*] An ancient Nobleman, who continued this practice long after his legs were difabled by the gout. Upon the death of Prince George of Denmark, he demanded an audience of the Queen, to advife her to preferve her health and difpel her grief by *dancing*.   .   P.

VER. 241. *Then bring the jowl.*] It is remarkable that a fimilar ftory may be found in the eighth book of Athenæus, concerning the poet Philoxenus, a writer of dithyrambics, who grew fick by eating a whole polypus, except the head; and who, when his phyfician told him he would never recover from his furfeit, called out, " Bring me then the head of the polypus." It is not here infinuated that Pope was a reader of Athenæus; but he evidently copied this ludicrous inftance of gluttony from La Fontaine:

    " Puis qu'il faut que je meure
       Sans faire tant de façon,
     Qu'on m'apporte tout à l'heure
      Le refte de mon poiffon."

VER. 242. *The frugal Crone, &c.*] A fact told him, by Lady Bolingbroke of an old Countefs at Paris.

Collects her breath, as ebbing life retires,
For one puff more, and in that puff expires. 245
" Odious! in woollen! 'twould a Saint provoke,"
(Were the laſt words that poor Narciſſa ſpoke,)
" No, let a charming Chintz and Bruſſels lace
" Wrap my cold limbs, and ſhade my lifeleſs face;
" One would not, ſure, be frightful when one's
  " dead— 250
" And—Betty—give this Cheek a little Red."
The Courtier ſmooth, who forty years had ſhin'd
An humble ſervant to all human kind,
Juſt brought out this, when ſcarce his tongue could
  ſtir,
" If—where I'm going—I could ſerve you, Sir?"
" I give and I deviſe" (old Euclio ſaid, 256
And ſigh'd) " my lands and tenements to Ned."
Your money, Sir? " My money, Sir, what all?
" Why,—if I muſt—(then wept) I give it Paul."
                                              The

NOTES.

VER. 245. *Expires.*] He repeated theſe four lines to Mr. J. Richardſon many years before they were here inſerted.

VER. 247. *The laſt words that poor Narciſſa ſpoke*] This ſtory, as well as the others, is founded on faɗt, though the author had the goodneſs not to mention the names. Several attribute this in particular to a very celebrated Aɗtreſs, who, in deteſtation of the thought of being buried in woollen, gave theſe her laſt orders with her dying breath. P.

The Betty here mentioned was Mrs. Saunders, Mrs. Oldfield's friend and confidante; a good aɗtreſs in parts of decayed widows and old maids.

The Manor, Sir?—" The Manor! hold," he cry'd,
" Not that,—I cannot part with that"—and dy'd.
  And you! brave COBHAM, to the lateſt breath,
Shall feel your Ruling Paſſion ſtrong in death:
Such in thoſe moments as in all the paſt;
" Oh, ſave my Country, Heav'n," ſhall be your laſt. 265

NOTES.

VER. 261. *And dy'd.*] Sir William Bateman uſed theſe very words on his death-bed. No comic nor ſatyric writer has ever carried their deſcriptions of avarice or gluttony ſo far as what has happened in real life. Other vices have been exaggerated; theſe two never have been.

EPISTLE II.

TO A LADY.

Of the CHARACTERS *of* WOMEN.

NOTHING so true as what you once let fall,
" Most Women have no Characters at all."
Matter too soft a lasting mark to bear,
And best distinguish'd by black, brown, or fair.

How

NOTES.

Of the Characters of WOMEN.] There is nothing in Mr. Pope's Works more highly finished, or written with greater spirit, than this Epistle: Yet its success was in no proportion to the pains he took in composing it, or the effort of genius displayed in adorning it. Something he chanced to drop in a short advertisement prefixed to it, on its first publication, may perhaps account for the small attention the Public gave to it. He said, that *no one Character in it was drawn from the Life.* They believed him on his word; and expressed little curiosity about a satire in which there was nothing personal. W.

VER. 1. *Nothing so true*] Bolingbroke, a judge of the subject, thought this Epistle the master-piece of Pope. But the bitterness of the satire is not always concealed in a laugh. The characters are lively, though uncommon. I scarcely remember one of them in our comic writers of the best order. The ridiculous is heightened by many strokes of humour, carried even to the borders of extravagance, as much as the two last lines of Boileau, quoted in the next page. The female foibles have been the subject of perhaps more wit, in every language, than any other topic that can be named. The sixth satire of Juvenal, though detestable for its obscenity,

How many pictures of one Nymph we view, 5
All how unlike each other, all how true!
Arcadia's Countefs, here, in ermin'd pride,
Is there, Paftora by a fountain fide.

Here

NOTES.

obfcenity, is undoubtedly the moft witty of all his fixteen, and is curious for the picture it exhibits of the private lives of the Roman ladies. If this Epiftle yields, in any refpect, to the tenth fatire of Boileau on the fame fubject, it is in the delicacy and variety of the tranfitions by which the French writer paffes from one character to another, always connecting each with the foregoing. It was a common faying of Boileau, fpeaking of La Bruyere, that one of the moft difficult parts of compofition was the art of tranfition. That we may fee how happily Pope has caught the manner of Boileau, let us furvey one of his portraits: it fhall be that of his learned lady:

" Qui s'offrira d'abord? c'eft cette Scavante,
Qu'eftime Roberval, et que Sauveur frequente.
D'où vient qu'elle a l'œil trouble, et le teint fi terni?
C'eft que fur le calcal, dit-on, de Caffini,
Un Aftrolabe en main, elle a dans fa goûtiere
Il fuivre Jupiter paffé le nuit entiere:
Gardons de la troubler. Sa fcience, fe croy,
Aura par s'occuper ce jour plus d'un employ.
D'un nouveau microfcope ou doit en fa préfence
Tantot chez Dalancé faire l'experience;
Puis d'une femme morte avec fon embryon,
Il faut chez Du Vernay voir la diffection."

None of Pope's female characters excel the Doris of Congreve in delicate touches of raillery and ridicule.

VER. 5. *How many pictures*] The Poet's purpofe here is to fhew, that the characters of Women are generally inconfiftent with themfelves: and this he illuftrates by fo happy a fimilitude, that we fee the folly, defcribed in it, arifes from that very principle which gives birth to this inconfiftency of character. W.

VER. 7, 8, 10, &c. *Arcadia's Countefs,—Paftora by a fountain,—Leda with a Swan,—Magdalen,—Cecilia*—] Attitudes in which

feveral

Here Fannia, leering on her own good man,
And there, a naked Leda with a Swan.   10
Let then the Fair one beautifully cry,
In Magdalen's loofe hair and lifted eye,
Or dreft in fmiles of fweet Cecilia fhine,
With fimp'ring Angels, Palms, and Harps divine;
Whether the Charmer finner it, or faint it,   15
If Folly grow romantic, I muft paint it.
   Come then, the colours and the ground prepare!
Dip in the Rainbow, trick her off in Air;
Chufe a firm Cloud, before it fall, and in it   19
Catch, ere fhe change, the Cynthia of this minute.
                                         Rufa,

NOTES.

feveral ladies affected to be drawn, and fometimes one lady in them all.—The Poet's politenefs and complaifance to the fex is obfervable in this inftance, amongft others, that whereas in the *Characters of Men* he has fometimes made ufe of real names, in the *Characters of Women* always fictitious.   P.

   But notwithftanding all the Poet's caution and complaifance, this general fatire, or rather moral analyfis of human nature, as it appears in the two fexes, will be always received very differently by them. The Men bear a general fatire moft heroically; the Women with the utmoft impatience. This is not from any ftronger confcioufnefs of guilt, for I believe the fum of Virtue in the female world does (from many accidental caufes) far exceed the fum of Virtue in the male; but from the fear that fuch reprefentations may hurt the fex in the opinion of the men: whereas the men are not at all apprehenfive that their follies or vices would prejudice them in the opinion of the women.   W.

   VER. 20. *Catch, ere fhe change, the Cynthia of this minute.*] Alluding in the expreffion to the precept of *Frefnoy*,
         —" formæ veneres captando fugaces."   W.
   " Like a dove's neck fhe fhifts her tranfient charms."
                                         Young, Sat. 5.

Rufa, whofe eye quick-glancing o'er the Park,
Attracts each light gay meteor of a Spark,
Agrees as ill with Rufa ftudying Locke,
As Sappho's di'monds with her dirty fmock;
Or Sappho at her toilet's greafy talk,   25
With Sappho fragrant at an ev'ning Mafk:
                                                           So

NOTES.

VER. 21. Inftances of contrarieties, given even from fuch characters as are moft ftrongly marked, and feemingly therefore moft
confiftent: As, I. In the *Affected*, Ver. 21, &c.   P.

VER. 21. *Rufa, whofe eye*] This character of Rufa, and the
fucceeding ones of Silia, Papillia, Narciffa, and Flavia, are precifely and entirely in the ftyle and manner of the portraits Young
has given us in his Fifth Satire on Women. - The pictures of
Young are fketched with a lighter and more fportive pencil;
thofe of our Author with a firmer hand and a chafter manner.
Pope put forth all his ftrength to excel his witty rival in this the
beft part of the Univerfal Paffion; and he has fucceeded accordingly. Both Pope and Boileau (fee his tenth fatire) have been
cenfured for their feverity on the fair fex. They have been reckoned as bad as Euripides; but furely they have not been quite fo
naughty as an old comic poet, Eubultus, in a fragment preferved
in that moft entertaining book, the Excerpta ex Trag. et Comœd.
of Grotius; 4to, p. 659. who, after mentioning Medæa, Clytemneftra, and Phædra, fuddenly ftops, and wickedly pretends
that his memory fails him in enabling him to mention any one
good character among women. The ladies of France revenged
themfelves on Boileau, by faying he was made incapable of love
and marriage, by an accident that befel him in his early youth.

VER. 23. *Agrees as ill*] This thought is expreffed with great
humour in the following ftanza, faid to mean Q. Caroline:

" Tho' Artemefia talks, by fits,
Of councils, claffics, fathers, wits;
    Reads Malbranche, Boyle, and Locke;
Yet in fome things, methinks, fhe fails,
'Twere well, if fhe would pair her nails,
    And wear a cleaner fmock."

So morning Infects that in muck begun,
Shine, buzz, and fly-blow in the setting sun.
  How soft is Silia! fearful to offend;
The frail one's advocate, the weak one's friend.   30
To her, Califta prov'd her conduct nice;
And good Simplicius asks of her advice.
Sudden, she storms! she raves! You tip the wink,
But spare your censure; Silia does not drink.
All eyes may see from what the change arose,   35
All eyes may see —— a pimple on her nose.
  Papillia, wedded to her am'rous spark,
Sighs for the shades!—" How charming is a Park!"
A Park is purchas'd, but the Fair he sees   39
All bath'd in tears—" Oh odious, odious Trees!"
  Ladies, like variegated Tulips, show;
'Tis to their Changes half their charms we owe;
Fine by defect, and delicately weak,
Their happy Spots the nice admirer take.
'Twas thus Calypso once each heart alarm'd,   45
Aw'd without Virtue, without Beauty charm'd;
Her Tongue bewitch'd as odly as her eyes;
Less Wit than Mimic, more a Wit than wife.
Strange graces still, and stranger flights she had,
Was just not ugly, and was just not mad;   50
Yet ne'er so sure our passion to create,
As when she touch'd the brink of all we hate.
                                          Narcissa's

NOTES.
  VER. 29 and 37. II. Contrarieties in the *Soft-natured.*   P.
  VER. 45. III. Contrarieties in the *Cunning* and *Artful.*   P.
  VER. 52. *As when she touch'd the brink of all we hate.*] Her charms consisted in the singular turn of her vivacity; consequently

Narcissa's nature, tolerably mild,
To make a wash, would hardly stew a child;
Has ev'n been prov'd to grant a Lover's pray'r, 55
And paid a Tradesman once to make him stare;
Gave alms at Easter, in a Christian trim,
And made a Widow happy, for a whim.
Why then declare Good-nature is her scorn,
When 'tis by that alone she can be born? 60
Why pique all mortals, yet affect a name?
A fool to Pleasure, yet a slave to Fame:
Now deep in Taylor and the Book of Martyrs,
Now drinking Citron with his Grace and Chartres:
Now Conscience chills her, and now Passion burns:
And Atheism and Religion take their turns; 66
                                                A very

NOTES.

the stronger she exerted this vivacity, the more forcible was her attraction. But when her vivacity arose to that height in which it was most attractive, it was upon the *brink* of Excess; the point where the delicacy of sensuality disappears, and all the coarseness of it stands exposed.   W.

VER. 53. IV. In the *Whimsical*.   P.

VER. 54. *Would hardly stew a child;*] This hyperbolical ridicule is carried to a great height, but in an image too disgusting. Juvenal, in his sixth satire, speaking of a great female talker, uses a pleasant hyperbole;

  " Una laboranti poterit succurrere lunæ."

VER. 57. *In a Christian trim,*] This is finely expressed; implying that her very charity was as much an exterior of Religion, as the ceremonies of the season. It was not even in a *Christian humour*, it was only *in a Christian trim:* not so much as *habit*, only *fashion*.   W.

VER. 58. *And made a Widow happy,*] There are some female characters sketched with exquisite delicacy and deep knowledge of nature, in a book where one would not expect to find them, Law's Christian Perfection.

A very Heathen in the carnal part,
Yet ſtill a ſad, good Chriſtian at her heart.
See Sin in State, majeſtically drunk;
Proud as a Peereſs, prouder as a Punk;   70
Chaſte to her Huſband, frank to all beſide,
A teeming Miſtreſs, but a barren Bride.
What then? let Blood and Body bear the fault,
Her Head's untouch'd, that noble ſeat of thought;
Such this day's doctrine — in another fit   75
She ſins with Poets through pure Love of Wit.
What has not fir'd her boſom or her brain?
Cæſar and Tall-boy, Charles and Carlema'ne.

As

VARIATIONS.

VER. 77. *What has not fir'd, &c.*] In the MS.
In whoſe mad brain the mixt ideas roll
Of Tall-boy's breeches, and of Cæſar's ſoul.

NOTES.

VER. 65. *Now Conſcience chills her,*] Madame de Montespan, during her criminal intercourſe with Louis XIV. kept her Lents ſo ſtrictly, that ſhe uſed to have her bread weighed out to her.

VER. 68. *Yet ſtill a ſad,*] I have been informed, on good authority, that this character was deſigned for the then Ducheſs of Hamilton.

VER. 69. V. In the *Lewd* and *Vicious*.   P.

VER. 70. *Proud as a Peereſs,*] Deſigned for the Ducheſs of Marlborough, who ſo much admired Congreve; and after his death cauſed a figure in wax-work to be made of him, and placed frequently at her table. This connexion is particularly hinted at in ver. 76.

She ſins with Poets———
Our Author's declaration, therefore, that no particular character was aimed at, is not true.

As Helluo, late Dictator of the Feaſt,
The Noſe of Hautgout and the Tip of Taſte, 80
Critiqu'd your wine, and analyz'd your meat,
Yet on plain Pudding deign'd at home to eat:
So Philomedé, lect'ring all mankind,
On the ſoft Paſſion, and the Taſte refin'd,
Th' Addreſs, the Delicacy—ſtoops at once, 85
And makes her hearty meal upon a Dunce.

Flavia's a Wit, has too much ſenſe to pray;
To toaſt our wants and wiſhes, is her way;
Nor aſks of God, but of her Stars, to give
The mighty bleſſing, " While we live, to live." 90
Then all for Death, that Opiate of the ſoul!
Lucretia's dagger, Roſamonda's bowl.
Say, what can cauſe ſuch impotence of mind?
A Spark too fickle, or a Spouſe too kind.
Wiſe Wretch! with pleaſures too refin'd to pleaſe;
With too much Spirit to be e'er at eaſe: 96
With too much Quickneſs ever to be taught;
With too much Thinking to have common Thought:
You purchaſe Pain with all that Joy can give,
And die of nothing but a Rage to live. 100

Turn then from Wits; and look on Simo's Mate,
No Aſs ſo meek, no Aſs ſo obſtinate.
Or her, that owns her faults, but never mends,
Becauſe ſhe's honeſt, and the beſt of Friends.
Or her, whoſe life the Church and Scandal ſhare,
For ever in a Paſſion or a Pray'r. 106
Or

NOTES.

VER. 87. VI. Contrarieties in the *Witty* and *Refined*.   P.

Or her, who laughs at Hell, but (like her Grace)
Cries, " Ah! how charming if there's no fuch place!"
Or who in fweet villicitude appears,
Of Mirth and Opium, Ratafie and Tears, 110
The daily Anodine, and nightly Draught,
To kill thofe foes to fair ones, Time and Thought.
Woman and Fool are too hard things to hit;
For true No-meaning puzzles more than Wit.
  But what are thefe to great Atoffa's mind? 115
Scarce once herfelf, by turns all Womankind!
Who, with herfelf, or others, from her birth
Finds all her life one warfare upon earth:
Shines in expofing Knaves, and painting Fools,
Yet is, whate'er fhe hates and ridicules. 120
                                                No

NOTES.

VER. 107. *Or her, who laughs at Hell,*]
  " Shall pleafures of a fhort duration chain
    A Lady's foul in everlafting pain?
    Will the Great Author us poor worms deftroy
    For now and then a fip of tranfient joy?
    No; He's for ever in a fmiling mood;
    He's like themfelves; or how could he be good?
From Young, Sat. 5. The perfon Pope intended to ridicule was the Duchefs of Montague.

VER. 115. *Great Atoffa's mind?* Atoffa is a name mentioned in Herodotus, and faid to be a follower of Sappho. She was daughter of Cyrus and fifter of Cambyfes, and married Darius. She is alfo named in the Perfæ of Æfchylus. She is faid to be the firft that wrote Epiftles. See Benfley on Phalaris, p. 385. and Dodwell againft Bentley.

VER. 120. *Yet is, whate'er fhe hates*] Thefe fpirited lines, that paint a fingular character, are defigned for the famous Duchefs of Marlborough, whom Swift had alfo feverely fatirized in the Examiner. Her beauty, her abilities, her political intrigues, are fufficiently

No thought advances, but her Eddy Brain
Whisks is about, and down it goes again.
Full

VARIATIONS.

After Ver. 122. in the MS.
    Oppress'd with wealth and wit, abundance sad!
    One makes her poor, the other makes her mad.

NOTES.

ficiently known. The violence of her temper frequently broke out into wonderful and ridiculous indecencies. In the last illness of the great Duke her husband, when Dr. Mead left his chamber, the Duchess, disliking his advice, followed him down stairs, swore at him bitterly, and was going to tear off his periwig. Her friend Dr. Hoadley, Bishop of Winchester, was present at this scene. These lines were shewn to her Grace as if they were intended for the portrait of the Duchess of Buckingham; but she soon stopped the person who was reading them to her, as the Duchess of Portland informed me, and called out aloud, " I cannot be so imposed upon: I see plainly enough for whom they are designed:" and abused Pope most plentifully on the subject, though she was afterwards reconciled to him, and courted him, and gave him a thousand pounds to suppress this portrait, which he accepted, it is said, by the persuasion of Mrs. M. Blount; and, after the Duchess's death, it was printed in a folio sheet, 1746, and afterwards here inserted with those of Philomedé and Cloe. This is the greatest blemish in our Poet's moral character. These three portraits are all animated with the most poignant wit. That of Cloe is particularly just and happy, who is represented as content merely and only to dwell in decencies, and satisfied to avoid giving offence; and is one of those many insignificant and useless beings,

    " Who want, as thro' blank life they dream along,
    Sense to be right, and passion to be wrong."

As says the ingenious author of the Universal Passion; a work that abounds in wit, observation on life, pleasantry, delicacy, urbanity, and the most well-bred raillery, without a single mark of spleen and ill-nature. These were the first characteristical satires in our language, and are written with an ease and familiarity of style very different from this author's other works. The four first were published in folio, in the year 1725; and the fifth and sixth, 1727.

Full fixty years the World has been her Trade,
The wifeft Fool much Time has ever made.
From lovelefs Youth to unrefpected Age, 125
No Paffion gratify'd, except her Rage.
So much the Fury ftill out-ran the Wit,
The Pleafure mifs'd her, and the Scandal hit.
Who breaks with her, provokes Revenge from Hell,
But he's a bolder man who dares be well. 130
Her ev'ry turn with Violence purfu'd,
No more a ftorm her Hate than Gratitude:
To that each Paffion turns, or foon or late;
Love, if it makes her yield, muft make her hate:
Superiors? death! and Equals? what a curfe! 135
But an Inferior not dependant? worfe.
Offend her, and fhe knows not to forgive;
Oblige her, and fhe'll hate you while you live:
But die, and fhe'll adore you—Then the Buft
And Temple rife— then fall again to duft. 140

Laft

NOTES.

VER. 139. *But die, and fhe'll adore you*—] " It is feldom," fays Mr. Walpole, " the public receives information on princes and favourites from the fountain-head. Flattery or invective is apt to pervert the relation of others. It is from their pens alone, whenever they are fo gracious, like the lady in queftion, as to have a paffion for fame and approbation, that we learn exactly how trifling, and foolifh, and ridiculous their views and actions were, and how often the mifchief they did proceeded from the moft inadequate caufes. We happen to know indeed, though he was no author, that the Duke of Buckingham's repulfes, in very impertinent amours, involved King James and King Charles in national quarrels with Spain and France. From her Grace of Marlborough we may collect, that Queen Anne was driven to change her miniftry, and, in confequence, the fate of Europe, becaufe fhe dared

to

Laſt night, her Lord was all that's good and great;
A Knave this morning, and his Will a Cheat.
Strange! by the Means defeated of the Ends,
By Spirit robb'd of Pow'r, by warmth of Friends,
By Wealth of follow'rs! without one diſtreſs   145
Sick of herſelf through very ſelfiſhneſs!
Atoſſa, curs'd with ev'ry granted pray'r,
Childleſs with all her Children, wants an Heir.

To

VARIATIONS.

After Ver. 148. in the MS.
This Death decides, nor lets the bleſſing fall
On any one ſhe hates, but on them all.
Curs'd chance! this only could afflict her more,
If any part ſhould wander to the poor.

NOTES.

to affect one bed-chamber woman as ſhe had done another. The Ducheſs could not comprehend how the couſins, Sarah Jennings and Abigail Hill, could ever enter into competition, though the one did but kneel to gather up the clue of favour which the other had haughtily toſſed away, and which ſhe could not recover by putting the Whole Duty of Man into the Queen's hands to teach her friendſhip. This favourite Ducheſs, who, like the proud Duke of Eſpernon, lived to brave the ſucceſſors in a court where ſhe had domineered, wound up her capricious life, where it ſeems ſhe had begun it, with an apology for her conduct. The piece, though weakened by the prudence of thoſe who were to correct it, though maimed by her Grace's own corrections, and though great part of it is rather the annals of a wardrobe than of a reign, yet has ſtill curious anecdotes, and a few of thoſe ſallies of wit which fourſcore years of arrogance could not fail to produce in ſo fantaſ- tic an underſtanding: And yet, by altering her memoirs as often as her will, ſhe diſappointed the public as much as her own family. However, the chief objects remain; and one ſees exactly how Europe and the back-ſtairs took their places in her imagination and in her narrative. The Revolution left no impreſſion on her mind, but of Queen Mary turning up bed-clothes; and the Proteſtant

Hero,

To Heirs unknown, defcends th' unguarded ftore,
Or wanders, Heav'n-directed, to the Poor.   150
    Pictures like thefe, dear Madam, to defign,
Afks no firm hand, and no unerring line;
Some wand'ring touches, fome reflected light,
Some flying ftroke alone can hit 'em right:
For how could equal Colours do the knack?   155
Cameleons who can paint in white and black?
    " Yet Cloe fure was form'd without a fpot."—
Nature in her then err'd not, but forgot.
" With ev'ry pleafing, ev'ry prudent part,   159
" Say, what can Cloe want?"—She wants a heart.
She fpeaks, behaves, and acts juft as fhe ought;
But never, never, reach'd one gen'rous Thought.
                                        Virtue

NOTES.

Hero, but of a felfifh glutton who devoured a difh of peas from his fifter-in-law. Little circumftances indeed convey the moft characteriftical ideas; but the choice of them may as often paint the genius of the writer as of the perfon reprefented. Mrs. Abigail Hill is not the only perfon tranfmitted to pofterity with marks of the Duchefs's refentment. Lord Oxford, " honeft Jack Hill, the ragged boy, the Quebec General," and others, make the fame figure in her hiftory that they did in her mind :—Sallies of paffion not to be wondered at in one who has facrificed even the private letters of her miftrefs and benefactrefs. The Queen gave her a picture in enamel, fet with diamonds. The Duchefs took off the diamonds, and gave the picture to a Mrs. Higgins to be fold."

VER. 151. *Pictures like thefe,*] A lady of wit and literature obferved to me, that fuch an Epiftle as this fhould be written every five years, fo many new and unimaginable female characters (I am afraid fhe faid foibles and follies) daily arife.

VER. 159. *With ev'ry pleafing,*] " Thefe two lines," Lord Huntingdon one day faid to me, " exactly paint the character of my old friend, Fontenelle." Tacitus fays, that Galba was rather without vices than really virtuous.

Virtue she finds too painful an endeavour,
Content to dwell in Decencies for ever.
So very reasonable, so unmov'd, 165
As never yet to love, or to be lov'd.
She, while her Lover pants upon her breast,
Can mark the figures on an Indian chest:
And when she sees her Friend in deep despair,
Observes how much a Chintz exceeds Mohair. 170
Forbid it, Heav'n, a Favour or a Debt
She e'er should cancel!—but she may forget.
Safe is your Secret still in Cloe's ear;
But none of Cloe's shall you ever hear.
Of all her Dears she never slander'd one, 175
But cares not if a thousand are undone.
Would Cloe know if you're alive or dead?
She bids her Footman put it in her head.
Cloe is prudent—Would you too be wise?
Then never break your heart when Cloe dies. 180

 One certain Portrait may (I grant) be seen,
Which Heav'n has varnish'd out, and made a *Queen:*
THE SAME FOR EVER! and describ'd by all
With Truth and Goodness, as with Crown and Ball.
Poets heap Virtues, Painters Gems at will, 185
And shew their zeal, and hide their want of skill.
            'Tis

NOTES.

VER. 180. *When Cloe dies.*] This highly-finished portrait was intended for Lady Suffolk, with whom, at the time he wrote it, he lived in a state of intimacy. At ver. 178. he alludes to a particular circumstance: Pope, being at dinner with her, heard her order her footman to put her in mind to send to know how Mrs. Blount, who was ill, had passed the night.

'Tis well—but, Artifts! who can paint or write,
To draw the Naked is your true delight.
That Robe of Quality fo ftruts and fwells,
None fee what Parts of Nature it conceals: 190
Th' exacteft traits of Body or of Mind,
We owe to models of an humble kind.
If QUEENSBERRY to ftrip there's no compelling,
'Tis from a Handmaid we muft take a Helen.
From Peer or Bifhop 'tis no eafy thing 195
To draw the Man who loves his God, or King:
Alas! I copy (or my draught would fail)
From honeft Mah'met, or plain Parfon Hale.
But grant, in Public, Men fometimes are fhown,
A Woman's feen in Private Life alone: 200
Our

VARIATIONS.

After Ver. 198. in the MS.
 Fain I'd in Fulvia fpy the tender Wife;
 I cannot prove it on her, for my life:
 And, for a noble pride, I blufh no lefs,
 Inftead of Berenice to think on Befs.
 Thus while immortal Cibber only fings
 (As * and H**y preach) for queens and kings,
 The nymph, that ne'er read Milton's mighty line,
 May, if fhe love, and merit verfe, have mine.

NOTES.

VER. 190. *Conceals :*] A bad rhyme to fwells. Such blemifhes fhould be noted.

VER. 198. *Mah'met*, fervant to the late King, faid to be the fon of a Turkifh Baffa, whom he took at the fiege of Buda, and conftantly kept about his perfon. P.

VER. 198. Dr. *Stephen Hale;* not more eftimable for his ufeful difcoveries as a natural Philofopher, than for his exemplary life and paftoral charity as a parifh prieft. W.

VER. 199. *But grant, in Public, &c.*] In the former Editions, between this and the foregoing lines, a want of Connexion might

Our bolder Talents in full light difplay'd;
Your Virtues open faireft in the fhade.
Bred to difguife, in Public 'tis you hide;
There, none diftinguifh 'twixt your Shame or Pride,
                                                    Weak-

NOTES.

be perceived, occafioned by the omiffion of certain *Examples* and *Illuftrations* to the Maxims laid down; and though fome of thefe have fince been found, viz. the Characters of *Philomedé*, *Atoffa*, *Cloe*, and fome verfes following, others are ftill wanting, nor can we anfwer that thefe are exactly inferted.   P.

VER. 201. *Light difplay'd;*] That is, are difplayed.

VER. 202. *Your Virtues open*] To balance the many fevere things our Author has faid of Women in this Epiftle, I cannot forbear adding a paffage from a writer who has been ufually thought by no means a friend to the fair fex. And it may occafion furprife to find fuch a paffage from Dean Swift. " The degeneracy of converfation, with the pernicious confequences thereof upon our humours and difpofitions, hath been owing, among other caufes, to the cuftom arifen, for fome time paft, of excluding women from any fhare in our fociety, further than in parties at play, or dancing, or in the purfuit of an amour. I take the higheft period of politenefs in *England* (and it is of the fame date in *France*) to have been the peaceable part of King *Charles* the Firft's reign; and from what we read of thofe times, as well as from the accounts I have formerly met with from fome who lived in that court, the methods then ufed for raifing and cultivating converfation were altogether different from ours; feveral ladies, whom we find celebrated by the poets of that age, had affemblies at their houfes, where perfons of the beft underftanding, and of both fexes, met to pafs the evenings in difcourfing upon whatever agreeable fubjects were occafionally ftarted; and although we are apt to ridicule the fublime platonic notions they had, or perfonated, in love and friendfhip, I conceive their refinements were grounded upon reafon, and that a little grain of the romance is no ill ingredient to preferve and exalt the dignity of human nature, without which it is apt to degenerate into every thing that is fordid, vicious, and low. If there were no other ufe in the converfation of ladies, it is fufficient that it would lay a reftraint upon thofe odious topics of immodefty and indecencies into which the rudenefs of our northern genius is fo apt to fall."

Ep. II. MORAL ESSAYS.

Weaknefs or Delicacy; all fo nice,   205
That each may feem a Virtue, or a Vice.
In Men, we various Ruling Paffions find;
In Women, two almoft divide the Kind;
Thofe, only fix'd, they firft or laft obey,
The Love of Pleafure, and the Love of Sway.   210
That, Nature gives; and where the leffon taught
Is but to pleafe, can Pleafure feem a fault?
Experience, this; by Man's oppreffion curft,
They feek the fecond not to lofe the firft.
                                                Men,

VARIATIONS.

VER. 207. in the firft Edition,
In fev'ral Men, we fev'ral Paffions find;
In Women, two almoft divide the Kind.

NOTES.

VER. 203. *Bred to difguife, in Public 'tis you hide;*] There is fomething apparently exceptionable in the turn of this affertion, which makes their *difguifing in public* the natural effect of their being *bred to difguife:* but if we confider that female education is the art of teaching, not to *be* but to *appear*, we fhall have no reafon to find fault with the exactnefs of the expreffion.   W.

VER. 207. The former part having fhewn, that the *particular Characters* of Women are more various than thofe of Men, it is neverthelefs obferved, that the *general* Characteriftic of the fex, as to the *ruling Paffion*, is more uniform.   P.

VER. 208. *In Women, two*] I cannot think our Author would fuffer by a minute comparifon of this Epiftle with the moft fhining and applauded morfels of the tenth fatire of Boileau, which undoubtedly are his portraits of the affected female Pedant, ver. 439. The Gamefter, ver. 215. His Jealous Lady, ver. 378. The Haughty Lady of Family, ver. 470. And above all, what Boileau himfelf valued moft, the Devout Lady and her Director, ver. 558. Boileau was feverely attacked for this epiftle by Perrault; but was powerfully defended by the great Arnauld, a rigid moralift, and alfo by La Bruyere.

VER. 211. This is occafioned partly by their *Nature*, partly by their *Education*, and in fome degree by *Neceffity*.   P.

Men, some to Bus'ness, some to Pleasure take;
But ev'ry Woman is at heart a Rake: 216
Men, some to Quiet, some to public Strife;
But ev'ry Lady would be Queen for life.
  Yet mark the fate of a whole sex of Queens!
Pow'r all their end, but Beauty all the means: 220
In Youth they conquer, with so wild a rage,
As leaves them scarce a subject in their Age:
For foreign glory, foreign joy, they roam;
No thought of peace or happiness at home.
But Wisdom's triumph, is well-tim'd Retreat,   225
As hard a science to the Fair as Great!
Beauties, like Tyrants, old and friendless grown,
Yet hate repose, and dread to be alone,
Worn out in public, weary ev'ry eye,
Nor leave one sigh behind them when they die. 230
  Pleasures the sex, as children Birds, pursue,
Still out of reach, yet never out of view;

Sure,

NOTES.

VER. 216. *But ev'ry Woman is at heart a Rake:*] This line has given offence: but in behalf of the Poet we may observe, that what he says amounts only to this, " Some men take to business, some to pleasure; but every woman would willingly make *pleasure her business;*" which being the proper periphrasis of a *Rake*, he uses that word, but of course includes in it no more of the Rake's ill qualities than is implied in this definition, of *one who makes pleasure his business.*   W.

VER. 219. What are the *Aims* and the *Fate* of this sex.—I. As to power.   P.

VER. 229. *Worn out in public,*] Copied from Young, Satire 5. written eight years before this Epistle appeared;

" Worn in the public eye, give cheap delight
  To throngs, and tarnish to the sated sight."

VER. 231.——II. As to *Pleasure.*   P.

Sure, if they catch, to fpoil the Toy at moft,
To covet flying, and regret when loft:
At laft, to follies Youth could fcarce defend, 235
It grows their Age's prudence to pretend;
Afham'd to own they gave delight before,
Reduc'd to feign it, when they give no more:
As Hags hold Sabbaths lefs for joy than fpight,
So thefe their merry, miferable Night; 240
Still round and round the Ghofts of Beauty glide,
And haunt the places where their honour dy'd.
See how the World its Veterans rewards!
A Youth of Frolics, an old Age of Cards;

Fair

NOTES.

VER. 234. *To covet flying*,] It is impoffible not to recollect the witty fimile of Young, Sat. 5.

" Pleafures are few, and fewer we enjoy;
Pleafure, like quickfilver, is bright and coy;
We ftrive to grafp it with our utmoft fkill,
Still it eludes us, and it glitters ftill;
If feiz'd at laft, compute your mighty gains,
What is it, but rank poifon in your veins?"

VER. 244. *A Youth of Frolics*,] The antithefis, fo remarkably ftrong in thefe lines, was a very favourite figure with our Poet: he has indeed ufed it but in too many parts of his Works; nay, even in his tranflation of the Iliad, where it ought to have been admitted, and which Dryden has but rarely ufed in his Virgil. Our Author feldom writes many words together without an antithefis. It muft be allowed fometimes, to add ftrength to a fentiment by an oppofition of images: but, too frequently repeated, it becomes tirefome and difgufting. Rhyme has almoft a natural tendency to betray a writer into it: but the pureft authors have defpifed it, as an ornament pert and puerile, and epigrammatic. Seneca, Pliny, Tacitus, and later authors, abound in it. Quintilian has fometimes ufed it with much fuccefs, as when he fpeaks of ftyle;
" magna, non nimia; fublimis, non abrupta; fevera, non triftis;
læta,

Fair to no purpose, artful to no end, 245
Young without Lovers, old without a Friend;
A Fop their Passion, but their Prize a Sot,
Alive, ridiculous, and dead, forgot!
Ah! Friend! to dazzle let the Vain design;
To raise the Thought, and touch the Heart, be thine! 250
That Charm shall grow, while what fatigues the Ring,
Flaunts and goes down, an unregarded thing:
So when the Sun's broad beam has tir'd the sight,
All mild ascends the Moon's more sober light,
                                        Serene

NOTES.

læta, non luxuriosa; plena, non tumida." And sometimes Tully; as, " vicit pudorem libido, timorem audacia, rationem amentia." But these writers fall into this mode of speaking but seldom, and do make it their constant and general manner. Those moderns, who have not acquired a true taste for the simplicity of the best antients, have generally run into a frequent use of point, opposition, and contrast. They who begin to study painting, are struck at first with the pieces of the most vivid colouring; they are almost ashamed to own that they do not relish and feel the modest and reserved beauties of Raphael. The exact proportion of St. Peter's at Rome occasions it not to appear so great as it really is. It is the same in writing; but by degrees we find that Lucan, Martial, Juvenal, Q. Curtius, and Florus, and others of that stamp, who abound in figures that contribute to the false florid, in luxuriant metaphors, in pointed conceits, in lively antitheses, unexpectedly darting forth, are contemptible for the very causes which once excited our admiration. It is then we relish Terence, Cæsar, and Xenophon.

    VER. 249. *Advice for their true Interest.*   P.

    VER. 253. *So when the Sun's*] There are not perhaps, in the whole compass of the English language, four lines more exquisitely finished; not a syllable can be altered for the better; every word

Serene in Virgin Modesty she shines, 255
And unobserv'd the glaring Orb declines.
Oh! blest with Temper, whose unclouded ray
Can make to-morrow chearful as to-day;
She, who can love a Sister's charms, or hear
Sighs for a Daughter with unwounded ear; 260
She, who ne'er answers till her Husband cools,
Or, if she rules him, never shows she rules;
Charms by accepting, by submitting sways,
Yet has her humour most, when she obeys;
Let Fops or Fortune fly which way they will; 265
Disdains all loss of Tickets, or Codille;
Spleen, Vapours, or Small-pox, above them all,
And Mistress of herself, though China fall.
And yet, believe me, good as well as ill,
Woman's at best a Contradiction still. 270
Heav'n,

NOTES.

word seems to be the only proper one that could have been used. So pure and pellucid is the style,

" Ut pura nocturno renidet
Luna mari!"

VER. 268. *Though China fall.*] Addison has touched this subject with his usual exquisite humour, in the Lover, No. 10. p. 291. of his Works, 4to. quoting Epictetus to comfort a lady that labours under this heavy calamity.

VER. 269. The picture of an estimable woman, with the best kind of contrarieties created out of the Poet's imagination: who therefore feigned those circumstances of a husband, a daughter, and *love for a sister*, to prevent her being mistaken for any of his acquaintance. And having thus made his *Woman*, he did, as the antient Poets were wont, when they had made their *Muse*, invoke, and address his poem to her. W.

VER. 270. *A Contradiction still.*] So also has he shewn Man to be in the Essay.

Heav'n, when it ſtrives to poliſh all it can
Its laſt beſt work, but forms a ſofter Man;
Picks from each ſex, to make the Fav'rite bleſt,
Your love of Pleaſure, our deſire of Reſt:
Blends, in exception to all gen'ral rules,   275
Your Taſte of Follies, with our Scorn of Fools:
Reſerve with Frankneſs, Art with Truth ally'd,
Courage with Softneſs, Modeſty with Pride;
Fix'd Principles, with Fancy ever new;
Shakes all together, and produces——You.   280

Be this a Woman's Fame: with this unbleſt,
Toaſts live a ſcorn, and Queens may die a jeſt.
This Phœbus promis'd (I forget the year)
When thoſe blue eyes firſt open'd on the ſphere;
Aſcendant Phœbus watch'd that hour with care, 285
Averted half your Parents' ſimple Pray'r;
And gave you Beauty, but deny'd the Pelf
That buys your Sex a Tyrant o'er itſelf.
The gen'rous God, who Wit and Gold refines,
And ripens Spirits as he ripens Mines,   290
Kept Droſs for Ducheſſes, the world ſhall know it,
To you gave Senſe, Good-humour, and a Poet.

NOTES.

VER. 280. *And produces—You.*] The turn of theſe lines is exactly the ſame with thoſe of Mrs. Biddy Floyd; Swift's Miſcellanies, vol. iv. p. 142.

   " Jove mix'd up all, and his beſt clay employ'd,
       Then call'd the happy compoſition—Floyd."

Mrs. Patty Blount was always, at firſt, ſuppoſed to be the lady here addreſſed—" produces You."

VER. 291. *The world ſhall know it,*] This is an unmeaning expreſſion, and a poor expletive, into which our Poet was unfortunately forced by the rhyme.

                                               " Maudit

"Maudit foit le premier, dont la verve infenfée,
Dans les bornes d'un vers renferma fa penfée,
Et donnant à fes mots une étroite prifon,
Voulut avec la rime enchaîner la raifon."
Boileau, Sat. ii. v. 53.

Rhyme alfo could alone be the occafion of the following faulty expreſſions; taken, too, from fome of his moſt finifhed pieces:

" Not Cæfar's emprefs would I *deign to prove*"——
" If Queenfberry to ftrip *there's no compelling*"——
" Rapt into future times the *bard begun*"——
" Know all the noife the bufy *world can keep*"——
" If true, a woful likenefs, and *if lyes*"——
" Nothing fo true as what you once *let fall*"——
" For Virtue's felf may too much *zeal be had*"——
————————" can no *wants endure*"——
" Nay half in Heav'n *except what's mighty odd*"——
————————" can have no *flaw*"——
————————" on fuch a world *we fall*"——
————————" take fcandal *at a fpark*"——
————————" do *the knack*, and—do *the feat*"——

And more inſtances might be added, if it were not difagreeable to obferve thefe ftraws in amber. But if rhyme occafions fuch inconveniencies and improprieties in fo exact a writer as our Author, what can be expected from inferior verfifiers? It is not my intention to enter into a trite and tedious difcuſſion of the feveral merits of rhyme and blank verfe. Perhaps rhyme may be propereft for fhorter pieces; for lyric, elegiac, and fatiric poems; for pieces where clofenefs of expreſſion and fmartnefs of ftyle are expected; but for fubjects of a higher order, where any enthufiafm or emotion is to be expreſſed, or for poems of a greater length, blank verfe is undoubtedly preferable. An epic poem in rhyme appears to be fuch a fort of thing as the Æneid would have been if it had been written, like Ovid's Fafti, in hexameter and pentameter verfes; and the reading it would have been as tedious as the travelling through the one long, ftrait avenue of firs that leads from Mofcow to Peterfburgh. I will give the reader Mr. Pope's own opinion on this fubject, and in his own words, as delivered to Mr. Spence: " I have nothing to fay for rhyme; but that I doubt if a poem can fupport itfelf without it in our language, unlefs it be ftiffened with fuch ftrange words as are likely to deftroy our language itfelf. The high ftyle that is affected fo much in blank verse would not have been supported even in Milton, had not his subject turned so much on such strange and out-of-the-world things as it does." May we not, however, venture to observe, that more of that true harmony, which will best support a poem, will result from a variety of pauses, and from an intermixture of those different feet (iambic and trochaic particularly) into which our language naturally falls, than from the uniformity of similar terminations. " There can be no music," says Cowley, " with only one note." See Mr. Webb's excellent Observations on Rhyme and Blank Verse, in his Beauties of Poetry.

Dr. Adam Smith, as well as Fontenelle, thought that much of the pleasure we receive from the imitative arts arose from the difficulty of imitation. Voltaire also, in the preface to his Œdipus, talks of the pleasure arising from the difficulté surmontée with respect to rhyme. But Smith, with whom I lived many years in a state of intimacy, was always a lover of French poetry, as was his friend David Hume. After all, we cannot subscribe to the authoritative decision of a certain noted critic, " that our epic compositions are found most pleasing when clothed in rhyme: And that the generality of readers, if left to themselves, and were not prejudiced by their admiration of the Greek and Latin languages, would be more delighted with Milton, if, besides his various pause and measured quantity, he had enriched his numbers with rhyme." This may remind us of the opinion of another learned prelate, who says, " that Paradise Lost was much admired, though the author affected to write it in blank verse." Burnet's Hist. vol. i.

EPISTLE III.

TO

ALLEN LORD BATHURST.

ARGUMENT.

Of the Use *of* RICHES.

THAT it is known to few, most falling into one of the extremes Avarice *or* Profusion, Ver. 1, &c. *The Point discussed, whether the invention of Money has been more commodious, or pernicious to Mankind,* Ver. 21 to 77. *That Riches either to the* Avaricious *or the* Prodigal, *cannot afford Happiness, scarcely necessaries,* Ver. 89 to 160. *That Avarice is an absolute Frenzy, without an End or Purpose,* Ver. 113, &c. 152. *Conjectures about the Motives of Avaricious Men,* Ver. 121 to 153. *That the conduct of Men, with respect to Riches, can only be accounted for by the* ORDER OF PROVIDENCE, *which works the general Good out of Extremes, and brings all to its great End by perpetual Revolutions,* Ver. 161 to 178. *How a* Miser *acts upon Principles which appear to him reasonable,* Ver. 179. *How a* Prodigal *does the same,* Ver. 199. *The due Medium, and true Use of Riches,* Ver. 219. *The* Man *of* Rofs, Ver. 250. *The fate of the* Profuse *and the* Covetous, *in two examples; both miserable in Life and in Death,* Ver. 300, &c. *The Story of* Sir Balaam, Ver. 339 *to the End.*

EPISTLE III.

P. Who shall decide, when Doctors disagree,
And soundest Casuists doubt, like you and me?
You hold the word, from Jove to Momus giv'n,
That Man was made the standing jest of Heav'n;
And Gold but sent to keep the fools in play, 5
For some to heap, and some to throw away.
But I, who think more highly of our kind,
(And surely, Heav'n and I are of a mind,)
           Opine,

VARIATIONS.

EPISTLE III.] This epistle was written after a violent outcry against our Author, on suspicion that he had ridiculed a worthy nobleman merely for his wrong taste. He justified himself upon that article in a letter to the Earl of Burlington; at the end of which are these words: " I have learnt that there are some who would rather be wicked than ridiculous; and therefore it may be safer to attack vices than follies. I will therefore leave my betters in the quiet possession of their idols, their groves, and their high places, and change my subject from their pride to their meanness, from their vanities to their miseries; and as the only certain way to avoid misconstructions, to lessen offence, and not to multiply ill-natured applications, I may probably, in my next, make use of real names instead of fictitious ones."   P.

VER. 2. *Like you and me?*] A most unaccountable piece of false English—me for I. It is not for the sake of making petty objections that it is thought necessary to hint at these inaccuracies in so correct a writer, but merely to prevent their becoming authorities for errors. " In the Epistles to Lords Bathurst and Burlington," says Johnson, " Warburton has endeavoured to find a train of thought which was never in the writer's head; and, to support his hypothesis, has printed that first which was published last.

Opine, that Nature, as in duty bound,
Deep hid the shining mischief under ground: 10
But when by Man's audacious labour won,
Flam'd forth this rival to its Sire, the Sun,
Then careful Heav'n supply'd two sorts of Men,
To squander These, and Those to hide agen.

Like Doctors thus, when much dispute has past,
We find our tenets just the same at last. 16
Both fairly owning, Riches, in effect,
No grace of Heav'n, or token of th' Elect;
Giv'n to the Fool, the Mad, the Vain, the Evil,
To Ward, to Waters, Chartres, and the Devil. 20
B. What

NOTES.

VER. 20. JOHN WARD of Hackney, Esq. Member of Parliament, being prosecuted by the Duchess of Buckingham, and convicted of Forgery, was first expelled the House, and then stood on the pillory on the 17th of March, 1727. He was suspected of joining in a conveyance with Sir John Blunt, to secrete fifty thousand pounds of that Director's estate, forfeited to the South-Sea Company by Act of Parliament. The Company recovered the fifty thousand pounds against Ward; but he set up prior conveyances of his real estate to his brother and son, and concealed all his personal, which was computed to be one hundred and fifty thousand pounds. These conveyances being also set aside by a bill in Chancery, Ward was imprisoned, and hazarded the forfeiture of his life, by not giving in his effects till the last day, which was that of his examination. During his confinement, his amusement was to give poison to dogs and cats, and see them expire by slower or quicker torments. To sum up the *worth* of this gentleman, at the several æras of his life: At his standing in the Pillory, he was *worth above two hundred thousand pounds;* at his commitment to Prison, he was *worth one hundred and fifty thousand;* but has been since so far diminished in his reputation, as to be thought a *worse man* by *fifty or sixty thousand.* P.

FR. CHARTRES, a man infamous for all manner of vices. When he was an ensign in the army, he was drummed out of the regiment

B. What Nature wants, commodious Gold beſtows,
'Tis thus we eat the bread another ſows.
P. But

NOTES.

ment for a cheat; he was next baniſhed Bruſſels, and drummed out of Ghent, on the ſame account. After a hundred tricks at the gaming-tables, he took to lending of money at exorbitant intereſt and on great penalties, accumulating premium, intereſt, and capital into a new capital, and ſeizing to a minute when the payments became due; in a word, by a conſtant attention to the vices, wants, and follies of mankind, he acquired an immenſe fortune. His houſe was a perpetual bawdy-houſe. He was twice condemned for rapes, and pardoned; but the laſt time not without impriſonment in Newgate, and large confiſcations. He died in Scotland in 1731, aged 62. The populace at his funeral raiſed a great riot, almoſt tore the body out of the coffin, and caſt dead dogs, &c. into the grave along with it. The following Epitaph contains his character very juſtly drawn by Dr. Arbuthnot:

HERE continueth to rot
The Body of FRANCIS CHARTRES,
Who, with an INFLEXIBLE CONSTANCY,
and INIMITABLE UNIFORMITY of Life
PERSISTED,
In ſpite of AGE and INFIRMITIES,
In the Practice of EVERY HUMAN VICE,
Excepting PRODIGALITY and HYPOCRISY:
His inſatiable AVARICE exempted him from the firſt,
His matchleſs IMPUDENCE from the ſecond.
Nor was he more ſingular
in the undeviating *Pravity* of his *Manners,*
Than ſucceſsful
in *Accumulating* WEALTH;
For, without TRADE or PROFESSION,
Without TRUST of PUBLIC MONEY,
And without BRIBE-WORTHY Service,
He acquired, or more properly created,
A MINISTERIAL ESTATE.
He was the only Perſon of his Time,
Who could CHEAT without the Maſk of HONESTY,
Retain his Primeval MEANNESS

When

P. But how unequal it beſtows, obſerve,
'Tis thus we riot, while, who ſow it, ſtarve:
                                          What

NOTES.

When poſſeſſed of TEN THOUSAND a Year,
And having daily deſerved the GIBBET for what he *did*,
Was at laſt condemned to it for what he *could* not *do*.
Oh indignant Reader!
Think not his Life uſeleſs to Mankind!
PROVIDENCE connived at his execrable Deſigns,
To give to After-ages
A conſpicuous PROOF and EXAMPLE,
Of how ſmall Eſtimation is EXORBITANT WEALTH
In the Sight of GOD,
By his beſtowing it on the moſt UNWORTHY of ALL MORTALS.

This fine reflection has been much admired; it is alſo found in La Bruyere; but he evidently borrowed it from Seneca: " Non funt divitiæ bonum; nullo modo magis poteſt Deus concupita traducere, quam ſi ille ad perpiſſimos defert, ab optimis abigit."
                    Cur Bonis Viris mala fiunt, cap. v.

This paſſage was pointed out to me by an amiable friend, equally ſkilled in all parts of uſeful and ornamental learning in matters both of taſte and philoſophy, Dr. Heberden.

The figure of Chartres is introduced by Hogarth in the firſt plate of his Rake's Progreſs, and behind him ſtands a man whom he always had about him, and was his pimp.

This Gentleman, it was ſaid, was *worth ſeven thouſand pounds a year* eſtate in Land, and about *one hundred thouſand* in Money.

Mr. WATERS, the third of theſe worthies, was a man no way reſembling the former in his military, but extremely ſo in his civil capacity; his great fortune having been raiſed by the like diligent attendance on the neceſſities of others. But this gentleman's hiſtory muſt be deferred till his death, when his *worth* may be known more certainly.   P.

VER. 20. *Chartres and the Devil.*] Alluding to the vulgar opinion, that all mines of metal and ſubterraneous treaſures are in the guard of the Devil: which ſeems to have taken its riſe from the pagan fable of Plutus the God of Riches. W.——No ſuch alluſion was intended!

What Nature wants (a phrafe I muft diftruft) 25
Extends to Luxury, extends to Luft:.
Ufeful, I grant, it ferves what life requires,
But dreadful too, the dark Affaffin hires.
B. Trade it may help, Society extend.
P. But lures the Pyrate, and corrupts the Friend. 30
B. It raifes Armies in a Nation's aid.
P. But bribes a Senate, and the Land's betray'd.
In vain may Heroes fight, and Patriots rave;
If fecret Gold fap on from knave to knave.

Once,

NOTES.

VER. 21. *What Nature wants,* commodious *Gold beflows,*] The epithet *commodious* gives us the very proper idea of a *Bawd* or *Pander;* and this thought produced the two following lines, which were in all the former editions, but, for their bad reafoning, omitted :

" And if we count amongft the needs of life
Another's Toil, why not another's Wife?" W.

VER. 29. *Trade it may help,*] What is here put into the mouth of Bathurft might be, with equal propriety, transferred to Pope; and fo, indeed, may many other lines.

VER. 33. *And Patriots rave;*] The character of modern pa_triots was, in the opinion of our Poet, very equivocal; as the name was undiftinguifhingly beftowed on every one who was in op-pofition to the court; of this he gives a hint in Ver. 139. of this Epiftle. And agreeable to thefe fentiments is the equivocal turn of his expreffion here,

" In vain—may Patriots rave;"

which they may do either in earneft or in jeft; and, in the opinion of *Sempronius* in the Play, it is beft done in jeft. W.

VER. 34. *If fecret Gold* fap *on from knave to knave.*] The ex-preffion is fine, and gives us the image of a Place invefted; where the approaches are made by communications, which fupport one another: juft as the connexions amongft knaves, after they have been taken in by a ftate-engineer, ferve to fcreen and encourage each other's private corruptions. W.

Once, we confess, beneath the Patriot's cloak, 35
From the crack'd bag the dropping Guinea spoke,
And gingling down the back-stairs, told the crew,
" Old Cato is as great a Rogue as you."
Blest paper-credit! last and best supply!
That lends Corruption lighter wings to fly! 40
Gold

NOTES.

VER. 35. *Beneath the Patriot's cloak,*] This is a true story, which happened in the reign of William III. to an unsuspected old Patriot, who coming out at the back-door from having been closetted by the King, where he had received a large bag of Guineas, the bursting of the bag discovered his business there. P.

" Sir Christopher Musgrave, the wisest man of the party (the Tories), died before the last Session; and, by their conduct after his death, it appeared that they wanted his direction: He had been at the head of the opposition that was made in the last reign, from the beginning to the end; but he gave up many points of great importance in the critical minute; for which I have good reason to believe that he had twelve thousand pounds from the late King, at different times." *Burnet under the year* 1705.

VER. 39. *Blest paper-credit!*] " None of my Works," said Pope to Mr. Spence, " was more laboured than my Epistle on the Use of Riches." It does indeed abound in knowledge of life, and in the justest satire. The lines above quoted have also the additional merit of touching on a subject that never occurred to former satirists. And though it was difficult to say any thing new about avarice, " a vice that has been so pelted," says Cowley, " with good sentences," yet has our Author done it so successfully, that this Epistle, together with Lord Bacon's thirty-third Essay, contains almost all that can be said on the use and abuse of Riches, and the absurd extremes of avarice and profusion. But our Poet has enlivened his precepts with so many various characters, pictures, and images, as may entitle him to claim the preference over all that have treated on this tempting subject, down from the time of the Plutus of Aristophanes. That very lively and amiable old nobleman, the late Lord Bathurst, told me, " that he was much surprised to see, what he had with repeated pleasure so often read as an epistle addressed to himself, in this edition converted into a dialogue,

Ep. III. MORAL ESSAYS.

Gold imp'd by thee, can compafs hardeft things,
Can pocket States, can fetch or carry Kings;
A fingle leaf fhall wait an Army o'er,
Or fhip off Senates to a diftant fhore;
A leaf, like Sibyl's, fcatter to and fro   45
Our fates and fortunes, as the winds fhall blow:
Pregnant with thoufands flits the Scrap unfeen,
And filent fells a King, or buys a Queen.
                                                              Oh!

NOTES.

logue, in which," faid he, " I perceive I make but a fhabby and indifferent figure, and contribute very little to the fpirit of the dialogue, if it muft be a dialogue; and I hope I had generally more to fay for myfelf in the many charming converfations I ufed to hold with Pope and Swift, and my old poetical friends." In truth we may make the fame objection that Perrault is faid to have done to the tenth fatire of Boileau; " l'auteur oublie quelquefois que c'eft un dialogue qu'il compofe." I cannot forbear adding, that Cicero gives to his friend Atticus a very fmall fhare in thofe dialogues in which he himfelf is reprefented as a fpeaker.

VER. 42. *Fetch or carry Kings;*] In our Author's time, many Princes had been fent about the world, and great changes of Kings projected in Europe. The partition treaty had difpofed of Spain; France had fet up a King for England, who was fent to Scotland, and back again; King Staniflaus was fent to Poland, and back again; the Duke of Anjou was fent to Spain, and Don Carlos to Italy.   P.

VER. 44. *Or fhip off Senates to a diftant Shore;*] Alludes to feveral Minifters, Counfellors, and Patriots banifhed in our times to Siberia, and to that MORE GLORIOUS FATE of the PARLIAMENT of PARIS, banifhed to Pontoife in the year 1720.   P.

VER. 47. *Pregnant with thoufands flits the Scrap unfeen,*] The imagery is very fublime, and alludes to the courfe of a deftroying peftilence. The Pfalmift, in his expreffion of *the Peftilence that walketh in darknefs,* fupplied him with the grandeur of his idea.   W.

VER. 48. *Buys a Queen.*] A fly ftroke of fatire on a character he frequently fatirized; but not fo feverely as Swift in Verfes on his own Death.

VOL. III.   R

Oh! that such bulky Bribes as all might see,
Still, as of old, incumber'd Villainy! 50
Could France or Rome divert our brave designs,
With all their brandies or with all their wines?
What could they more than Knights and Squires
   confound,
Or water all the Quorum ten miles round?
A Statesman's slumbers how this speech would spoil!
" Sir, Spain has sent a thousand jars of oil; 56
" Huge bales of British cloth blockade the door;
" A hundred oxen at your levee roar."
   Poor Avarice one torment more would find;
Nor could Profusion squander all in kind. 60
Astride his cheese Sir Morgan might we meet;
And Worldly crying coals from street to street,
Whom with a wig so wild, and mien so maz'd,
Pity mistakes for some poor tradesman craz'd.
Had Colepepper's whole wealth been hops and hogs,
Could he himself have sent it to the dogs? 66
                                          His

VARIATIONS.

After Ver. 50. in the MS.
   To break a trust were Peter brib'd with wine,
   Peter! 'twould pose as wise a head as thine.

NOTES.

VER. 62. Some Misers of great wealth, proprietors of the coal mines, had entered at this time into an Association to keep up coals to an extravagant price, whereby the poor were reduced almost to starve, till one of them, taking the advantage of underselling the rest, defeated the design. One of these Misers was *worth ten thousand,* another *seven thousand* a year.   P.

VER. 65. *Colepepper,*] Sir WILLIAM COLEPEPPER, Bart. a Person of an antient family, and ample fortune, without one other
                                                    quality

His Grace will game: to White's a Bull be led,
With fpurning heels and with a butting head.
To White's be carry'd, as to ancient games,
Fair Courfers, Vafes, and alluring Dames.   70
Shall then Uxorio, if the ftakes he fweep,
Bear home fix Whores, and make his Lady weep?
Or foft Adonis, fo perfum'd and fine,
Drive to St. James's a whole herd of fwine?
Oh filthy check on all induftrious fkill,   75
To fpoil the nation's laft great trade, Quadrille!
Since then, my Lord, on fuch a world we fall,
What fay you? B. Say? Why take it, Gold and all.
P. What Riches give us let us then enquire:
Meat, Fire, and Clothes. B. What more? P. Meat,
    Clothes, and Fire.   80
Is this too little? would you more than live?
Alas! 'tis more than Turner finds they give.
                                        Alas!

VARIATIONS.

VER. 77. *Since then, &c.*] In the former Editions,
    Well then, fince with the world we ftand or fall,
    Come take it as we find it, Gold and all.

NOTES.

quality of a Gentleman, who, after ruining himfelf at the Gaming-table, paft the reft of his days in fitting there to fee the ruin of others; preferring to fubfift upon borrowing and begging, rather than to enter into any reputable method of life, and refufing a Poft in the army which was offered him.   P.

VER. 65. *Had Colepepper's*] Thus in former Editions,
    Had Hawley's fortune lay'n in hops and hogs,
    Scarce Hawley's felf had fent it to the dogs.

VER. 82. *Turner*] One who, being poffeffed of three hundred thoufand pounds, laid down his coach, becaufe Intereft was reduced

Alas! 'tis more than (all his Vifions paft)
Unhappy Wharton, waking, found at laft!
What can they give? to dying Hopkins, Heirs; 85
To Chartres, Vigour; Japhet, Nofe and Ears?
Can they, in gems bid pallid Hippia glow,
In Fulvia's buckle cafe the throbs below:
Or heal, old Narfes, thy obfcener ail,
With all th' embroid'ry plaifter'd at thy tail?   90
They

NOTES.

duced from five to four *per cent.* and then put feventy thoufand into the Charitable corporation for better Intereft; which fum having loft, he took it fo much to heart that he kept his chamber ever after. It is thought he would not have outlived it, but that he was heir to another confiderable eftate, which he daily expected, and that by this courfe of life he faved both clothes and all other expences. P.

VER. 84. *Unhappy Wharton,*] A Nobleman of great qualities, but as unfortunate in the application of them, as if they had been vices and follies. See his Character in the firft Epiftle. P.

VER. 85. *Hopkins,*] A Citizen, whofe rapacity obtained him the name of *Vulture Hopkins*. He lived worthlefs, but died *worth three hundred thoufand pounds*, which he would give to no perfon living, but left it fo as not to be inherited till after the fecond generation. His counfel reprefenting to him how many years it muft be before this could take effect, and that his money could only lie at intereft all that time, he expreffed great joy thereat, and faid, " They would then be as long in fpending as he had been in getting it." But the Chancery afterwards fet afide the will, and gave it to the heir at law. P.

VER. 86. *Japhet, Nofe and Ears?*] JAPHET CROOK, alias Sir *Peter Stranger*, was punifhed with the lofs of thofe parts, for having forged a conveyance of an eftate to himfelf, upon which he took up feveral thoufand pounds. He was at the fame time fued in Chancery for having fraudulently obtained a Will, by which he poffeffed another confiderable eftate, in wrong of the brother of the deceafed. By thefe means he was *worth* a great fum, which (in reward for the fmall lofs of his ears) he enjoyed in prifon till his death, and quietly left to his executor. P.

They might (were Harpax not too wife to spend)
Give Harpax felf the blessing of a friend ;
Or find some Doctor that would save the life
Of wretched Shylock, spite of Shylock's Wife:
But thousands die, without or this or that, 95
Die, and endow a College, or a Cat.
To some, indeed, Heav'n grants the happier fate,
T' enrich a Baftard, or a Son they hate.
  Perhaps you think the Poor might have their part?
Bond damns the Poor, and hates them from his
  heart: 100
                                                   The

NOTES.

VER. 90. *With all*] An image infufferably filthy, and unworthy of fuch a writer! Boileau has no fuch images.

VER. 96. *Die, and endow a College, or a Cat.*] A famous Duchefs of *R.* in her laft Will left confiderable legacies and annuities to her Cats. P.

This benefactrefs was no other than La Belle Stuart of the Comte de Grammont ; and her endowment was not a proper object of fatire. The real truth was, that fhe left annuities to certain female friends, with the burden of maintaining fome of her cats ; a delicate way of providing for poor, and probably, proud gentlewomen, without making them feel that they owed their livelihood to her mere liberality.

VER. 100. *Bond damns the Poor, &c.*] This Epiftle was written in the year 1730, when a corporation was eftablifhed to lend money to the poor upon pledges, by the name of the *Charitable Corporation ;* but the whole was turned only to an iniquitous method of enriching particular people, to the ruin of fuch numbers, that it became a parliamentary concern to endeavour the relief of thofe unhappy fufferers ; and three of the managers, who were members of the Houfe, were expelled. By the report of the Committee appointed to inquire into that iniquitous affair, it appears, that when it was objected to the intended removal of the office, that the Poor, for whofe ufe it was erected, would be hurt by it, Bond, one of the Directors, replied, *Damn the Poor.* That
" God

The grave Sir Gilbert holds it for a rule
That ev'ry man in want is knave or fool:
" God cannot love (fays Blunt, with tearlefs eyes)
" The wretch he ftarves"—and pioufly denies:
But the good Bifhop, with a meeker air, 105
Admits, and leaves them, Providence's care.
Yet, to be juft to thefe poor men of pelf,
Each does but hate his neighbour as himfelf:
Damn'd

NOTES.

" God hates the poor," and, " That every man in want is either knave or fool," &c. were the genuine apothegms of fome of the Perfons here mentioned. P.

VER. 105. *But the good Bifhop, &c.*] In the place of this imaginary *Bifhop*, and in the firft Dialogue of 1738, the Poet had named a very worthy Perfon of condition, who, for a courfe of many years, had fhined in public ftations much to the honour and advantage of his country. But being at once oppreffed by popular prejudice and a public cenfure, it was no wonder the Poet, to whom he was perfonally a ftranger, fhould think hardly of him. I had the honour to be well known to that truly illuftrious Perfon, and to be greatly obliged by him. From my intimate knowledge of his character, I was fully perfuaded of his innocence, and that he was unwarily drawn in by a pack of infamous Cheats, to his great lofs of fortune as well as reputation. At my requeft and information, therefore, the Poet with much fatisfaction retracted, and ftruck out, in both places, his ill-grounded cenfure. I have fince had the pleafure to underftand, from the beft authority, that thefe favourable fentiments of him have of late been fully juftified in the courfe of fome proceedings in the High Court of Chancery, the moft unerring inveftigator of Truth and Falfehood. W.——
This proceeding certainly does great honour to Dr. Warburton's gratitude and friendfhip. Sir R. gave him the living of Brandbroughton; and the letter he wrote in his vindication appears in p. 144. of his Life by Bifhop Hurd.

VER. 105. *But the good Bifhop,*] Formerly thus;
    But rev'rend Sutton, with a fofter air
    Admits and leaves them——

Damn'd to the Mines, an equal fate betides
The Slave that digs it, and the Slave that hides.
B. Who suffer thus, mere Charity should own, 111
Must act on motives pow'rful, tho' unknown.
P. Some War, some Plague, or Famine they foresee,
Some Revelation hid from you and me. 114
Why Shylock wants a meal, the cause is found,
He thinks a Loaf will rise to fifty pound.
What made Directors cheat in South-sea year?
To live on Ven'son when it sold so dear.
Ask you why Phryne the whole Auction buys?
Phryne foresees a general Excise. 120
Why she and Sappho raise that monstrous sum?
Alas! they fear a man will cost a plum.
Wise Peter sees the World's respect for Gold,
And therefore hopes this Nation may be sold:

Glorious

NOTES.

VER. 109. *Damn'd to the Mines,*] This is plainly taken from the causes of the Decay of Christian Piety. "It has always been held," says this excellent writer, "the severest treatment of slaves and malefactors, *damnare ad metalla*, to force them to dig in the mines: now this is the covetous man's lot, from which he is never to expect a release."

VER. 118. *To live on Ven'son*] In the extravagance and luxury of the South-sea year, the price of a haunch of Venison was from three to five pounds. P.

VER. 120. *General Excise.*] Many people, about the year 1733, had a conceit that such a thing was intended, of which it is not improbable this lady might have some intimation. P.

VER. 123. *Wise Peter*] PETER WALTER, a person not only eminent in the wisdom of his profession, as a dextrous attorney, but allowed to be a good, if not a safe, conveyancer; extremely respected by the Nobility of this land, though free from all man-

Glorious Ambition! Peter, fwell thy ftore, 125
And be what Rome's great Didius was before.
The Crown of Poland, venal twice an age,
To juft three millions ftinted modeft Gage.
                                              But

NOTES.

ner of luxury and oftentation: his Wealth was never feen, and his Bounty never heard of, except to his own fon, for whom he procured an employment of confiderable profit, of which he gave him as much as was *neceffary*. Therefore the taxing this gentleman with any Ambition, is certainly a great wrong to him.   P.

VER. 126. *Rome's great Didius*] A Roman Lawyer, fo rich as to purchafe the Empire when it was fet to fale upon the death of Pertinax.   P.

VER. 127. *The Crown of Poland, &c.*] The two perfons here mentioned were of Quality, each of whom in the Miffiffippi defpifed to realize above *three hundred thoufand pounds*; the Gentleman with a view to the purchafe of the Crown of Poland, the Lady on a vifion of the like royal nature. They fince retired into Spain, where they are ftill in fearch of gold in the mines of the Afturies.   P.

A country devoted to ruin by its ambitious and unjuft neighbours; who deferve the fevereft ftrokes of fuch a fatirift as our Author.

VER. 128. *Stinted modeft Gage.*] "The names of thefe two perfons were Mr. Gage, and Lady Mary Herbert, daughter of William Marquis of Powis, who, dying October 1745, left in the hands of his executors and truftees an annuity of 200 l. a year to be paid to the ufe of this daughter, not for the payment of her many debts which fhe had contracted, but to keep her from wanting neceffaries. William Marquis of Powis, fon of the former, litigated the faid will, but died while the fuit was pending in the Ecclefiaftical Court, leaving the refidue of the lands and profits of his eftates, after his debts fhould be paid, in the hands of truftees for the ufe of the Right Honourable Henry Arthur, then Lord Herbert, afterwards Earl of Powis, with whom he had no relation, friendfhip, or acquaintance, which Arthur afterwards married Barbara Herbert, niece and heir at law of the latter Earl Powis. This man, by fair promifes and threats, got the truftees
                                                                  of

But nobler fcenes Maria's dreams unfold,
Hereditary Realms, and worlds of Gold. 130
Congenial fouls! whofe life one Av'rice joins,
And one fate buries in the Afturian Mines.
Much injur'd Blunt! why bears he Britain's hate?
A wizard told him in thefe words our fate:
" At

NOTES.

of the firft Earl to agree in obtaining adminiftration with the will
and codicil of the Marquis the father, annexed in May 1749, and
then repented paying the annuity of 200 l. to Mary Herbert,
daughter of the faid Marquis. As fhe now refided in France, fhe
had obtained a promife there of being made Dame of Honour to
the Queen of France; which Lord Herbert hearing of, went out
of England to diffuade her from accepting it, as being a difgrace
to her and the family; and promifed he would pay her all the arrears of the annuity of 200 l. due by her father's will, and would
give her, over and above, 200 l. a year more. This he never performed, till after feveral fuits of law the caufe was brought to the
Houfe of Lords, who decreed both her annuities to be paid, with
all arrears due in the year 1766. Throughout a long life, fo little
difference has this lady found between dreams and realities."
From MSS. notes of Mr. Bowyer.

VER. 133. *Much injur'd Blunt!*] Sir JOHN BLUNT, originally
a fcrivener, was one of the firft projectors of the South-fea Company, and afterwards one of the directors and chief managers of
the famous fcheme in 1720. He was alfo one of thofe who fuf-
fered moft feverely by the bill of pains and penalties on the faid directors. He was a diffenter of a moft religious deportment, and
profeffed to be a great believer. Whether he did really credit the
prophecy here mentioned is not certain, but it was conftantly in
this very ftyle he declaimed againft the corruption and luxury of
the Age, the partiality of Parliaments, and the mifery of Party-
fpirit. He was particularly eloquent againft *Avarice* in great and
noble perfons, of which he had indeed lived to fee many miferable
examples. He died in the year 1732. P.

VER. 134. *A wizard told him*] Is there fuch a thing as a calm
and candid fpectator of our prefent manners to be found, who will
inform us, whether the direful prophecy of this wizard be founded
on truth or not?

" At length Corruption, like a gen'ral flood,　135
" (So long by watchful Ministers withstood,)
" Shall deluge all; and Avarice creeping on,
" Spread like a low-born mist, and blot the Sun;
" Statesman and Patriot ply alike the stocks,
" Peeress and Butler share alike the Box,　140
" And Judges job, and Bishops bite the town,
" And mighty Dukes pack cards for half a crown.
" See Britain sunk in lucre's sordid charms,
" And France reveng'd of ANNE's and EDWARD's
" arms!"
'Twas no Court-badge, great Scriv'ner! fir'd thy brain,
Nor lordly Luxury, nor City Gain:　146
No, 'twas thy righteous end, asham'd to see
Senates degen'rate, Patriots disagree,
And nobly wishing Party-rage to cease,
To buy both sides, and give thy Country peace.　150
" All this is madness," cries a sober sage:
But who, my friend, has reason in his rage?
" The Ruling Passion, be it what it will,
" The Ruling Passion conquers Reason still."

Less

NOTES.

VER. 137.———*Av'rice creeping on,*
Spread like a low-born *mist, and blot the* Sun;] The similitude is extremely apposite, implying that this vice is of base and mean original; hatched and nursed up among Scriveners and Stock-jobbers, and unknown, till of late, to the Nobles of this land: But now, in the fulness of time, she rears her head, and aspires to cover the most illustrious stations in her dark and pestilential shade. The Sun, and other luminaries of Heaven, signifying, in the high eastern style, the Grandees and Nobles of the earth.　SCRIBL.———A strained interpretation.

VER. 145. *Fir'd thy brain,*] A court-badge firing the brain, is surely an uncouth and improper expression.

Less mad the wildest whimsey we can frame, 155
Than ev'n that Passion, if it has no Aim;
For though such motives Folly you may call,
The Folly's greater to have none at all.
 Hear then the truth: " 'Tis Heav'n each Passion
  " sends,
" And diff'rent men directs to diff'rent ends. 160
" Extremes in Nature equal good produce,
" Extremes in Man concur to gen'ral use."
Ask me what makes one keep, and one bestow?
That Pow'r who bids the Ocean ebb and flow,
Bids seed-time, harvest, equal course maintain, 165
Through reconcil'd extremes of drought and rain,
Builds Life on Death, on Change Duration founds,
And gives th' eternal wheels to know their rounds.
 Riches, like insects, when conceal'd they lie,
Wait but for wings, and in their season fly. 170
Who sees pale Mammon pine amidst his store,
Sees but a backward steward for the Poor;
This year a Reservoir, to keep and spare;
The next, a Fountain, spouting through his Heir,

In

NOTES.

VER. 154. *Conquers Reason still.*] See what is said before of the pernicious tenet of a Ruling Passion.

VER. 158. *The Folly's greater*] Verbatim from Rochefoucault.

VER. 162. *Extremes in Man*] See the fine passage quoted above, in Essay on Man, from Dr. Bulguy's Treatise on Divine Benevolence, p. 100.

VER. 173. *This year a Reservoir,*] The same comparison was before used by Young, Sat. vi. line 34. Pope collected gold from many a dunghill; for this allusion is taken from Fuller's Church History, p. 28.

In lavish streams to quench a Country's thirst, 175
And men and dogs shall drink him till they burst.
  Old Cotta sham'd his fortune and his birth,
Yet was not Cotta void of wit or worth:
What though (the use of barb'rous spits forgot)
His kitchen vy'd in coolness with his grot? 180
His court with nettles, moats with cresses stor'd,
With soups unbought and sallads bless'd his board?
                                                          If

NOTES.

VER. 181. *His court with nettles,*] The use, the force, and the excellence of language, certainly consists in raising clear, complete, and circumstantial images, and in turning readers into spectators. Here is an eminent example of this excellence, of all others the most essential in poetry. Every epithet here used paints its object, and paints it distinctly. After having passed over the moat full of cresses, do you not actually find yourself in the middle court of this forlorn and solitary mansion, overgrown with docks and nettles? And do you not hear the dog that is going to assault you? Among the other fortunate circumstances that attended Homer, it was not one of the least that he wrote before general and abstract terms were invented. Hence his muse (like his own Helen standing on the walls of Troy) points out every person and thing accurately and forcibly. All the views and prospects he lays before us appear as fully and perfectly to the eye as that which engaged the attention of Neptune when he was sitting (Iliad, b. xiii. v. 12.)

Ύψῶ ἐπ' ἀκροτάτης κορυφῆς Σάμου ὑλησσης,
Θρηκίης· ἔνθεν γὰρ ἐφαίνετο πᾶσα μὲν Ἴδη,
Φαίνετο δὲ Πριάμοιο πόλις, καὶ νῆες Ἀχαιῶν.

Those who are fond of generalities may think the number of natural, little circumstances, introduced in the beautiful narration of the expedition of Dolon and Diomed, (book the tenth,) too particular and trifling, and below the dignity of epic poetry. But
                                                                                every

IMITATIONS.

VER. 182. *With soups unbought*]
  " —dapibus mensas onerabat inemptis."   VIRG. P.

If Cotta liv'd on pulfe, it was no more
Than Bramins, Saints, and Sages did before;
To

NOTES.

every reader of a juft tafte will always admire the minute defcription of the helmet and creft, at verfe 257; the clapping of the wings of the heron which they could not fee; the fquatting down among the dead bodies till Dolon had paffed; Ulyffes hiffing to Diomed as a fignal; the ftriking the horfes with his bow, becaufe he had forgotten to bring his whip with him; and the innumerable circumftances which make this narration fo lively, fo dramatic, and fo interefting. Half the Iliad and the Odyffey might be quoted as examples of this way of writing: fo different from the unfinifhed, half-formed figures prefented to us by many modern writers. How much is the pathetic heightened by Sophocles, when, fpeaking of Deianira determined to deftroy herfelf, and taking leave of her palace, he adds, a circumftance that Voltaire would have difdained,

—— Κλαιε δ' οργανων ετε
Ψαυσειεν, οις εχρητο δειλαια παρος.

Among the Roman poets, Lucretius will furnifh many inftances of this fort of ftrong painting. Witnefs his portrait of a jealous man, book iv. v. 1130.

" Aut quod in ambiguo verbum jaculata reliquit;
Aut nimium jactare oculos, aliumve pueri
Quod putat, in vultûque videt veftigia rifûs."

Of Iphigenia going to be facrificed, at the moment, when,

——" Mœftum ante aras aftare parentum
Senfit, et hunc propter ferrum celare miniftros."

Of fear, in book iii. v. 155.

" Sudorem itaque et pellorem exiftere toto
Corpore; et infringi linguam; vocemque aboriri;
Caligare occulos; fonere aures; fuccidere artus."

Without fpecifying the various ftrokes of nature with which Virgil has defcribed the prognoftics of the weather in his firft Georgic, let us only confider with what energy he has enumerated and particularized the geftures and attitudes of his dying Dido. No five verfes ever contained more images more diftinctly expreffed:

" Illa

To cram the Rich was prodigal expence,   185
And who would take the Poor from Providence?
                                              Like

NOTES.

" Illa graves oculos conata attolere, rurfus
Deficit; infixum ftridet fub pectore vulnus;
Ter revoluta toro eft; oculifque errantibus, alto
Quæfivit cœlo lucem, ingemutique repertâ."

The words of Virgil have here painted the dying Dido as powerfully as the pencil of Reynolds has done when fhe is juft dead. I once faw Mr. Garrick gefticulate every circumftance in this fine defcription. But none of the Roman writers has difplayed a greater force and vigour of imagination than Tacitus, who was in truth a great poet. With what an affemblage of mafterly ftrokes has he exhibited the diftrefs of the Roman army under Cæcina, in the firft book of the Annals! " Nox per diverfa inquies; cum barbari feftis epulis, læto cantu, aut truci fonore, fubjecta vallium ac refultantes faltus, complerent. Apud Romanos, invalidi ignes, interruptæ voces, atque ipfi paffim adjacerent vallo, oberrarent tentoriis, infomnes magis quam pervigiles, ducemque terruit dira quies." And what a fpectre he then immediately calls up, in the ftyle of Michael Angelo! " Nam Quintilium Varum, fanguine oblitum, et paludibus emerfum, cernere et audire vifus eft, velut vocantem, non tamen obfecutos, et manum intendentis repuliffe."

A celebrated foreigner, the Count Algarotti, has paffed the following cenfure on our poetry, as deficient in this refpect:

" La poefia dei populi fettentrionali pare a me, che, generalménte parlando, confifta più di penfieri, che d'immagini, fi compiaccia delle riffeffione equalmente che dei fentimenti: non fia cofi particolareggiata, e pittorefca come e la noftra. Virgilio a cagione d'efempio rapprefentando Didone, quando efce alla caccia fa una tal defcrizione del fuo veftimento, che tutti i ritrattifti, leggendo quel paffo, la veftirebbono a un modo:

' Tandem progreditur, magnâ ftipante caterva,
' Sidoniam picto chlamydem circumdata limbo;
' Cui pharetra ex auro, crines nodantur in aurum,
' Aurea purpuream fubnectit fibuli veftum.'

Non cofi Miltono quando defcrive la nuda bellezza di Eva:

' Grace was in all her fteps, heav'n in her eye,
' In every gefture, dignity and love.'

Con

Like some lone Chartreux stands the good old Hall,
Silence without, and fasts within the wall;
                                            No

* NOTES.

Con quella parole generale, e astratte idee di grazia, cielo, amore, e maestà non pare a lei che ognuno si formi in mente una Eva a posta sua?"

It must indeed be granted, that this passage gives no distinct and particular idea of the person of Eve; but in how many others has Milton drawn his figures, and expressed his images, with energy and distinctness?

"Under a coronet his flowing hair
In curls on either cheek play'd; wings he wore
Of many a colour'd plume sprinkled with gold;
His habit fit for speed succinct, and held
Before his decent steps a silver wand."

"Dire was the tossing, deep the groans; Despair
Tended the sick, busiest from couch to couch;
And over them triumphant Death his dart
Shook, but delay'd to strike."

"From his slack hand the garland, wreath'd for Eve,
Down dropt, and all the faded roses shed;
Speechless he stood, and pale."

And Spencer, the master of Milton, so much abounds in portraits peculiarly marked, and strongly created, that it is difficult to know which to select from this copious magazine of the most lively painting. The same may be said of Shakespeare, whose little touches of nature it is no wonder Voltaire could not relish, who affords no example of this beauty in his Henriade, and gives no proofs of a picturesque fancy, in a work that abounds more in declamation, in moral and political reflections, than in poetic images, in which there is little character and less nature, and in which the author himself appears throughout the piece, and is himself the hero of his poem.

I have dwelt the longer on this subject, because I think I can perceive many symptoms, even among writers of eminence, of departing from these true, and lively, and minute representations of Nature, and of dwelling in generalities. To these I oppose the testimony of, perhaps, the most judicious and elegant critic among the antients: " Proculdubio qui dicit expugnatam esse civitatem,

com-

No rafter'd roofs with dance and tabor found,
No noon-tide bell invites the country round :   190
Tenants with fighs the fmoaklefs tow'rs furvey,
And turn th' unwilling fteeds another way :
Benighted wanderers, the foreft o'er,
Curfe the fav'd candle, and unop'ning door;
While the gaunt maftiff, growling at the gate,   195
Affrights the beggar whom he longs to eat.
  Not fo his Son, he mark'd this overfight,
And then miftook reverfe of wrong for right.
(For what to fhun will no great knowledge need,
But what to follow is a tafk indeed.)   200
Yet fure, of qualities deferving praife,
More go to ruin Fortunes, than to raife.
                                        What

NOTES.

complectitur omnia quæcunque talis fortuna recipit : fed in affec-
tus minus penetrat brevis hic velut nuntius. At fi aperias hæc
quæ verbo uno inclufa erant, apparebunt effufa per domos ac tem-
pla flammæ, et ruentium tectorum fragor, et ex diverfis clamori-
bus unus quidam fonus; aliorum fuga incerta; alii in extremo
complexû fuorum cohærentes, et infantium fæminarumque plora-
tus, et malè ufque in illum diem fervati fato fenes; tum illa pro-
fanorum facrorumque direptio, efferentium prædas, repetentiumque
difcurfus, et acti ante fuum quifque prædonem catenati, et conata
retinere infantem fuum mater, et ficubi majus lucrum eft, pugna
inter victores.   Licet enim hæc omnia, ut dixi, complectatur ever-
fio, minus eft tamen totum dicere quam omnia."

  VER. 200. Here I found two lines in the Poet's MS.
    " Yet fure, of qualities deferving praife,
       More go to ruin Fortunes, than to raife."
which, as they feemed to be neceffary to do juftice to the imaginary Character going to be defcribed, I advifed him to infert in
their place. W.——The expreffion of " more qualities go," is
furely faulty.

What flaughter'd hecatombs, what floods of wine,
Fill the capacious 'Squire, and deep Divine!
Yet no mean motive this profufion draws, 205
His oxen perifh in his country's caufe;
'Tis GEORGE and LIBERTY that crowns the cup,
And Zeal for that great Houfe which eats him up.
The woods recede around the naked feat,
The fylvans groan—no matter—for the Fleet : 210
Next goes his wool—to clothe our valiant bands;
Laft, for his Country's Love, he fells his Lands.
To town he comes, completes the nation's hope,
And heads the bold Train-bands, and burns a Pope.
And fhall not Britain now regard his toils, 215
Britain, that pays her Patriots with her Spoils?
In vain at Court the Bankrupt pleads his caufe,
His thanklefs Country leaves him to her Laws.

The Senfe to value Riches, with the Art
T' enjoy them, and the Virtue to impart, 220
Not meanly, nor ambitioufly purfu'd,
Not funk by floth, nor rais'd by fervitude;
To balance Fortune by a juft expence,
Join with Economy, Magnificence; 224
With

VARIATIONS.

After Ver. 218. in the MS.
Where one lean herring furnifh'd Cotta's board,
And nettles grew, fit porridge for their Lord;
Where mad good-nature, bounty mifapply'd,
In lavifh Curio blaz'd a-while and dy'd;
There Providence once more fhall fhift the fcene,
And fhewing H—Y, teach the golden mean.

With Splendor, Charity; with Plenty, Health;
Oh teach us, BATHURST! yet unspoil'd by wealth!
That secret rare, between th' extremes to move
Of mad Good-nature, and of mean Self-love.

B. To Worth or Want well weigh'd, be Bounty
     giv'n,
And ease, or emulate, the care of Heav'n ; 230
(Whose measure full o'erflows on human race;)
Mend Fortune's fault, and justify her grace.
Wealth in the gross is death, but life diffus'd;
As Poison heals, in just proportion us'd :
In heaps, like Ambergrise, a stink it lies, 235
But well dispers'd, is Incense to the Skies.

P. Who starves by Nobles, or with Nobles eats?
The Wretch that trusts them, and the Rogue that
     cheats.
Is there a Lord, who knows a chearful noon
Without a Fiddler, Flatt'rer, or Buffoon? 240
Whose table, Wit, or modest Merit share,
Un-elbow'd by a Gamester, Pimp, or Play'r?
Who copies Yours, or OXFORD's better part,
To ease th' oppress'd, and raise the sinking heart?
                                              Where'er

VARIATIONS.

After Ver. 226. in the MS.
  That secret rare, with affluence hardly join'd,
  Which W——n lost, yet B——y ne'er could find;
  Still miss'd by Vice, and scarce by Virtue hit,
  By G——'s goodness, or by S——'s wit.

NOTES.

VER. 243. OXFORD's *better part,*] Edward Harley, Earl of
Oxford. The son of Robert, created Earl of Oxford and Earl of
                                              Mortimer

Where'er he shines, oh Fortune, gild the scene, 245
And Angels guard him in the golden Mean!
There, English Bounty yet a-while may stand,
And Honour linger ere it leaves the land.
But all our praises why should Lords engross?
Rise, honest Muse! and sing the MAN of Ross: 250
Pleas'd

VARIATIONS.

After Ver. 250. in the MS.
Trace humble worth beyond Sabrina's shore,
Who sings not him, oh may he sing no more!

NOTES.

Mortimer by Queen Anne. This Nobleman died regretted by all men of letters, great numbers of whom had experienced his benefits. He left behind him one of the most noble Libraries in Europe. P.

VER. 246. *And Angels guard him in the* GOLDEN MEAN!] This was a friendly hint, and not useless, as ill well known. The idea of this Guard was prettily imagined, being taken from the Supporters of his Lordship's Arms. W.——Pope did not, could not, think of this prettiness.

VER. 250. *Rise, honest Muse!*] These lines, which are eminently beautiful, particularly 267, containing a fine prosopopæia, have conferred immortality on a plain, worthy, and useful citizen of Herefordshire, Mr. John Kyrle, who spent his long life in advancing and contriving plans of public utility. The Howard of his time; who deserves to be celebrated more than all the heroes of Pindar. The particular reason for which I mention them, is to observe the pleasing effect that the use of common and familiar words and objects, judiciously managed, produce in poetry. Such as are here the words, *causeway, seats, spire, market-place, alms-house, apprentic'd*. A fastidious delicacy, and a false refinement, in order to avoid meanness, have deterred our writers from the introduction of such words; but Dryden often hazarded it, and gave by it a secret charm, and a natural air to his verses, well knowing of what consequence it was sometimes to soften and subdue his hints, and not to paint and adorn every object he touched, with perpetual pomp and unremitted splendor. Mr. Kyrle was enabled to effect

Pleas'd Vaga echoes through her winding bounds,
And rapid Severn hoarse applause resounds.
Who hung with woods yon mountain's sultry brow?
From the dry rock who bade the waters flow?
Not to the skies in useless columns tost, 255
Or in proud falls magnificently lost,
But clear and artless, pouring through the plain
Health to the sick, and solace to the swain.
Whose Cause-way parts the vale with shady rows?
Whose Seats the weary Traveller repose? 260
Who taught that Heav'n-directed spire to rise?
" The MAN of Ross," each lisping babe replies.
Behold the Market-place with poor o'erspread!
The MAN of Ross divides the weekly bread;
He feeds yon Alms-house, neat, but void of state,
Where Age and Want sit smiling at the gate: 266
Him portion'd maids, apprentic'd orphans blest,
The young who labour, and the old who rest.
Is any sick? the MAN of Ross relieves,
Prescribes, attends, the med'cine makes, and gives.
Is there a variance? enter but his door, 271
Balk'd are the Courts, and contest is no more.
Despairing Quacks with curses fled the place,
And vile Attornies, now an useless race.

B. Thrice

NOTES.

many of his benevolent purposes by the assistance of liberal subscriptions, which his character easily procured. This circumstance was communicated by Mr. Victor.

VER. 267. *Orphans blest,*] The tenses are here unluckily changed, contrary to grammatical propriety. Blest, is the time past; labour and rest, in the next line, the time present.

B. Thrice happy man! enabl'd to purſue 275
What all ſo wiſh, but want the pow'r to do!
Oh ſay, what ſums that gen'rous hand ſupply?
What mines, to ſwell that boundleſs charity?
P. Of Debts, and Taxes, Wife and Children clear,
This man poſſeſt ——— five hundred pounds a
   year.   280
Bluſh, Grandeur, bluſh! proud Courts, withdraw
   your blaze!
Ye little Stars! hide your diminiſh'd rays.
B. And what? no monument, inſcription, ſtone?
His race, his form, his name almoſt unknown?
P. Who builds a church to God, and not to Fame,
Will never mark the marble with his Name: 286
Go, ſearch it there, where to be born and die,
Of rich and poor, makes all the hiſtory;
                                    Enough,

VARIATIONS.

VER. 287. thus in the MS.
   The Regiſter inrolls him with his Poor,
   Tells he was born and dy'd, and tells no more.
   Juſt as he ought, he fill'd the ſpace between;
   Then ſtole to reſt, unheeded and unſeen.

NOTES.

VER. 275. *Thrice happy man!*] At laſt Lord Bathurſt is allowed to interpoſe a few words: and aſk a queſtion.

VER. 281. *Bluſh, Grandeur, bluſh! proud Courts, withdraw your blaze, &c.*] In this ſublime apoſtrophe, *proud Courts* are not bid to *bluſh* becauſe *outſtript* in virtue; for no ſuch contention is ſuppoſed: but for being *outſhined* in their own proper pretentions to Splendor and Magnificence.   SCRIBL.

VER. 286. *Will never mark*] As Voltaire did at Ferney, with this inſcription: " Deo erexit Voltaire."

VER. 287. *Go, ſearch it there,*] The Pariſh regiſter.

Enough, that Virtue fill'd the space between;
Prov'd, by the ends of being, to have been. 290
When Hopkins dies, a thousand lights attend
The wretch, who living sav'd a candle's end:
Should'ring God's altar a vile image stands,
Belies his features, nay extends his hands;
That live-long wig which Gorgon's self might own,
Eternal buckle takes in Parian stone. 296
Behold what blessings Wealth to life can lend!
And see, what comfort it affords our end.

In the worst inn's worst room, with mat half-hung,
The floors of plaister, and the walls of dung, 300
On once a flock-bed, but repair'd with straw,
With tape-ty'd curtains, never meant to draw,
The George and Garter dangling from that bed
Where tawdry yellow strove with dirty red,
Great Villers lies—alas! how chang'd from him,
That life of pleasure, and that soul of whim! 306
Gallant

NOTES.

VER. 296. *Eternal buckle takes in Parian stone.*] The Poet ridicules the wretched taste of carving large perriwigs on bustos, of which there are several vile examples in the tombs at Westminster and elsewhere. P.

VER. 305. *Great Villers lies—*] This Lord, yet more famous for his vices than his misfortunes, having been possessed of about 50,000 l. a year, and passed through many of the highest posts in the kingdom, died in the year 1687, in a remote inn in Yorkshire, reduced to the utmost misery. P.

" When this extraordinary man, with the figure and genius of Alcibiades, could equally charm the presbyterian Fairfax, and the dissolute Charles; when he alike ridiculed that witty king, and his
solemn

Gallant and gay, in Cliveden's proud alcove,
The bow'r of wanton Shrewfbury and love;
Or juſt as gay, at Council, in a ring
Of mimick Stateſmen, and their merry King. 310
                                                                                    No

NOTES.

folemn chancellor; when he plotted the ruin of his country with a cabal of bad miniſters; or equally unprincipled fupported its caufe with bad patriots; one laments that fuch parts fhould have been devoid of every virtue. But when Alcibiades turns chymiſt; when he is a real bubble, and a vifionary mifer; when ambition is but a frolic; when the worſt defigns are for the foolifheſt ends; contempt extinguifhes all reflections on his character. The portrait of this duke has been drawn by four maſterly hands: Burnet has hewn it with a rough chiffel: Count Hamilton touched it with that flight delicacy that finifhes while it feems to fketch: Dryden catched the living likenefs: Pope completed the hiſtorical refemblance. Yet the abilities of this Lord appear in no inſtance more amazing, than that being expofed by two of the greateſt Poets, he has expofed one of them ten times more feverely. Zimri is an admirable portrait; but Bayes an original creation. Dryden fatirized Buckingham; but Villers made Dryden fatirize himfelf." Catalogue of Noble Authors, vol. ii. p. 77.

VER. 307. *Cliveden*] A delightful palace, on the banks of the Thames, built by the D. of Buckingham. P.

VER. 308. *Shrewſbury*] The Countefs of Shrewfbury, a woman abandoned to gallantries. The Earl her hufband was killed by the Duke of Buckingham in a duel; and it has been faid, that during the combat fhe held the Duke's horfes in the habit of a page. P.

VER. 308. *The bow'r*] This very infamous Countefs of Shrewfbury was eldeſt daughter of Robert Brudenel Earl of Cardigan. Her hufband was killed March 16, 1667. She afterwards married George Rodney Bridges Efq. fecond fon of Sir Thomas Bridges of Keynſham in Somerfetſhire, Knt. and died April 20, 1702. The noble houfe of Cliveden, fo delightfully and fuperbly fituated on the banks of the Thames, which had been the refidence of Frederick Prince of Wales, who lived in it for many years with a proper dignity and magnificence, attended by many

No Wit to flatter, left of all his ſtore!
No Fool to laugh at, which he valu'd more.
There, Victor of his health, of fortune, friends,
And fame; this lord of uſeleſs thouſands ends.
 His Grace's fate ſage Cutler could foreſee, 315
And well (he thought) advis'd him, " Live like me."
As well his Grace reply'd, " Like you, Sir John?
" That I can do, when all I have is gone."
Reſolve me, Reaſon, which of theſe is worſe,
Want with a full, or with an empty purſe? 320
Thy life more wretched, Cutler, was confeſs'd,
Ariſe, and tell me, was thy death more bleſs'd?
Cutler ſaw tenants break, and houſes fall,
For very want; he could not build a wall.
His only daughter in a ſtranger's pow'r, 325
For very want; he could not pay a dow'r.
A few grey hairs his rev'rend temples crown'd,
'Twas very want that ſold them for two pound.
What ev'n deny'd a cordial at his end,
Baniſh'd the doctor, and expell'd the friend? 330
What but a want, which you perhaps think mad,
Yet numbers feel, the want of what he had!
            Cutler

NOTES.

of the firſt geniuſes of the age, was unfortunately burnt to the ground in May 1795, and nothing of its elegant furniture preſerved from the flames but the fine tapeſtry that repreſented the Duke of Marlborough's victories. The beautiful Maſk of Alfred was written and acted at Clivedon in 1744. In the duel mentioned above, the Duke of Buckingham had for his two ſeconds, captain Holmes and Mr. Jenkins. The Earl of Shrewſbury's ſeconds were Sir John Talbot of Laycock, and Mr. Bernard Howard. The Duke of Buckingham mortally wounded the Earl.

Cutler and Brutus, dying, both exclaim,
" Virtue! and Wealth! what are ye but a name!"
Say, for fuch worth are other worlds prepar'd?
Or are they both, in this their own reward? 336
A knotty point! to which we now proceed.
But you are tir'd—I'll tell a tale—B. Agreed.
P. Where London's column, pointing at the fkies
Like a tall bully, lifts the head, and lies; 340
There dwelt a Citizen of fober fame,
A plain good man, and Balaam was his name;
                                            Religious,

VARIATIONS.
VER. 337. in the former Editions,
   That knotty point, my Lord, fhall I c. fcufs,
   Or tell a tale?—A Tale.—It follows thus.

NOTES.
VER. 333. Cutler *and* Brutus, *dying, both exclaim,*
   " *Virtue! and Wealth! what are ye but a name!*"]
There is a greater beauty in this comparifon than the common reader is aware of. *Brutus* was, in *morals*, at leaft, a *Stoic*, like his uncle. And how much addicted to that fect in general, appears from his profeffing himfelf of the old Academy, and being a moft paffionate admirer of *Antiochus Afcalonites,* an effential *Stoic,* if ever there was any. Now *Stoical virtue* was, as our author truly tells us, not *exercife,* but apathy, *Contracted all, retiring to the breaft.* In a word, like Sir *J. Cutler's purfe,* nothing for ufe, but kept clofe fhut, and centered all within himfelf.—Now *virtue* and *wealth,* thus circumftanced, are, indeed, no other than mere *names.* W.——A moft tortured meaning!

VER. 339. *Where London's column,*] The Monument built in memory of the fire of London, with an infcription importing that city to have been burnt by the Papifts.   P.

VER. 340. *Like a tall* bully, *lifts the head, and lies* ;] It were to be wifhed, the *City monument* had been compared to fomething of more dignity: As, to the *Court-champion,* for inftance, fince, like him, it only fpoke the fenfe of the Government.   SCRIBL.

VER. 341. *There dwelt a Citizen*] This tale of Sir Balaam, his progrefs and change of manners, from being a plodding, fober, plain,

Religious, punctual, frugal, and so forth;
His word would pass for more than he was worth.
One solid dish his week-day meal affords, 345
And adding pudding solemniz'd the Lord's:
Constant at Church, and 'Change; his gains were sure,
His givings rare, save farthings to the poor.
  The Dev'l was piqu'd such saintship to behold,
And long'd to tempt him like good Job of old: 350
But Satan now is wiser than of yore,
And tempts by making rich, not making poor.
  Rous'd by the Prince of Air, the whirlwinds sweep
The surge, and plunge his Father in the deep;
Then full against his Cornish lands they roar, 355
And two rich shipwrecks bless the lucky shore.

Sir

NOTES.

plain, and punctual citizen, to his becoming a debauched and dissolute courtier and senator, abounds in much knowledge of life, and many strokes of true humour, and will bear to be compared to the exquisite history of Eugenio and Corusodes in one of Swift's Intelligencers.

  VER. 351. *But Satan*] Sherlock is of opinion, that Moses would not mention Satan as an agent, in his History of the Temptation, least it should communicate or countenance the notion of two independent principles of good and evil. And yet afterwards, he asserts, that the Book of Job, in which Satan is openly named and introduced, is of an age prior to the writings of Moses. Disc. on Prophecy.

  VER. 355. *Cornish*] The Author has placed the scene of these shipwrecks in Cornwall, not only from their frequency on that coast, but from the inhumanity of the inhabitants to those to whom that misfortune arrives: When a ship happens to be stranded there, they have been known to bore holes in it, prevent its getting off: to plunder, and sometimes even to massacre the people: Nor has the Parliament of England been yet able wholly to suppress these barbarities.   P.

Sir Balaam now, he lives like other folks,
He takes his chirping pint, and cracks his Jokes:
" Live like yourfelf," was foon my Lady's word;
And lo ! two puddings fmoak'd upon the board. 360
 Afleep and naked as an Indian lay,
An honeft factor ftole a Gem away:
He pledg'd it to the Knight, the Knight had wit,
So kept the Di'mond, and the rogue was bit. 364
Some fcruple rofe, but thus he eas'd his thought,
" I'll now give fixpence where I gave a groat;
" Where once I went to church, I'll now go twice—
" And am fo clear too of all other vice."
 The Tempter faw his time; the work he ply'd;
Stocks and Subfcriptions pour on ev'ry fide, 370
Till all the Demon makes his full defcent
In one abundant fhow'r of Cent per Cent,
Sinks deep within him, and poffeffes whole,
Then dubs Director, and fecures his foul.
 Behold Sir Balaam, now a man of fpirit, 375
Afcribes his gettings to his parts and merit;
What late he call'd a Bleffing, now was Wit,
And God's good Providence, a lucky Hit.

Things

NOTES.

VER. 377. *What late he call'd a Bleffing, now was Wit, &c.*]
This is an admirable picture of human nature: In the entrance
into life, all, but coxcombs-born, are modeft; and efteem the favours of their fuperiors as marks of their benevolence: But if
thefe favours happen to increafe; then, inftead of advancing in
gratitude to our benefactors, we only improve in the good opinion
of ourfelves; and the conftant returns of fuch favours make us
confider them no longer as accommodations to our wants, or the
hire of our fervice, but debts due to our merit: Yet, at the fame
time, to do juftice to our common nature, we fhould obferve,
that

Things change their titles, as our manners turn:
His Compting-houfe employ'd the Sunday-morn;
Seldom at Church ('twas fuch a bufy life) 381
But duly fent his family and wife.
There (fo the Dev'l ordain'd) one Chriftmas-tide
My good old Lady catch'd a cold, and dy'd.

   A Nymph of Quality admires our Knight; 385
He marries, bows at Court, and grows polite:
Leaves the dull Cits, and joins (to pleafe the fair)
The well-bred cuckolds in St. James's air:
Firft, for his Son a gay Commiffion buys,
Who drinks, whores, fights, and in a duel dies: 390
His Daughter flaunts a Vifcount's tawdry wife;
She bears a Coronet and P—x for life.
In Britain's Senate he a feat obtains,
And one more Penfioner St. Stephen gains.

   My

NOTES.

that this does not proceed fo often from downright vice as is imagined, but frequently from mere infirmity; of which the reafon is evident; for, having fmall knowledge, and yet an exceffive opinion of ourfelves, we eftimate our merit by the paffions and caprice of others; and this perhaps would not be fo much amifs, were we not apt to take their favours for a declaration of their fenfe of our merits. How often, for inftance, has it been feen, in the three learned profeffions, that a Man, who, had he continued in his primeval meannefs, would have circumfcribed his knowledge within the modeft limits of Socrates; yet, being *pufhed up*, as the phrafe is, has felt himfelf growing into a *Hooker*, a *Hales*, or a *Sydenham;* while, in the rapidity of his courfe, he imagined he faw, at every new ftation, a new door of fcience opening to him, without fo much as ftaying for a Flatterer to let him in?

    " ——Beatus enim jam
Cum pulchris tunicis fumet nova confilia." W.

IMITATIONS.

VER. 394. *And one more Penfioner St. Steven gains.*]
    " ——atque unum civem donare *Sibyllæ*." Juv.

My Lady falls to play; so bad her chance, 395
He muſt repair it; takes a bribe from France;
The Houſe impeach him; Coningſby harangues;
The Court forſake him, and Sir Balaam hangs:
Wife, ſon, and daughter, Satan! are thy own,
His wealth, yet dearer, forfeit to the Crown: 400
The Devil and the King divide the Prize,
And ſad Sir Balaam curſes God and dies.

VER. 401. *The Devil and the King divide the Prize,*] This is to be underſtood in a very ſober and *decent* ſenſe; as a Satire only on ſuch Miniſters of State (which hiſtory informs us have been found) who aided the *Devil* in his *temptations*, in order to foment, if not to make, Plots for the ſake of confiſcations. So ſure always, and juſt, is our Author's ſatire, even in thoſe places where he ſeems moſt to have indulged himſelf only in an elegant *badinage*. But this Satire on the abuſe of the general laws of forfeiture for high-treaſon, which laws all well-policied communities have found neceſſary, is by no means to be underſtood as a reflection on the Laws themſelves; whoſe neceſſity, equity, and even lenity have been excellently well vindicated in that very learned and elegant Diſcourſe, intitled, *Some Conſiderations on the Law of Forfeiture for High Treaſon. Third Edition,* London, 1748. W.

Methinks it was better in the former Editions, becauſe ſhorter:
Wife, ſon, and daughter, Satan! are thy prize,
And ſad Sir Balaam curſes God and dies.

VER. 402. *Curſes God*] Alluding to the ſecond chapter of the Book of Job; on which paſſage Warburton made (Divine Legation, Book vi.) the following remarkable obſervation: " The wife of Job acts a ſmall part in this drama, but a very ſpirited one. Then ſaid his wife unto him, ‘ Doſt thou ſtill retain thy integrity? Curſe God and die.' Tender and pious! He might ſee by this prelude of his ſpouſe, what he was to expect from his friends. The Devil, indeed, aſſaulted Job, but he ſeems to have got poſſeſſion of his wife." p. 261.

EPISTLE IV.

TO

RICHARD BOYLE, EARL OF BURLINGTON.

ARGUMENT.

Of the Use *of* RICHES.

THE Vanity of Expence in People of Wealth and Quality. The abuse of the Word Taste, Ver. 13. *That the first Principle and foundation in this, as in every thing else, is* Good Sense, Ver. 40. *The chief proof of it is to* follow Nature, *even in works of mere Luxury and Elegance. Instanced in* Architecture *and* Gardening, *where all must be adapted to the* Genius *and* Use *of the* Place, *and the Beauties not forced into it, but resulting from it,* Ver. 50. *How men are disappointed in their most expensive undertakings, for want of this true Foundation, without which nothing can please long, if at all; and the best* Examples *and* Rules *will be but perverted into something* burdensome *and* ridiculous, Ver. 65, &c. to 92. *A description of the* false Taste *of* Magnificence; *the first grand Error of which is to imagine that* Greatness *consists in the* Size *and* Dimension, *instead of the* Proportion *and* Harmony *of the* whole, Ver. 97. *and the second, either in joining together* Parts incoherent, *or too* minutely resembling, *or in the* Repetition *of the same too frequently,* Ver. 105, &c. *A word or two of false Taste in* Books, *in* Music, *in* Painting, *even in* Preaching *and* Prayer, *and lastly*

lastly in Entertainments, Ver. 133, &c. *Yet* PROVIDENCE *is justified in giving Wealth to be squandered in this manner, since it is dispersed to the Poor and laborious part of mankind,* Ver. 169. [*recurring to what is laid down in the first book, Ep.* ii. *and in the Epistle preceding this,* Ver. 159. &c.] *What are the* proper Objects *of Magnificence, and a proper field for the Expence of* Great Men, Ver. 177, &c. *and finally the Great and Public Works which become a* Prince, Ver. 191. to the end.

EPISTLE IV.

'TIS ſtrange, the Miſer ſhould his Cares employ
To gain thoſe Riches he can ne'er enjoy:
Is it leſs ſtrange, the Prodigal ſhould waſte
His wealth, to purchaſe what he ne'er can taſte?
Not for himſelf he ſees, or hears, or eats; 5
Artiſts muſt chuſe his Pictures, Muſic, Meats:
He buys for Topham, Drawings and Deſigns,
For Pembroke, Statues, dirty Gods, and Coins;
Rare monkiſh Manuſcripts for Hearne alone,
And Books for Mead, and Butterflies for Sloane. 10

Think

NOTES.

VER. 1. *'Tis ſtrange,*] This Epiſtle was written and publiſhed before the preceding one; and the placing it after the third, has occaſioned ſome aukward anachroniſms and inconſiſtencies.

VER. 7. *Topham,*] A Gentleman famous for a judicious collection of Drawings. P.

VER. 8. *For Pembroke, Statues,*] "The ſoul of Inigo Jones," ſays Mr. Walpole, "which had been patronized by the anceſtors of Henry Earl of Pembroke, ſeemed ſtill to hover over its favourite Wilton, and to have aſſiſted the Muſes of Arts in the education of this noble perſon. The towers, the chambers, the ſcenes which Holbein, Jones, and Vandyck had decorated, and which Earl Thomas had enriched with the ſpoils of the beſt ages, received the laſt touches of beauty from Earl Henry's hand.

VER. 10. *And Books for Mead, and Butterflies for Sloane.*] Two eminent Phyſicians; the one had an excellent Library, the other the fineſt collection in Europe of natural curioſities; both men of great learning and humanity. P.

Think we all thefe are for himfelf? no more
Than his fine Wife, alas! or finer Whore.
For what has Virro painted, built, and planted?
Only to fhow, how many Taftes he wanted.
What brought Sir Vifto's ill-got wealth to wafte? 15
Some Demon whifper'd, " Vifto! have a Tafte."
Heav'n vifits with a Tafte the wealthy fool,
And needs no Rod but Ripley with a Rule.
See! fportive fate, to punifh aukward pride,
Bids Bubo build, and fends him fuch a Guide: 20
A ftanding fermon, at each year's expence,
That never Coxcomb reach'd Magnificence!
                                        You

VARIATIONS.

After Ver. 22. in the MS.
    Muft Bifhops, Lawyers, Statefmen have the fkill
    To build, to plant, judge paintings, what you will?
    Then why not Kent as well our treaties draw,
    Bridgman explain the Gofpel, Gibbs the Law?

NOTES.

VER. 11. *Think we all thefe*] The oftentation of this man of falfe tafte is only here ridiculed; he has no enjoyment of either of the two objects of falfe magnificence here mentioned.

VER. 17. *Heav'n vifits with a Tafte the wealthy fool,*] The prefent rage of *Tafte*, in this overflow of general Luxury, may be very properly reprefented by a *defolating peftilence*, alluded to in the word *vifit*.   W.

VER. 18. *Ripley*] This man was a carpenter, employed by a firft Minifter, who raifed him to an Architect, without any genius in the art; and after fome wretched proofs of his infufficiency in public Buildings, made him Comptroller of the Board of Works. P.
——But Mr. Walpole fpeaks more favourably of this architect.

VER. 19. *See! fportive fate, to punifh aukward pride,*] Pride is one of the greateft mifchiefs, as well as higheft abfurdities of our nature; and therefore, as appears both from profane and facred Hiftory, has ever been the more peculiar object of divine vengeance.

You fhow us, Rome was glorious, not profufe,
And pompous buildings once were things of Ufe.
                                                Yet

NOTES.

geance. But *aukward Pride* intimates fuch abilities in its owner, as eafes us of the apprehenfion of much mifchief from it; fo that the Poet fuppofes fuch a one fecure from the ferious refentment of Heaven, though it may permit *fate* or *fortune* to bring him into that public contempt and ridicule which his natural badnefs of heart fo well deferves.   W.

VER. 23. The Earl of Burlington was then publifhing the Defigns of Inigo Jones, and the Antiquities of Rome by Palladio. P.

VER. 23. *You fhow us, Rome*] Thus our Author addreffes the Earl of Burlington, who was then publifhing the Defigns of Inigo Jones, and the Antiquities of Rome by Palladio. " Never was protection and great wealth *," fays an able judge of the fubject, " more generoufly and judicioufly diffufed than by this great perfon, who had every quality of a genius and artift, except envy. Though his own defigns were more chafte and claffic than Kent's, he entertained him in his houfe till his death, and was more ftudious to extend his friend's fame than his own. As we have few famples of architecture more antique and impofing than the colonnade within the court of his houfe in Piccadilly, I cannot help mentioning the effect it had on myfelf. I had not only never feen it, but had never heard of it, at leaft with any attention, when, foon after my return from Italy, I was invited to a ball at Burlington-houfe. As I paffed under the gate by night, it could not ftrike me. At day-break, looking out of the window to fee the fun rife, I was furprifed with the vifion of the colonnade that fronted me. It feemed one of thofe edifices in Fairy tales, that are raifed by genii in a night's time." Pope having appeared an excellent moralift in the foregoing Epiftles, in this appears to be as excellent a connoiffeur, and has given not only fome of our firft, but our beft rules and obfervations on architecture and gardening, but particularly on the latter of thefe ufeful and entertaining arts, on which he has dwelt more largely, and with rather more knowledge of the fubject. The following is copied *verbatim* from a little paper which he gave to Mr. Spence : " Arts are taken from

---

* Mr. Walpole, p. 108. Anecdotes of Painting, vol. iv.

nature :

Yet shall (my Lord) your just, your noble rules, 25
Fill half the land with Imitating-Fools;
                                                    Who

NOTES.

nature; and, after a thousand vain efforts for improvements, are best when they return to their first simplicity. A sketch or analysis of the first principles of each art, with their first consequences, might be a thing of most excellent service. Thus, for instance, all the rules of architecture might be reducible to three or four heads; the justness of the openings; bearings upon bearings; the regularity of the pillars, &c. That which is not just in buildings is disagreeable to the eye, (as a greater upon a lesser, &c.) and this may be called *the reasoning of the eye*. In laying out a garden, the first and chief thing to be considered is the genius of the place. Thus at Riskins, now called Piercy Lodge, Lord *** should have raised two or three mounts, because his situation is all a plain, and nothing can please without variety."

Mr. Walpole, in his elegant and entertaining History of Modern Gardening, has clearly proved that Kent was the artist to whom the English nation was chiefly indebted for diffusing a taste in laying out grounds, of which the French and Italians have no idea. But he adds, much to the credit of our Author, that Pope undoubtedly contributed to form Kent's taste. The design of the Prince of Wales's garden at Carlton House was evidently borrowed from the Poet's at Twickenham. There was a little affected modesty in the latter, when he said, of all his Works he was most proud of his garden. And yet it was a singular effort of art and taste to impress so much variety and scenery on a spot of five acres. The passing through the gloom from the grotto to the opening day, the retiring and again assembling shades, the dusky groves, the larger lawn, and the solemnity of the termination at the cypresses that lead up to his mother's tomb, are managed with exquisite judgment; and though Lord Peterborough assisted him

" To form his quincunx, and to rank his vines,"

those were not the most pleasing ingredients of his little perspective. I do not know whether the disposition of the garden at Rousham, laid out by General Dormer, and, in my opinion, the most engaging of all Kent's works, was not planned on the model of Mr. Pope's, at least in the opening and retiring " shades of Venus's Vale."

It

Who random drawings from your sheets shall take,
And of one beauty many blunders make;
Load

NOTES.

It ought to be observed, that many years before this Epistle was written, and before Kent was employed as an improver of grounds, even so early as the year 1713, Pope seems to have been the very first person that censured and ridiculed the formal French, Dutch, false and unnatural mode in gardening, by a paper in the Guardian, No. 173, levelled against capricious operations of art, and every species of verdant sculpture and inverted nature; which paper abounds with wit as well as taste, and ends with a ridiculous catalogue of various figures cut in evergreens. Neither do I think that these four lines in this Epistle,

> Here Amphitrite sails thro' myrtle bow'rs;
> There gladiators fight, or die in flow'rs:
> Unwater'd see the drooping sea-horse mourn,
> And swallows roost on Nilus' dusty urn;

do at all excel the following passage in his Guardian:

" A citizen is no sooner proprietor of a couple of yews, but he entertains thoughts of erecting them into giants, like those of Guildhall. I know of an eminent cook who beautified his country-seat with a coronation dinner in greens, where you see the champion flourishing on horseback at the end of the table, and the queen in perpetual youth at the other."

But it was the vigorous and creative imagination of Milton, superior to the prejudices of his times, that exhibited in his Eden the first hints and outlines of what a beautiful garden should be; for even his beloved Ariosto and Tasso, in their luxuriant pictures of the gardens of Alcina and Armida, shewed they were not free from the unnatural and narrow taste of their countrymen; and even his master, Spencer, has an artificial fountain in the midst of his bowre of blifs.

I cannot forbear taking occasion to remark in this place, that in the sacred drama, intitled L'Adamo, written and published at Milan, in the year 1617, by Gio Battista Andreini, a Florentine, which Milton certainly had read, (and of which Voltaire has given so false and so imperfect an account in his Essays on the Epic Poets,) the prints that are to represent Paradise are full of clipt hedges, square parterres, strait walks, trees uniformly lopt, regular knots and carpets of flowers, groves nodding at groves, marble fountains,

Load some vain Church with old Theatric state,
Turn Arcs of Triumph to a Garden-gate;   30
                                        Reverse

NOTES.

fountains, and water-works. And yet these prints were designed by Carlo Antonio Proccachini, a celebrated landscape painter of his time, and of the school of the Carraches: many of those works are still admired at Milan. To every scene of this drama is prefixed a print of this artist's designing. The poem, though wild and incorrect, has many strokes of genius. The author was an actor.

It hence appears, that this enchanting art of modern gardening, in which this kingdom claims a preference over every nation in Europe, chiefly owes its origin and its improvements to two great poets, Milton and Pope. May I be suffered to add, in behalf of a favourite author, and who would have been a first-rate poet, if his style had been equal to his conceptions, that the Seasons of Thomson have been very instrumental in diffusing a general taste for the beauties of nature and landscape?

VER. 28. *And of one beauty many blunders make;*] Because the road to *Taste*, like that to Truth, is but one; and those to Error and Absurdity a thousand.

VER. 29. *Load some vain Church with old Theatric state,*] In which there is a complication of absurdities, arising both from their different *natures* and *forms:* For the one being for *religious service,* and the other only for *civil amusement,* it is impossible that the profuse and lascivious ornaments of the latter should become the modesty and sanctity of the other. Nor will any examples of this vanity of dress in the sacred buildings of antiquity justify this imitation; for those ornaments might be very suitable to a Temple of Bacchus, or Venus, which would ill become the sobriety and purity of the Christian Religion.

Besides, it should be considered, that the form of a Theatre would not permit the architectonic ornaments to be placed but on the outward face; whereas those of a *Church* may be as commodiously, and are more properly put within; particularly in great and close pent-up Cities, where the incessant driving of the smoke, in a little time, corrodes and destroys all outward ornaments of this kind; especially if the members, as in the common taste, be small and little.

Our

Reverſe your Ornaments; and hang them all
On ſome patch'd dog-hole ek'd with ends of wall;
                                                    Then

NOTES.

Our Gothic anceſtors had juſter and manlier notions of magnificence, on Greek and Roman ideas, than theſe Mimics of *Taſte*, who profeſs to ſtudy only claſſic elegance. And becauſe the thing does honour to the genius of thoſe Barbarians, I ſhall endeavour to explain it. All our antient Churches are called, without diſtinction, *Gothic*; but erroneouſly. They are of two ſorts; the one built in the *Saxon* times; the other in the *Norman*. Several *Cathedral* and *Collegiate* Churches of the firſt ſort are yet remaining, either in whole or in part: of which, this was the Original: When the Saxon kings became Chriſtian, their piety (which was the piety of the times) confiſted in building Churches at home, and performing pilgrimages abroad, eſpecially to the Holy Land: and theſe ſpiritual Exerciſes aſſiſted and ſupported one another. For the moſt venerable as well as moſt elegant models of religious edifices were then in Paleſtine. From theſe, our Saxon Builders took the whole of their ideas, as may be ſeen by comparing the drawings which travellers have given us of the churches yet ſtanding in that country, with the Saxon remains of what we find at home; and particularly in that ſameneſs of ſtyle in the *later* religious edifices of the Knights Templars (profeſſedly built upon the model of the church of the Holy Sepulchre at Jeruſalem) with the earlier remains of our Saxon Edifices. Now the architecture of the Holy Land was Grecian, but greatly fallen from its antient elegance. Our Saxon performance was indeed a bad copy of it; and as much inferior to the works of St. Helene and Juſtinian, as theirs were to the Grecian models they had followed: Yet ſtill the footſteps of antient art appeared in the circular arches, the entire columns, the diviſion of the entablature, into a ſort of Architrave, Frize, and Corniche, and a ſolidity equally diffuſed over the whole maſs. This, by way of diſtinction, I would call the SAXON Architecture.

But our Norman works had a very different original. When the *Goths* had conquered Spain, and the genial warmth of the climate, and the religion of the old inhabitants, had ripened their wits, and inflamed their miſtaken piety, (both kept in exerciſe by the neighbourhood of the Saracens, through emulation of their ſcience and averſion to their ſuperſtition,) they ſtruck out a new
                                                    ſpecies

Then clap four slices of Pilaster on't,
That, lac'd with bits of rustic, makes a Front.
Shall

NOTES.

species of Architecture unknown to Greece and Rome; upon original principles and ideas much nobler than what had given birth even to classical magnificence: For this northern people having been accustomed, during the gloom of paganism, to worship the Deity in GROVES, (a practice common to all nations,) when their new religion required covered edifices, they ingeniously projected to make them resemble *Groves,* as nearly as the distance of Architecture would permit; at once indulging their old prejudices, and providing for their present conveniencies, by a cool receptacle in a sultry climate. And with what skill and success they executed the project by the assistance of Saracen Architects, whose exotic style of building very luckily suited their purpose, appears from hence, That no attentive observer ever viewed a regular Avenue of well-grown trees, intermixing their branches over head, but it presently put him in mind of the long Visto through a Gothic Cathedral; or ever entered one of the larger and more elegant Edifices of this kind, but it represented to his imagination an Avenue of trees. And this alone is what can be truly called the GOTHIC style of Building.

Under this idea, of so extraordinary a species of Architecture, all the irregular transgressions against art, all the monstrous offences against nature, disappear; every thing has its reason, every thing is in order, and an harmonious Whole arises from the studious application of means, proper and proportioned to the end. For could the *Arches* be otherwise than *pointed* when the Workman was to imitate that curve which branches of two opposite trees make by their interfection with one another? Or could the *Columns* be otherwise than split into distinct shafts, when they were to represent the Stems of a clump of Trees growing close together? On the same principles they formed the spreading ramification of the stone-work in the windows, and the stained glass in the interstices; the one to represent the branches, and the other the leaves, of an opening Grove; and both concurred to preserve that gloomy light which inspires religious reverence and dread. Lastly, we see the reason of their studied aversion to *apparent* solidity in these stupendous masses, deemed so absurd by men accustomed to the *apparent* as well as *real* strength of Grecian Architecture.
Had

Shall call the winds through long arcades to roar, 35
Proud to catch cold at a Venetian door;
                                            Conscious

NOTES.

Had it been only a wanton exercise of the Artist's skill, to shew he could give real strength without the appearance of any, we might indeed admire his superior science, but we must needs condemn his ill judgment. But when one considers, that this surprising lightness was necessary to complete the execution of his idea of a Sylvan place of worship, one cannot sufficiently admire the ingenuity of the contrivance.

This too will account for the contrary qualities in what I call the *Saxon Architecture*. These artists copied, as has been said, from the churches in the Holy Land, which were built on the models of the Grecian Architecture; but corrupted by prevailing barbarism; and still further depraved by a religious idea. The first places of Christian worship were Sepulchres and subterraneous caverns, low and heavy from necessity. When Christianity became the Religion of the State, and sumptuous Temples began to be erected, they yet, in regard to the first pious ages, preserved the massive Style; made still more venerable by the *Church of the Holy Sepulchre;* where this style was, on a double account, followed and aggravated.

Such as is here described was GOTHIC ARCHITECTURE. And it would be no discredit to the warmest admirers of *Jones* and *Palladio* to acknowledge it hath its merit. They must at least confess it had a nobler birth, though an humbler fortune, than the GREEK and ROMAN ARCHITECTURE.—The Reader may see Sir Christopher Wren's account of this matter from some papers of his, published since the printing this, in a book called *Parentalia*, page 273—297—306-7-8—355, and then judge for himself. W. —See Wren's Parentalia, the Preface to Bentham's History of Ely Cathedral, in which it is said he was assisted by Gray. A fuller history of Gothic and Saxon Architecture, on another idea, is expected from an able hand.

VER. 30. *Turn Arcs of Triumph to a Garden-gate;*] This absurdity seems to have arisen from an injudicious imitation of what these Builders might have heard of, at the entrance of the antient Gardens of Rome: But they do not consider, that those were
                                                                            public

Conscious they act a true Palladian part,
And if they starve, they starve by rules of art.
Oft have you hinted to your brother Peer,
A certain truth, which many buy too dear: 40
Something there is more needful than Expence,
And something previous ev'n to Taste—'tis Sense:
Good Sense, which only is the gift of Heav'n,
And though no Science, fairly worth the seven:
A Light, which in yourself you must perceive; 45
Jones and Le Nôtre have it not to give.

To build, to plant, whatever you intend,
To rear the Column, or the Arch to bend,
To swell the Terras, or to sink the Grot;
In all, let Nature never be forgot. 50
But treat the Goddess like a modest fair,
Nor over-dress, nor leave her wholly bare;
             Let

NOTES.

public Gardens, given to the people by some great man after a triumph; to which, therefore, Arcs of this kind were very suitable ornaments. W.

 Ver. 36. *Proud to catch cold at a Venetian door;*] In the foregoing instances, the Poet exposes the absurd imitation of foreign and discordant *manners* in *public* buildings; here he turns to the still greater absurdity of taking their models from a discordant *climate*, in their *private:* which folly, he supposes, may be more easily redressed, as men will be sooner brought to feel for themselves than to see for the public. W.

 Ver. 46. *Le Nôtre*] The architect of the groves and grottos of Versailles: He came hither on a mission to improve our taste. He planted St. James's and Greenwich Parks: no great monuments of his invention." Walpole on Gardening, p. 278.

 Ver. 50. *In all, let Nature*] In Castell's Villas of the Antients, folio, London, 1728, may be seen how much the celebrated Tuscan villa resembled our gardens, as they were planned a few years ago. Pliny's villa was like his genius.

Ep. IV. MORAL ESSAYS.

Let not each beauty ev'ry where be fpy'd,
Where half the fkill is decently to hide.
He gains all points, who pleafingly confounds, 55
Surprizes, varies, and conceals the Bounds.
Confult the Genius of the Place in all ;
That tells the Waters or to rife, or fall;

Or

NOTES.

VER. 53. *Let not each beauty ev'ry where be fpy'd,*] For when the fame beauty obtrudes itfelf upon you over and over ; when it meets you full at whatever place you ftop, or to whatever point you turn, then Nature lofes her proper charms of a *modeft fair;* and you begin to hate and naufeate her as a proftitute. W.

VER. 54. *Where half the fkill is decently to hide.*] If the Poet was right in comparing the true drefs of *Nature* to that of a *modeft fair*, it is a plain confequence, that one half of the defigner's art muft be, *decently to hide;* as the other half is *gracefully to difcover.* W.

VER. 57. *Confult the Genius of the Place, &c.* to *defigns,* Ver. 64.] The perfonalizing, or rather *deifying,* the Genius *of the place,* in order to be confulted as an *Oracle,* has produced one of the nobleft and moft fublime defcriptions of *Defign* that Poetry could exprefs. Where this *Genius,* while prefiding over the work, is reprefented by little and little, as advancing from a fimple *advifer,* to a *creator* of all the beauties of improved Nature, in a variety of bold metaphors and allufions, all rifing one above another, till they complete the unity of the general idea.

Firft, the *Genius* of the place *tells the waters,* or only fimply gives directions : Then he *helps th' ambitious hill,* or is a fellowlabourer : Then again he *fcoops the circling Theatre,* or works alone, or in chief. Afterwards, rifing faft in our idea of dignity, he *calls in the country,* alluding to the orders of princes in their progrefs, when accuftomed to difplay all their ftate and magnificence : His character then grows facred, he *joins willing woods,* a metaphor taken from one of the offices of the priefthood ; till at length he becomes a Divinity, and creates and prefides over the whole :

" Now breaks, or now directs, th' intending lines ;
 Paints as you plant, and, as you work, defigns."

Much

Or helps th' ambitious Hill the Heav'ns to scale,
Or scoops in circling theatres the Vale; 60
Calls in the Country, catches op'ning Glades,
Joins willing Woods, and varies Shades from Shades;
Now breaks, or now directs, th' intending Lines;
Paints as you plant, and, as you work, designs.
  Still follow Sense, of ev'ry art the soul, 65
Parts answ'ring parts shall slide into a whole,
                                          Spon-

NOTES.

Much in the same manner as the *plastic Nature* is supposed to do in the work of generation. W.——Not a single remark will I make on this supposed string of fanciful metaphors and allusions here ascribed to the Poet, but leave it to the derision and astonishment of the reader, or rather his regret and concern, at seeing so considerable a writer as this commentator trifle so egregiously, and endeavour to mislead the reader, and expose the Poet; who would have been ridiculous enough if these extorted meanings could be justly imputed to him.

VER. 58. *That tells the Waters*] Would it not give life and vigour to this noble *prosopopœia*, if we were to venture to alter only one word, and read, in the second line,

    He tells the Waters——

instead of

    That tells?——

Our Author is never happier than in his allusions to painting, an art he so much admired and understood: So below, at Ver. 81.

    The wood *supports* the plain, the parts *unite*,
    And *strength* of *shade* contends with *strength* of *light*.

Indeed, the two arts in question differ only in the materials which they employ. And it is neither exaggeration or affectation to call Mr. BROWN a great *painter*; for he has realized

    Whate'er LORRAIN light-touch'd with softening hue,
    Or savage ROSA, or learned POUSSIN drew.

VER. 66. *Parts answ'ring parts, shall slide into a whole*,] *i. e.* shall not be *forced*, but *go of themselves;* as if both the parts and whole were not of *yours,* but of *Nature*'s making. The metaphor

4   is

Spontaneous beauties all around advance,
Start ev'n from Difficulty, strike from Chance;
Nature shall join you; Time shall make it grow
A Work to wonder at—perhaps a STOW. 70
Without it, proud Versailles! thy glory falls;
And Nero's Terraces desert their walls:
The vast Parterres a thousand hands shall make,
Lo! COBHAM comes, and floats them with a Lake:
                                                Or

NOTES.

is taken from a piece of mechanism finished by some great master, where all the parts are so previously fitted, as to be easily put together by any ordinary workman: and each part slides into its place, as it were through a groove ready made for that purpose. W.

VER. 69. *Nature shall join you;*] I recollect no antient that had so just a taste as Atticus, who preferred Tully's house at Arpinum to all his other houses; declaring a contempt of the laboured magnificence, marble pavements, artificial canals, and forced streams of the villas of Italy, compared with the natural beauties of this place. De Legibus, lib. ii.

Every reader of taste, we presume, must be acquainted with the English garden of Mr. Mason, and with the commentary and notes upon it by Mr. Burgh.

VER. 70. The seat and gardens of the Lord Viscount Cobham in Buckinghamshire. P.

VER. 71. *Proud Versailles!*] Every instance of false taste and false magnificence is to be found at Versailles; a true picture of the spurious greatness of its vain, gaudy, unnatural, ostentatious owner, Louis XIV.

VER. 72. This line is obscure; it is difficult to know what is meant by the terraces *deserting* their walls. In line 172, below, is another obscurity, " his hard heart denies,"—it does not immediately occur *whose* heart. In line 71, " Without *it*," is obscure. Without what? Good sense, he means, which is too far disjoined in the context.

VER. 74. *Lo!* COBHAM *comes, and floats them with a Lake:*] An high compliment to the noble person on whom it is bestowed, as making him the *substitute of good Sense*.—This office, in the original

Or cut wide views through Mountains to the Plain,
You'll wish your hill or shelter'd seat again. 76
Ev'n in an ornament its place remark,
Nor in an Hermitage set Dr. Clarke.
                                        Behold

NOTES.

ginal plan of the Poem, was given to another Man of Taste, Bridgman; who not having the Sense to see that a compliment was intended him, it convinced the Poet that it did not belong to him.   W.

"Magnificence and splendour are the characteristics of Stow; it is like one of those places celebrated in antiquity, which were devoted to the purposes of religion, and filled with sacred groves, hallowed fountains, and temples dedicated to several deities; the resort of distant nations, and the object of veneration to half the heathen world: this *pomp* is at *Stow*, blended with *beauty;* and the place is equally distinguished by its *amenity* and *grandeur.*"
        Observations on Modern Gardening, p. 213.

Among the many edifices with which these gardens are decorated, one of the most striking is the Temple of the British Worthies, filled with the following Bustoes, with inscriptions containing their respective characters: Pope, Sir Thomas Gresham, Ignatius Jones, John Milton, William Shakespeare, John Locke, Sir Isaac Newton, Sir Francis Bacon, King Alfred, Edward Prince of Wales, Queen Elizabeth, King William III. Sir Walter Raleigh, Sir Francis Drake, John Hampden, Sir John Barnard. Of these characters and inscriptions the two most remarkable are those of Locke and Hampden, which are drawn with great energy, and a strong spirit of liberty.

VER. 75, 76. *Or cut wide views thro' Mountains to the Plain, You'll wish your hill or shelter'd seat again.*] This was done in Hertfordshire by a wealthy citizen, at the expence of above 5000 l. by which means (merely to overlook a dead plain) he let in the north wind upon his house and parterre, which were before adorned and defended by beautiful woods.   P.

VER. 77. *Ev'n in an ornament*] These lines are as ill-placed, and as injudicious, as the busto they were designed to censure. Pope imbibed an aversion to this excellent man from Bolingbroke, who hated Clarke, not only because he had written a book which this declamatory philosopher could not confute, but because he
                                                                    was

Behold Villario's ten-years toil complete;
His Quincunx darkens, his Efpaliers meet; 80
The Wood fupports the Plain, the parts unite,
And ftrength of Shade contends with ftrength of
.Light;
A waving Glow the bloomy beds difplay,
Blufhing in bright diverfities of day,
With filver-quiv'ring rills meander'd o'er— 85
Enjoy them, you! Villario can no more;
Tir'd of the fcene Parterres and Fountains yield,
He finds at laft, he better likes a Field.

Through

NOTES.

was a favourite of Queen Caroline. In Pope's MSS. were two lines on Dr. *Alured Clarke*, Dean of *Exeter*, who muft not be confounded with the *Rector* of *St. James's*:

 " Let Clarke tire half his days the Poor's fupport,
 But let him pafs the other half at Court;"

for he was inftrumental in building our two firft county hofpitals at Winchefter and at Exeter.

VER. 78. *Set Dr. Clarke.*] Dr. S. Clarke's bufto placed by the Queen in the Hermitage, while the Doctor duly frequented the Court. P.—But he fhould have added—with the innocence and difintereftednefs of an hermit. W.

VER. 82. *And ftrength of Shade*] After celebrating Kent as very inftrumental in promoting the new and juft tafte in gardening, Mr. Walpole adds; " Juft as the encomiums are that I have beftowed on Kent, he was neither without affiftance or faults. Whoever would fearch for his faults will find an ample crop in a very favourite work of his, the Prints for Spenfer's Fairy Queen. As the drawings were exceedingly cried up by his admirers, the blame was unjuftly thrown on the engraver. His celebrated monument of Shakefpeare in the Abbey was prepofterous.

VER. 83. *A waving Glow*] Thefe three lines are full of gay and florid epithets, well adapted to the fubject.

VER. 88. *He better likes a Field.*] The late Earl of Leicefter, being complimented upon the completion of his great defign at
Holkham,

Through his young Woods how pleas'd Sabinus stray'd,
Or sat delighted in the thick'ning shade, 90
With annual joy the red'ning shoots to greet,
Or see the stretching branches long to meet!
His Son's fine Taste an op'ner Vista loves,
Foe to the Dryads of his Father's groves;
One boundless Green, or flourish'd Carpet views, 95
With all the mournful family of Yews;
The thriving plants, ignoble broomsticks made,
Now sweep those Alleys they were born to shade.

At Timon's Villa let us pass a day,
Where all cry out, "What sums are thrown away!"
So

NOTES.

Holkham, replied, "It is a melancholy thing to stand alone in one's country. I look round; not a house is to be seen but mine. I am the giant of Giant-castle, and have ate up all my neighbours."

VER. 95. The two extremes in parterres, which are equally faulty; a *boundless Green*, large and naked as a field, or a *flourish'd Carpet*, where the greatness and nobleness of the piece is lessened by being divided into too many parts, with scroll'd works and beds, of which the examples are frequent. P.

VER. 95. *Carpet views,*] His fine *taste*, views, is an inaccurate expression, and hardly grammar; at least, an harsh combination of words. Is a total banishment of evergreens right? Has not this fashion of banishing them been carried too far?

VER. 96. *Mournful family of Yews;*] Touches upon the ill taste of those who are so fond of Evergreens (particularly Yews, which are the most tonsile) as to destroy the nobler Forest-trees to make way for such little ornaments as Pyramids of dark green continually repeated, not unlike a Funeral procession. P.

VER. 99. *At* Timon's *Villa*] This description is intended to comprize the principles of a false Taste of Magnificence, and to exemplify what was said before, that nothing but Good Sense can attain it. P.

So proud, fo grand; of that ſtupendous air,   101
Soft and Agreeable come never there.
Greatneſs, with Timon, dwells in ſuch a draught
As brings all Brobdignag before your thought.
To compaſs this, his building is a Town,   105
His pond an Ocean, his parterre a Down :
Who but muſt laugh, the Maſter when he ſees,
A puny infect, ſhiv'ring at a breeze!
Lo, what huge heaps of littleneſs around!
The whole, a labour'd Quarry above ground.   110
                                                Two

NOTES.

VER. 103. *Greatneſs, with Timon,*] The firſt edition of this Epiſtle was in folio, 1731. A ſpurious one was publiſhed in octavo, 1732, with many ſevere remarks by Concanen and Welſted, as was ſuppoſed; to which was prefixed a print deſigned by Hogarth, in which Pope is repreſented ſtanding on a builder's high ſtage, and white-waſhing the great gate-way of Burlington-houſe, and at the ſame time beſpattering the coach of the Duke of Chandos paſſing by. Hogarth ſuppreſſed this print, which is now become very valuable. It is remarkable our Author never once names Hogarth, though he had ſo many opportunities of doing it.

VER. 104. *All Brobdignag*] It is worth mentioning, that two pieces of burleſque poetry, one on *Pygmies,* by Moreau the preceptor of Scarron, and the other by Scarron himſelf, on *Giants,* bear a cloſe reſemblance to the Lilliput and the Brobdignac of Swift.

VER. 109. *Lo, what huge heaps of littleneſs around!*] Grandeur in building, as in the human frame, does not take its denomination from the body, but the ſoul of the work : when the ſoul therefore is loſt or incumbered in its envelope, the unanimated parts, how *huge* ſoever, are not members of grandeur, but mere *heaps of littleneſs.*   W.

VER. 110. *A labour'd Quarry*] In his letters he applies this expreſſion to Blenheim; the maſſy magnificence of which Sir Joſhua Reynolds always defended againſt the common cant of its being *heavy.* By Brown's late improvements, Blenheim is become one of the fineſt examples of laying out grounds judiciouſly.

Two Cupids fquirt before: a Lake behind
Improves the keennefs of the Northern wind.
His Gardens next your admiration call,
On ev'ry fide you look, behold the Wall!
No pleafing Intricacies intervene, 115
No artful wildnefs to perplex the fcene;
Grove nods at grove, each Alley has a brother,
And half the platform juft reflects the other.
The fuff'ring eye inverted Nature fees,
Trees cut to Statues, Statues thick as trees; 120
With here a Fountain, never to be play'd;
And there a Summer-houfe, that knows no fhade;
Here Amphitrite fails through myrtle bow'rs;
There Gladiators fight, or die in flow'rs;
Unwater'd fee the drooping fea-horfe mourn, 125
And fwallows rooft in Nilus' dufty Urn.

My Lord advances with majeftic mien,
Smit with the mighty pleafure, to be feen:
But foft—by regular approach—not yet—
Firft thro' the length of yon hot Terrace fweat; 130
And·

NOTES.

VER. 121. *With here a Fountain,*] It is amufing to fee how far our tafte in gardening has fpread. The prefent Emprefs of Ruffia writes thus to Voltaire, June 25, 1772: "J'aime à la folie préfentement les jardins à l'Anglaife, les lignes courbes, les pentes douces, les étangs en forme de lacs, les archipels en terre ferme; et j'ai un profond mepris pour les lignes droits, les allées jumelles. Je hais les fontaines qui donnent la torture a l'eau pour lui faire prendre un cours contraire à fa nature; les ftatues font reléquées dans les galeries, les veftibules, &c. En un môt, l'Anglomanie domine dans ma plantomanie."

VER. 124. The two Statues of the *Gladiator pugnans,* and *Gladiator moriens.* P.

VER. 124. *Die in flow'rs;*] This is more finical and puerile than his ufual manner.

And when up ten deep flopes you've drag'd your
    thighs,
Juft at his Study-door he'll blefs your eyes.
His Study! with what Authors is it ftor'd?
In Books, not Authors, curious is my Lord;
To all their dated backs he turns you round;   135
Thefe Aldus printed, thofe Du Sućil has bound!
Lo, fome are Vellom, and the reft as good
For all his Lordfhip knows, but they are Wood.
For Locke or Milton 'tis in vain to look,
Thefe fhelves admit not any modern book.   140
And now the Chapel's filver bell you hear,
That fummons you to all the Pride of Pray'r:
                                                    Light

NOTES.

VER. 130. The *Approaches* and *Communication* of houfe with garden, or one part with another, ill-judged, and inconvenient. P.

VER. 133. *His Study! &c.*] The falfe Tafte in books; a fatire on the vanity in collecting them, more frequent in men of Fortune than the ftudy to underftand them. Many delight chiefly in the elegance of the print, or of the binding; fome have carried it fo far, as to caufe the upper fhelves to be filled with painted books of wood; others pique themfelves fo much upon books in a language they do not underftand, as to exclude the moft ufeful in one they do.   P.

VER. 138. *But they are Wood.*] There is a flatnefs and infipidity in this couplet, much below the ufual manner of our Author. Young has been more fprightly and poignant on the fame fubject.
                    UNIVERSAL PASSION, Sat. 3.

VER. 139. *Or Milton*] This is one of the few places in which our Author feems to fpeak highly of Milton.

VER. 142. The falfe tafte in *Mufic*, improper to the fubjects, as of light airs in churches, often practifed by the organift, &c.   P.

VER. 142. *That fummons you to all the* Pride *of Pray'r:*] This abfurdity is very happily expreffed; *Pride*, of all human follies,
                                                    being

Light quirks of Mufic, broken and uneven,
Make the foul dance upon a Jig to Heav'n.
On painted Cielings you devoutly ftare,   145
Where fprawl the Saints of Verrio or Laguerre,
                                                      On

NOTES.

being the firft we fhould leave behind us when we approach the facred altar.—But he who could take Meannefs for Magnificence, might eafily miftake Humility for Meannefs.   W.

VER. 145.—And in *Painting* (from which even Italy is not free) of naked figures in churches, &c. which has obliged fome Popes to put draperies on fome of thofe of the beft mafters.   P.

VER. 146. *Where* fprawl *the Saints of Verrio or Laguerre*,] This was not only faid to deride the indecency and aukward pofition of the figures, but to infinuate the want of dignity in the fubjects. Raphael's pagans, as the devils in Milton, act a nobler part than the *Gods* and *Saints* of ordinary poets and painters. The cartons at Hampton-Court are talked of by every body; they have been copied, engraved, and criticifed; and yet fo little ftudied or confidered, that in the nobleft of them, of which likewife more has been faid than of all the reft, we are as much ftrangers to St. Paul's audience in the Areopagus, as to thofe before whom he preached at Theffalonica or Beroea.

The ftory from whence the painter took his fubject is this:— " St. Paul came to Athens,—was encountered by the Epicureans and Stoics,—taken up by them to the court of Areopagus,—before which he made his apology; and amongft his converts at this time, were Dionyfius the Areopagite, and a woman named Damaris." On this fimple plan he exercifes his invention. Paul is placed on an eminence in the act of fpeaking, the audience round him in a circle; and a ftatue of Mars, in the front of his temple, denotes the Scene of Action.

The firft figure has been taken notice of for the force of its expreffion. We fee all the marks of conviction and refignation to the direction of the divine Meffenger. But I do not know that it has been fufpected that a particular character was here reprefented. And yet the Platonic countenance, and the female attendant, fhew plainly, that the painter defigned DIONYSIUS, whom Eccleſiaſtical ſtory makes of this ſect; and to whom ſacred
                                                           hiftory

On gilded clouds in fair expanſion lie,
And bring all Paradiſe before your eye.

To

NOTES.

hiſtory has given this companion. For the woman is DAMARIS, mentioned with him, in the *Acts*, as a joint convert. Either the Artiſt miſtook his text, and ſuppoſed her to be converted with him at this audience; or, what is more likely, he purpoſely committed the indecorum of bringing a woman into the Areopagus, the better to mark out his *Dionyſius*; a character of great fame in the Romiſh Church, from a myſtic voluminous impoſtor, who has aſſumed his titles. Next to this PLATONIST of open mien, is a figure deeply collected within himſelf, immerſed in thought, and ruminating on what he hears. Conformable to his ſtate, his arms are buried in his garment, and his chin repoſing on his boſom; in a word, all his lineaments denote the STOIC; he ſays as plainly, *Ne te quæſiveris extra*, as if the Painter had drawn this Symbol of his Sect out of his mouth on a label. Adjoining to him is an old man, with a ſqualid beard and habit, leaning on his crouch, and turning his eyes upwards on the Apoſtle; but with a countenance ſo four and canine, that one cannot heſitate a moment in pronouncing him a CYNIC. The next who follows, by his elegance of dreſs, and placid air of raillery and neglect, proclaims himſelf an EPICUREAN: As the other which ſtands cloſe by him, with his finger on his lips, denoting *ſilence*, plainly marks out a follower of PYTHAGORAS. After theſe come a groupe of figures, cavilling in all the rage of diſputation, as criticiſing the divine Speaker. Theſe plainly deſign the ACADEMICS, the genius of whoſe ſchool was to debate *de quolibet ente*, and never come to a concluſion. Without the Circle, and behind the principal figures, are a number of young faces, to repreſent the ſcholars and diſciples of the ſeveral ſects. Theſe are all fronting the Apoſtle. Behind him are two other figures: one regarding the Apoſtle's action, with his face turned upwards: in which the paſſions of malicious zeal and diſappointed rage are ſo ſtrongly marked, that we needed not the *red bonnet*, to ſee he was a Jewiſh Rabbi. The other is a pagan prieſt, full of anxiety for the danger of the eſtabliſhed Worſhip.

Thus has this great Maſter, in order to heighten the dignity of his ſubject, brought in the heads of every ſect of philoſophy and religion

To reft, the Cufhion and foft Dean invite,
Who never mentions Hell to ears polite. 150
But hark! the chiming Clocks to dinner call;
A hundred footfteps fcrape the marble Hall:
The rich Buffet well-colour'd Serpents grace,
And gaping Tritons fpew to wafh your face.

Is

NOTES.

religion which were moft averfe to the principles, and moft oppofite to the fuccefs of the Gofpel; fo that one may truly efteem
this carton as the greateft effort of his divine genius. W.

I have the authority of two fuch eminent artifts as Sir Jofhua
Reynolds and Nathaniel Dance Efq. to fay, that this whole criticifm, on the cartons of Raphael, is ill-grounded, and fanciful to
the laft degree.

VER. 146. *Where* fprawl] This fingle verb has marked with felicity and force the diftorted attitudes, the indecent fubjects, the
want of nature and grace fo vifible in the pieces of thefe two artifts, employed to adorn our royal palaces and chapels. " I cannot help thinking," fays Pope to Mr. Allen, in Letter lxxxix.
vol. ix. "and I know you will join with me, who have been making an altar-piece, that the zeal of the firft reformers was ill-
placed, in removing pictures (that is to fay, examples) out of
churches; and yet fuffering epitaphs (that is to fay, flatteries and
falfe hiftory) to be a burthen to church-walls, and the fhame as
well as derifion of all honeft men." This is a fentiment, it may
be faid, of a papiftical poet; and yet it appears to be founded on
good fenfe, and religion well underftood. Notwithftanding the
many juft and well-founded arguments againft popery, yet I hope
we may ftill, one day, fee our places of worfhip beautified with
proper ornaments, and the generofity and talents of our living
artifts perpetuated on the naked walls of St. Paul's.

VER. 146. *Verrio or Laguerre,*] Verrio (Antonio) painted
many cielings, &c. at Windfor, Hampton-Court, &c. and Laguerre at Blenheim-caftle, and other places. P.

VER. 150. *Who never mentions Hell to ears polite.*] This is a
fact; a reverend Dean, preaching at Court, threatened the finner
with punifhment in "a place which he thought it not decent to
name in fo polite an affembly." P.

Is this a dinner? this a Genial room? 155
No, 'tis a Temple, and a Hecatomb.
A folemn Sacrifice, perform'd in ftate,
You drink by meafure, and to minutes eat.
So quick retires each flying courfe, you'd fwear
Sancho's dread Doctor, and his Wand were there.
Between each Act the trembling falvers ring, 161
From foup to fweet-wine, and God blefs the King.
In plenty ftarving, tantaliz'd in ftate,
And complaifantly help'd to all I hate,
Treated, carefs'd, and tir'd, I take my leave, 165
Sick of his civil Pride from Morn to Eve;
I curfe fuch lavifh coft, and little fkill,
And fwear no Day was ever paft fo ill.
  Yet hence the Poor are cloath'd, the hungry fed;
Health to himfelf, and to his Infants bread 170
The

NOTES.

VER. 153. Taxes the incongruity of *Ornaments*, (though fometimes practifed by the ancients) where an open mouth ejects the water into a fountain, or where the fhocking images of ferpents, &c. are introduced into Grottos or Buffets. P.

VER. 155. *Is this a dinner, &c.*] The proud Feftivals of fome men are here fet forth to ridicule, where pride deftroys the eafe, and formal regularity all the pleafurable enjoyment of the entertainment. P.

VER. 156. *A Hecatomb.*] Alluding to the *hundred footfteps* before. W.——This obfervation is very ridiculoufly ftrained.

VER. 160. Sancho'*s dread Doctor*,] See Don Quixote, chap. xlvii. P.

VER. 169. *Yet hence the Poor, &c.*] This is the *Moral* of the whole; where PROVIDENCE is juftified in giving Riches to thofe who fquander them in this manner. A bad Tafte employs more hands, and diffufes wealth more ufefully than a good one. This recurs to what is laid down in Book I. Ep. ii. Ver. 230—7, and in the Epiftle preceding this, Ver. 161, &c. P.

The Lab'rer bears : What his hard Heart denies,
His charitable Vanity supplies.
 Another Age shall see the golden Ear
Imbrown the Slope, and nod on the Parterre,
Deep Harvests bury all his pride has plann'd, 175
And laughing Ceres re-assume the land.
 Who then shall grace, or who improve the Soil?
Who plants like BATHURST, or who builds like
  BOYLE.
Tis Use alone that sanctifies Expence,
And Splendor borrows all her rays from Sense. 180

His

NOTES.

 This reflection is very different from the flagitious principle of Mandevill, that private vices are public benefits. Of whom, says Hume very shrewdly, " Is it not very inconsistent for an author to assert in one page, that moral distinctions are inventions of politicians for public interest ; and in the next page maintain, that vice is advantageous to the public ?"

 VER. 173. *Another Age, &c.*] Had the Poet lived but three years longer, he had seen his general prophecy against all ill-judged magnificence fulfilled in a very particular instance. W.

 In the edition of 1751, this note ran thus : " Had the Poet lived three years longer he had seen this prophecy fulfilled :" which so plainly pointed at what had happened at Canons, that it was altered as it here stands.

 VER, 176. *And laughing Ceres re-assume the land.*] The great beauty of this line is an instance of the art peculiar to our Poet ; by which he has so disposed a trite classical figure, as not only to make it do its vulgar office, of representing a very *plentiful harvest*, but also to assume the personage of *Nature*, re-establishing herself in her rights, and mocking the vain efforts of magnificence, which would keep her out of them. W.

 VER. 179, 180. *'Tis Use alone that* sanctifies *Expence,*
  And Splendor borrows all her rays from Sense.]
Here the Poet, to make the *examples* of good Taste the better understood,

His Father's Acres who enjoys in peace,
Or makes his Neighbours glad, if he encreafe:
Whofe chearful Tenants blefs their yearly toil,
Yet to their Lord owe more than to the foil;
Whofe ample Lawns are not afham'd to feed 185
The milky heifer, and deferving fteed;
Whofe rifing Forefts, not for pride or fhow,
But future Buildings, future Navies, grow:
Let his plantations ftretch from down to down,
Firft fhade a Country, and then raife a Town. 190
 You too proceed! make falling Arts your care,
Erect new wonders, and the old repair;

Jones

NOTES.

derftood, introduces them with a fummary of his *Precepts*, in thefe two fublime lines; for, the confulting *Ufe* is *beginning with Senfe*, and the making *Splendor* or *Tafte borrow all its rays* from thence, is *going on with Senfe*, after fhe has led us up to *Tafte*. The art of this difpofition of the thought can never be fufficiently admired. But the Expreffion is equal to the Thought. This *fanctifying* of expence gives us the idea of fomething confecrated and fet apart for facred ufes; and indeed it is the idea under which it may be properly confidered: for wealth employed according to the intention of Providence is its true confecration; and the real ufes of humanity were certainly *firft* in its intention. W.

Lord Chefterfield wrote the following lines, intending to fhew that Lord Burlington did not always attend to this rule of our Poet:

Poffeft of one great hall for ftate,
Without one room to fleep or eat,
How well you build, let flattery tell,
And all mankind, how ill you dwell.

VER. 182. *If he encreafe:*] Badly expreffed.

VER. 185. *Not afham'd to feed*] Cattle, and not deer.

VER. 191. *You too proceed!*] This is not fulfome adulation, but only fuch honeft praife as the noble Lord, whom he addreffed,

Jones and Palladio to themselves reftore,
And be whate'er Vitruvius was before:
Till Kings call forth th' Ideas of your mind,   195
(Proud to accomplish what fuch hands defign'd)
Bid Harbours open, public Ways extend,
Bid Temples, worthier of the God, afcend;
                                              Bid

NOTES.

ftrictly deferved; who inherited all that love of fcience and ufeful knowledge for which his family has been fo famous. The name of Boyle is indeed aufpicious to literature. That fublime genius and good man, Bifhop Berkley, owed his preferment chiefly to this accomplifhed peer: For it was he that recommended him to the Duke of Grafton, in the year 1721, who took him over with him to Ireland when he was Lord Lieutenant, and promoted him to the deanery of Derry in the year 1724. Berkley gained the patronage and friendfhip of Lord Burlington, not only by his true politenefs, and the peculiar charms of his converfation, which was exquifite, but by his profound and perfect fkill in architecture; an art which he had very particularly and accurately ftudied in Italy, when he went and continued abroad four years with Mr. Afhe, fon of the Bifhop of Clogher. With an infatiable and philofophic attention, Berkley furveyed and examined every object of curiofity. He not only made the ufual tour, but went over Apulia and Calabria, and even travelled on foot through Sicily, and drew up an account of that very claffical ground; which was loft in a voyage to Naples, and cannot be fufficiently regretted. His generous project for erecting an univerfity at Bermudas, the effort of a mind truly active, benevolent, and patriotic, is fufficiently known.

VER. 193. *Jones*] See an accurate and judicious account of his Works in Walpole's Anecdotes, vol. ii. from page 261 to page 280. full of curious particulars. Dr. Clarke, of All Souls College, Oxford, had Jones's Palladio, with his own notes and obfervations in Italian, which the Doctor bequeathed to Worcefter College.

VER. 195, 197, &c. *Till Kings—Bid Harbours open, &c.*] The Poet, after having touched upon the proper objects of Magnificence

Bid the broad Arch the dang'rous Flood contain,
The mole projected break the roaring Main ; 200
Back

NOTES.

cence and Expence, in the private works of great men, comes to thofe great and public works which become a prince. This Poem was publifhed in the year 1732, when fome of the new-built churches, by the act of Queen Anne, were ready to fall, being founded in boggy land, (which is fatirically alluded to in our Author's imitation of Horace, Lib. ii. Sat. 2.

" Shall half the new-built Churches round thee fall)."

Others were vilely executed, through fraudulent cabals between undertakers, officers, &c. Dagenham-breach had done very great mifchiefs ; many of the Highways throughout England were hardly paffable ; and moft of thofe which were repaired by Turnpikes were made jobs for private lucre, and infamoufly executed, even to the entrance of London itfelf. The propofal of building a Bridge at Weftminfter had been petitioned againft and rejected ; but in two years after the publication of this poem, an Act for building a Bridge paffed through both Houfes. After many debates in the committee, the execution was left to the carpenter above mentioned, who would have made it a *wooden one ;* to which our Author alludes in thefe lines,

" Who builds a Bridge that never drove a pile ?
Should Ripley venture, all the world would fmile."

See the notes on that place. P.

VER. 197. *Bid Harbours open,*] No country has been enriched and adorned, within a period of thirty or forty years, with fo many works of public fpirit, as Great Britain has been ; witnefs our many extenfive roads, our inland navigations, (fome of which excel the boafted canal of Languedoc,) the lighting, and the paving, and beautifying our cities, and our various and magnificent edifices. A general good tafte has been diffufed in gardening, planting, and building. The ruins of Palmyra, the antiquities of Athens and Spalatro, and the Ionian antiquities, by Wood, Stuart, Adam, and Chandler, are fuch magnificent monuments of learned curiofity as no country in Europe can equal. Let it be remembered, that thefe fine lines of Pope were written when we had no Wyatt or Brown, Brindley or Reynolds ; no Weftminfter
Bridge,

Back to his bounds their subject Sea command,
And roll obedient Rivers through the Land:
These Honours, Peace to happy BRITAIN brings,
These are Imperial Works, and worthy Kings.

NOTES.

Bridge, no Pantheon, no Royal Academy, no king that is at once a judge and a patron of all those fine arts, which ought to be employed in raising and beautifying a palace equal to his dignity and his taste.

On the whole, this Epistle contains rather strictures on the false taste, than illustrations of the true; which circumstance gave room to Mr. Mason to treat the subject in a more open and ornamental manner, and with more picturesque and poetical imagery in his English Garden.

VER. 203. *These Honours, Peace*] One of the chief sources of the great riches of this country was the long Peace which was enjoyed during the ministry of Sir Robert Walpole; who, however he may have been censured, deserved high praise on this account.

EPISTLE V.

TO MR. ADDISON.

Occafioned by his Dialogues on MEDALS.

SEE the wild Wafte of all-devouring years!
How Rome her own fad Sepulchre appears!
With nodding arches, broken temples fpread!
The very Tombs now vanifh'd like their dead!
                                        Imperial

NOTES.

THIS was originally written in the year 1715, when Mr. Addifon intended to publifh his book of Medals; it was fome time before he was Secretary of State; but not publifhed till Mr. Tickel's Edition of his works: at which time the verfes on Mr. Craggs, which conclude the poem, were added, viz. in 1720. P.

VER. 1. *See the wild Wafte*] This treatife on Medals was written by Addifon in that pleafing form of compofition, fo unfuccefsfully attempted by many modern authors, Dialogues. In no one fpecies of writing have the antients fo indifputable a fuperiority over us. The dialogues of Plato and Cicero, efpecially the former, are perfect dramas; where the characters are supported with confiftency and nature, and the reafoning fuited to the characters.

" There are in Englifh three dialogues, and but three," fays a learned and ingenious author, who has himfelf practifed this agreeable way of writing, " that deferve commendation, namely, the Moralifts in Lord Shaftefbury, Mr. Addifon's Treatife on Medals, and the Minute Philofophy of Bifhop Berkley." Alciphron did, indeed, well deferve to be mentioned on this occafion; notwithftanding it has been treated with contempt by writers much inferior to Berkley in learning, genius, and tafte. Omitting thofe paffages in the fourth dialogue, where he has introduced

Imperial wonders rais'd on Nations spoil'd,   5
Where mix'd with Slaves the groaning Martyr toil'd:

Huge

NOTES.

duced his fanciful and whimsical opinions about *vision*, an attentive reader will find that there is scarce a single argument that can be urged in defence of Revelation, but what is here placed in the clearest light, and in the most beautiful diction: In this work there is a happy union of reasoning and imagination. The two different characters of the two different sorts of free-thinkers, the sensual and the refined, are strongly contrasted with each other, and with the plainness and simplicity of Euphranor.

These dialogues of Addison are written with that sweetness and purity of style which constitute him one of the first of our prose-writers. The Pleasures of Imagination, the Essay on the Georgics, and his last papers in the Spectator and Guardian, are models of language. And some late writers, who seem to have mistaken stiffness for strength, and are grown popular by a pompous rotundity of phrase, make one wish that the rising generation may abandon this unnatural, false, inflated, and florid style, and form themselves on the chaster model of Addison. The chief imperfection of his Treatise on Medals, is, the persons introduced as speakers, in direct contradiction to the practice of the antients, are *fictitious* not *real;* for Cynthio*, Philander, Palæmon, Eugenio, and Theocles, cannot equally excite and engage the attention of the reader, with Socrates and Alcibiades, Atticus and Brutus, Cowley and Spratt, Maynard and Somers. It is somewhat singular, that so many of the modern dialogue-writers should have failed in this particular, when so many of the most celebrated wits of modern Italy had given them eminent examples of the contrary proceeding, and closely following the steps of the antients, constantly introduced living and real persons in their numerous compositions of this sort; in which they were so fond of delivering their sentiments, both on moral and critical subjects; witness the Il Cortegiano of B. Castiglione, the Asolani of P. Bembo, Dialoghi

---

* How ill the forms, and ceremonies, and compliments of modern good-breeding would bear to be exactly represented; see Characteristics, vol. i. p. 209.

del

Huge Theatres, that now unpeopled Woods,
Now drain'd a diftant country of her Floods:
Fanes, which admiring Gods with pride furvey,
Statues of Men, fcarce lefs alive than they! 10
Some felt the filent ftroke of mould'ring age,
Some hoftile fury, fome religious rage.
Barbarian blindnefs, Chriftian zeal confpire,
And Papal piety, and Gothic fire.
Perhaps, by its own ruins fav'd from flame, 15
Some bury'd marble half preferves a name;
That Name the Learn'd with fierce difputes purfue,
And give to Titus old Vefpafian's due.

         Ambition

NOTES.

del S. Sperone, and the great Galileo, the Naugerius of Fracaf-
torius, and Lil. Gyraldus de Poetis, and many others. In all
which pieces the famous and living geniufes of Italy are introduced
difcuffing the feveral different topics before them.

 VER. 2. *Her own fad Sepulchre*] St. Jerome fays, " Roma
quondam orbis caput, poftea populi Romani fepulchrum."

 VER. 6. *Where mix'd with Slaves the groaning Martyr toil'd:*]
Palladio, fpeaking of the Baths of Dioclefian, fays, " Nell' edifi-
catione delle quali, Dioclefiano tenne molti enni 140 mila Chrifti-
ani a edificarle."   W.

 VER. 6. *Groaning Martyr*] Dodwell, in his Differtationes Cy-
prianicæ, has undertaken to prove that the number of Martyrs was
far lefs than hath been ufually imagined. His opinion is com-
bated by Mofheim in the 5th chapter of his excellent Hiftory of
the Church.

 VER. 7. *Huge Theatres,*] Is this equal or fuperior to what Ad-
difon fays on the fame fubject?
  " That on its public fhews unpeopled Rome,
   And held *uncrowded* nations in its womb."

 VER. 18. *And give to Titus old Vefpafian's due.*] A fine infinua-
tion of the want both of tafte and learning in Antiquaries; whofe
                    ignorance

Ambition sigh'd : She found it vain to trust
The faithless Column, and the crumbling Bust : 20
Huge moles, whose shadow stretch'd from shore to shore,
Their ruins perish'd, and their place no more !
Convinc'd, she now contracts her vast design,
And all her Triumphs shrink into a Coin.
A narrow ORB each crowded conquest keeps, 25
Beneath her Palm here sad Judea weeps.
Now scantier limits the proud Arch confine,
And scarce are seen the prostrate Nile or Rhine ;
A small Euphrates through the piece is roll'd,
And little Eagles wave their wings in gold. 30
The Medal, faithful to its charge of fame,
Through climes and ages bears each form and name:
In one short view subjected to our eye
Gods, Emp'rors, Heroes, Sages, Beauties, lie.
With

NOTES.

ignorance of characters misleads them (supported only by a name) against reason and history.

VER. 19. *Ambition sigh'd:*] Such short *personifications* have a great effect. " Silence was pleas'd," says Milton ; which personification is taken, though it happens not to have been observed by any of his commentators, from the Hero and Leander of Musæus, v. 280.

VER. 25. *A narrow* ORB *each crowded* Conquest *keeps,*] A ridicule on the pompous title of *Orbis Romanus,* which the Romans gave to their Empire. W.———No ridicule was nor could be here intended.

VER. 27. *The proud Arch*] i. e. The triumphal Arch, which was generally an enormous mass of building.

VER. 29. *A small Euphrates*] The two first-mentioned rivers, the Nile and Rhine, having been personified, the Euphrates should not have been spoken of as a mere river. The circumstance in line 30. is very puerile and little.

Ep. IV. MORAL ESSAYS.

With sharpen'd sight pale Antiquaries pore, 35
Th' inscription value, but the rust adore.
This the blue varnish, that the green endears,
The sacred rust of twice ten hundred years!
To gain Pescennius one employs his Schemes,
One grasps a Cecrops in ecstatic dreams. 40
Poor Vadius, long with learned spleen devour'd,
Can taste no pleasure since his Shield was scour'd:
And Curio, restless by the Fair One's side,
Sighs for an Otho, and neglects his bride.

Theirs

NOTES.

VER. 35. *With* sharpen'd sight *pale Antiquaries pore,*] Microscopic glasses, invented by Philosophers to discover the beauties in the minuter works of Nature, ridiculously applied by Antiquaries to detect the cheats of counterfeit medals. W.

VER. 37. *This the blue varnish, that the green endears,*] *i. e.* This a collector of silver; that, of brass coins. W.

VER. 39. *To gain Pescennius*] The lively and ingenious Young says, in his 4th Satire,

" How his eyes languish! how his thoughts adore
That painted coat which Joseph never wore!
He shews, on holidays, a sacred pin,
That touch'd the ruff that touch'd Queen Bess's chin."

How much wit has been wasted and misplaced in endeavouring to ridicule antiquarians, whose studies are not only pleasing to the imagination, but attended with many advantages to society, especially since they have been improved, as they lately have been, with singular taste and propriety, in elucidating what, after all, is the most interesting and important part of *all* history—the *history* of *manners!*

VER. 41. *Poor Vadius,*] See his history, and that of his Shield, in the *Memoirs of Scriblerus.* W.

VER. 43. *And Curio, restless, &c.*] The Historian Dio has given us a very extraordinary instance of this Virtuoso-taste. He tells

Theirs is the Vanity, the Learning thine: 45
Touch'd by thy hand, again Rome's glories shine;
Her Gods, and godlike Heroes rise to view,
And all her faded garlands bloom a-new.

Nor

NOTES.

tells us, that one Vibius Rufus, who, in the reign of Tiberius, was the fourth husband to Cicero's widow, Terentia, then upwards of an hundred years old, used to value himself on his being possessed of the two noblest pieces of Antiquity in the world, TULLY'S WIDOW and CÆSAR'S CHAIR, that Chair in which he was assassinated in full Senate. W.

VER. 44. *Sighs for an Otho,*] Charles Patin was banished from the Court because he sold Louis XIV. an Otho that was not genuine. Patin's Treatise on Medals is a good one. Ficorini, the celebrated virtuoso at Florence, said to Mr. Spence, "Addison did not go any great depth in the study of medals; all the knowledge he had of that kind, I believe, he received of me; and I did not give him above twenty lessons on that subject."

VER. 48. *Her faded*] In Winkelman's History of Art among the Ancients, is to be found perhaps the best account of the gradual decay of painting, architecture, and medals, that can be read; abounding with many instances of the fate that has befallen many exquisite pieces of art. Among the rest he says, that when the Austrians took Madrid, Lord Galloway searched for a very celebrated Busto of Caligula, that he knew Cardinal G. Colonna had conveyed to Spain; which fine Busto he at last found in the Escurial, where it served for a weight of the church-clock. What Winkelman says of the Laocoon, vol. ii. sect. 3. is a capital piece of criticism and just taste; which he finishes by mentioning a matchless absurdity, worthy of the country where it is to be found, that in the Castle of St. Ildephonso in Spain, there is a Relief of this group of Laocoon and his sons, with a figure of Cupid fluttering over their heads, as if flying to their assistance. As to the revival of arts in Italy, we have lately been gratified with a curious account of this important event, in the elegant History of the Life of Lorenzo de Medici, their chief restorer and protector. See particularly, chapter ix. p. 196.

Nor blush, these studies thy regard engage;
These pleas'd the Fathers of poetic rage;   50
The verse and sculpture bore an equal part,
And Art reflected images to Art.

Oh when shall Britain, conscious of her claim,
Stand emulous of Greek and Roman fame?
In living medals see her wars enroll'd,   55
And vanquish'd realms supply recording gold?
Here, rising bold, the Patriot's honest face;
There Warriors frowning in historic brass:
Then future ages with delight shall see
How Plato's, Bacon's, Newton's looks agree;   60
Or in fair series laurel'd Bards be shown,
A Virgil there, and here an Addison.

Then

NOTES.

VER. 49. *Nor blush, these studies thy regard engage;*] A senseless affectation, which some Authors of eminence have betrayed; who, when fortune or their talents have raised them to a condition to do without those arts, for which only they gained our esteem, have pretended to think letters below their character. This false shame M. Voltaire has very well, and with proper indignation, exposed in his account of Mr. Congreve: " He had one defect, which was, his entertaining too mean an idea of his first profession, (that of a Writer,) though it was to this he owed his fame and fortune. He spoke of his works as of trifles that were beneath him; and hinted to me, in our first conversation, that I should visit him upon no other foot than that of a gentleman, who led a life of plainness and simplicity. I answered, that had he been so unfortunate as to be a mere gentleman, I should never have come to see him; and I was very much disgusted at so unseasonable a piece of vanity." *Letters concerning the English Nation*, xix.   W.

VER. 53. *Oh when shall Britain, &c.*] A compliment to one of Mr. Addison's papers in the Spectator, on this subject.   W.

VER. 62. *A Virgil there,*] Copied evidently from Tickell to Addison on his Rosamond;

" Which gain'd a Virgil and an Addison."

Then ſhall thy CRAGGS (and let me call him mine)
On the caſt ore, another Pollio, ſhine;
With aſpect open, ſhall erect his head, 65
And round the orb in laſting notes be read,
" Stateſman, yet friend to Truth! of ſoul ſincere,
" In action faithful, and in honour clear;
                                                    " Who

NOTES.

This elegant copy of Verſes was ſo acceptable to Addiſon, that it was the foundation of a laſting friendſhip betwixt them. Tickell deſerves a higher place among poets than is uſually allotted to him.

VER. 67. *Stateſman, yet friend to Truth, &c.*] It ſhould be remembered, that this poem was compoſed to be printed before Mr. Addiſon's *Diſcourſe on Medals*, in which there is the following cenſure of *long legends* upon coins: " The firſt fault I find with a modern legend is its diffuſiveneſs. You have ſometimes the whole ſide of a medal over-run with it. One would fancy the Author had a deſign of being Ciceronian—but it is not only the tedioufneſs of theſe inſcriptions that I find fault with; ſuppoſing them of a moderate length, why muſt they be in verſe? We ſhould be ſurpriſed to ſee the title of a ſerious book in rhyme." *Dial.* iii. W.

VER. 67. *Stateſman,*] Theſe nervous and finiſhed lines were afterwards inſcribed as an epitaph on this worthy man's monument in Weſtminſter Abbey, with the alteration of two words in the laſt verſe; which there ſtands thus:

" Prais'd, wept, and honour'd by the Muſe he lov'd."

It was Craggs, who raiſed himſelf by his abilities, his father being a barber, that, in the moſt friendly and alluring manner, offered our Author a penſion of three hundred pounds per annum; which if he had accepted we ſhould have been deprived of his beſt ſatires. Poets have a high ſpirit of liberty and independence. They neither ſeek or expect rewards.

Mecænaſes do *not* create geniuſes. Neither Spenſer, nor Milton, nor Dante, nor Taſſo, nor Corneille, were patronized by the governments under which they lived. And Horace, and Virgil,

and

"Who broke no promife, ferv'd no private end,
"Who gain'd no title, and who loft no friend; 70
"Ennobled by himfelf, by all approv'd,
"And prais'd unenvy'd, by the Mufe he lov'd."

NOTES.

and Boileau were formed before they had an opportunity of flattering Auguftus and Lewis XIV.

Though Pope enlifted under the banner of Bolingbroke, in what was called the country party, and in violent oppofition to the meafures of Walpole, yet his clear and good fenfe enabled him to fee the follies and virulence of all parties; and it was his favourite maxim, that, however factious men thought proper to diftinguifh themfelves by names, yet when they got into power, they all acted much in the fame manner; faying,

"I know how like Whig minifters to Tory."

And among his manufcripts were four very fenfible, though not very poetical lines, which contain the moft folid apology that can be made for a minifter of this country:

"Our minifters like gladiators live:
'Tis half their bufinefs blows to ward, or give:
The good their virtue would effect, or fenfe,
Dies between exigents and felf-defence."

Yet he appears fometimes to have forgotten this candid reflection.

VER. ult. *And prais'd unenvy'd, by the Mufe he lov'd.*] It was not likely that men acting in fo different fpheres, as were thofe of Mr. Craggs and Mr. Pope, fhould have their friendfhip difturb'd by envy. We muft fuppofe then that fome circumftances in the friendfhip of Mr. Pope and Mr. Addifon are hinted at in this place. W.

APPENDIX.

APPENDIX.

AN

ESSAY ON SATIRE,

OCCASIONED BY

THE DEATH OF MR POPE.

Infcribed to Mr. WARBURTON.

By J. BROWN, A. M.

CONTENTS.

PART I.

OF the End and Efficacy of Satire. *The Love of Glory and Fear of Shame universal*, Ver. 29. *This Passion, implanted in Man as a Spur to Virtue, is generally perverted*, Ver. 41. *And thus becomes the Occasion of the greatest Follies, Vices, and Miseries*, Ver. 61. *It is the Work of* Satire *to rectify this Passion, to reduce it to its proper Channel, and to convert it into an Incentive to Wisdom and Virtue*, Ver. 89. *Hence it appears, that* Satire *may influence those who defy all Laws Human and Divine*, Ver. 99. *An Objection answered*, Ver. 131.

PART II.

Rules for the Conduct of Satire. *Justice and Truth its chief and essential Property*, Ver. 169. *Prudence in the Application of Wit and Ridicule, whose Province is, not to explore* unknown *but to enforce* known *Truths*, Ver. 191. *Proper Subjects of* Satire *are the Manners of present Times*, Ver. 239. *Decency of Expression recommended*, Ver. 255. *The different Methods in which Folly and Vice ought to be chastised*, Ver. 269. *The Variety of Style and Manner which these two Subjects require*, Ver. 277. *The Praise of Virtue may be admitted with Propriety*, Ver. 315. *Caution with regard to Panegyric*, Ver. 329. *The Dignity of* true Satire, Ver. 341.

PART

CONTENTS.

PART III.

The History of Satire. Roman *Satirists*, Lucilius, Horace, Persius, Juvenal, Ver. 357, &c. *Causes of the Decay of Literature, particularly of* Satire, Ver. 389. *Revival of* Satire, Ver. 401. Erasmus *one of its principal Restorers*, Ver. 405. Donne, Ver. 411. *The Abuse of* Satire *in* England, *during the licentious Reign of* Charles II. Ver. 415. Dryden, 429. *The true Ends of* Satire *pursued by* Boileau *in* France, Ver. 439; *and by* Mr. Pope *in* England, Ver. 445.

PART I.

FATE gave the word; the cruel arrow fped;
    And POPE lies number'd with the mighty Dead!
Refign'd he fell; fuperior to the dart,
That quench'd its rage in YOURS and BRITAIN's
    Heart: 4
You mourn: but BRITAIN, lull'd in reft profound,
(Unconfcious BRITAIN!) flumbers o'er her wound.
Exulting dullnefs ey'd the fetting Light,
And flapp'd her wing, impatient for the Night:
Rous'd at the fignal, Guilt collects her train,
And counts the Triumphs of her growing Reign: 10
With inextinguifhable rage they burn;
And fnake-hung ENVY hiffes o'er his Urn:
Th' envenom'd Monfters fpit their deadly foam,
To blaft the Laurel that furrounds his Tomb.
    But YOU, O WARBURTON! whofe eye refin'd 15
Can fee the greatnefs of an honeft mind;
Can fee each Virtue and each Grace unite,
And tafte the Raptures of a *pure* Delight;
YOU vifit oft his awful Page with Care,
And view that bright Affemblage treafur'd there; 20
You trace the Chain that links his deep defign,
And pour new Luftre on the glowing Line:
                                 Yet

Yet deign to hear the efforts of a Muse,
Whose eye, not wing, his ardent flight pursues:
Intent from this great Archetype to draw 25
SATIRE's bright Form, and fix her equal law;
Pleas'd if from hence th' unlearn'd may compre-
    hend,
And rev'rence HIS and SATIRE's gen'rous End.

   In ev'ry breast there burns an active flame,
The love of Glory, or the dread of Shame: 30
The Passion ONE, tho' various it appear,
As brighten'd into Hope, or dimm'd by Fear.
The lisping Infant, and the hoary Sire,
And Youth and Manhood feel the heart-born fire:
The Charms of Praise the Coy, the Modest woo, 35
And only fly, that Glory may pursue:
She, Pow'r resistless, rules the wise and great;
Bends ev'n reluctant Hermits at her feet;
Haunts the proud City, and the lowly Shade,
And sways alike the Sceptre and the Spade. 40

   Thus Heav'n in Pity wakes the friendly Flame,
To urge Mankind on Deeds that merit Fame:
But Man, vain Man, in folly only wise,
Rejects the Manna sent him from the Skies:
With rapture hears corrupted Passion's call, 45
Still proudly prone to mingle with the stall.
As each deceitful shadow tempts his view,
He for the *imag'd* Substance quits the *true;*
Eager to catch the visionary Prize,
In quest of Glory, plunges deep in Vice; 50
                              Till

ESSAY ON SATIRE.

Till madly zealous, impotently vain,
He forfeits ev'ry Praise he pants to gain.
 Thus still imperious NATURE plies her part;
And still her Dictates work in ev'ry heart.
Each Pow'r that sov'reign Nature bids enjoy, 55
Man may corrupt, but Man can ne'er destroy:
Like mighty rivers, with resistless force
The Passions rage, obstructed in their course;
Swell to new heights, forbidden paths explore,
And drown those Virtues which they fed before. 60
 And sure, the deadliest Foe to Virtue's flame,
Our worst of Evils, is *perverted shame*.
Beneath this load what abject numbers groan,
Th' entangled Slaves to folly not their own!
Meanly by fashionable fear oppres'd, 65
We seek our Virtues in each other's breast;
Blind to ourselves, adopt each foreign Vice,
Another's weakness, int'rest, or caprice.
Each Fool to low Ambition, poorly great,
That pines in splendid wretchedness of state, 70
Tir'd in the treach'rous Chace, would nobly yield,
And, but for shame, like SYLLA, quit the field:
The demon *Shame* paints strong the ridicule,
And whispers close, " The World will call you Fool."
 Behold yon Wretch, by impious fashion driv'n, 75
Believes and trembles while he scoffs at Heav'n.
By weakness strong, and bold through fear alone,
He dreads the sneer by shallow coxcombs thrown;

         Dauntless

Dauntless pursues the path *Spinoza* trod;
To Man a *Coward*, and a *Brave* to God.   80
  Faith, Justice, Heav'n itself now quit their hold,
When to false Fame the captiv'd heart is sold:
Hence, blind to truth, relentless *Cato* dy'd;
Nought could subdue his Virtue, but his Pride.
Hence chaste *Lucretia*'s Innocence betray'd   85
Fell by that Honour which was meant its aid.
Thus Virtue sinks beneath unnumber'd woes,
When Passions, born her friends, revolt her foes.
  Hence SATIRE's pow'r: 'tis her corrective part,
To calm the wild disorders of the heart.   90
She points the arduous height where Glory lies,
And teaches mad Ambition to be wise:
In the dark bosom wakes the fair desire,
Draws good from ill, a brighter flame from fire;
Strips black Oppression of her gay disguise,   95
And bids the Hag in native horror rise;
Strikes tow'ring Pride, and lawless Rapine dead,
And plants the wreath on Virtue's awful head.
  Nor boasts the Muse a vain imagin'd pow'r,
Tho' oft she mourn those ills she cannot cure.   100

The

IMITATIONS.

VER. 80. *To Man a Coward, &c.*]

  " Vois tu ce Libertin en public intrepide,
  " Qui preche contre un Dieu que dans son Ame il croit?
  " Il iroit embrasser la Verité, qu'il voit;
  " Mais de ses faux Amis il craint la Raillerie,
  " Et ne brave ainsi Dieu que par Poltronnerie."
                                    BOILEAU, Ep. iii.

Part I.   ESSAY ON SATIRE.

The Worthy court her, and the Worthlefs fear:
Who fhun her piercing eye, that eye revere.
Her awful voice the Vain and Vile obey,
And ev'ry foe to Wifdom feels her fway.
Smarts, Pedants, as fhe fmiles, no more are vain;
Defponding Fops refign the *clouded cane:*   106
Hufh'd at her voice, pert Folly's felf is ftill,
And Dulnefs wonders while fhe drops her quill.
Like the arm'd BEE, with art moft fubtly true,
From pois'nous Vice fhe draws a healing dew: 110
Weak are the ties that civil arts can find,
To quell the ferment of the tainted mind:
Cunning evades, fecurely wrapt in wiles;
And Force ftrong finew'd rends th' unequal toils:
The ftream of Vice impetuous drives along,   115
Too deep for Policy, for Pow'r too ftrong,
Ev'n fair Religion, Native of the fkies,
Scorn'd by the Crowd, feeks refuge with the Wife;
The Crowd with laughter fpurns her awful train,
And Mercy courts, and Juftice frowns in vain.   120
But SATIRE's fhaft can pierce the harden'd breaft:
She plays a *ruling paffion* on the reft:
Undaunted ftorms the batt'ry of his pride,
And awes the *Brave* that Earth and Heav'n defy'd.

When

IMITATIONS.

VER. 110. *From pois'nous Vice, &c.*] Alluding to thefe lines of Mr. Pope;

"In the nice Bee what Art fo fubtly true
"From pois'nous Herbs extracts a healing Dew?"

When fell Corruption, by her vaſſals crown'd, 125
Derides fall'n Juſtice proſtrate on the ground;
Swift to redreſs an injur'd People's groan,
Bold SATIRE ſhakes the Tyrant on her throne;
Pow'rful as Death, defies the ſordid train,
And Slaves and Sycophants ſurround in vain. 130
 But with the friends of Vice, the foes of SATIRE,
All truth is Spleen; all juſt reproof, Ill-nature.
Well may they dread the Muſe's fatal ſkill;
Well may they tremble, when ſhe draws her quill:
Her magic quill, that, like ITHURIEL's ſpear, 135
Reveals the cloven hoof, or lengthen'd ear:
Bids Vice and Folly take their nat'ral ſhapes,
Turns Ducheſſes to ſtrumpets, Beaux to apes;
Drags the vile Whiſp'rer from his dark abode,
Till all the Demon ſtarts up from the toad. 140
 O ſordid maxim, form'd to ſcreen the vile,
That true good-nature ſtill muſt wear a ſmile!
In frowns array'd her beauties ſtronger riſe,
When love of Virtue makes her ſcorn of Vice:
Where Juſtice calls, 'tis Cruelty to ſave; 145
And 'tis the Law's good-nature hangs the Knave.
Who combats Virtue's foe is Virtue's friend;
Then judge of SATIRE's merit by her end:
To Guilt alone her vengeance ſtands confin'd,
The object of her love is all Mankind. 150
Scarce more the friend of Man, the wiſe muſt own,
Ev'n ALLEN's bounteous hand, than SATIRE's frown.
This to chaſtize, as That to bleſs, was giv'n;
Alike the faithful Miniſters of Heav'n.

           Oft

ESSAY ON SATIRE.

Oft in unfeeling hearts the shaft is spent: 155
Tho' strong th' example, weak the punishment.
They least are pain'd, who merit Satire most;
Folly the *Laureat*'s, Vice was *Chartres*' boast:
Then where's the wrong, to gibbet high the name
Of Fools and Knaves already dead to shame? 160
Oft SATIRE acts the faithful Surgeon's part;
Gen'rous and kind, tho' painful is her art:
With caution bold, she only strikes to heal;
Tho' folly raves to break the friendly steel.
Then sure no fault impartial SATIRE knows, 165
Kind ev'n in Vengeance, kind to Virtue's foes.
Whose is the crime, the scandal too be theirs:
The Knave and Fool are their own Libellers.

PART II.

<small>D</small>*ARE* nobly then: But confcious of your truft,
   As ever warm and bold, be ever juft: 170
Nor court applaufe in thefe degen'rate days:
The Villain's cenfure is extorted praife.
   But chief, be fteady in a noble end,
And fhew mankind that Truth has yet a friend.
'Tis mean for empty praife of wit to write,   175
As Foplings grin to fhew their teeth are white:
To brand a doubtful folly with a fmile,
Or madly blaze unknown defects, is vile:
'Tis doubly vile, when, but to prove your art,
You fix an arrow in a blamelefs heart.   180
O loft to honour's voice, O doom'd to fhame,
Thou Fiend accurft, thou Murderer of Fame!
Fell Ravifher, from Innocence to tear
That name, than liberty, than life more dear!
Where fhall thy bafenefs meet its juft return!   185
Or what repay thy guilt, but endlefs fcorn?
And know, immortal Truth fhall mock thy toil:
Immortal Truth fhall bid the fhaft recoil;
With rage retorted, wing the deadly dart;
And empty all its poifon in thy heart.   190
   With caution next, the dang'rous pow'r apply;
An eagle's talon afks an eagle's eye:

Part II.   ESSAY ON SATIRE.

Let SATIRE then her proper object know,
And ere she strike, be sure she strike a foe.
Nor fondly deem the real fool confest,   195
Because blind *Ridicule* conceives a jest:
Before whose altar Virtue oft hath bled,
And oft a destin'd Victim shall be led:
Lo, *Shaftsb'ry* rears her high on Reason's throne,
And loads the Slave with honours not her own: 200
Big-swoln with folly, as her smiles provoke,
Prophaneness spawns, pert Dunces nurse the joke!
Come, let us join a while this titt'ring crew,
And own the *Ideot Guide* for once is *true;*
Deride our weak forefathers' musty rule,   205
Who *therefore* smil'd, *because* they saw a Fool;
Sublimer logic now adorns our isle,
We *therefore* see a Fool, *because* we smile.
Truth in her gloomy Cave why fondly seek?
Lo, gay she sits in Laughter's dimple cheek: 210
Contemns each surly academic foe,
And courts the spruce Freethinker and the Beau.
Dædalion arguments but few can trace,
But all can read the language of grimace.
Hence mighty Ridicule's all-conqu'ring hand   215
Shall work *Herculean* wonders through the Land:
Bound in the magic of her cob-web chain,
You, mighty WARBURTON, shall rage in vain,
In vain the trackless maze of Truth you scan,
And lend th' informing Clue to erring Man: 220
No more shall Reason boast her pow'r divine,
Her Base eternal shook by Folly's mine!

Truth's facred Fort th' exploded laugh fhall win;
And Coxcombs vanquifh BERKLEY by a grin.

But you, more fage, reject th' inverted rule, 225
That Truth is e'er explor'd by Ridicule:
On truth, on falfehood let her colours fall,
She throws a dazzling glare alike on all;
As the gay Prifm but mocks the flatter'd eye,
And gives to ev'ry object ev'ry dye. 230
Beware the mad Advent'rer: bold and blind
She hoifts her fail, and drives with ev'ry wind;
Deaf as the ftorm to finking Virtue's groan,
Nor heeds a Friend's deftruction, or her own.
Let clear-ey'd Reafon at the helm prefide, 235
Bear to the wind, or ftem the furious tide;
Then Mirth may urge, when Reafon can explore,
This point the way, *that* waft us glad to fhore.

Tho' diftant Times may rife in SATIRE's page,
Yet chief 'tis Her's to draw the *prefent Age:* 240
With Wifdom's luftre, Folly's fhade contraft,
And judge the reigning Manners by the paft:
Bid *Britain*'s Heroes (awful Shades!) arife,
And ancient Honour beam on modern Vice:
Point back to minds ingenuous, actions fair, 245
Till the Sons blufh at what their Fathers were:
Ere yet 'twas beggary the great to truft;
Ere yet 'twas quite a folly to be juft;
When *low-born* Sharpers only dar'd a lie,
Or falfify'd the card, or cogg'd the die; 250
Ere Lewdnefs the ftain'd garb of Honour wore,
Or Chaftity was carted for the Whore;

Vice

Vice flutter'd, in the plumes of freedom drefs'd;
Or public Spirit was the public jeft.
  Be ever, in a juft expreffion, bold,   255
Yet ne'er degrade fair SATIRE to a Scold:
Let no unworthy mien her form debafe,
But let her fmile, and let her frown with grace:
In mirth be temp'rate, temp'rate in her fpleen;
Nor, while fhe preaches modefty, obfcene.   260
Deep let her wound, not rankle to a fore,
Nor call his Lordfhip ———, her Grace a ——:
The Mufe's charms refiftlefs then affail,
When wrapt in *Irony*'s tranfparent veil:
Her beauties half conceal'd, the more furprize,
And keener luftre fparkles in her eyes.   266
Then be your line with fharp encomiums grac'd:
Style *Clodius* honourable, *Bufa* chafte.
  Dart not on Folly an indignant eye:
Whoe'er difcharg'd Artillery on a Fly?   270
Deride not Vice: Abfurd the thought and vain,
To bind the Tiger in fo weak a chain.
Nay more: when flagrant crimes your laughter move,
The Knave exults: to fmile is to approve.
The Mufe's labour then fuccefs fhall crown,   275
When Folly feels her fmile, and Vice her frown.
  Know next what Meafures to each Theme belong,
And fuit your thoughts and numbers to your fong:
On wing proportion'd to your quarry rife,
And ftoop to earth, or foar among the fkies.   280
Thus when a modifh folly you rehearfe,
Free the expreffion, fimple be the verfe.

In artless numbers paint th' ambitious Peer
That mounts the box, and shines a Charioteer:
In strains familiar sing the midnight toil   285
Of Camps and Senates disciplin'd by *Hoyle;*
Patriots and Chiefs, whose deep design invades
And carries off the captive King—of *Spades!*
Let SATIRE here in milder vigour shine,
And gayly graceful sport along the line;   290
Bid courtly fashion quit her thin pretence,
And smile each Affectation into sense.

 Not so when Virtue by her Guards betray'd,
Spurn'd from her Throne, implores the Muse's aid:
When *crimes*, which erst in kindred darkness lay,
Rise frontless, and insult the eye of day;   295
Indignant *Hymen* veils his hallow'd fires,
And white-rob'd Chastity with tears retires;
When rank Adultery on the genial bed
Hot from *Cocytus* rears her baleful head: 300
When private Faith and public Trust are fold,
And Traitors barter Liberty for Gold:
When fell Corruption dark and deep, like fate,
Saps the foundation of a sinking State:
When Giant-Vice and Irreligion rise,   305
On mountain'd falsehoods to invade the skies:
Then warmer numbers glow thro' SATIRE's page,
And all her smiles are darken'd into rage:
On eagle-wing she gains *Parnassus'* height,
Not lofty EPIC soars a nobler flight: 310
Then keener indignation fires her eye;
Then flash her lightnings, and her thunders fly;

           Wide

Part II.   ESSAY ON SATIRE.

Wide and more wide her flaming bolts are hurl'd,
Till all her wrath involves the guilty World.
   Yet SATIRE oft affumes a gentler mien,   315
And beams on Virtue's friends a fmile ferene:
She wounds reluctant; pours her balm with joy;
Glad to commend where Worth attracts her eye.
But chief, when Virtue, Learning, Arts decline,
She joys to fee unconquer'd merit fhine;   320
Where burfting glorious, with departing ray,
True Genius gilds the clofe of Britain's day:
With joy fhe fees the ftream of Roman art
From MURRAY's tongue flow purer to the heart:
Sees YORKE to Fame, ere yet to Manhood known,
And juft to ev'ry Virtue but his own: 326
Hears unftain'd CAM with gen'rous pride proclaim
A SAGE's, CRITIC's, and a POET's name:
Behold, where WIDCOMBE's happy hills afcend,
Each orphan'd Art and Virtue find a friend: 330
To HAGLEY's honour'd Shade directs her view;
And culls each flow'r, to form a Wreath for YOU.
   But tread with cautious ftep this dangerous ground,
Befet with faithlefs precipices round: 334
Truth be your guide: difdain Ambition's call;
And if you fall with Truth, you greatly fall.
'Tis Virtue's *native luftre* that muft *fhine*;
The Poet can but *fet it* in his line:
And who unmov'd with laughter can behold
A *fordid pebble* meanly grac'd with *gold*?   340
Let *real* Merit then adorn your lays,
For Shame attends on proftituted praife;

And

And all your wit, your moſt diſtinguiſh'd art,
But makes us grieve you want an honeſt heart.

   Nor think the Muſe by SATIRE's Law confin'd: 345
She yields deſcription of the nobleſt kind.
Inferior art the Landſcape may deſign,
And paint the purple ev'ning in the line:
Her daring thought eſſays a higher plan;
Her hand delineates Paſſion, pictures Man.   350
And great the toil, the latent ſoul to trace,
To paint the heart, and catch internal grace;
By turns bid Vice or Virtue ſtrike our eyes,
Now bid a *Wolſey*, or a *Cromwell* riſe;
Now with a touch more ſacred and refin'd,   355
Call forth a CHESTERFIELD's or LONSDALE's mind.
Here ſweet or ſtrong may ev'ry Colour flow:
Here let the pencil warm, the canvaſs glow:
Of light and ſhade provoke the noble ſtrife,
And wake each ſtriking feature into life.   360

PART

PART III.

THROUGH Ages thus has SATIRE keenly ſhin'd,
The Friend to Truth, to Virtue, and Mankind:
Yet the bright flame from Virtue ne'er had ſprung,
And Man was guilty ere the Poet ſung.
This Muſe in ſilence joy'd each better Age,   365
Till glowing crimes had wak'd her into rage.
Truth ſaw her honeſt ſpleen with new delight,
And bade her wing her ſhafts, and urge their flight.
Firſt on the Sons of *Greece* ſhe prov'd her art,
And *Sparta* felt the fierce IAMBIC dart *.   370
To LATIUM next, avenging SATIRE flew:
The flaming faulchion rough LUCILIUS † drew;
With dauntleſs warmth in Virtue's cauſe engag'd,
And conſcious Villains trembled as he rag'd.
   Then ſportive HORACE ‡ caught the gen'rous fire;
For SATIRE's bow reſign'd the ſounding lyre: 376
                                                               Each

NOTES.
* " Archilochum proprio rabies armavit Iambo."   HOR.
† " Enſe velut ſtricto quoties Lucilius ardens
   " Infremuit, rubet auditor cui frigida mens eſt
   " Criminibus, tacita ſudant præcordia culpa."   JUV. S. i.
‡ " Omne vafer vitium ridenti Flaccus amico
   " Tangit, et admiſſus circum præcordia ludit,
   " Callidus excuſſo populum ſuſpendere naſo."   PERS. S. i.

Each arrow polish'd in his hand was seen,
And, as it grew more polish'd, grew more keen.
His art, conceal'd in study'd negligence,
Politely sly, cajol'd the foes of sense: 380
He seem'd to sport and trifle with the dart,
But while he sported, drove it to the heart.

  In graver strains majestic PERSIUS wrote,
Big with a ripe exuberance of thought:
Greatly sedate, contemn'd a Tyrant's reign,   385
And lash'd Corruption with a calm disdain.

  More ardent eloquence, and boundless rage,
Inflame bold JUVENAL's exalted page,
His mighty numbers aw'd corrupted Rome,
And swept audacious Greatness to its doom;   390
The headlong torrent thund'ring from on high,
Rent the proud rock that lately brav'd the sky.

  But lo! the fatal Victor of Mankind!
Swoln *Luxury!*—pale *Ruin* stalks behind!
As countless Insects from the north-east pour,   395
To blast the Spring, and ravage ev'ry flow'r:
So barb'rous Millions spread contagious death:
The sick'ning Laurel wither'd at their breath.
Deep Superstition's night the skies o'erhung,
Beneath whose baleful dews the Poppy sprung.   400
No longer Genius woo'd the Nine to love,
But Dulness nodded in the Muse's grove:
Wit, Spirit, Freedom, were the sole offence,
Nor aught was held so dangerous as Sense.

                                At

ESSAY ON SATIRE.

At length, again fair Science shot her ray, 405
Dawn'd in the skies, and spoke returning day.
Now, SATIRE, triumph o'er thy flying foe,
Now, load thy quiver, string thy slacken'd bow!
Tis done!—See, great ERASMUS breaks the spell,
And wounds triumphant Folly in her cell! 410
(In vain the solemn Cowl surrounds her face,
Vain all her bigot cant, her sour grimace,)
With shame compell'd her leaden throne to quit,
And own the force of Reason urg'd by Wit.
'Twas then plain DONNE in honest vengeance rose,
His Wit harmonious, tho' his Rhyme was prose:
He 'midst an age of Puns and Pedants wrote 417
With genuine sense, and Roman strength of thought.

Yet scarce had SATIRE well relum'd her flame,
(With grief the Muse records her Country's shame,)
Ere Britain saw the foul revolt commence, 421
And treach'rous Wit began her war with Sense.
Then rose a shameless mercenary train,
Whom latest Time shall view with just disdain:
A race fantastic, in whose gaudy line 425
Untutor'd thought, and tinsel beauty shine;
Wit's shatter'd Mirror lies in fragments bright,
Reflects not Nature, but confounds the sight.
Dry Morals the Court-Poet blush'd to sing:
'Twas all his praise to say, " *the oddest thing.*"
Proud for a jest obscene, a Patron's nod, 431
To martyr Virtue, or blaspheme his God.

Ill-fated

Ill-fated DRYDEN! who unmov'd can fee
Th' extremes of wit and meannefs join'd in Thee!
Flames that could mount, and gain their kindred fkies,
Low creeping in the putrid fink of vice;   436
A Mufe whom Wifdom woo'd, but woo'd in vain,
The Pimp of Pow'r, the Proftitute to Gain:
Wreaths that fhould deck fair Virtue's form alone,
To Strumpets, Traitors, Tyrants vilely thrown:
Unrival'd parts, the fcorn of honeft fame;   441
And Genius rife, a Monument of fhame!

More happy *France:* immortal BOILEAU there
Supported Genius with a Sage's care:
Him with her love propitious SATIRE bleft,   445
And breath'd her airs divine into his breaft:
Fancy and Senfe to form his line confpire,
And faultlefs Judgment guides the pureft Fire.

But fee at length the *Britifh* Genius fmile,
And fhow'r her bounties o'er her favour'd Ifle: 450
Behold for POPE fhe twines the laurel crown,
And centers ev'ry Poet's pow'r in *one:*
Each *Roman*'s force adorns his various page,
Gay fmiles, corrected ftrength, and manly rage.
Defpairing Guilt and Dulnefs loath the fight,   455
As Spectres vanifh at approaching light:
In this clear Mirror with delight we view
Each image juftly fine, and boldly true:
Here Vice, dragg'd forth by Truth's fupreme decree,
Beholds and hates her own deformity: 460

While-

ESSAY ON SATIRE.

While felf-feen Virtue in the faithful line
With modeſt joy furveys her form divine.
But oh, what thoughts, what numbers ſhall I find,
But faintly to exprefs the Poet's mind!
Who yonder Star's effulgence can difplay, 465
Unlefs he dip his pencil in the ray?
Who paint a God, unlefs the God infpire?
What catch the Lightning, but the fpeed of fire?
So, mighty POPE, to make thy Genius known,
All pow'r is weak, all numbers — but thy own. 470
Each Mufe for thee with kind contention ſtrove,
For thee the Graces left th' IDALIAN grove;
With watchful fondnefs o'er thy cradle hung,
Attun'd thy voice, and form'd thy infant-tongue.
Next, to her Bard majeftic Wifdom came; 475
The Bard enraptur'd caught the heav'nly flame:
With tafte fuperior fcorn'd the venal tribe,
Whom fear can fway, or guilty Greatnefs bribe;
At Fancy's call, who rear the wanton fail,
Sport with the ſtream, and trifle in the gale: 480
Sublimer views *thy* daring Spirit bound;
Thy mighty Voyage was Creation's round;
Intent new Worlds of Wifdom to explore,
And blefs Mankind with Virtue's facred ſtore;
A nobler joy than Wit can give, impart; 485
And pour a moral tranfport o'er the heart.
Fantaftic Wit ſhoots momentary fires,
And, like a Meteor, while we gaze, expires:

Wit kindled by the fulph'rous breath of Vice,
Like the blue Light'ning, while it fhines, deftroys:
But Genius, fir'd by Truth's eternal ray,   491
Burns clear and conftant, like the fource of day:
Like this, its beam prolific and refin'd,
Feeds, warms, infpirits, and exalts the mind;
Mildly difpels each wintry Paffion's gloom,   495
And opens all the Virtues into bloom.
This Praife, immortal POPE, to thee be giv'n:
Thy Genius was indeed a *Gift* from Heav'n.
Hail, Bard unequal'd, in whofe deathlefs line
Reafon and Wit, with ftrength collected fhine;   500
Where matchlefs Wit but wins the fecond praife,
Loft, nobly loft, in Truth's fuperior blaze.
Did FRIENDSHIP e'er miflead thy wand'ring Mufe?
That Friendfhip fure may plead the *great* excufe:
That facred Friendfhip which infpir'd thy Song,
Fair in defect, and *amiably* wrong.   506
Error like this ev'n Truth can fcarce reprove;
'Tis almoft Virtue when it flows from Love.

Ye deathlefs Names, ye Sons of endlefs praife,
By Virtue crown'd with never-fading bays!   510
Say, fhall an artlefs Mufe, if you infpire,
Light her pale lamp at your immortal fire?
Or if, O WARBURTON, infpir'd by You,
The daring Mufe a nobler path purfue,
By You infpir'd, on trembling pinion foar,   515
The facred founts of focial blifs explore,

In

ESSAY ON SATIRE.

In her bold numbers chain the Tyrant's rage,
And bid *her Country's Glory* fire her page:
If such her fate, do thou, fair *Truth*, descend,
And watchful guard her in an honest end:
Kindly severe, instruct her equal line
To court no Friend, nor own a Foe but *thine*.
But if her giddy eye should vainly quit
Thy sacred paths, to run the maze of wit;
If her apostate heart should e'er incline
To offer incense at Corruption's shrine;
Urge, urge thy pow'r, the black attempt confound,
And dash the smoaking Censer to the ground.
Thus aw'd to fear, instructed Bards may see,
That Guilt is doom'd to sink in Infamy.

A LETTER[a]

TO

A NOBLE LORD,

On occasion of some Libels written and propagated at Court, in the year 1732-3.

My LORD,   Nov. 30, 1733.

Your Lordſhip's [b] epiſtle has been publiſhed ſome days, but I had not the pleaſure and pain of ſeeing it till yeſterday: Pain, to think your Lordſhip ſhould attack me at all; Pleaſure, to find that you

---

[a] This Letter (which was firſt printed in the Year 1733) bears the ſame place in our Author's proſe that the Epiſtle to Dr. Arbuthnot does in his poetry. They are both Apologetical, repelling the libellous ſlanders on his Reputation: with this difference, that the Epiſtle to Dr. Arbuthnot, his friend, was chiefly directed againſt *Grub-ſtreet Writers*, and this letter to the Noble Lord, his enemy, againſt *Court Scriblers*. For the reſt, they are both Maſter-pieces in their kinds; *That* in verſe, more grave, moral, and ſublime; *This* in proſe, more lively, critical, and pointed; but equally conducive to what he had moſt at heart, the vindication of his moral Character: the only thing he thought worth his care in literary altercations; and the firſt thing he would expect from the good offices of a ſurviving Friend.   W.

[b] Intitled, *An Epiſtle to a Doctor of Divinity from a Nobleman at Hampton Court, Aug.* 28, 1733, and printed the November following for J. Roberts Fol.   W.

you can attack me so weakly. As I want not the humility, to think myself in every way but *one* your inferior, it seems but reasonable that I should take the only method either of self-defence or retaliation, that is left me against a person of your quality and power. And as by your choice of this weapon, your pen, you generously (and modestly too, no doubt) meant to put yourself upon a level with me; I will as soon believe that your Lordship would give a wound to a man unarmed, as that you would deny me the use of it in my own defence.

I presume you will allow me to take the same liberty in my answer to so *candid, polite,* and *ingenious* a Nobleman, which your Lordship took in yours, to so *grave, religious,* and *respectable* a clergyman [c]: As you answered his *Latin* in *English,* permit me to answer your *Verse* in *Prose.* And though your Lordship's reasons for not writing in *Latin* might be stronger than mine for not writing in Verse, yet I may plead *Two good* ones, for this conduct: the one that I want the talent of spinning *a thousand lines in a* Day [d], (which, I think, is as much *Time* as this subject deserves,) and the other, that I take your Lordship's *Verse* to be as much *Prose* as this letter. But no doubt it was your choice, in writing to a friend, to renounce all the pomp of Poetry, and give us this excellent model of the familiar.

When

---

[c] Dr. S.
[d] And Pope with justice of such lines may say,
  His Lordship spins a thousand in a day.   Epist. p. 6.

A NOBLE LORD.

When I confider the *great difference* betwixt the rank your Lordfhip holds in the *World*, and the rank which your *writings* are like to hold in the *learned world*, I prefume that diftinction of ftyle is but neceffary, which you will fee obferved through this letter. When I fpeak of *you*, my Lord, it will be with all the deference due to the inequality which Fortune has made between you and myfelf: but when I fpeak of your *writings*, my Lord, I muft, I can do nothing but trifle.

I fhould be obliged indeed to leffen this *Refpect*, if all the Nobility (and efpecially the elder brothers) are but fo many hereditary fools [e], if the privilege of Lords be to want brains [f], if noblemen can hardly write or read [g], if all their bufinefs is but to drefs and vote [h], and all their employment in court, to tell lies, flatter in public, flander in private, be falfe to each other, and follow nothing but felf-intereft [i]. Blefs me,

---

[e] That to good blood by old prefcriptive rules,
Gives right hereditary to be Fools.

[f] Nor wonder that my Brain no more affords,
But recollect the privilege of Lords.

[g] And when you fee me fairly write my name;
For *England*'s fake wifh all could do the fame.

[h] Whilft all our bufinefs is to drefs and vote.   Epift. p. 6.

[i] Courts are only larger families,
The growth of each, few truths, and many lies:
    in private fatyrize, in public flatter.
Few to each other, all to one point true;
Which one I fhan't, nor need explain.   Adieu.   P. ult.

me, my Lord, what an account is this you give of them? and what would have been said of me, had I immolated, in this manner, the whole body of the Nobility, at the stall of a well-fed Prebendary?

Were it the mere *Excess* of your Lordship's *Wit*, that carried you thus triumphantly over all the bounds of decency, I might consider your Lordship on your *Pegasus*, as a sprightly hunter on a mettled horse; and while you were trampling down all our works, patiently suffer the injury, in pure admiration of the *Noble Sport*. But should the case be quite otherwise, should your Lordship be only like a *Boy* that is *run away with;* and run away with by a *Very Foal;* really common charity, as well as respect for a noble family, would oblige me to stop your career, and to *help you down* from *this Pegasus*.

Surely the little praise of a *Writer* should be a thing below your ambition: You, who are no sooner born, but in the lap of the Graces; no sooner at school, but in the arms of the Muses; no sooner in the World, but you practised all the skill of it; no sooner in the Court, but you possessed all the art of it! Unrival'd as you are, in making a figure, and in making a speech, methinks, my Lord, you may well give up the poor talent of turning a Distich. And why this fondness for Poetry? Prose admits of the two excellencies you most admire, Diction and Fiction: It admits of the talents you chiefly possess, a most fertile invention, and most florid expression; it is with prose,

nay

A NOBLE LORD. 343

nay the plaineſt proſe, that you beſt could teach our nobility to vote, which you juſtly obſerve, is half at leaſt of their Buſineſs [k] : And give me leave to prophesy, it is to your talent in proſe, and not in verſe, to your ſpeaking, not your writing, to your art at court, not your art of poetry, that your Lordſhip muſt owe your future figure in the world.

My Lord, whatever you imagine, this is the advice of a Friend, and one who remembers he formerly had the honour of ſome profeſſion of Friendſhip from you: Whatever was his *real ſhare* in it, whether ſmall or great, yet as your Lordſhip could never have had the leaſt *Loſs* by continuing it, or the leaſt *Intereſt* by withdrawing it; the misfortune of loſing it, I fear, muſt have been owing to his own *deficiency* or *neglect*. But as to any *actual fault* which deſerved to forfeit it in ſuch a degree, he proteſts he is to this day guiltleſs, and ignorant. It could at moſt be but a fault of *omiſſion*; but indeed by omiſſions, men of your Lordſhip's uncommon merit may ſometimes think themſelves ſo injured, as to be capable of an inclination to injure another; who, though very much below their quality, may be above the injury.

I never heard of the leaſt diſpleaſure you had conceived againſt me, till I was told that an imitation I had made of [l] *Horace* had offended ſome perſons, and among

---

[k] All their buſ'neſs is to dreſs, and vote.
[l] The firſt Satire of the ſecond Book, printed in 1732.

among them your Lordship. I could not have apprehended that a few *general strokes* about a *Lord scribling carelessly* [m], a *Pimp*, or a *Spy* at Court, a *Sharper* in a gilded chariot, &c. that these, I say, should be ever applied as they have been, by *any malice* but that which is the gerateft in the world, *the Malice of Ill people to themselves*.

Your Lordship so well knows, (and the whole Court and Town through your means so well know,) how far the resentment was carried upon that imagination, not only in the *Nature* of the *Libel* [n] you propagated against me, but in the extraordinary *manner*, *place*, and *presence*, in which it was propagated [o]; that I shall only say, it seemed to me to exceed the bounds of justice, common sense, and decency.

I wonder yet more, how a *Lady*, of great wit, beauty, and fame for her poetry, (between whom and your Lordship there is a *natural*, a *just*, and a *well-grounded esteem*,) could be prevailed upon to take a part in that proceeding. Your resentments against me indeed might be equal, as my offence to you both was the same; for neither had I the least misunderstanding with that Lady, till after I was the *Author* of my own misfortune in discontinuing her
acquaint-

---

[m] He should have added, that he called this Nobleman, who scribled so carelessly, *Lord Fanny*.

[n] *Verses to the Imitator of Horace*, afterwards printed by J. Roberts, 1732, Fol.

[o] It was for this reason that this Letter, as soon as it was printed, was communicated to the Queen.

A NOBLE LORD.

acquaintance. I may venture to own a truth, which cannot be unpleasing to either of you; I assure you my reason for so doing, was merely that you had both *too much wit* for me [p]; and that I could not do with *mine*, many things which you could with *yours*. The injury done you in withdrawing myself could be but small, if the value you had for me was no greater than you have been pleased since to profess. But surely, my Lord, one may say, neither the Revenge, nor the Language you held, bore any *proportion* to the pretended offence: The appellation of [q] *Foe* to *humankind*, an *Enemy* like the *Devil* to all that have *Being; ungrateful, unjust,* deserving to be *whipt, blanketed, kicked,* nay *killed:* a *Monster*, an *Assassin*, whose conversation every man ought to *shun*, and against whom *all doors* should be shut; I beseech you, my Lord, had you the least right to give, or to encourage or justify any other in giving such language as this to me? Could I be treated in terms more strong or more atrocious, if during my acquaintance with you I had been a *Betrayer*, a *Backbiter*, a *Whisperer*, an *Eves-dropper*, or an *Informer?* Did I in all that time ever throw *a false Dye*, or palm *a foul Card* upon you? Did I ever *borrow, steal,* or accept, either *Money, Wit,* or *Advice* from you? Had I ever the honour to join with either of you in one

Ballad,

---

[p] Once, and but once, his heedless youth was bit,
And lik'd that dang'rous thing a female Wit.
  See *the Letter to Dr.* ARBUTHNOT, *amongst the Variations.*

[q] See the aforesaid *Verses to the Imitator of Horace.*

Ballad, Satire, Pamphlet, or *Epigram,* on any person *living* or *dead?* Did I ever do you so great an *injury* as to put off *my own verses* for *yours,* especially on *those Persons* whom they might *most offend?* I am confident you cannot answer in the affirmative; and I can truly affirm, that ever since I lost the happiness of your conversation, I have not published or written one syllable of or to either of you; never hitched your *names* in a *Verse,* or trifled with your *good names in company.* Can I be honestly charged with any other crime but an *Omission* (for the word *Neglect,* which I used before, slipped my pen unguardedly) to continue my admiration of you all my life, and still to contemplate, face to face, your many excellencies and perfections? I am persuaded you can reproach me truly with no great *Faults,* except my *natural ones,* which I am as ready to own, as to do all justice to the contrary *Beauties* in you. It is true, my Lord, I am short, not well shaped, generally ill-dressed, if not sometimes dirty: Your Lordship and Ladyship are still in bloom; your figures such, as rival the *Apollo* of *Belvedere,* and the *Venus* of *Medicis;* and your faces so finished, that neither sickness or passion can deprive them of *Colour;* I will allow your own in particular to be the finest that ever *Man* was blest with: preserve it, my Lord, and reflect, that to be a Critic, would cost it too many *frowns,* and to be a Statesman, too many *wrinkles!* I further confess, I am now somewhat old; but so your Lordship and this

excel-

excellent Lady, with all your beauty, will (I hope) one day be. I know your Genius and hers fo perfectly *tally*, that you cannot but join in admiring each other, and by confequence in the contempt of all fuch as myfelf. You have both, in my regard, been like—(your Lordfhip, I know loves a *Simile*, and it will be one fuitable to your *Quality*)—you have been like *Two Princes*, and I like a *poor Animal* facrificed between them to cement a lafting league: I hope I have not bled in vain; but that fuch an amity may endure for ever! For though it be what common *underftandings* would hardly conceive, Two *Wits* however may be perfuaded that it is in friendfhip as in enmity, The more *danger* the more *honour*.

Give me the liberty, my Lord, to tell you, why I never replied to thofe *Verfes* on the *Imitator* of *Horace*? They regarded nothing but my *Figure*, which I fet no value upon; and my *Morals*, which, I knew, needed no defence: Any honeft man has the pleafure to be confcious, that it is out of the power of the *Wittieft*, nay the *Greateft Perfon* in the kingdom, to leffen him *that way*, but at the expence of his own *Truth*, *Honour*, or *Juftice*.

But though I declined to explain myfelf juft at the time when I was fillily threatened, I fhall now give your Lordfhip a frank account of the offence you imagined to be meant to you. *Fanny* (my Lord) is the plain Englifh of *Fannius*, a real perfon, who was a foolifh Critic, and an enemy of *Horace*: perhaps a

Noble one, so (if your Latin be gone in earnest[r]) I must acquaint you, the word *Beatus* may be construed;

> *Beatus Fannius! ultro*
> *Delatis capsis et imagine.*

This *Fannius* was, it seems, extremely fond both of his *Poetry* and his *Person*, which appears by the pictures and *Statues* he caused to be made of himself, and by his great diligence to propagate *bad Verses* at *Court*, and get them admitted into the library of *Augustus*. He was moreover of a delicate or *effeminate complexion*, and constant at the Assemblies and Operas of those days, where he took it into his head to *slander poor Horace;*

> *Ineptus*
> Fannius, *Hermogenis* lædat *conviva Tigelli;*

till it provoked him at last just to *name* him, give him a *lash*, and send him whimpering to the *Ladies*.

> Discipularum *inter jubeo plorare cathedras.*

So much for *Fanny*, my Lord. The word *spins*, (as Dr. *Freind* or even Dr. *Sherwin* could assure you,) was the literal translation of *deduci ;* a metaphor taken from a *Silk-worm*, my Lord, to signify any *slight, silken,* or (as your Lordship and the Ladies call it) [s] *slimsy* piece of work. I presume your Lordship has enough of this, to convince you there was nothing

personal

---

[r] All I learn'd from Dr. Freind at school,
Has quite deserted this poor John Trot-head,
And left plain native English in its stead.   Epist. p. 2.

[s] Weak texture of his flimsy brain.

A NOBLE LORD. 349

perſonal but to *that Fannius*, who (with all his fine accompliſhments) had never been heard of, but for *that Horace* he injured.

In regard to the right honourable Lady, your Lordſhip's friend, I was far from deſigning a perſon of her condition by a name ſo derogatory to her, as that of *Sappho;* a name proſtituted to every infamous Creature that ever wrote Verſe or Novels. I proteſt I never *applied* that name to her in any verſe of mine, *public* or *private;* (and I firmly believe) not in any *Letter* or *Converſation.* Whoever could invent a Falſehood to ſupport an accuſation, I pity; and whoever can believe ſuch a Character to be theirs, I pity ſtill more. God forbid the Court or Town ſhould have the complaiſance to *join* in that opinion! Certainly I meant it only of ſuch modern *Sappho's*, as imitate much more the *Lewdneſs* than the *Genius* of the ancient one; and upon whom their wretched brethren frequently beſtow both the *Name* and the *Qualification* there mentioned [t].

There was another reaſon why I was ſilent as to that paper—I took it for a *Lady's*, (on the printer's word in the title page,) and thought it too preſuming, as well as indecent, to contend with one of that *Sex* in *altercation:* For I never was ſo mean a creature as to commit my Anger againſt a *Lady* to *paper*, though but

[t] From furious Sappho ſcarce a milder fate,
Pox'd by her love, or libell'd by her hate.
1 Sat. B. ii. Hor.

but in a *private Letter*. But soon after, her denial of it was brought to me by a Noble person of *real Honour* and *Truth*. Your Lordship indeed said you had it from a Lady, and the Lady said it was your Lordship's; some thought the beautiful by-blow had *Two Fathers*, or (if one of them will hardly be allowed a man) *Two Mothers*; indeed I think *both Sexes* had a share in it, but which was *uppermost*, I know not: I pretend not to determine the exact method of this *Witty Fornication:* and if I call it *Yours*, my Lord, it is only because, whoever *got* it, you *brought it forth*.

Here, my Lord, allow me to observe, the different proceeding of the *Ignoble Poet*, and his *Noble Enemies*. What he has written of *Fanny* [u], *Adonis*, *Sappho*, or who

---

[u] All the topics of contempt, ridicule, and satire that are used in this letter against Lord Hervey, had been used before, 1731, by the Author of a Reply to a late Scurrilous Libel; particularly the topics of the delicacy of his manners, and the foppery of his dress, and effeminacy of his person. He is there said, "to be such a composition of the two sexes, that it is difficult to distinguish which is most predominant." My friend Horace hath described him much better than I can :

"Quem si puellarum insereres choro,
 Mire sagaces falleret hospites
  Discrimen obscurum, solutis
   Crinibus, ambiguoque vultû."

And it is added, "Though it would be barbarous to handle such a delicate hermaphrodite, such a pretty little master-miss, too roughly, yet you must give me leave, my dear, to give you a little gentle correction for your good." Page 6.

Lord Hervey left behind him Memoirs of his own Times, said to be full of curious matter, and which it is to be hoped will one day be published, for Hans Stanley told me he had read them.

In

who you will, he owned he publifhed, he fet his name to: What they have *publifhed* of him, they have denied to have *written;* and what they have *written* of him, they have denied to have *publifhed.* One of thefe was the cafe in the paſt Libel, and the other in the prefent. For though the parent has owned it to a few choice friends, it is fuch as he has been obliged to deny in the moſt particular terms, to the great perfon whofe opinion *concerned him moft.* Yet, my Lord, this Epiftle was a piece not written in *hafte,* or in a *paffion,* but many months after all pretended provocations; when you was at *full leifure* at Hampton-court, and I the object *fingled,* lake a *Deer out of Seafon,* for fo ill-timed and ill-placed a diverfion. It was a *deliberate* work, directed to a *Reverend Perfon*[w], of the moſt *ferious and facred* character, with whom you are known to cultivate a *ftrict correfpondence,* and to whom it will not be doubted but you open your *fecret Sentiments,* and deliver your *real judgment* of men and things. This, I fay, my Lord, with fubmiffion, could not but awaken all my *Reflection.*

In the fecond volume of the Letters of Voltaire, page 305, is a very long and curious letter to Lord Hervey, full of high encomiums on this Peer, and ſtill higher of Louis XIV. and his reign. From whence it appears that Lord Hervey had made fome objections to this work of Voltaire; and particularly for his intitling it, The Age of Louis XIV.

In a celebrated pamphlet, intitled, the Court Secret, written on occaſion of the death of Lord Scarborough, Lord Hervey was very feverely fatirized under the name of Ibrahim. 8vo. 1791.

[w] Dr. Sherwin.

ficction and *Attention*. Your Lordship's opinion of me as a *Poet*, I cannot help; it is yours, my Lord, and that were enough to mortify a poor man; but it is not yours *alone*, you must be content to share it with the Gentlemen of the *Dunciad*, and (it may be) with many *more innocent* and *ingenious men*. If your Lordship destroys my *poetical* character, *they* will claim their part in the glory: but, give me leave to say, if my *moral* character be ruined, it must be *wholly* the work of *your Lordship;* and will be hard even for you to do, unless I *myself co-operate*.

How can you talk (my most worthy Lord) of all *Pope*'s Works as so many *Libels*, affirm, that, *he has no invention* but in *Defamation* [x], and charge him with *selling another man's labours printed with his own name* [y]; Fye, my Lord, you forget yourself. He printed not his name before a line of the person's you mention; that person himself has told you and all the world in the book itself, what part he had in it, as may be seen at the conclusion of his notes to the Odyssey. I can only suppose your Lordship (not having at that time *forgot your Greek)* despised to look upon the *Translation;* and ever since entertained too mean an opinion of the Translator to cast an eye upon it. Besides, my Lord, when you said he *sold* another man's works, you ought in justice to have added that he

bought

---

[x] To his eternal shame
Prov'd he can ne'er invent but to defame.

[y] And sold Broom's labours printed with Pope's name. P. 7.

A NOBLE LORD.

bought them, which very much *alters the Cafe*. What he gave him was five hundred pounds: his receipt can be produced to your Lordſhip. I dare not affirm that he was as *well paid* as *ſome Writers* (much his inferiors) have been ſince; but your Lordſhip will reflect that I am no man of quality, either to *buy* or *ſell* ſcribling ſo high: and that I have neither *Place*, *Penſion*, nor Power to reward for *Secret Services*. It cannot be, that one of your rank can have the leaſt *Envy* to ſuch an author as I: but were that *poſſible*, it were much better gratified by employing *not your own*, but ſome of *thoſe low and ignoble pens* to do you this *mean office*. I dare engage you will have them for leſs than I gave Mr. Broom, if your friends have not raiſed the market: Let them drive the bargain for you, my Lord; and you may depend on ſeeing, every day in the week, as many (and now and then as pretty) Verſes, as theſe of your Lordſhip.

And would it not be full as well, that my poor perſon ſhould be abuſed by them, as by one of your rank and quality? Cannot *Curl* do the ſame? nay has he not done it before your Lordſhip, in the ſame *kind of Language*, and almoſt the *ſame words*? I cannot but think the worthy and *diſcreet clergyman* himſelf will agree, it is *improper*, nay *unchriſtian*, to expoſe the *perſonal* defects of our brother: that both ſuch perfect forms as yours, and ſuch unfortunate ones as mine, proceed from the hand of the ſame Maker; who *faſhioneth his Veſſels* as he pleaſeth, and that it is not from their *shape* we can tell whether they are made for *honour* or *dishonour*. In a word, he would teach you Charity to your greatest enemies; of which number, my Lord, I cannot be reckoned, since, though a Poet, I was never your flatterer.

Next, my Lord, as to the *Obscurity of [z] my Birth*, (a reflection copy'd also from Mr. *Curl* and his brethren,) I am sorry to be obliged to such a presumption as to name my *Family* in the same leaf with your Lordship's: but my Father had the honour in one instance to resemble you, for he was a *younger Brother*. He did not indeed think it a happiness to bury his *elder Brother*, though he had one who wanted some of those good qualities which *yours* possessed. How sincerely glad could I be, to pay to that young Nobleman's memory the debt I owed to his friendship, whose early death deprived your family of as much *Wit* and *Honour* as he left behind him in any branch of it. But as to my Father, I could assure you, my Lord, that he was no mechanic, (neither a hatter, nor, which might please your Lordship yet better, a Cobler,) but in truth, of a very tolerable family: And my Mother of an ancient one, as well born and educated as that *Lady*, whom your Lordship made choice of to be the *Mother of your own Children;* whose merit, beauty, and vivacity (if transmitted to your posterity) will be a *better present* than even the noble blood they derive *only* from *you*. A mother, on whom I was

---

[z] Hard as thy Heart, and as thy Birth obscure.

I was never obliged so far to reflect, as to say, she *spoiled me* [a]. And a Father, who never found himself obliged to say of me that he *disapproved my conduct.* In a word, my Lord, I think it enough that my parents, such as they were, never cost me a *Blush;* and that their Son, such as he is, never cost them a *Tear.*

I have purposely omitted to consider your Lordship's Criticisms on my *Poetry.* As they are exactly the same with those of the *forementioned Authors,* I apprehend they would justly charge me with partiality, if I gave to *you* what belongs to *them;* or paid more distinction to the *same things* when they are in your mouth, than when they were in theirs. It will be shewing both them and you (my Lord) a *more particular respect,* to observe how much they are honoured by *your imitation of them,* which indeed is carried through your whole Epistle. I have read somewhere at *School,* (though I make it no *Vanity* to have forgot where,) that *Tully* naturalized a few phrases at the instance of some of his friends. Your Lordship has done more in honour of these Gentlemen; you have authorized not only their *Assertions,* but their *Style.* For example, *A* Flow *that wants skill to restrain its ardour,—A* Dictionary *that gives us nothing at* its own expence.—*As luxuriant branches* bear *but little fruit,*

so

---

[a] A noble Father's heir spoil'd by his mother.
    His Lordship's account of himself, p. 7.

so Wit unprun'd is but raw fruit—While you rehearse ignorance, *you still* know enough *to do it in Verse— Wits* are *but glittering* ignorance.—The *account of* how *we pass our time*—and, *The Weight on Sir R. W—'s* brain, *You can* ever *receive from* no *head more than such a head* (as no head) *has to give:* Your Lordship would have said, *never* receive instead of *ever*, and *any head* instead of *no head:* but all this is perfectly new, and has greatly enriched our language.

You are merry, my Lord, when you say, *Latin* and *Greek*

> Have quite deserted your poor *John Trot-head*,
> And left plain native English in their stead;

for (to do you justice) this is nothing less than *plain English*. And as for your *John Trot-head*, I can't conceive why you should give it that name; for by some [b] papers I have seen sign'd with that name, it is certainly a head *very different* from your Lordship's.

Your Lordship seems determined to fall out with every thing you have learned at school: you complain next of a *dull Dictionary*,

> That gives us nothing at its own expence,
> But a few modern words for ancient Sense.

Your Lordship is the first man that ever carried the love of Wit so far, as to expect a *witty Dictionary*. A Dictionary that gives us *any thing but words*, must not only be an *expensive* but a very *extravagant Dictionary*.

---

[b] See some Treatises printed in the Appendix to the Craftsman, about that time.

tionary[c]. But what does your Lordſhip mean by its giving us but *a few modern words* for *ancient Senſe?* If by *Senſe* (as I fuſpect) you mean *words, (a miſtake not unuſual,)* I muſt do the Dictionary the juſtice to ſay, that it gives us *juſt as many modern words as ancient ones.* Indeed, my Lord, you have more need to complain of a bad Grammar than of a dull Dictionary.

Doctor *Freind*, I dare anſwer for him, never taught you to talk

of Sapphic, Lyric, and Iambic Odes.

Your Lordſhip might as well bid your preſent Tutor, your Taylor, make you a *Coat, Suit of Cloaths,* and *Breeches:* for you muſt have forgot your Logic, as well as Grammar, not to know, that Sapphic and Iambic are both included in Lyric; that being the *Genus,* and thoſe the *Species.*

For all cannot *invent* who can *tranſlate,*
No more than thoſe who *cloath* us, can *create.*

Here your Lordſhip ſeems in labour for a meaning. Is it that you would have Tranſlations, *Originals?* for it is the common opinion, that the *buſineſs* of a Tranſlator is to *tranſlate,* and not to *invent*; and of a

Taylor

---

[c] Yet we have ſeen many of theſe *extravagant* Dictionaries, and are likely to ſee many more, in an age ſo abounding in ſcience, that the ordinary vehicles of it being inſufficient to diſtribute it abroad, recourſe is had to this extraordinary method of conveyance.   W.

Taylor to *cloath*, and not to *create*. But why should you, my Lord, of all mankind, abuse a Taylor? not to say *blaspheme* him; if he can (as some think) at least go halves with God Almighty in the formation of a *Beau*. Might not Dr. *Sherwin* rebuke you for this, and bid you *Remember your* Creator *in the days of your youth?*

From a *Taylor*, your Lordship proceeds (by a beautiful gradation) to a *Silkman*.

> Thus *P—pe* we find
> The gaudy *Hinckcliff* of a beauteous mind.

Here too is some ambiguity. Does your Lordship use *Hinchcliff* as a *proper name?* or as the Ladies say a *Hinchcliff* or a *Colmar*, for a *Silk* or a *Fan?* I will venture to affirm, no Critic can have a perfect taste of your Lordship's works, who does not understand both your *Male Phrase* and your *Female Phrase*.

Your Lordship, to finish your Climax, advances up to a *Hatter;* a Mechanic, whose Employment, you inform us, is not (as was generally imagined) to *cover people's heads*, but to *dress their brains* [d]. A most useful Mechanic indeed! I cannot help wishing to have been one, for some people's sake.—But this too may be only another *Lady-Phrase:* Your Lordship and the Ladies may take a *Head-dress* for a *Head*, and understand, that to *adorn the Head* is the same thing as to *dress the Brains*.

Upon

---

[d] For this Mechanic's like the Hatter's pains,
Are but for dressing other people's brains.

Upon the whole, I may thank your Lordſhip for this high Panegyric: For if I have but *dreſſed* up *Homer*, as your *Taylor*, *Silkman*, and *Hatter have equipped your Lordſhip*, I muſt be owned to have dreſſed him *marvellouſly indeed*, and no wonder if he is *admired by the Ladies*ᵉ.

After all, my Lord, I really wiſh you would learn your *Grammar*. What if you put yourſelf awhile under the Tuition of your Friend *H———m?* May not I with all reſpect ſay to you, what was ſaid to *another Noble Poet* by Mr. Cowley, *Pray, Mr.* Howardᶠ, *if you did read your* Grammar, *what harm would it do you?* You yourſelf wiſh all Lords would *learn to write*ᵍ; though I do not ſee of what uſe it could be, if their whole buſineſs is to *give their Votes*ʰ: It could only be ſerviceable in *ſigning their Proteſts.* Yet ſurely this ſmall portion of learning might be indulged to your Lordſhip, without any Breach of that *Privilege*ⁱ you ſo generouſly aſſert to all thoſe of your rank, or too great an Infringement of that *Right*ᵏ which you claim as *Hereditary*, and

for

ᵉ by Girls admir'd. P. 6.
ᶠ The Honourable Mr. Edward Howard, celebrated for his poetry.
ᵍ And when you ſee me fairly write my name,
For England's ſake wiſh all Lords did the ſame.
ʰ — All our bus'neſs is to dreſs and vote. P. 4.
ⁱ The want of brains. Ibid.
ᵏ To be fools. Ibid.

A A 4

for which, no doubt, your Noble Father will thank you. Surely, my Lord, no Man was ever so bent upon depreciating himself!

All your Readers have obferved the following Lines:

> How oft we hear fome Witling pert and dull,
> By fafhion Coxcomb, and by nature Fool,
> With hackney Maxims, in dogmatic ftrain,
> Scoffing Religion and the Marriage chain?
> Then from his Common-place-book he repeats,
> The Lawyers all are rogues, and Parfons cheats,
> That Vice and Virtue's but a jeft,
> And all Morality Deceit well-dreft;
> That Life itfelf is like a wrangling game, &c.

The whole Town and Court (my good Lord) have heard *this Witling;* who is fo much every body's acquaintance but his own, that I will engage *they all name* the *fame Perfon.* But to hear *you* fay, that this is only——*of whipt Cream* a *frothy Store,* is a fufficient proof, that never mortal was endued with fo humble an opinion both of himfelf and his own Wit, as your Lordfhip: For, I do affure you, thefe are by much the beft Verfes in your whole Poem.

How unhappy is it for me, that a Perfon of your Lordfhip's *Modefty* and *Virtue,* who manifefts fo tender a regard to *Religion, Matrimony,* and *Morality;* who, though an ornament to the Court, cultivate an exemplary Correfpondence with the *Clergy;* nay, who

A NOBLE LORD.

who difdain not charitably to converfe with, and even affift, fome of the very worft of Writers (fo far as to caft a few *Conceits*, or drop a few *Antithefes*, even among the *Dear Joys* of the *Courant*); that you, I fay, fhould look upon Me alone as reprobate and unamendable! Reflect what *I was*, and what *I am*. I am even *annihilated* by your anger: For in thefe Verfes you have robbed me of *all power to think*[1], and, in your others, of the very *name* of a *Man!* Nay, to fhew that this is wholly your own doing, you have told us that before I wrote my *laft Epiftles*, (that is, before I unluckily mentioned *Fanny* and *Adonis*, whom, I proteft, I knew not to be your Lordfhip's Relations,) *I might have lived and died in glory*[m].

What would I not do to be well with your Lordfhip? Though, you obferve, I am a mere *Imitator* of *Homer*, *Horace*, *Boileau*, *Garth*, &c. (which I have the lefs caufe to be afhamed of, fince they were *Imitators of one another*), yet what if I fhould folemnly engage never to imitate *your* Lordfhip? May it not be one ftep towards an accommodation, that while you remark my *Ignorance in Greek*, you are fo good as to fay, you have *forgot your own?* What if I fhould confefs I tranflated from *D'Acier?* That furely could not but oblige your Lordfhip, who are known to prefer *French* to all the learned languages.

But

[l] P——e, who ne'er cou'd think. P. 7.
[m] In glory then he might have liv'd and dy'd. Ibid.

But allowing that in the space of *twelve years* acquaintance with *Homer*, I might unhappily contract as much *Greek* as your Lordship did in *Two* at the University, why may not I forget it again as happily?

Till such a reconciliation take effect, I have but one thing to entreat of your Lordship. It is, that you will not decide of my *Principles* on the same grounds as you have done of my *Learning:* Nor give the same account of my *Want of Grace*, after you have lost all acquaintance with my *Person*, as you do of my *Want of Greek*, after you have confessedly lost all acquaintance with the *Language*. You are too generous, my Lord, to follow the *Gentlemen* of the *Dunciad* quite so far, as to seek my *utter Perdition;* as *Nero* once did *Lucan*'s, merely for presuming to be a *Poet*, while one of so much greater quality was a *Writer*. I therefore make this humble request to your Lordship, that the next time you please *to write of me, speak of me,* or even *whisper of me* [n], you will recollect it is full *eight Years* since I had the honour of *any conversation* or *correspondence* with your Lordship, except *just half an hour* in a Lady's Lodgings at Court, and then I had the happiness of her being present all the time. It would therefore be difficult even for your Lordship's penetration to tell, to what, or from what *Principles*, *Parties*, or *Sentiments*, Moral, Political,

---

[n] " The *whisper*, that, to greatness still too near,
" Perhaps yet vibrates on his Sov'reign's ear."
Epist. to Dr. ARBUTHNOT.

Political, or Theological, I may have been converted, or perverted in all that time. I befeech your Lordfhip to confider the injury a Man of your *high Rank* and *Credit* may do to a *private Perfon*, under *Penal Laws* and many other difadvantages, not for want of *honefty* or *confcience*, but merely perhaps for having too *weak a head*, or too *tender a heart* °. It is by *thefe alone* I have hitherto lived excluded from all *pofts* of *Profit* or *Truft:* As I can interfere with the *Views* of *no man*, do not deny me, my Lord, *all that is left*, a little *Praife*, or the common Encouragement due, if not to my *Genius*, at leaft to my *Induftry*.

Above all, your Lordfhip will be careful not to wrong my *Moral Character* with THOSE [p] under whofe *Protection* I live, and through whofe *Lenity* alone I can live with Comfort. Your Lordfhip, I am confident, upon confideration, will think, you inadvertently went a little *too far* when you recommended to THEIR perufal, and ftrengthened by the weight of your Approbation, a *Libel*, mean in its reflections upon my poor *figure*, and fcandalous in thofe on my *Honour* and *Integrity:* wherein I was reprefented as " *an Enemy* to Human Race, a *Murderer*
" of Reputations, and a *Monfter* marked by God
" like *Cain*, deferving to wander accurfed through
" the world."

A ftrange

° See Letters to Bifhop ATTERBURY, Lett. iv,
[p] The K. and Q.

A ſtrange Picture of a Man, who had the good fortune to enjoy many friends, who will be always remembered as the firſt ornaments of their Age and Country; and no Enemies that ever contrived to be heard of, except Mr. *John Dennis*, and your Lordſhip: A Man, who never wrote a line in which the *Religion* or *Government* of his Country, the *Royal Family*, or their *Miniſtry* were diſreſpectfully mentioned; the Animoſity of any one Party gratify'd at the expence of another; or any Cenſure paſt, but upon *known Vice*, *acknowledged Folly*, or *aggreſſing Impertinence*. It is with infinite pleaſure he finds, that *ſome Men*, who ſeem *aſhamed* and *afraid* of *nothing elſe*, are ſo very ſenſible of *his Ridicule:* And it is for that very reaſon he reſolves (by the grace of God, and your Lordſhip's good leave)

> That while he breathes, no rich or noble knave
> Shall walk the world in credit to his grave.

This, he thinks, is rendering the beſt Service he can to the Public, and even to the good Government of his Country; and for this, at leaſt, he may deſerve ſome Countenance, even from the GREATEST PERSONS in it. Your Lordſhip knows OF WHOM I ſpeak. Their NAMES I ſhall be as ſorry, and as much aſhamed to place near *yours*, on ſuch an occaſion, as I ſhould be to ſee *You*, my Lord, placed ſo near *their* PERSONS, if you could ever make ſo ill an Uſe of their Ear [q] as to aſperſe or miſrepreſent any innocent man.

This

---

[q] " Cloſe at the ear of Eve." Ep. to Dr. ARBUTHNOT.

This is all I shall ever ask of your Lordship, except your pardon for this tedious Letter'. I have the honour to be, with equal *Respect* and *Concern*,

My Lord,

Your truly devoted Servant,

A. POPE.

The whole is so severe that we may say,
    Impressit memorem dente labris notam.

END OF THE THIRD VOLUME.

www.ingramcontent.com/pod-product-compliance
Lightning Source LLC
Chambersburg PA
CBHW020312240426
43673CB00039B/784